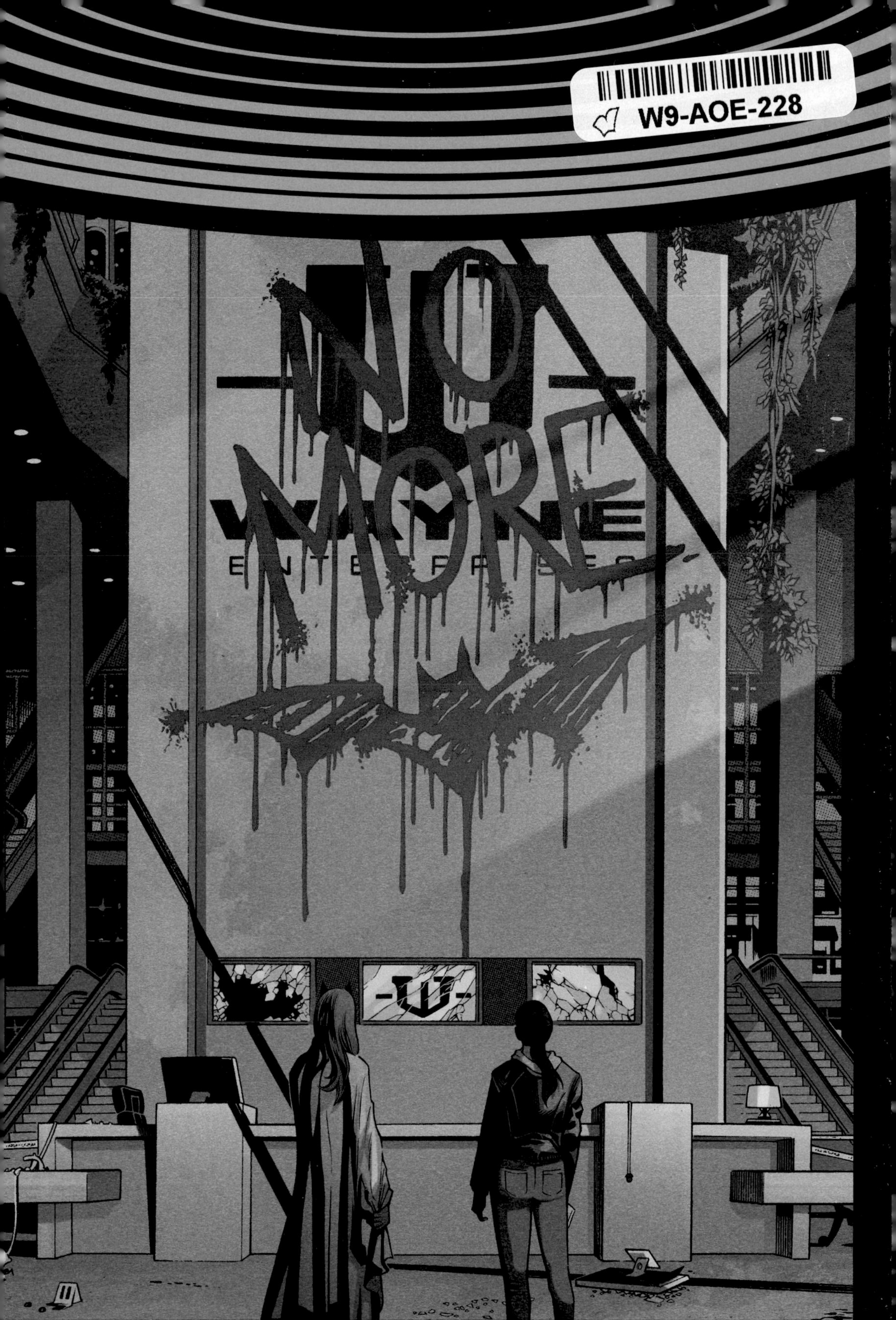
NO MORE

BATMAN: DETECTIVE COMICS

VOL.2 THE VICTIM SYNDICATE

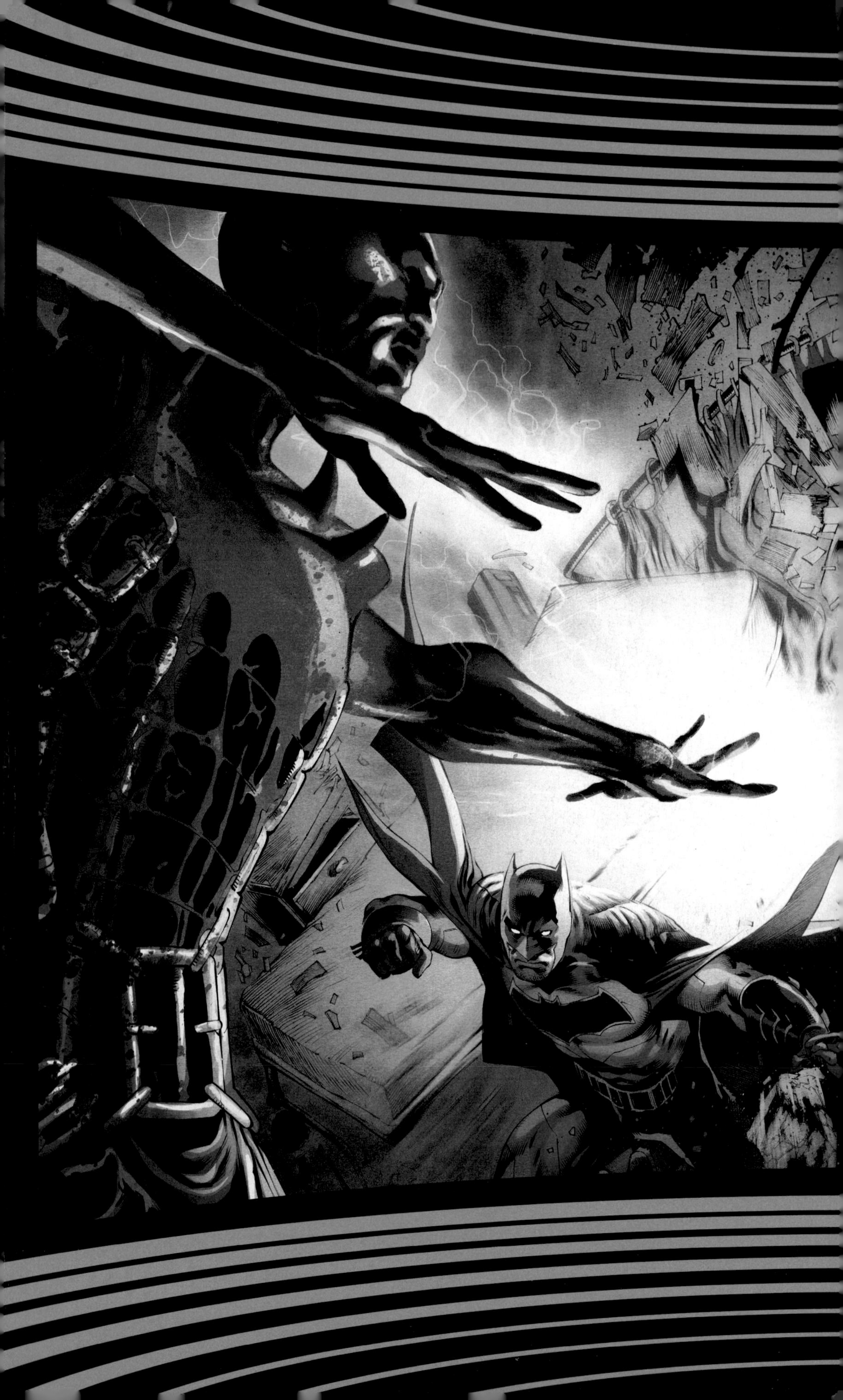

BATMAN: DETECTIVE COMICS
VOL.2 THE VICTIM SYNDICATE

JAMES TYNION IV
MARGUERITE BENNETT
writers

ALVARO MARTINEZ * **EDDY BARROWS** * **BEN OLIVER**
AL BARRIONUEVO * **CARMEN CARNERO** * **RAUL FERNANDEZ**
EBER FERREIRA * **SCOTT HANNA** * **JULIO FERREIRA** * **SZYMON KUDRANSKI**
artists

ADRIANO LUCAS * **BRAD ANDERSON** * **BEN OLIVER**
GABE ELTAEB * **HI-FI**
colorists

MARILYN PATRIZIO
letterer

JASON FABOK & BRAD ANDERSON
collection cover artists

BATMAN created by BOB KANE with BILL FINGER

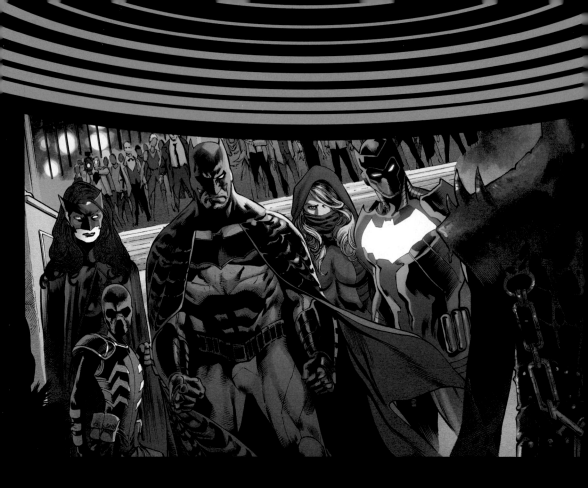

CHRIS CONROY Editor - Original Series * **DAVE WIELGOSZ** Assistant Editor - Original Series
JEB WOODARD Group Editor - Collected Editions * **ROBIN WILDMAN** Editor - Collected Edition
STEVE COOK Design Director - Books * **MONIQUE GRUSPE** Publication Design

BOB HARRAS Senior VP - Editor-in-Chief, DC Comics

DIANE NELSON President * **DAN DiDIO** Publisher * **JIM LEE** Publisher * **GEOFF JOHNS** President & Chief Creative Officer
AMIT DESAI Executive VP - Business & Marketing Strategy, Direct to Consumer & Global Franchise Management * **SAM ADES** Senior VP - Direct to Consumer
BOBBIE CHASE VP - Talent Development * **MARK CHIARELLO** Senior VP - Art, Design & Collected Editions
JOHN CUNNINGHAM Senior VP - Sales & Trade Marketing * **ANNE DePIES** Senior VP - Business Strategy, Finance & Administration
DON FALLETTI VP - Manufacturing Operations * **LAWRENCE GANEM** VP - Editorial Administration & Talent Relations
ALISON GILL Senior VP - Manufacturing & Operations * **HANK KANALZ** Senior VP - Editorial Strategy & Administration
JAY KOGAN VP - Legal Affairs * **THOMAS LOFTUS** VP - Business Affairs
JACK MAHAN VP - Business Affairs * **NICK J. NAPOLITANO** VP - Manufacturing Administration
EDDIE SCANNELL VP - Consumer Marketing * **COURTNEY SIMMONS** Senior VP - Publicity & Communications
JIM (SKI) SOKOLOWSKI VP - Comic Book Specialty Sales & Trade Marketing * **NANCY SPEARS** VP - Mass, Book, Digital Sales & Trade Marketing

BATMAN: DETECTIVE COMICS VOL. 2–THE VICTIM SYNDICATE

DC Comics, 2900 West Alameda Ave., Burbank, CA 91505. Printed by LSC Communications, Salem, VA, USA. 4/7/17.
First Printing. ISBN: 978-1-4012-6891-6

Library of Congress Cataloging-in-Publication Data is available.

PEFC Certified
Printed on paper from sustainably managed forests, controlled sources
PEFC/29-31-337
www.pefc.org

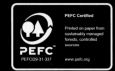

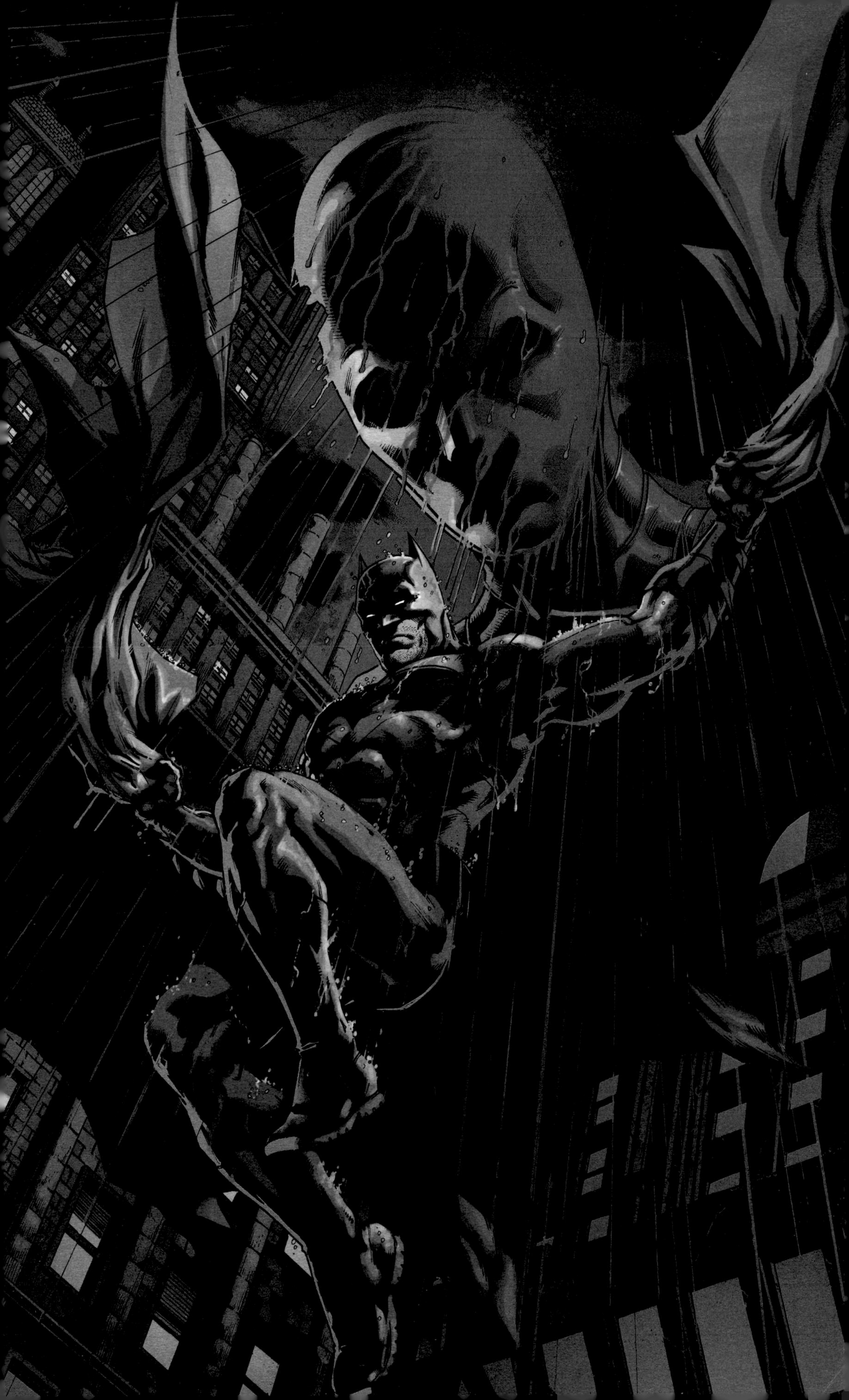

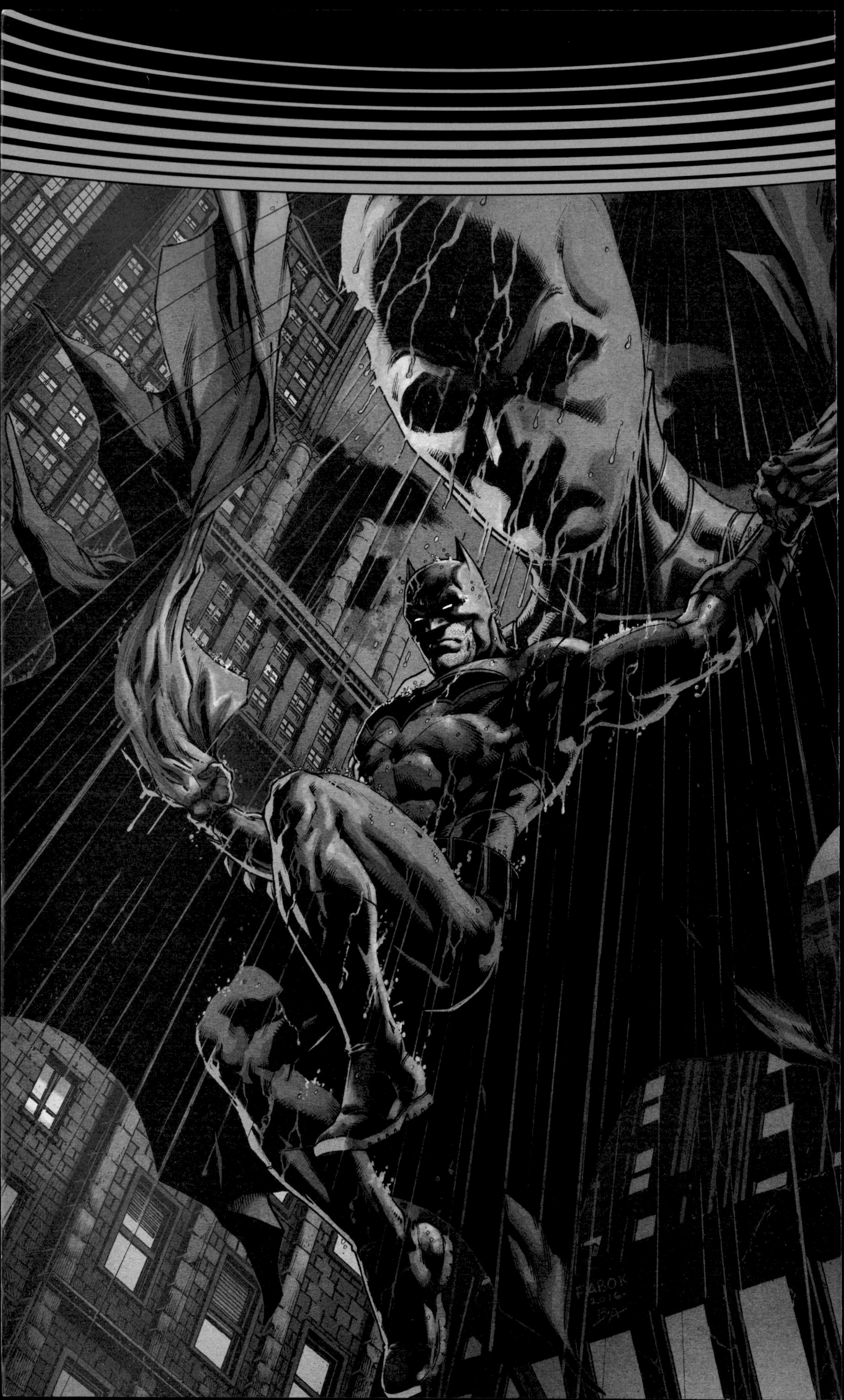

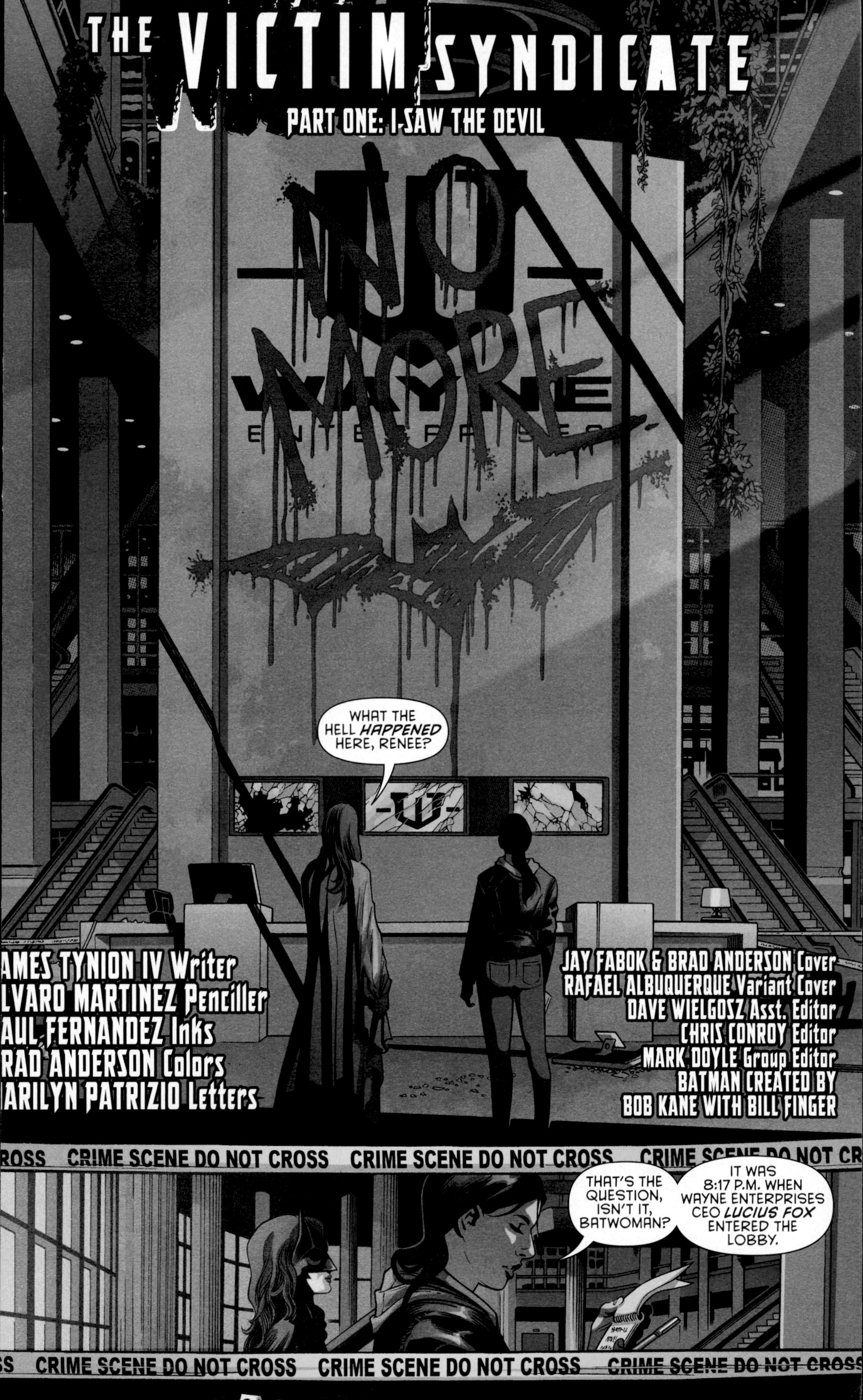
THE VICTIM SYNDICATE
PART ONE: I SAW THE DEVIL
NO MORE
WAYNE ENTERPRISES
WHAT THE HELL *HAPPENED* HERE, RENEE?
AMES TYNION IV Writer
LVARO MARTINEZ Penciller
AUL FERNANDEZ Inks
RAD ANDERSON Colors
ARILYN PATRIZIO Letters
JAY FABOK & BRAD ANDERSON Cover
RAFAEL ALBUQUERQUE Variant Cover
DAVE WIELGOSZ Asst. Editor
CHRIS CONROY Editor
MARK DOYLE Group Editor
BATMAN CREATED BY
BOB KANE WITH BILL FINGER
CROSS CRIME SCENE DO NOT CROSS CRIME SCENE DO NOT CROSS CRIME SCENE DO NOT CR
THAT'S THE QUESTION, ISN'T IT, BATWOMAN?
IT WAS 8:17 P.M. WHEN WAYNE ENTERPRISES CEO *LUCIUS FOX* ENTERED THE LOBBY.
SS CRIME SCENE DO NOT CROSS CRIME SCENE DO NOT CROSS CRIME SCENE DO NOT CROSS

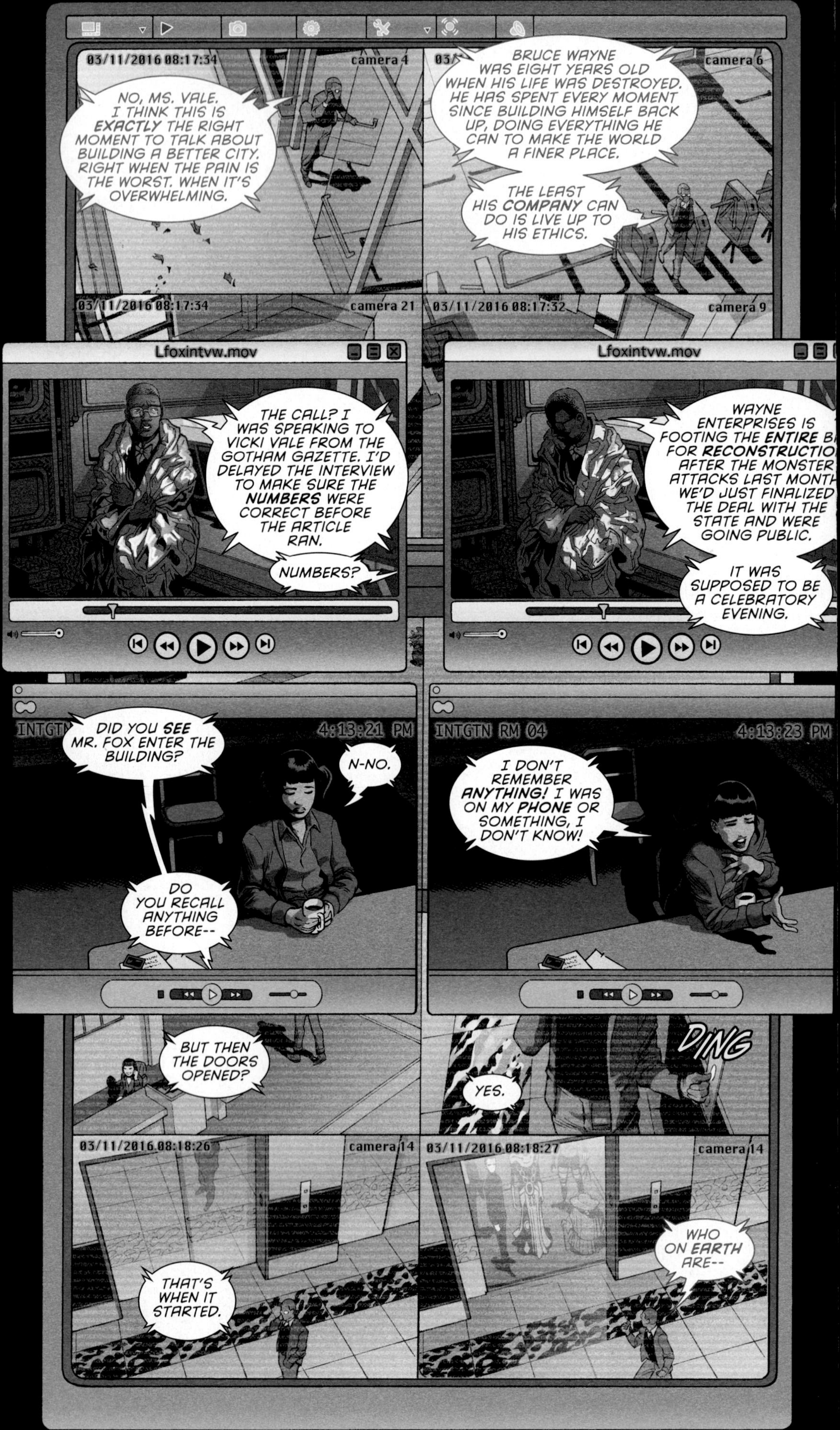
03/11/2016 08:17:34
camera 4
NO, MS. VALE. I THINK THIS IS EXACTLY THE RIGHT MOMENT TO TALK ABOUT BUILDING A BETTER CITY. RIGHT WHEN THE PAIN IS THE WORST. WHEN IT'S OVERWHELMING.
camera 6
BRUCE WAYNE WAS EIGHT YEARS OLD WHEN HIS LIFE WAS DESTROYED. HE HAS SPENT EVERY MOMENT SINCE BUILDING HIMSELF BACK UP, DOING EVERYTHING HE CAN TO MAKE THE WORLD A FINER PLACE.
THE LEAST HIS COMPANY CAN DO IS LIVE UP TO HIS ETHICS.
03/11/2016 08:17:34
camera 21
03/11/2016 08:17:32
camera 9
Lfoxintvw.mov
THE CALL? I WAS SPEAKING TO VICKI VALE FROM THE GOTHAM GAZETTE. I'D DELAYED THE INTERVIEW TO MAKE SURE THE NUMBERS WERE CORRECT BEFORE THE ARTICLE RAN.
NUMBERS?
Lfoxintvw.mov
WAYNE ENTERPRISES IS FOOTING THE ENTIRE BI FOR RECONSTRUCTIO AFTER THE MONSTER ATTACKS LAST MONTH WE'D JUST FINALIZED THE DEAL WITH THE STATE AND WERE GOING PUBLIC.
IT WAS SUPPOSED TO BE A CELEBRATORY EVENING.
4:13:21 PM
DID YOU SEE MR. FOX ENTER THE BUILDING?
N-NO.
DO YOU RECALL ANYTHING BEFORE--
INTGTN RM 04
4:13:23 PM
I DON'T REMEMBER ANYTHING! I WAS ON MY PHONE OR SOMETHING, I DON'T KNOW!
BUT THEN THE DOORS OPENED?
DING
YES.
03/11/2016 08:18:26
camera 14
THAT'S WHEN IT STARTED.
03/11/2016 08:18:27
camera 14
WHO ON EARTH ARE--

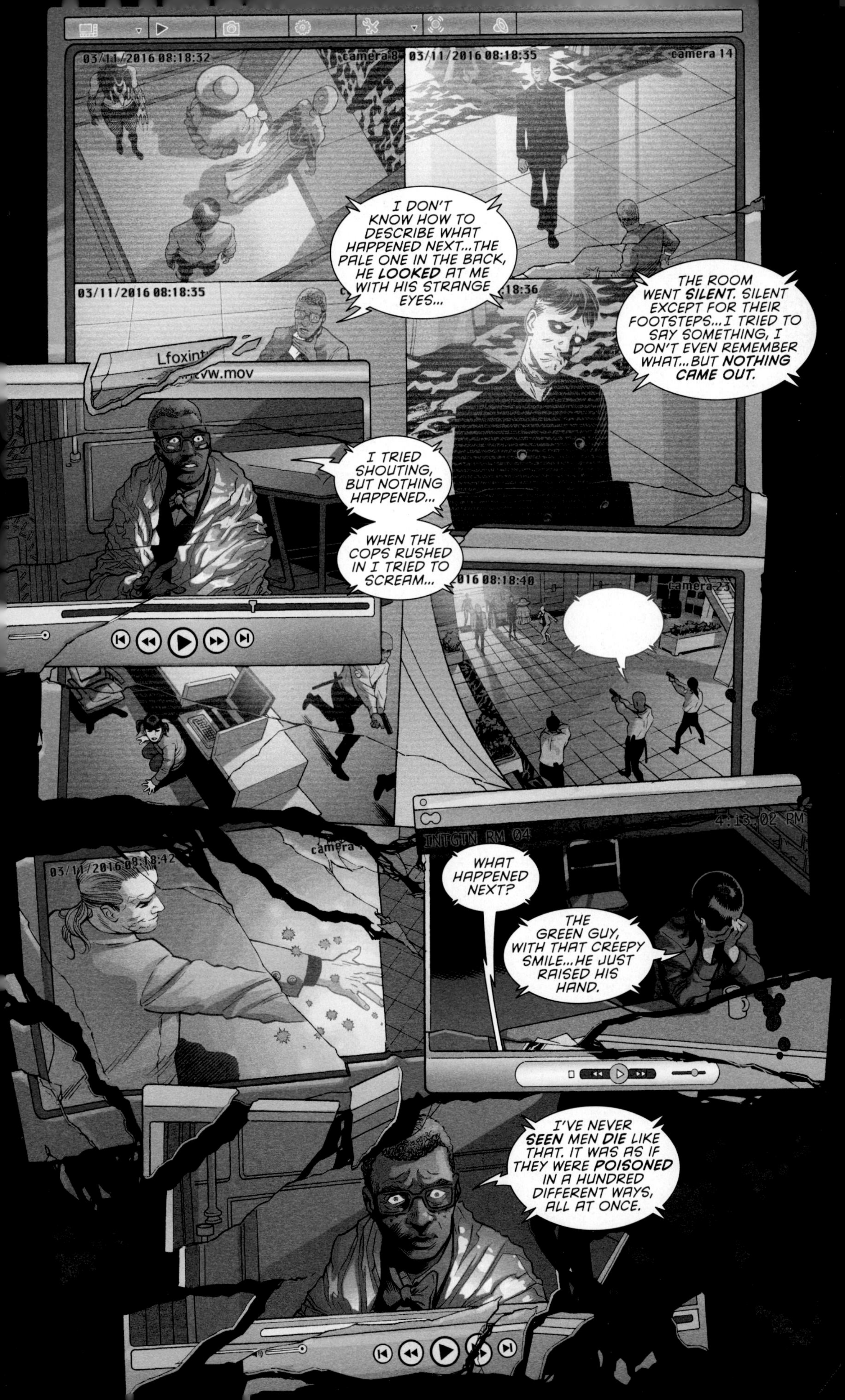

03/11/2016 08:18:32
camera 8
03/11/2016 08:18:35
camera 14
I DON'T KNOW HOW TO DESCRIBE WHAT HAPPENED NEXT...THE PALE ONE IN THE BACK, HE LOOKED AT ME WITH HIS STRANGE EYES...
03/11/2016 08:18:35
THE ROOM WENT SILENT. SILENT EXCEPT FOR THEIR FOOTSTEPS...I TRIED TO SAY SOMETHING, I DON'T EVEN REMEMBER WHAT...BUT NOTHING CAME OUT.
I TRIED SHOUTING, BUT NOTHING HAPPENED...
WHEN THE COPS RUSHED IN I TRIED TO SCREAM...
camera 23
03/11/2016 08:18:42
4:13:02 PM
INTGTN RM 04
WHAT HAPPENED NEXT?
THE GREEN GUY, WITH THAT CREEPY SMILE...HE JUST RAISED HIS HAND.
I'VE NEVER SEEN MEN DIE LIKE THAT. IT WAS AS IF THEY WERE POISONED IN A HUNDRED DIFFERENT WAYS, ALL AT ONCE.

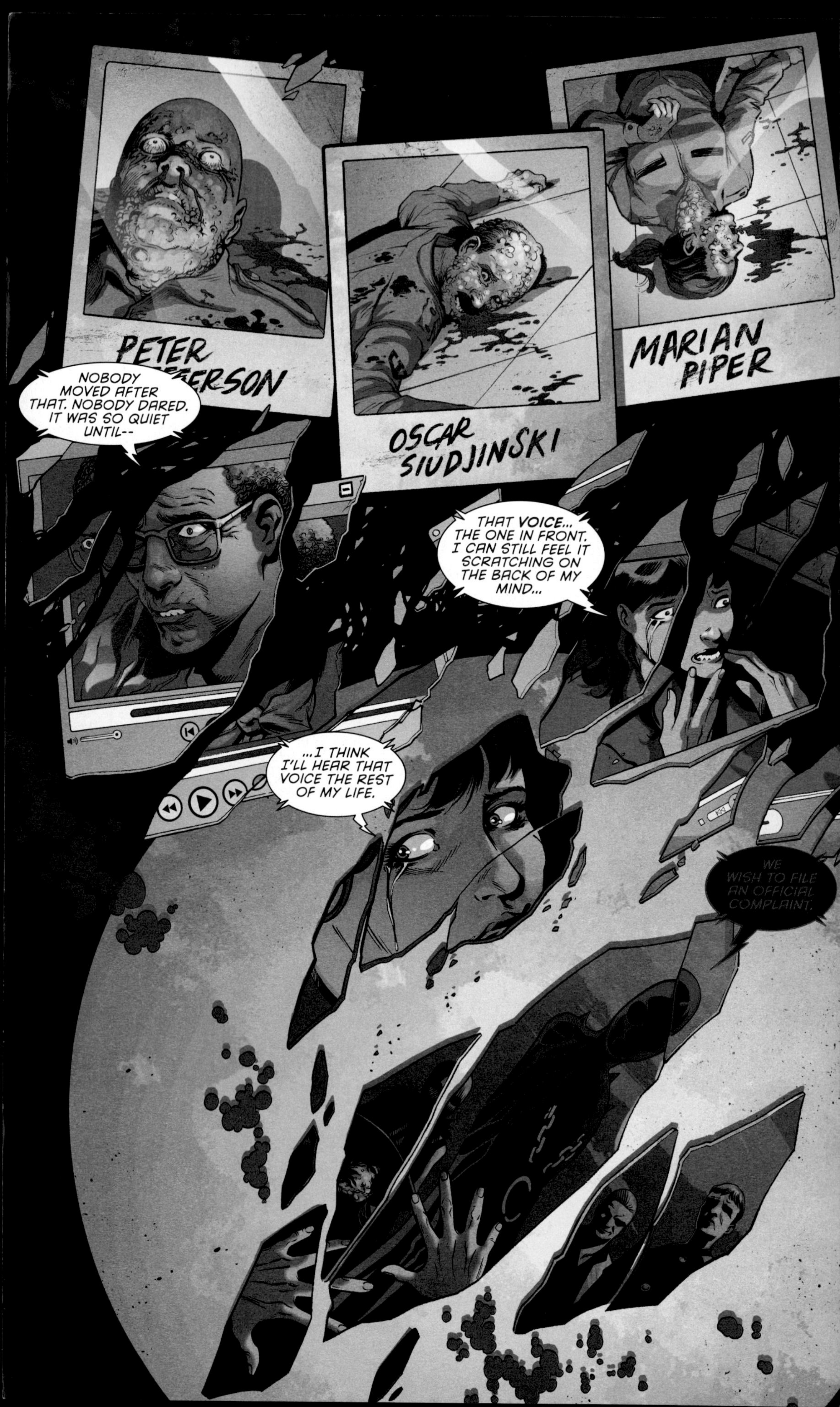
PETER
ERSON
OSCAR SIUDJINSKI
MARIAN PIPER
NOBODY MOVED AFTER THAT. NOBODY DARED. IT WAS SO QUIET UNTIL--
THAT VOICE... THE ONE IN FRONT. I CAN STILL FEEL IT SCRATCHING ON THE BACK OF MY MIND...
...I THINK I'LL HEAR THAT VOICE THE REST OF MY LIFE.
WE WISH TO FILE AN OFFICIAL COMPLAINT.

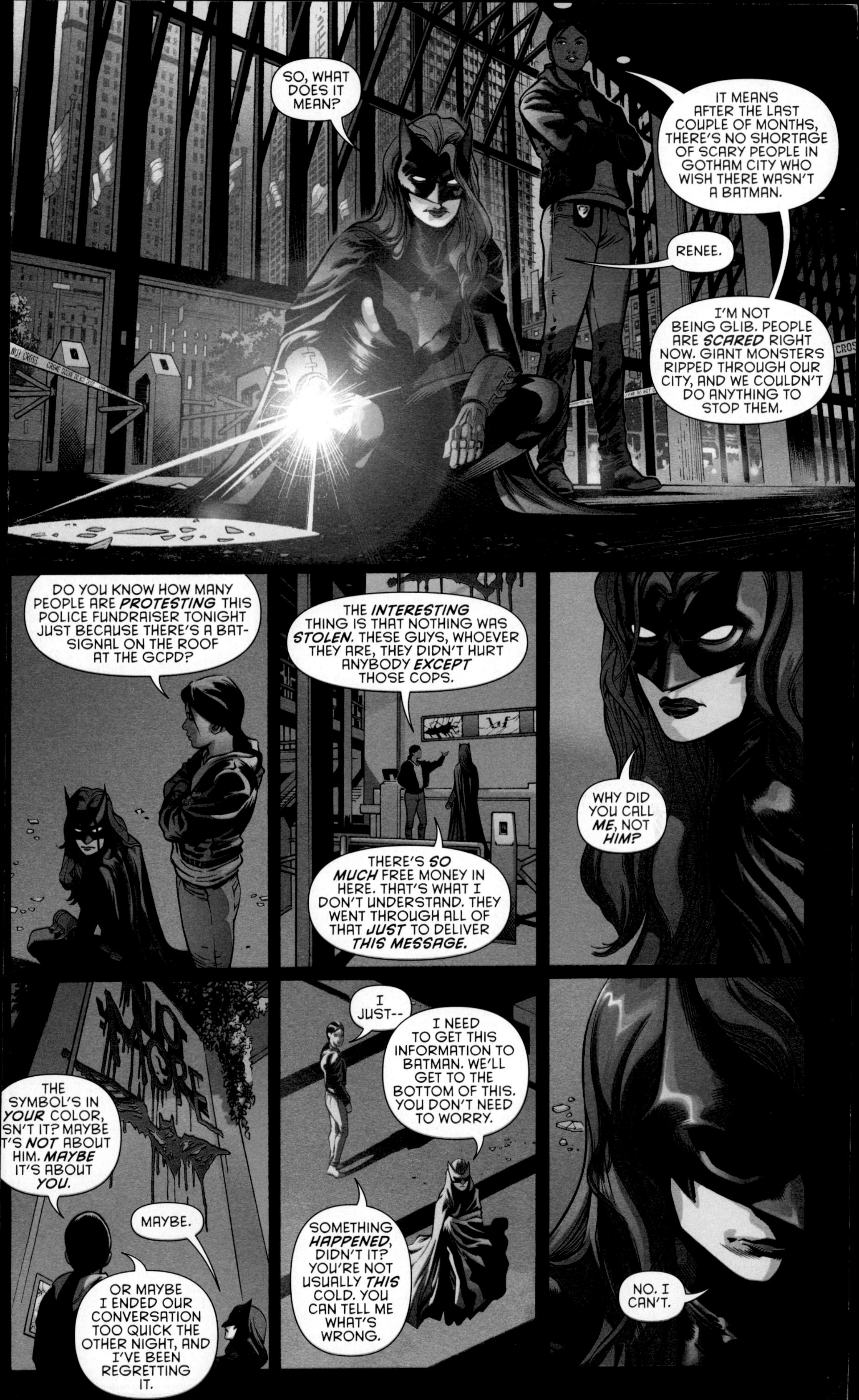
SO, WHAT DOES IT MEAN?
IT MEANS AFTER THE LAST COUPLE OF MONTHS, THERE'S NO SHORTAGE OF SCARY PEOPLE IN GOTHAM CITY WHO WISH THERE WASN'T A BATMAN.
RENEE.
I'M NOT BEING GLIB. PEOPLE ARE *SCARED* RIGHT NOW. GIANT MONSTERS RIPPED THROUGH OUR CITY, AND WE COULDN'T DO ANYTHING TO STOP THEM.
DO YOU KNOW HOW MANY PEOPLE ARE *PROTESTING* THIS POLICE FUNDRAISER TONIGHT JUST BECAUSE THERE'S A BAT-SIGNAL ON THE ROOF AT THE GCPD?
THE *INTERESTING* THING IS THAT NOTHING WAS *STOLEN*. THESE GUYS, WHOEVER THEY ARE, THEY DIDN'T HURT ANYBODY *EXCEPT* THOSE COPS.
THERE'S *SO MUCH* FREE MONEY IN HERE. THAT'S WHAT I DON'T UNDERSTAND. THEY WENT THROUGH ALL OF THAT *JUST* TO DELIVER *THIS MESSAGE.*
WHY DID YOU CALL *ME*, NOT *HIM?*
NO MORE
THE SYMBOL'S IN *YOUR* COLOR, SN'T IT? MAYBE T'S *NOT* ABOUT HIM. *MAYBE* IT'S ABOUT *YOU.*
MAYBE.
OR MAYBE I ENDED OUR CONVERSATION TOO QUICK THE OTHER NIGHT, AND I'VE BEEN REGRETTING IT.
I JUST--
I NEED TO GET THIS INFORMATION TO BATMAN. WE'LL GET TO THE BOTTOM OF THIS. YOU DON'T NEED TO WORRY.
SOMETHING *HAPPENED*, DIDN'T IT? YOU'RE NOT USUALLY *THIS* COLD. YOU CAN TELL ME WHAT'S WRONG.
NO. I CAN'T.

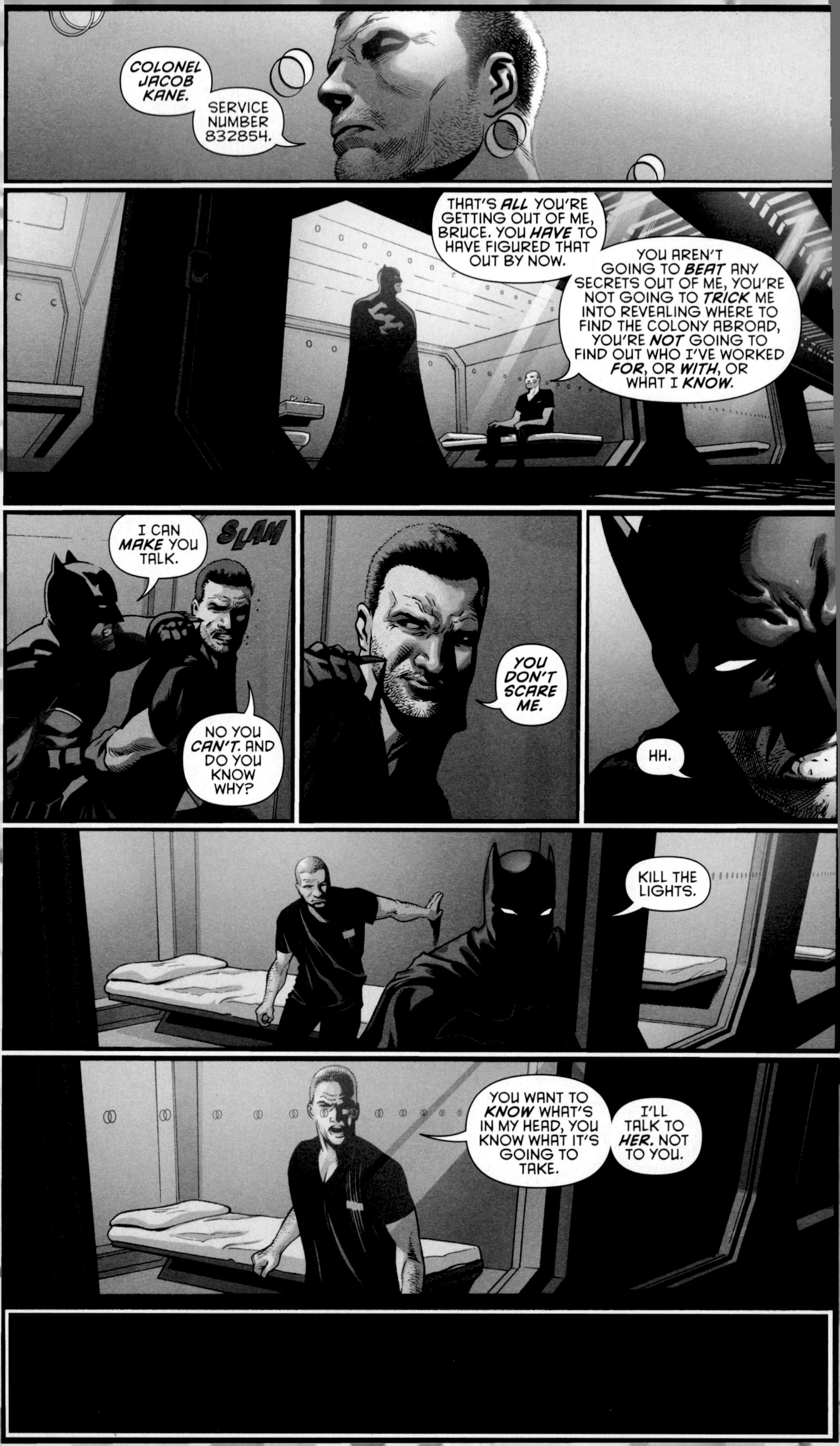
COLONEL JACOB KANE.
SERVICE NUMBER 832854.
THAT'S ALL YOU'RE GETTING OUT OF ME, BRUCE. YOU HAVE TO HAVE FIGURED THAT OUT BY NOW.
YOU AREN'T GOING TO BEAT ANY SECRETS OUT OF ME, YOU'RE NOT GOING TO TRICK ME INTO REVEALING WHERE TO FIND THE COLONY ABROAD, YOU'RE NOT GOING TO FIND OUT WHO I'VE WORKED FOR, OR WITH, OR WHAT I KNOW.
I CAN MAKE YOU TALK.
SLAM
NO YOU CAN'T. AND DO YOU KNOW WHY?
YOU DON'T SCARE ME.
HH.
KILL THE LIGHTS.
YOU WANT TO KNOW WHAT'S IN MY HEAD, YOU KNOW WHAT IT'S GOING TO TAKE.
I'LL TALK TO HER. NOT TO YOU.

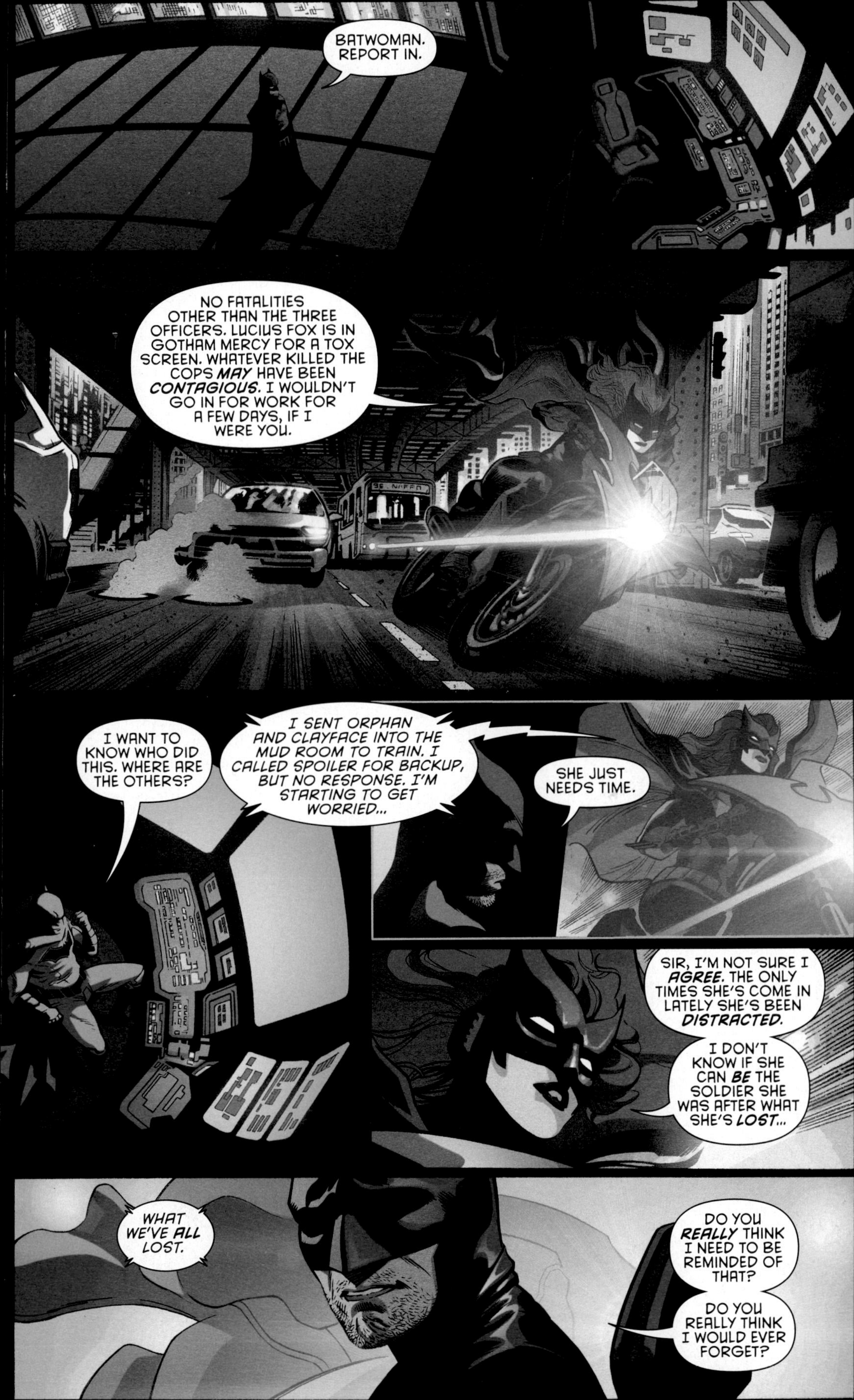
BATWOMAN. REPORT IN.
NO FATALITIES OTHER THAN THE THREE OFFICERS. LUCIUS FOX IS IN GOTHAM MERCY FOR A TOX SCREEN. WHATEVER KILLED THE COPS MAY HAVE BEEN CONTAGIOUS. I WOULDN'T GO IN FOR WORK FOR A FEW DAYS, IF I WERE YOU.
I WANT TO KNOW WHO DID THIS. WHERE ARE THE OTHERS?
I SENT ORPHAN AND CLAYFACE INTO THE MUD ROOM TO TRAIN. I CALLED SPOILER FOR BACKUP, BUT NO RESPONSE. I'M STARTING TO GET WORRIED...
SHE JUST NEEDS TIME.
SIR, I'M NOT SURE I AGREE. THE ONLY TIMES SHE'S COME IN LATELY SHE'S BEEN DISTRACTED.
I DON'T KNOW IF SHE CAN BE THE SOLDIER SHE WAS AFTER WHAT SHE'S LOST...
WHAT WE'VE ALL LOST.
DO YOU REALLY THINK I NEED TO BE REMINDED OF THAT?
DO YOU REALLY THINK I WOULD EVER FORGET?

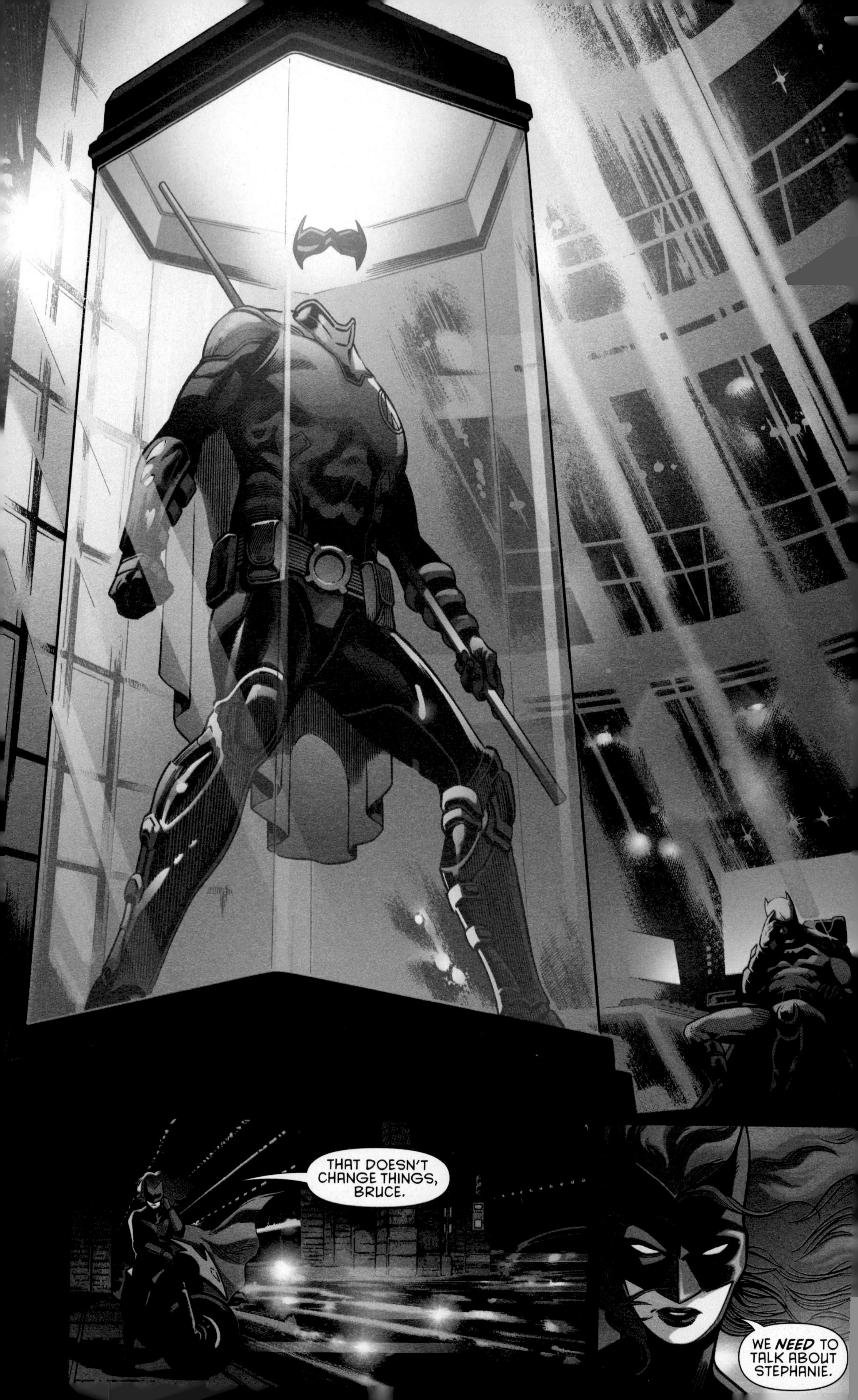
THAT DOESN'T CHANGE THINGS, BRUCE.
WE NEED TO TALK ABOUT STEPHANIE.

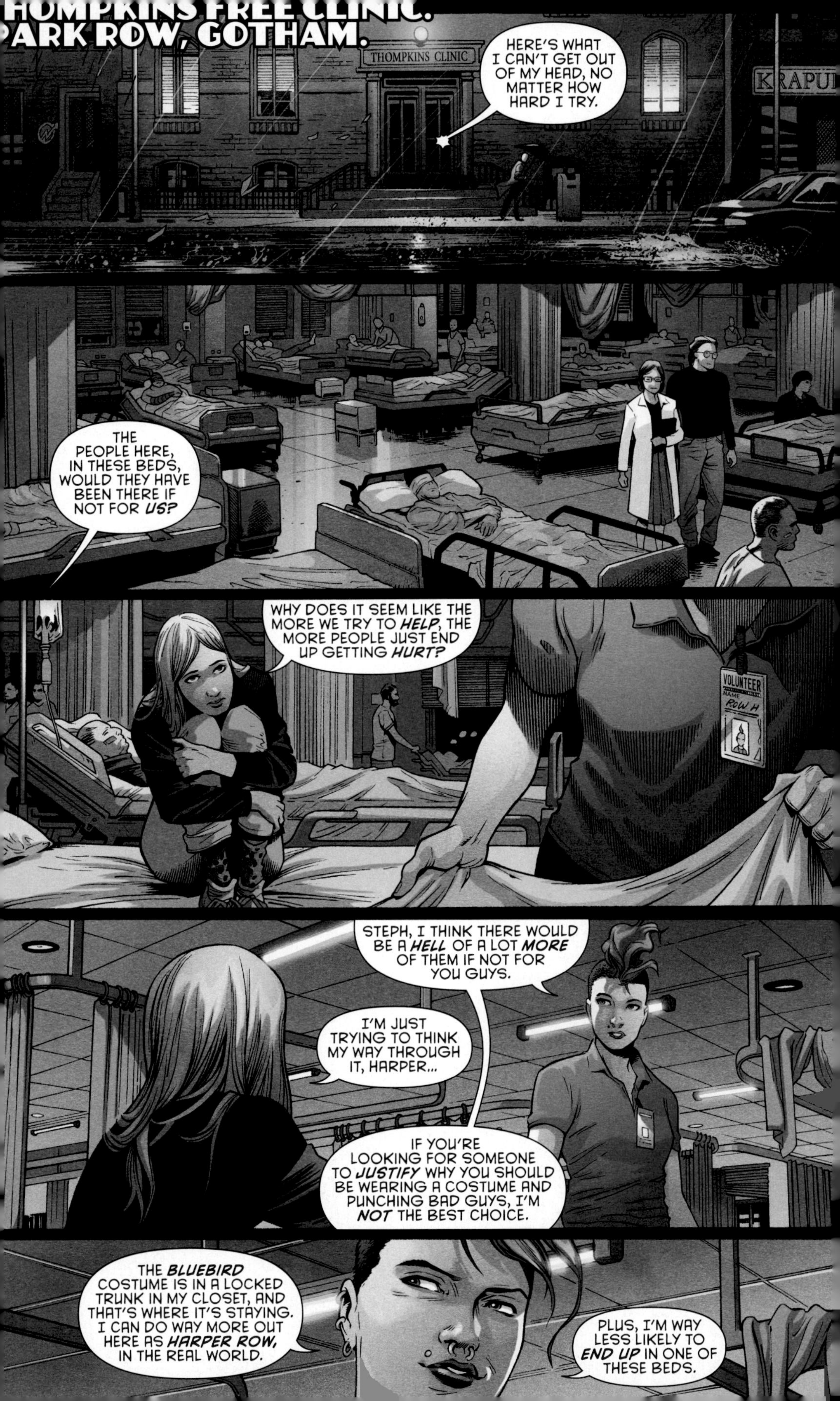
THOMPKINS FREE CLINIC. PARK ROW, GOTHAM.
THOMPKINS CLINIC
HERE'S WHAT I CAN'T GET OUT OF MY HEAD, NO MATTER HOW HARD I TRY.
THE PEOPLE HERE, IN THESE BEDS, WOULD THEY HAVE BEEN THERE IF NOT FOR *US?*
WHY DOES IT SEEM LIKE THE MORE WE TRY TO *HELP*, THE MORE PEOPLE JUST END UP GETTING *HURT?*
VOLUNTEER
NAME ROW H
STEPH, I THINK THERE WOULD BE A *HELL* OF A LOT *MORE* OF THEM IF NOT FOR YOU GUYS.
I'M JUST TRYING TO THINK MY WAY THROUGH IT, HARPER...
IF YOU'RE LOOKING FOR SOMEONE TO *JUSTIFY* WHY YOU SHOULD BE WEARING A COSTUME AND PUNCHING BAD GUYS, I'M *NOT* THE BEST CHOICE.
THE *BLUEBIRD* COSTUME IS IN A LOCKED TRUNK IN MY CLOSET, AND THAT'S WHERE IT'S STAYING. I CAN DO WAY MORE OUT HERE AS *HARPER ROW,* IN THE REAL WORLD.
PLUS, I'M WAY LESS LIKELY TO *END UP* IN ONE OF THESE BEDS.

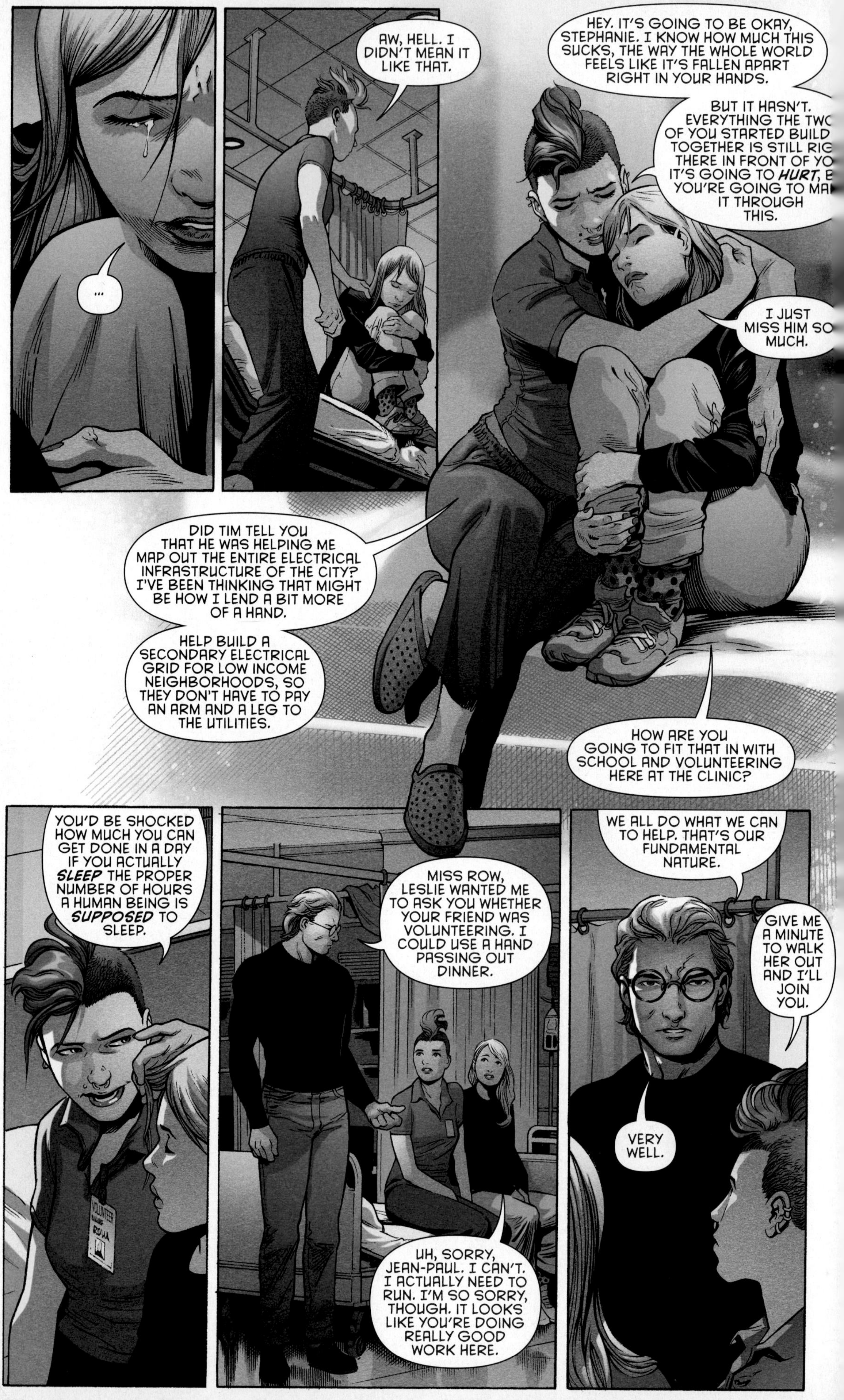

...
AW, HELL. I DIDN'T MEAN IT LIKE THAT.
HEY. IT'S GOING TO BE OKAY, STEPHANIE. I KNOW HOW MUCH THIS SUCKS, THE WAY THE WHOLE WORLD FEELS LIKE IT'S FALLEN APART RIGHT IN YOUR HANDS.
BUT IT HASN'T. EVERYTHING THE TWO OF YOU STARTED BUILD TOGETHER IS STILL RIG THERE IN FRONT OF YO IT'S GOING TO HURT, B YOU'RE GOING TO MA IT THROUGH THIS.
I JUST MISS HIM SO MUCH.
DID TIM TELL YOU THAT HE WAS HELPING ME MAP OUT THE ENTIRE ELECTRICAL INFRASTRUCTURE OF THE CITY? I'VE BEEN THINKING THAT MIGHT BE HOW I LEND A BIT MORE OF A HAND.
HELP BUILD A SECONDARY ELECTRICAL GRID FOR LOW INCOME NEIGHBORHOODS, SO THEY DON'T HAVE TO PAY AN ARM AND A LEG TO THE UTILITIES.
HOW ARE YOU GOING TO FIT THAT IN WITH SCHOOL AND VOLUNTEERING HERE AT THE CLINIC?
YOU'D BE SHOCKED HOW MUCH YOU CAN GET DONE IN A DAY IF YOU ACTUALLY SLEEP THE PROPER NUMBER OF HOURS A HUMAN BEING IS SUPPOSED TO SLEEP.
MISS ROW, LESLIE WANTED ME TO ASK YOU WHETHER YOUR FRIEND WAS VOLUNTEERING. I COULD USE A HAND PASSING OUT DINNER.
UH, SORRY, JEAN-PAUL. I CAN'T. I ACTUALLY NEED TO RUN. I'M SO SORRY, THOUGH. IT LOOKS LIKE YOU'RE DOING REALLY GOOD WORK HERE.
WE ALL DO WHAT WE CAN TO HELP. THAT'S OUR FUNDAMENTAL NATURE.
GIVE ME A MINUTE TO WALK HER OUT AND I'LL JOIN YOU.
VERY WELL.

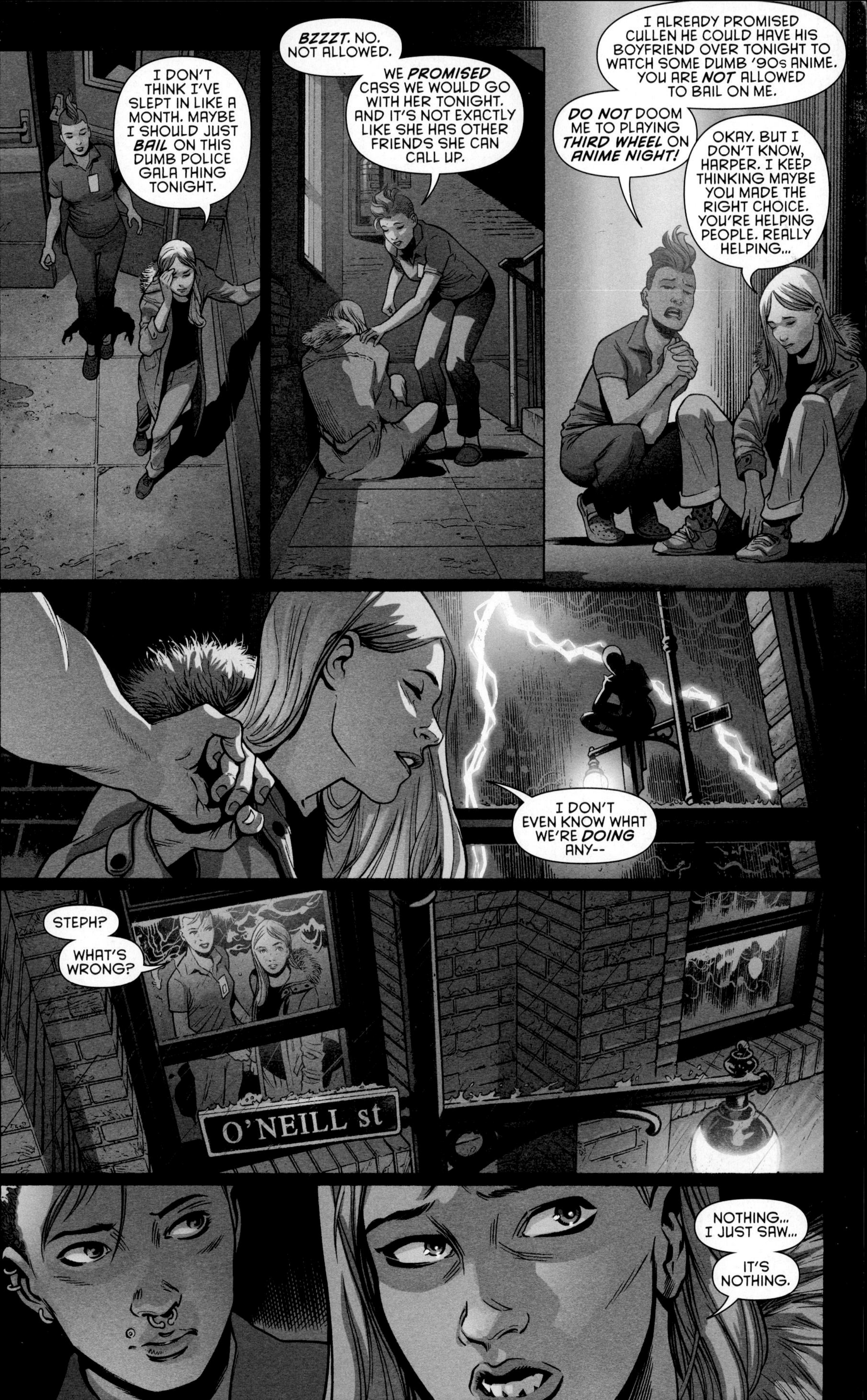

I DON'T THINK I'VE SLEPT IN LIKE A MONTH. MAYBE I SHOULD JUST BAIL ON THIS DUMB POLICE GALA THING TONIGHT.
BZZZT. NO. NOT ALLOWED.
WE PROMISED CASS WE WOULD GO WITH HER TONIGHT. AND IT'S NOT EXACTLY LIKE SHE HAS OTHER FRIENDS SHE CAN CALL UP.
I ALREADY PROMISED CULLEN HE COULD HAVE HIS BOYFRIEND OVER TONIGHT TO WATCH SOME DUMB '90s ANIME. YOU ARE NOT ALLOWED TO BAIL ON ME.
DO NOT DOOM ME TO PLAYING THIRD WHEEL ON ANIME NIGHT!
OKAY. BUT I DON'T KNOW, HARPER. I KEEP THINKING MAYBE YOU MADE THE RIGHT CHOICE. YOU'RE HELPING PEOPLE. REALLY HELPING...
I DON'T EVEN KNOW WHAT WE'RE DOING ANY--
STEPH?
WHAT'S WRONG?
O'NEILL st
NOTHING... I JUST SAW...
IT'S NOTHING.

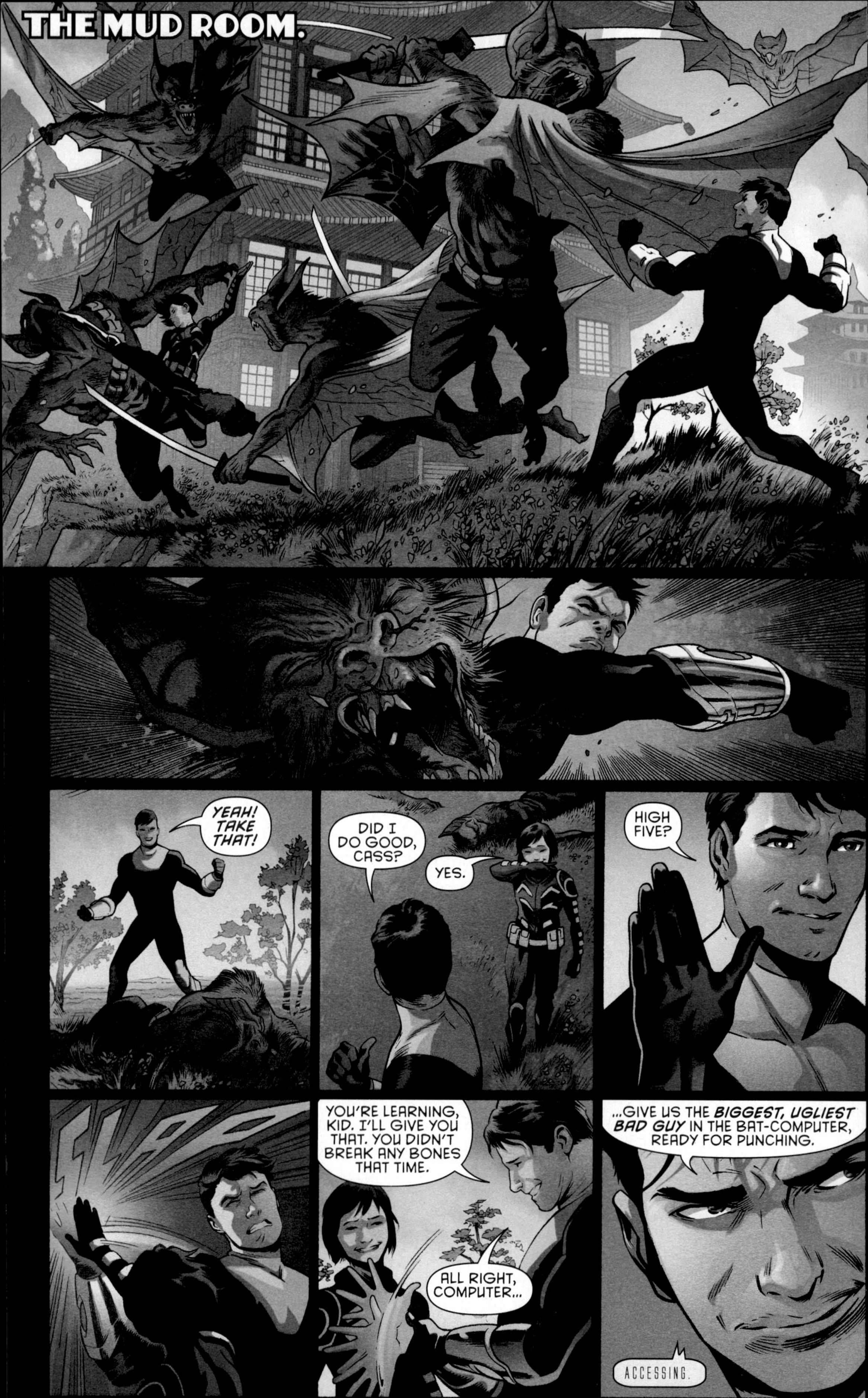
THE MUD ROOM.
YEAH! TAKE THAT!
DID I DO GOOD, CASS?
YES.
HIGH FIVE?
YOU'RE LEARNING, KID. I'LL GIVE YOU THAT. YOU DIDN'T BREAK ANY BONES THAT TIME.
ALL RIGHT, COMPUTER...
...GIVE US THE BIGGEST, UGLIEST BAD GUY IN THE BAT-COMPUTER, READY FOR PUNCHING.
ACCESSING.

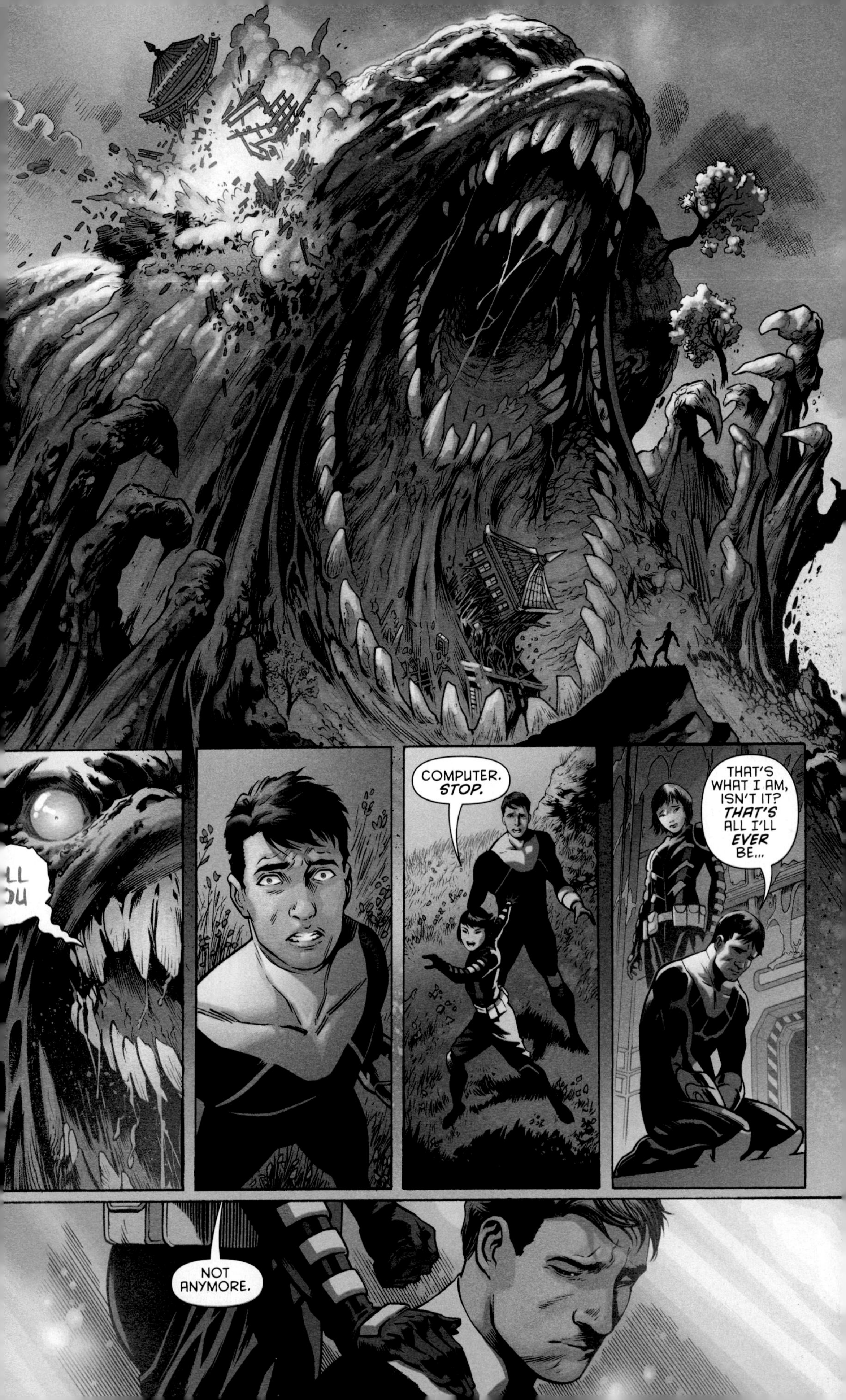
COMPUTER. STOP.
THAT'S WHAT I AM, ISN'T IT? THAT'S ALL I'LL EVER BE...
NOT ANYMORE.

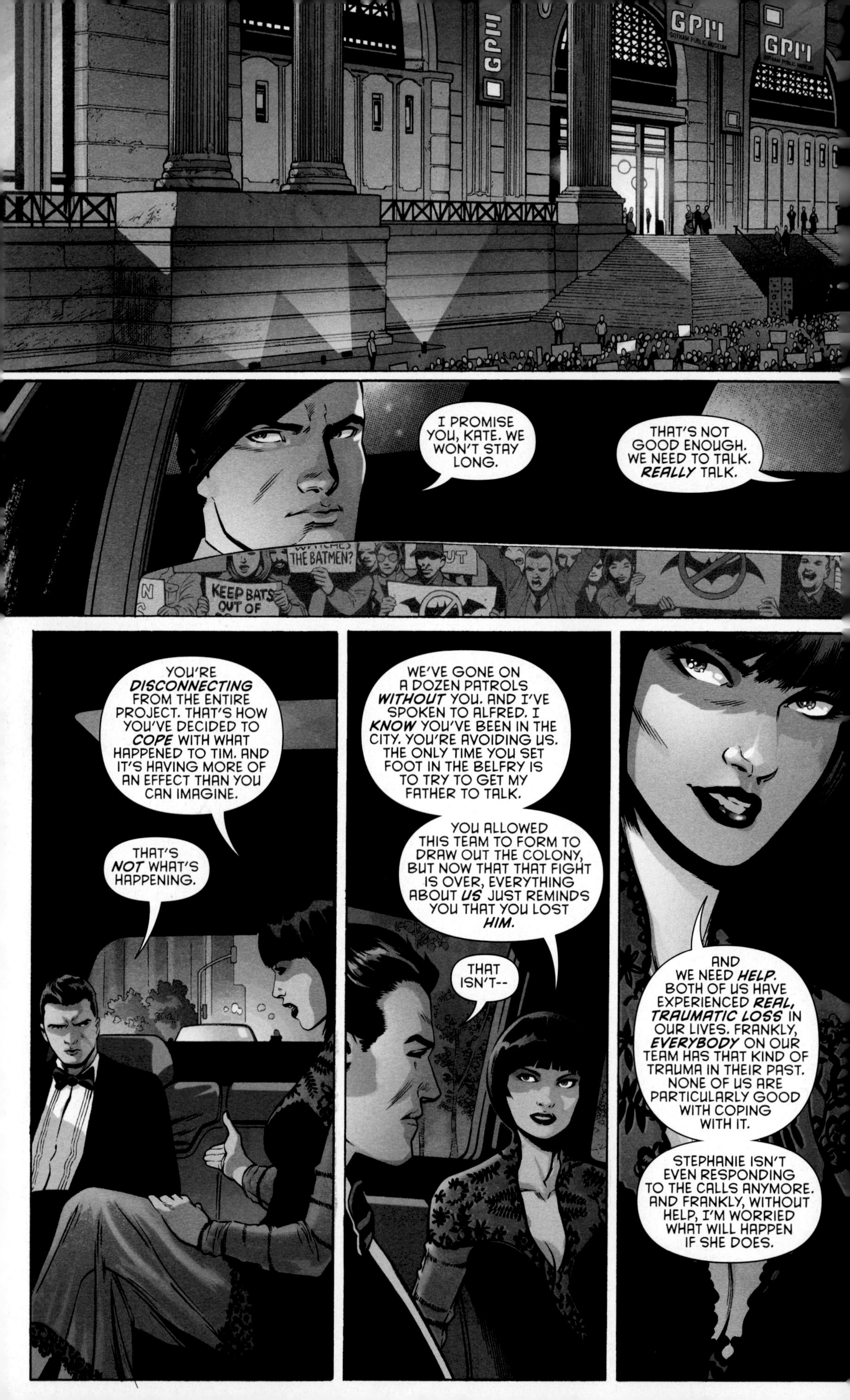
GPM
GOTHAM PUBLIC MUSEUM
I PROMISE YOU, KATE. WE WON'T STAY LONG.
THAT'S NOT GOOD ENOUGH. WE NEED TO TALK. *REALLY* TALK.
THE BATMEN?
KEEP BATS OUT OF
YOU'RE *DISCONNECTING* FROM THE ENTIRE PROJECT. THAT'S HOW YOU'VE DECIDED TO *COPE* WITH WHAT HAPPENED TO TIM. AND IT'S HAVING MORE OF AN EFFECT THAN YOU CAN IMAGINE.
THAT'S *NOT* WHAT'S HAPPENING.
WE'VE GONE ON A DOZEN PATROLS *WITHOUT* YOU. AND I'VE SPOKEN TO ALFRED. I *KNOW* YOU'VE BEEN IN THE CITY. YOU'RE AVOIDING US. THE ONLY TIME YOU SET FOOT IN THE BELFRY IS TO TRY TO GET MY FATHER TO TALK.
YOU ALLOWED THIS TEAM TO FORM TO DRAW OUT THE COLONY, BUT NOW THAT THAT FIGHT IS OVER, EVERYTHING ABOUT *US* JUST REMINDS YOU THAT YOU LOST *HIM*.
THAT ISN'T--
AND WE NEED *HELP*. BOTH OF US HAVE EXPERIENCED *REAL, TRAUMATIC LOSS* IN OUR LIVES. FRANKLY, *EVERYBODY* ON OUR TEAM HAS THAT KIND OF TRAUMA IN THEIR PAST. NONE OF US ARE PARTICULARLY GOOD WITH COPING WITH IT.
STEPHANIE ISN'T EVEN RESPONDING TO THE CALLS ANYMORE. AND FRANKLY, WITHOUT HELP, I'M WORRIED WHAT WILL HAPPEN IF SHE DOES.

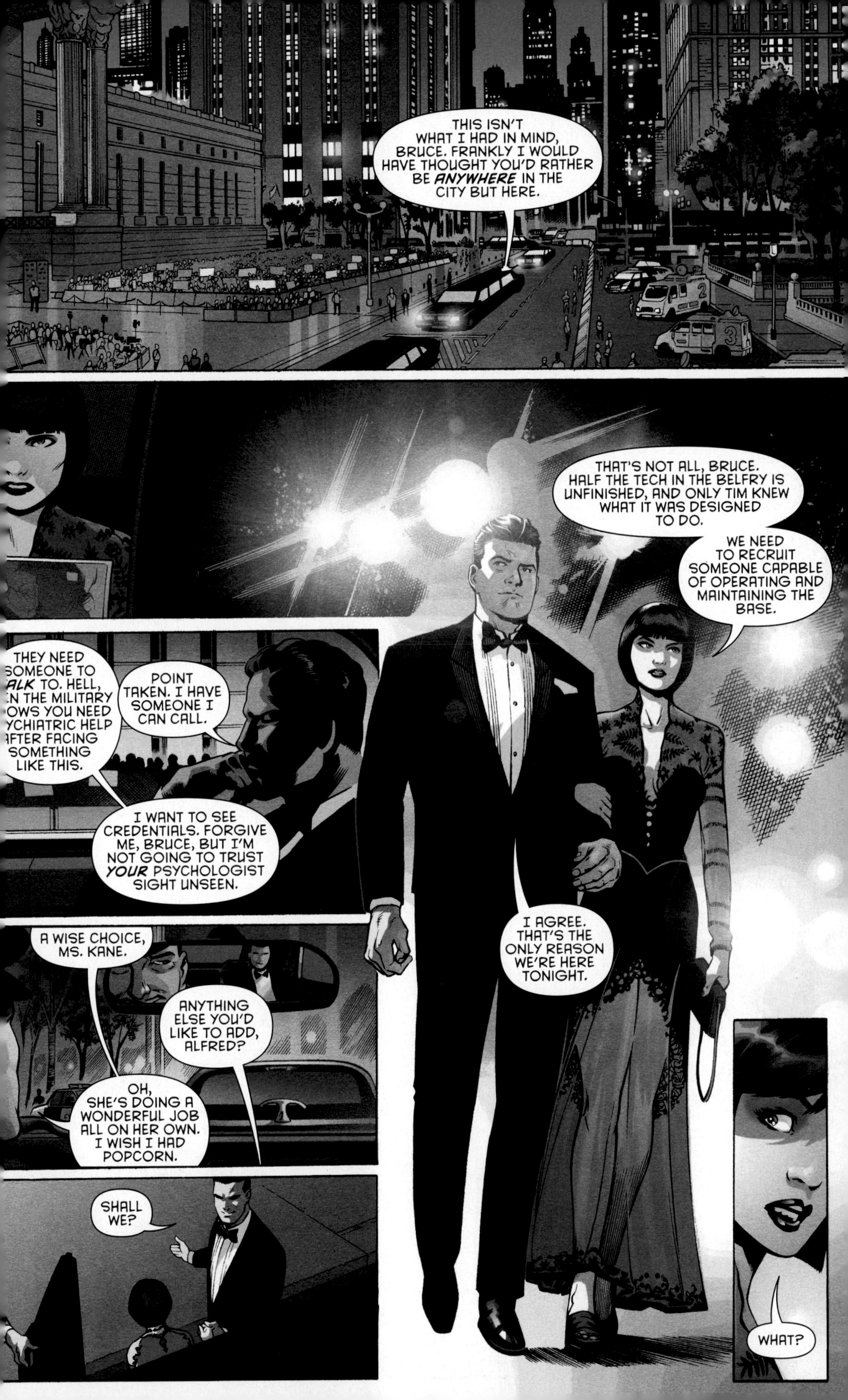

THIS ISN'T WHAT I HAD IN MIND, BRUCE. FRANKLY I WOULD HAVE THOUGHT YOU'D RATHER BE *ANYWHERE* IN THE CITY BUT HERE.
THAT'S NOT ALL, BRUCE. HALF THE TECH IN THE BELFRY IS UNFINISHED, AND ONLY TIM KNEW WHAT IT WAS DESIGNED TO DO.
WE NEED TO RECRUIT SOMEONE CAPABLE OF OPERATING AND MAINTAINING THE BASE.
THEY NEED SOMEONE TO ALK TO. HELL, N THE MILITARY OWS YOU NEED YCHIATRIC HELP AFTER FACING SOMETHING LIKE THIS.
POINT TAKEN. I HAVE SOMEONE I CAN CALL.
I WANT TO SEE CREDENTIALS. FORGIVE ME, BRUCE, BUT I'M NOT GOING TO TRUST *YOUR* PSYCHOLOGIST SIGHT UNSEEN.
I AGREE. THAT'S THE ONLY REASON WE'RE HERE TONIGHT.
A WISE CHOICE, MS. KANE.
ANYTHING ELSE YOU'D LIKE TO ADD, ALFRED?
OH, SHE'S DOING A WONDERFUL JOB ALL ON HER OWN. I WISH I HAD POPCORN.
SHALL WE?
WHAT?

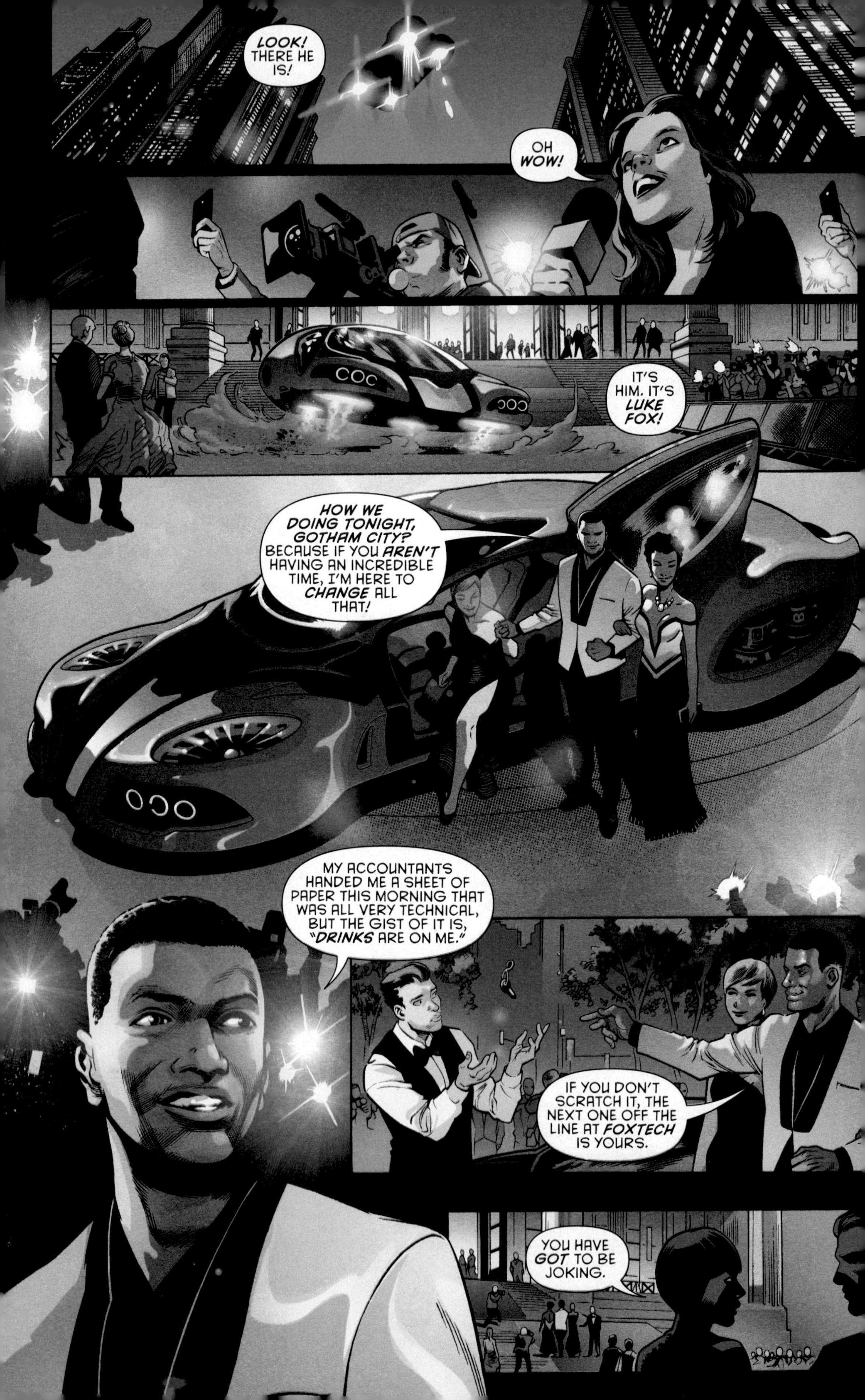
LOOK! THERE HE IS!
OH WOW!
IT'S HIM. IT'S LUKE FOX!
HOW WE DOING TONIGHT, GOTHAM CITY? BECAUSE IF YOU AREN'T HAVING AN INCREDIBLE TIME, I'M HERE TO CHANGE ALL THAT!
MY ACCOUNTANTS HANDED ME A SHEET OF PAPER THIS MORNING THAT WAS ALL VERY TECHNICAL, BUT THE GIST OF IT IS, "DRINKS ARE ON ME."
IF YOU DON'T SCRATCH IT, THE NEXT ONE OFF THE LINE AT FOXTECH IS YOURS.
YOU HAVE GOT TO BE JOKING.

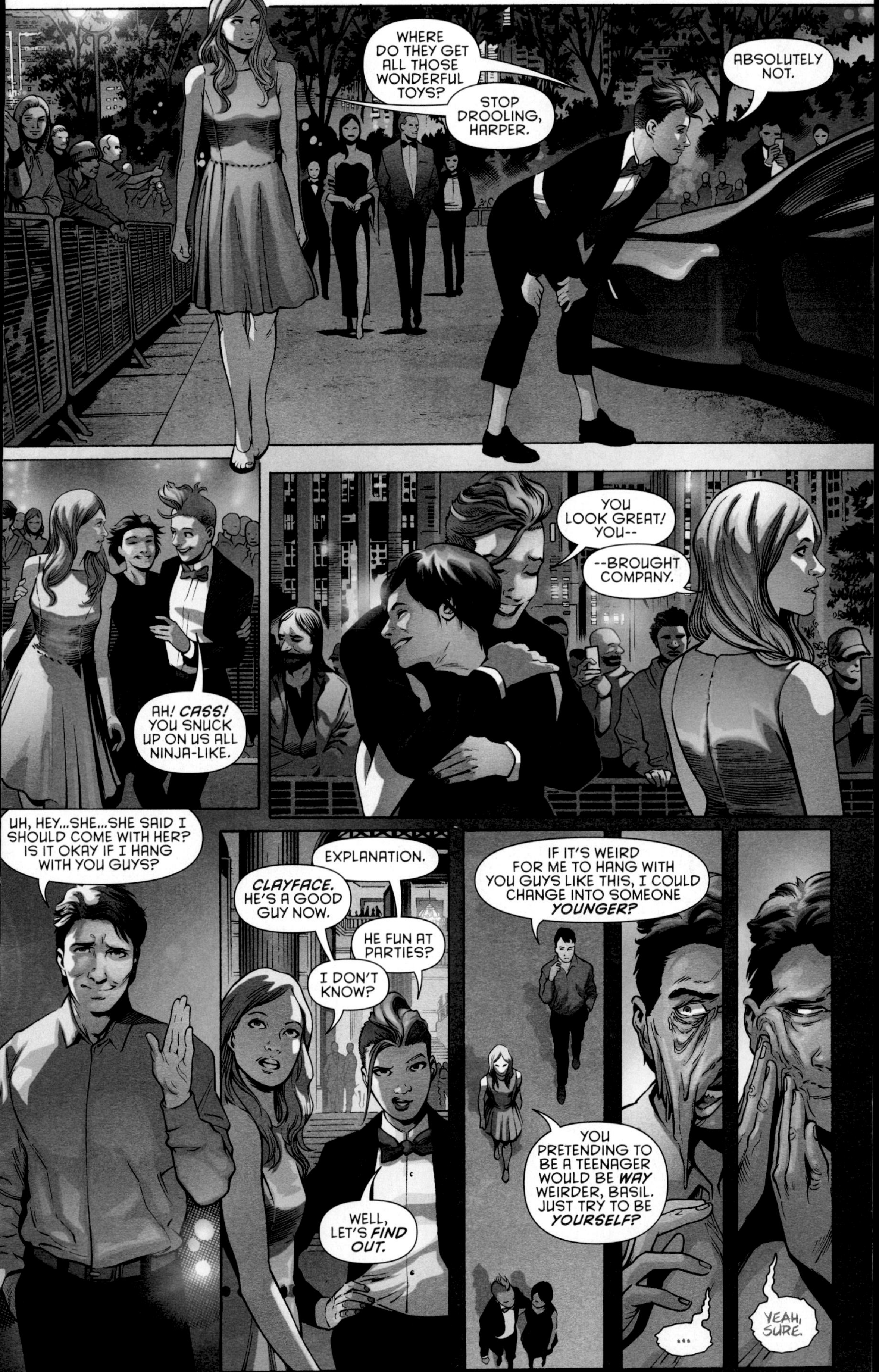
WHERE DO THEY GET ALL THOSE WONDERFUL TOYS?
STOP DROOLING, HARPER.
ABSOLUTELY NOT.
AH! CASS! YOU SNUCK UP ON US ALL NINJA-LIKE.
YOU LOOK GREAT! YOU--
--BROUGHT COMPANY.
UH, HEY...SHE...SHE SAID I SHOULD COME WITH HER? IS IT OKAY IF I HANG WITH YOU GUYS?
EXPLANATION.
CLAYFACE. HE'S A GOOD GUY NOW.
HE FUN AT PARTIES?
I DON'T KNOW?
WELL, LET'S FIND OUT.
IF IT'S WEIRD FOR ME TO HANG WITH YOU GUYS LIKE THIS, I COULD CHANGE INTO SOMEONE YOUNGER?
YOU PRETENDING TO BE A TEENAGER WOULD BE WAY WEIRDER, BASIL. JUST TRY TO BE YOURSELF?
...
YEAH, SURE.

MR. FOX. DO YOU HAVE ANY COMMENT ON THE *ATTACK* ON YOUR FATHER EARLIER TODAY AT WAYNE ENTERPRISES?

ACTUALLY, I JUST GOT OFF THE PHONE WITH HIM A FEW MINUTES AGO. HE TOL[D] ME TO TELL YOU THAT THE DOCTORS WERE VERY *ANGRY* WITH YO[U] FOR SNEAKING IN TO FINISH YOUR INTERVIEW THIS AFTERNOON.

SERIOUSL[Y] THOUGH. H[E'S] DOING GRE[AT] HE WISHES [HE] COULD B[E] HERE.

THAT SOUNDS A BIT LIKE THE M.O. OF THE VIGILANTE KNOWN AS *BATMAN*. THIS EVENT HAS BEEN CRITICIZED BY CITIZENS CONCERNED ABOUT THE RELATIONSHIP BETWEEN OUR POLICE FORCE AND A DANGEROUS *VIGILANTE*.

JUST THE OTHER WEEK BATMAN AND HIS ALLIES MANAGED TO SAVE THE ENTIRE CITY FROM A THREAT UNLIKE ANYTHING WE'VE EVER SEEN BEFORE.

I'M PROUD THAT GOTHAM CITY IS WHERE THE BATMAN HANGS UP HIS CAPE AND COWL.

IT'S LIKE I ALWAYS SAY, GOTHAM DOES THINGS BETTE[R] THAN *ANYWHER[E]* ELSE ON *EARTH* IT'S NO MISTAK[E] WE'VE GOT TH[E] WORLD'S *GREATEST SUPERHERO*.

AND WHO IS THIS LOVELY LADY RIGHT HERE?

NOT EVEN REMOTELY INTERESTED.

BRUCE, A WORD?

LUKE FOX HAS ONE OF THE BEST TECHNICAL MINDS IN GOTHAM CITY.

FUNNY HOW I SEE HIM ALL OVER THE TABLOIDS, AND NOT THE BUSINESS SECTION.

YO[U] COULD [SAY] THE SA[ME] FOR B[RUCE] WAYN[E]

HE WAS A CELEBRITY BEFORE H[E] EVER PUT ON A COSTU[ME] BRUCE. HE TURNED DO[WN] LUCRATIVE CAREER PAT[H] TO BECOME AN MM[A] FIGHTER, AND ONLY GAVE *THAT* UP TO PLAY AT BEING A SUPERHERO.

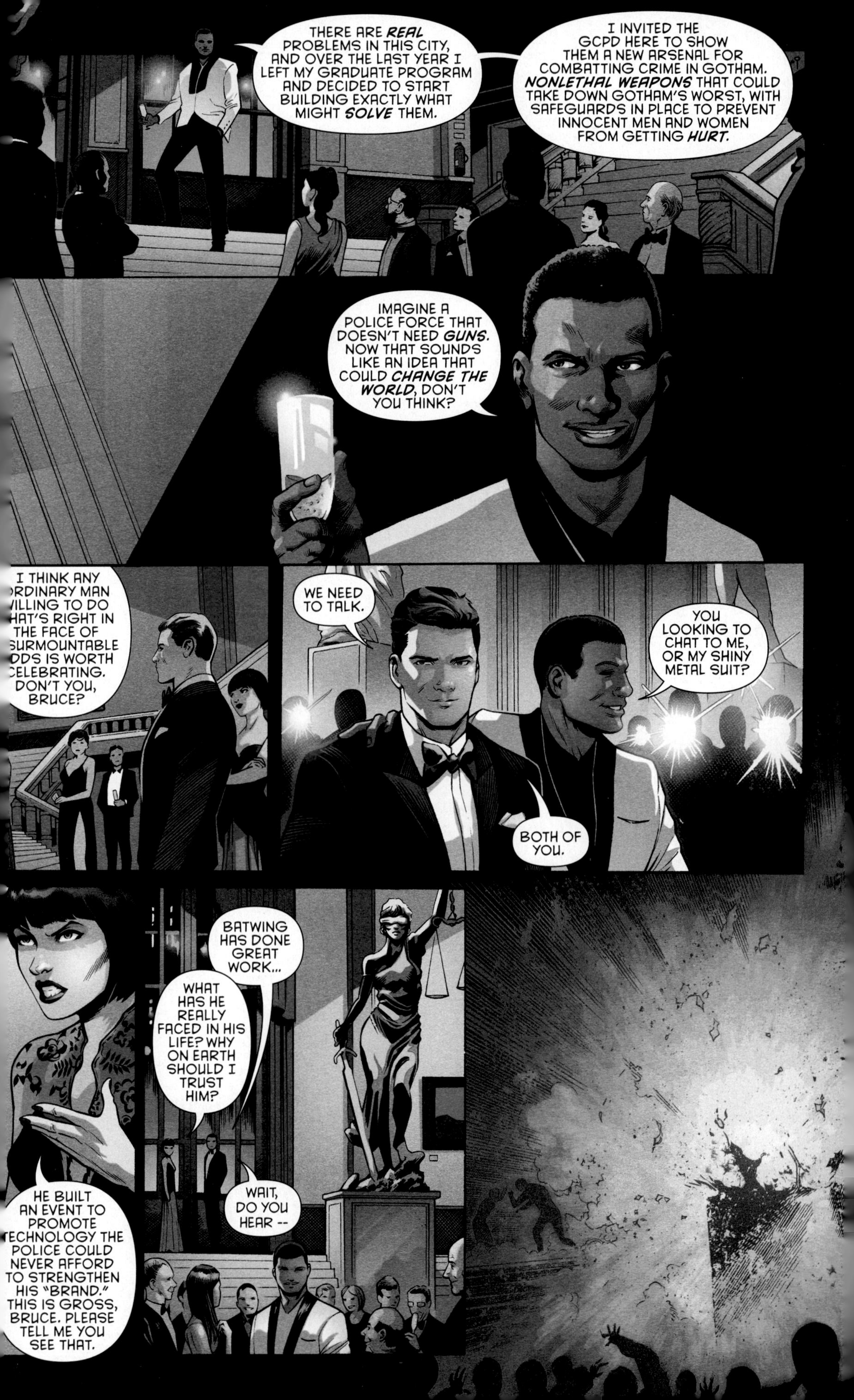
THERE ARE *REAL* PROBLEMS IN THIS CITY, AND OVER THE LAST YEAR I LEFT MY GRADUATE PROGRAM AND DECIDED TO START BUILDING EXACTLY WHAT MIGHT *SOLVE* THEM.
I INVITED THE GCPD HERE TO SHOW THEM A NEW ARSENAL FOR COMBATTING CRIME IN GOTHAM. *NONLETHAL WEAPONS* THAT COULD TAKE DOWN GOTHAM'S WORST, WITH SAFEGUARDS IN PLACE TO PREVENT INNOCENT MEN AND WOMEN FROM GETTING *HURT*.
IMAGINE A POLICE FORCE THAT DOESN'T NEED *GUNS*. NOW THAT SOUNDS LIKE AN IDEA THAT COULD *CHANGE THE WORLD*, DON'T YOU THINK?
I THINK ANY ORDINARY MAN WILLING TO DO WHAT'S RIGHT IN THE FACE OF INSURMOUNTABLE ODDS IS WORTH CELEBRATING. DON'T YOU, BRUCE?
WE NEED TO TALK.
YOU LOOKING TO CHAT TO ME, OR MY SHINY METAL SUIT?
BOTH OF YOU.
BATWING HAS DONE GREAT WORK...
WHAT HAS HE REALLY FACED IN HIS LIFE? WHY ON EARTH SHOULD I TRUST HIM?
HE BUILT AN EVENT TO PROMOTE TECHNOLOGY THE POLICE COULD NEVER AFFORD TO STRENGTHEN HIS "BRAND." THIS IS GROSS, BRUCE. PLEASE TELL ME YOU SEE THAT.
WAIT, DO YOU HEAR --

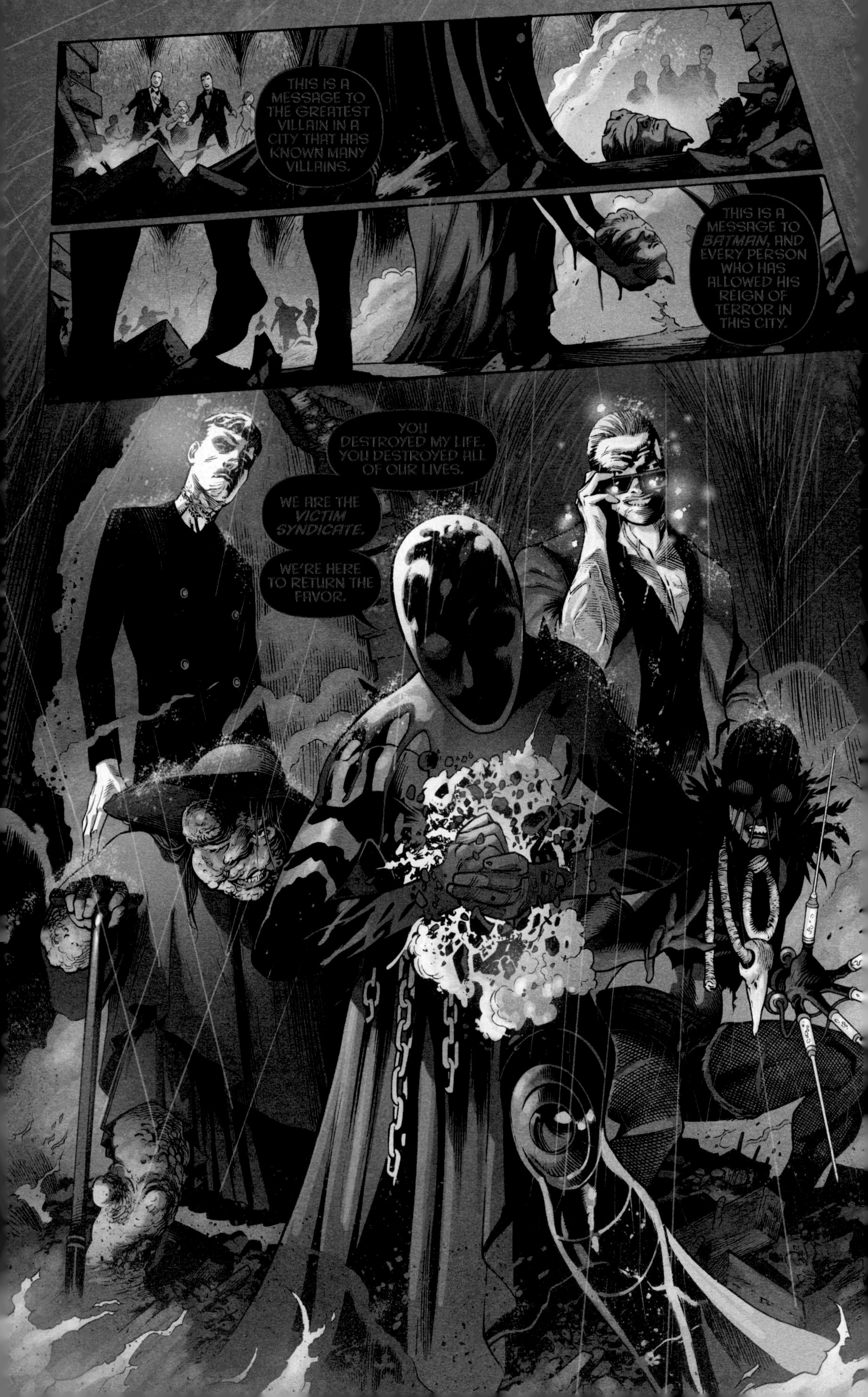
THIS IS A MESSAGE TO THE GREATEST VILLAIN IN A CITY THAT HAS KNOWN MANY VILLAINS.
THIS IS A MESSAGE TO *BATMAN*, AND EVERY PERSON WHO HAS ALLOWED HIS REIGN OF TERROR IN THIS CITY.
YOU DESTROYED MY LIFE. YOU DESTROYED ALL OF OUR LIVES.
WE ARE THE *VICTIM SYNDICATE.*
WE'RE HERE TO RETURN THE FAVOR.

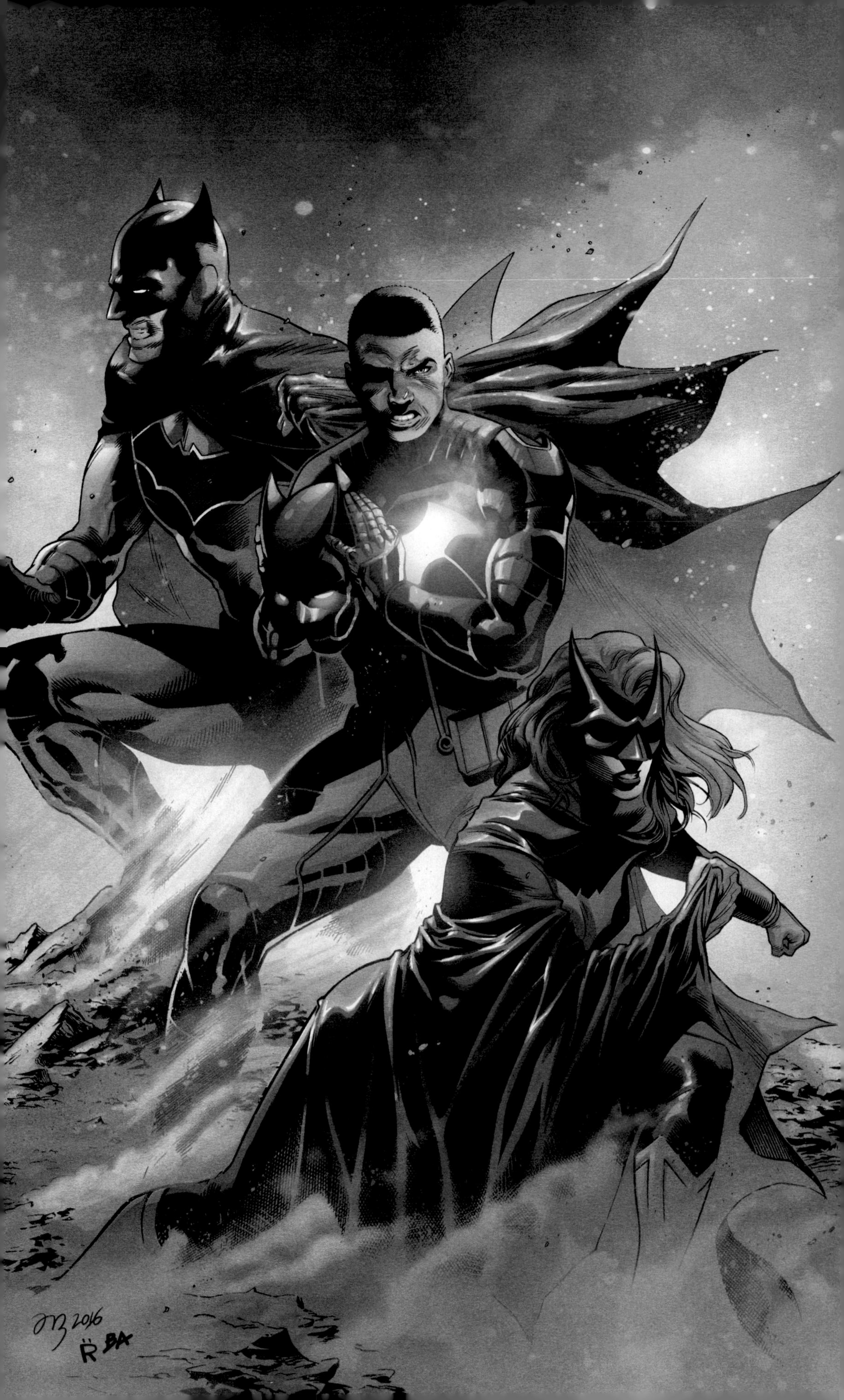

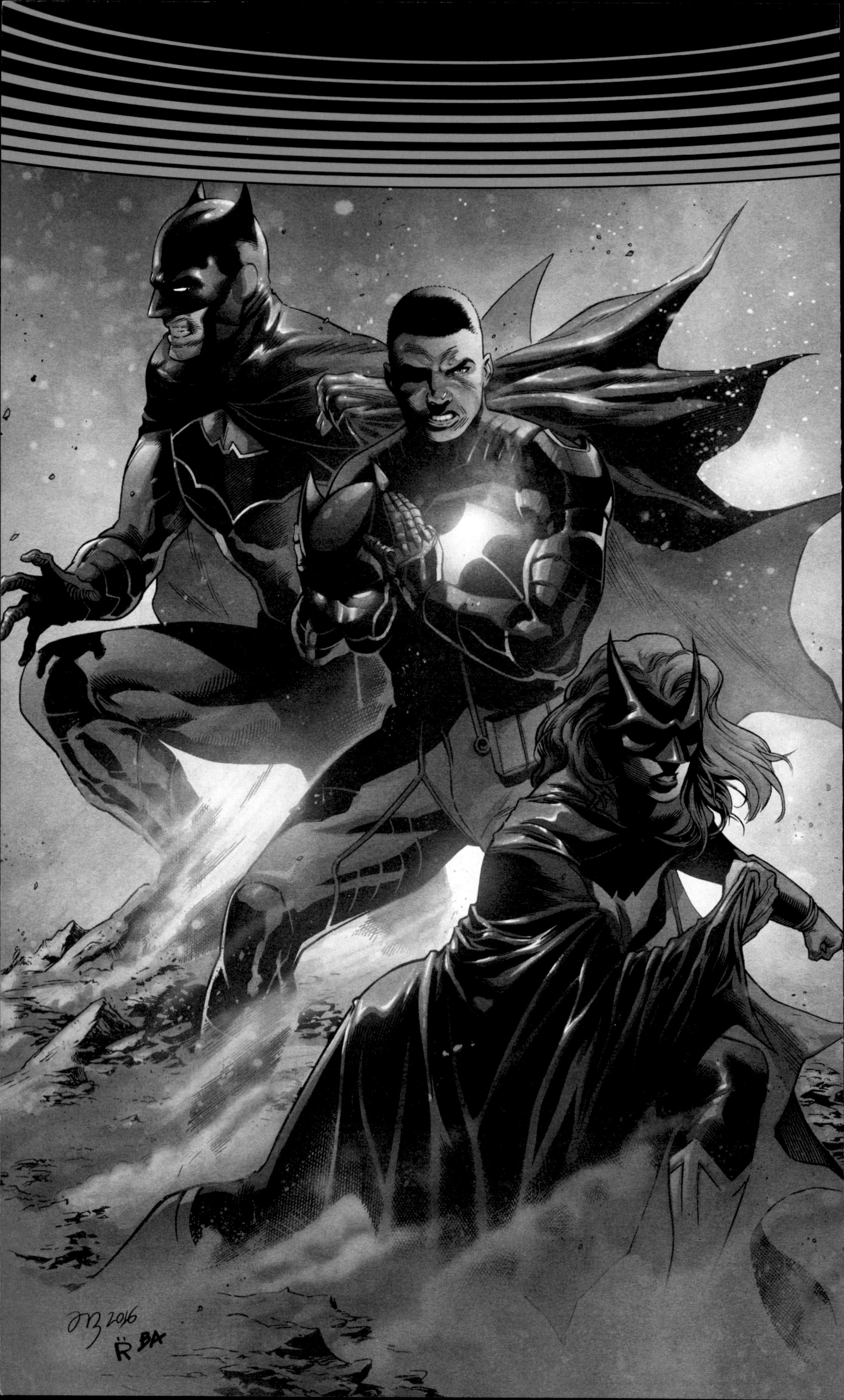

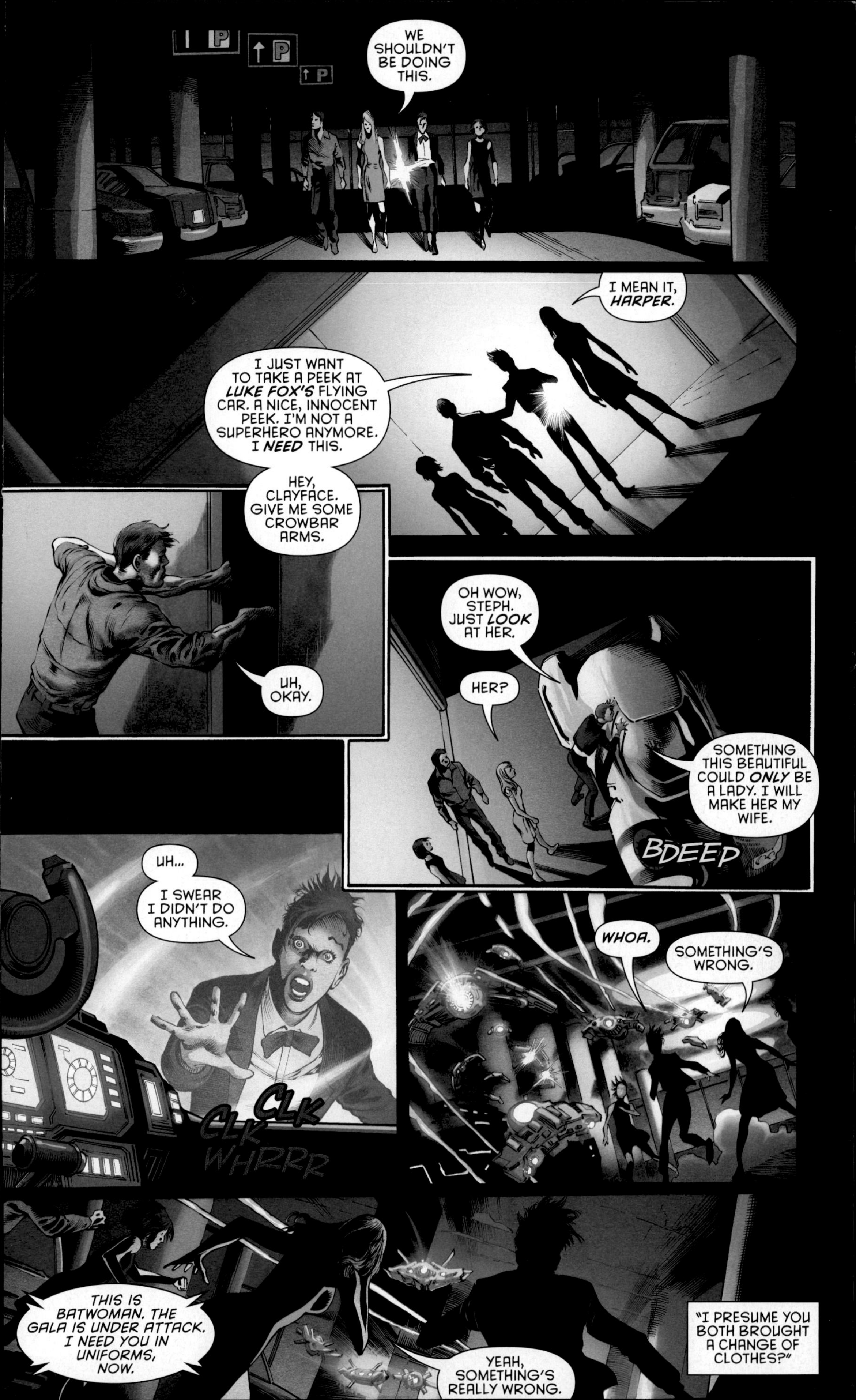
WE SHOULDN'T BE DOING THIS.
I MEAN IT, HARPER.
I JUST WANT TO TAKE A PEEK AT LUKE FOX'S FLYING CAR. A NICE, INNOCENT PEEK. I'M NOT A SUPERHERO ANYMORE. I NEED THIS.
HEY, CLAYFACE. GIVE ME SOME CROWBAR ARMS.
UH, OKAY.
OH WOW, STEPH. JUST LOOK AT HER.
HER?
SOMETHING THIS BEAUTIFUL COULD ONLY BE A LADY. I WILL MAKE HER MY WIFE.
BDEEP
UH...
I SWEAR I DIDN'T DO ANYTHING.
CLK
CLK
WHRRR
WHOA.
SOMETHING'S WRONG.
THIS IS BATWOMAN. THE GALA IS UNDER ATTACK. I NEED YOU IN UNIFORMS, NOW.
YEAH, SOMETHING'S REALLY WRONG.
"I PRESUME YOU BOTH BROUGHT A CHANGE OF CLOTHES?"

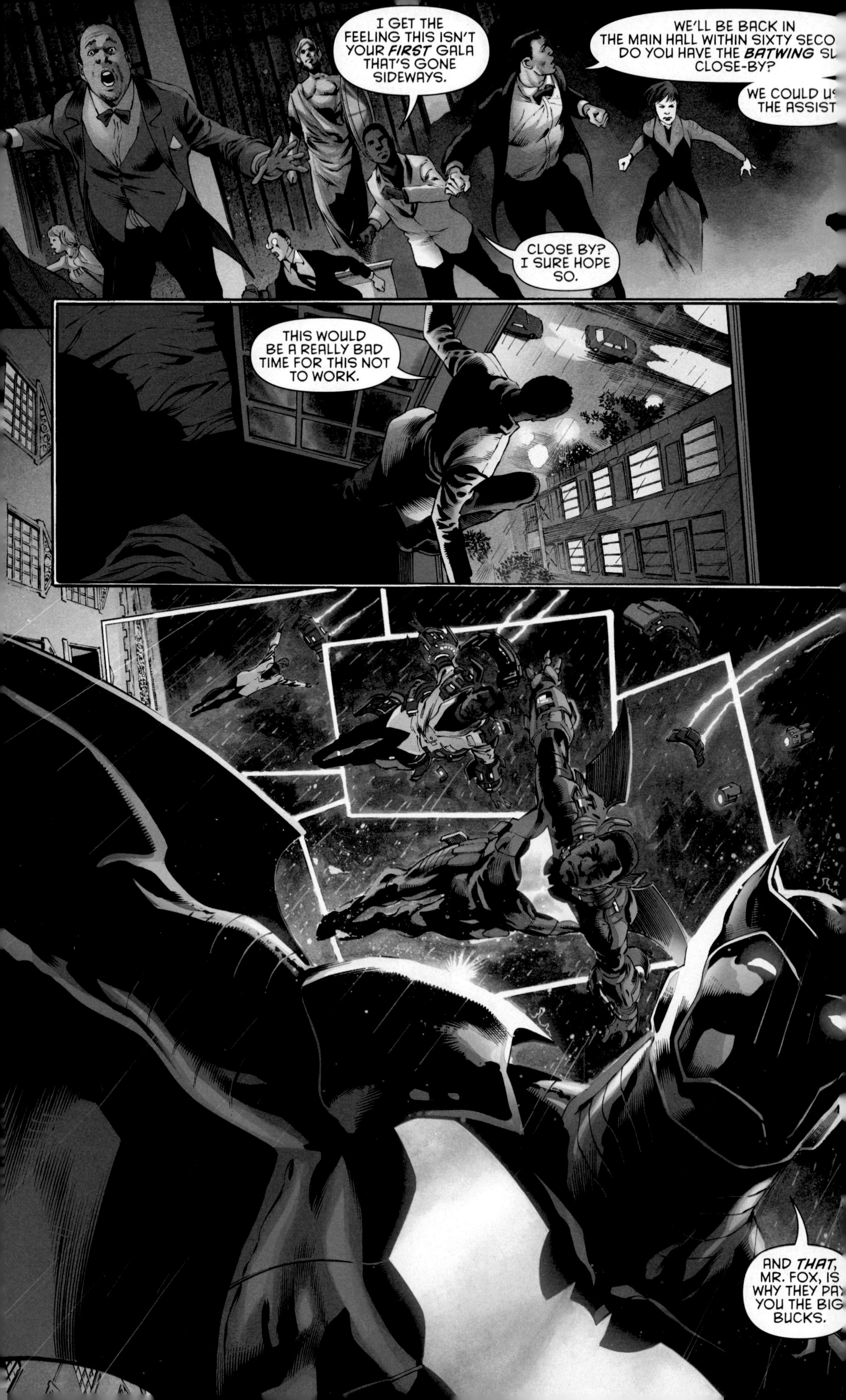
I GET THE FEELING THIS ISN'T YOUR *FIRST* GALA THAT'S GONE SIDEWAYS.
WE'LL BE BACK IN THE MAIN HALL WITHIN SIXTY SECO
DO YOU HAVE THE *BATWING* SL
CLOSE-BY?
WE COULD US
THE ASSIST
CLOSE BY? I SURE HOPE SO.
THIS WOULD BE A REALLY BAD TIME FOR THIS NOT TO WORK.
AND *THAT*, MR. FOX, IS WHY THEY PAY
YOU THE BIG
BUCKS.

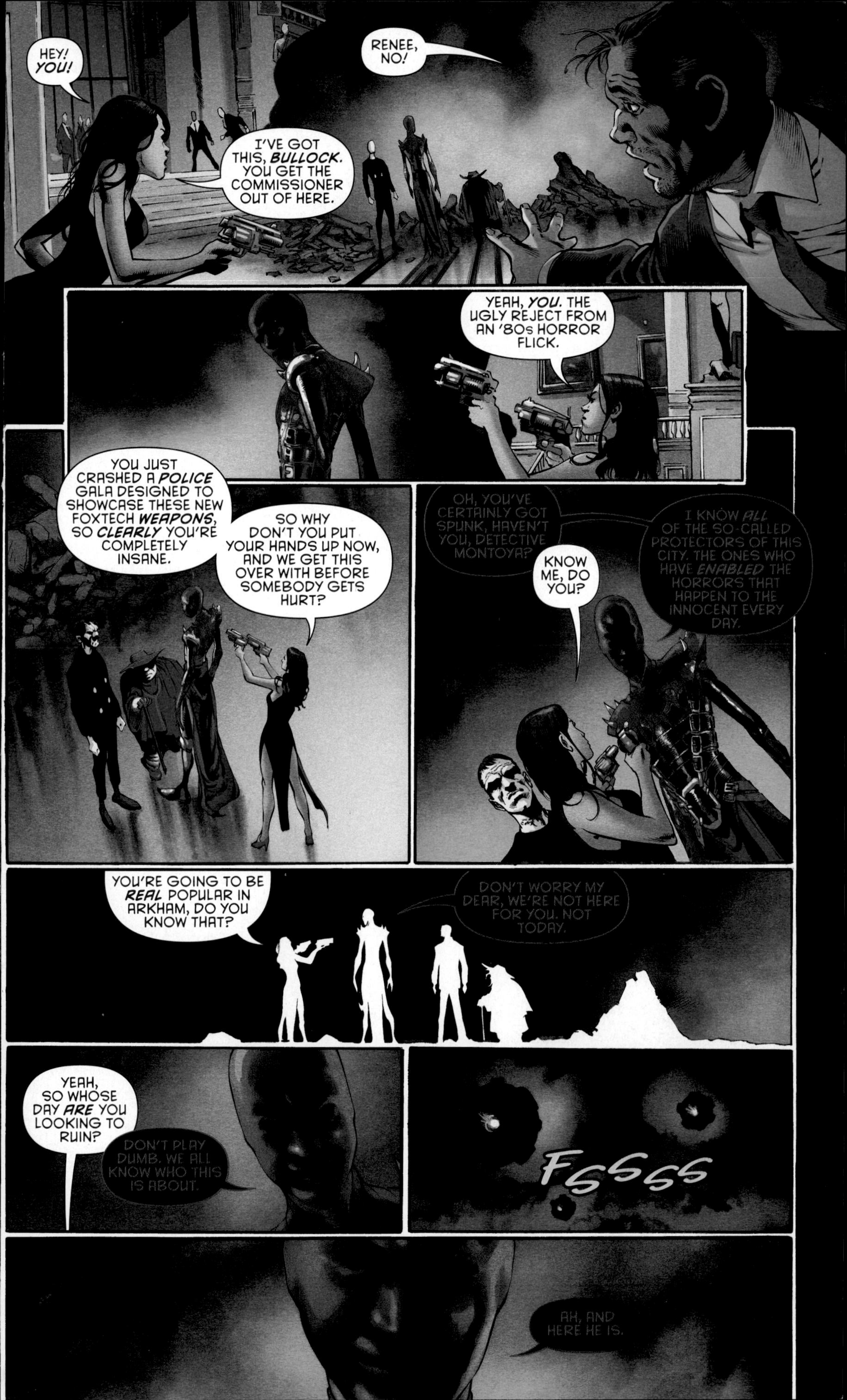

HEY! YOU!
RENEE, NO!
I'VE GOT THIS, BULLOCK. YOU GET THE COMMISSIONER OUT OF HERE.
YEAH, YOU. THE UGLY REJECT FROM AN '80s HORROR FLICK.
YOU JUST CRASHED A POLICE GALA DESIGNED TO SHOWCASE THESE NEW FOXTECH WEAPONS, SO CLEARLY YOU'RE COMPLETELY INSANE.
SO WHY DON'T YOU PUT YOUR HANDS UP NOW, AND WE GET THIS OVER WITH BEFORE SOMEBODY GETS HURT?
OH, YOU'VE CERTAINLY GOT SPUNK, HAVEN'T YOU, DETECTIVE MONTOYA?
KNOW ME, DO YOU?
I KNOW ALL OF THE SO-CALLED PROTECTORS OF THIS CITY. THE ONES WHO HAVE ENABLED THE HORRORS THAT HAPPEN TO THE INNOCENT EVERY DAY.
YOU'RE GOING TO BE REAL POPULAR IN ARKHAM, DO YOU KNOW THAT?
DON'T WORRY MY DEAR, WE'RE NOT HERE FOR YOU. NOT TODAY.
YEAH, SO WHOSE DAY ARE YOU LOOKING TO RUIN?
DON'T PLAY DUMB. WE ALL KNOW WHO THIS IS ABOUT.
FSSSS
AH, AND HERE HE IS.

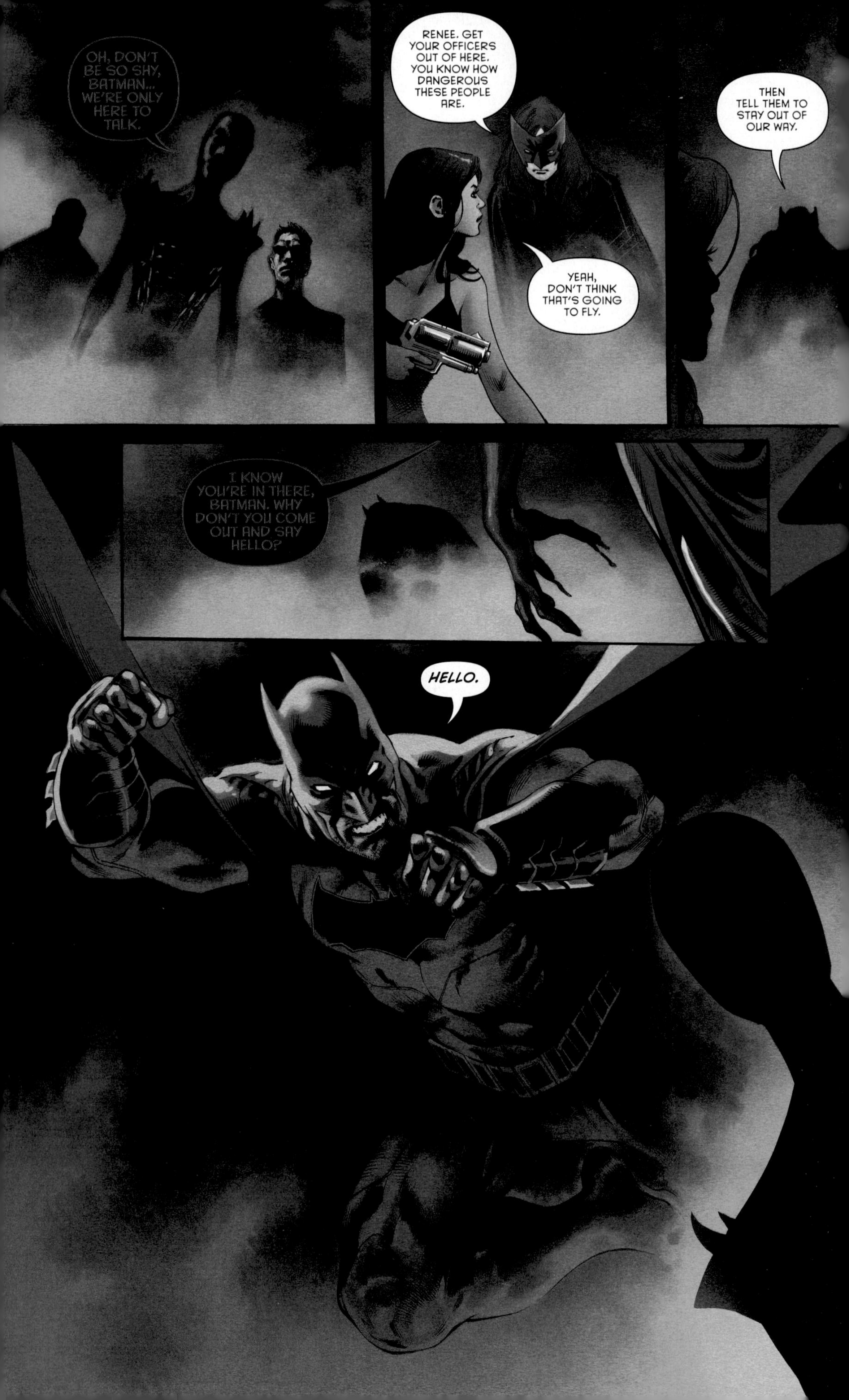
OH, DON'T BE SO SHY, BATMAN... WE'RE ONLY HERE TO TALK.
RENEE. GET YOUR OFFICERS OUT OF HERE. YOU KNOW HOW DANGEROUS THESE PEOPLE ARE.
YEAH, DON'T THINK THAT'S GOING TO FLY.
THEN TELL THEM TO STAY OUT OF OUR WAY.
I KNOW YOU'RE IN THERE, BATMAN. WHY DON'T YOU COME OUT AND SAY HELLO?
HELLO.

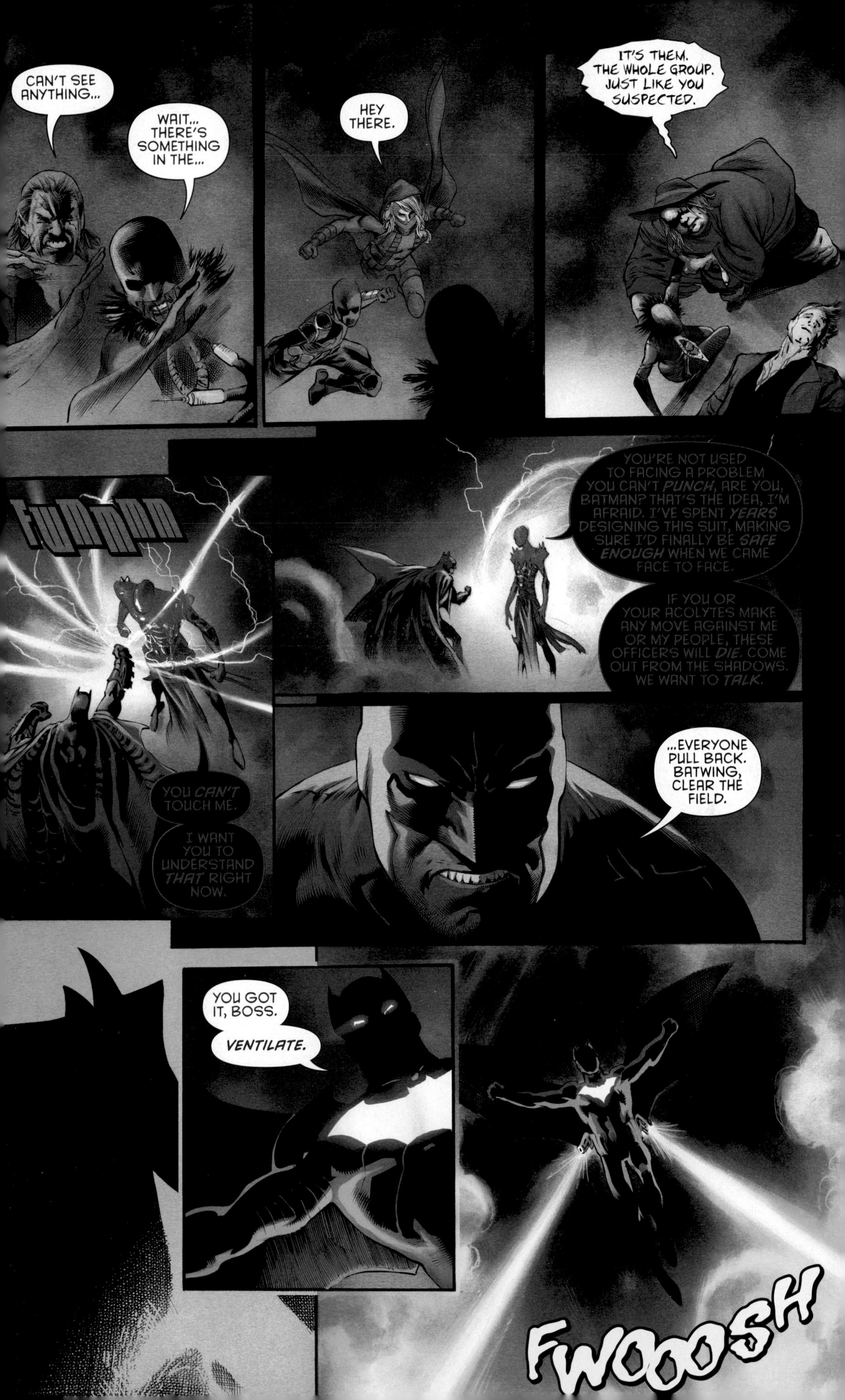

CAN'T SEE ANYTHING...
WAIT... THERE'S SOMETHING IN THE...
HEY THERE.
IT'S THEM. THE WHOLE GROUP. JUST LIKE YOU SUSPECTED.
TUNNNN
YOU CAN'T TOUCH ME.
I WANT YOU TO UNDERSTAND THAT RIGHT NOW.
YOU'RE NOT USED TO FACING A PROBLEM YOU CAN'T PUNCH, ARE YOU, BATMAN? THAT'S THE IDEA, I'M AFRAID. I'VE SPENT YEARS DESIGNING THIS SUIT, MAKING SURE I'D FINALLY BE SAFE ENOUGH WHEN WE CAME FACE TO FACE.
IF YOU OR YOUR ACOLYTES MAKE ANY MOVE AGAINST ME OR MY PEOPLE, THESE OFFICERS WILL DIE. COME OUT FROM THE SHADOWS. WE WANT TO TALK.
...EVERYONE PULL BACK. BATWING, CLEAR THE FIELD.
YOU GOT IT, BOSS.
VENTILATE.
FWOOOSH

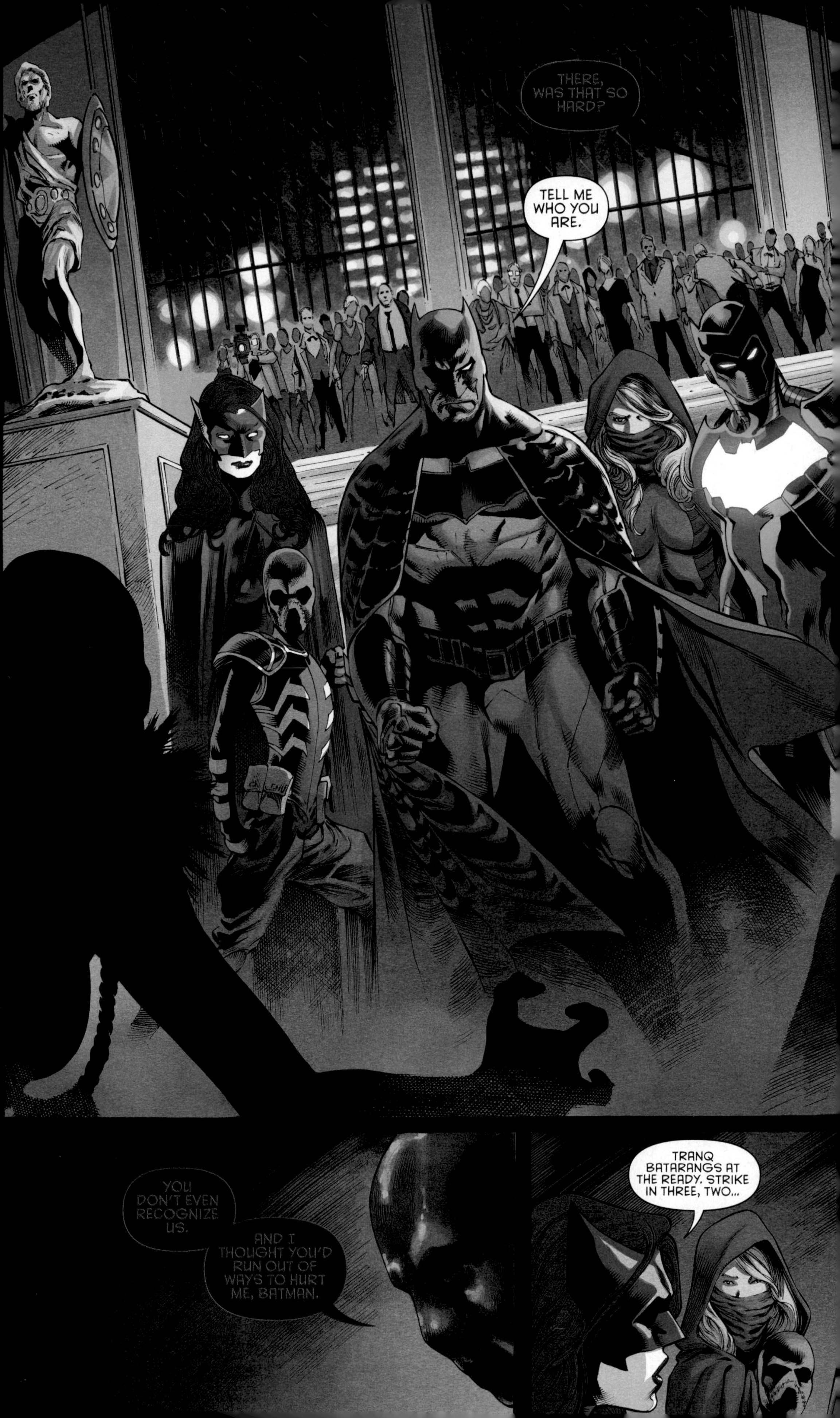
THERE, WAS THAT SO HARD?
TELL ME WHO YOU ARE.
YOU DON'T EVEN RECOGNIZE US.
AND I THOUGHT YOU'D RUN OUT OF WAYS TO HURT ME, BATMAN.
TRANQ BATARANGS AT THE READY. STRIKE IN THREE, TWO...

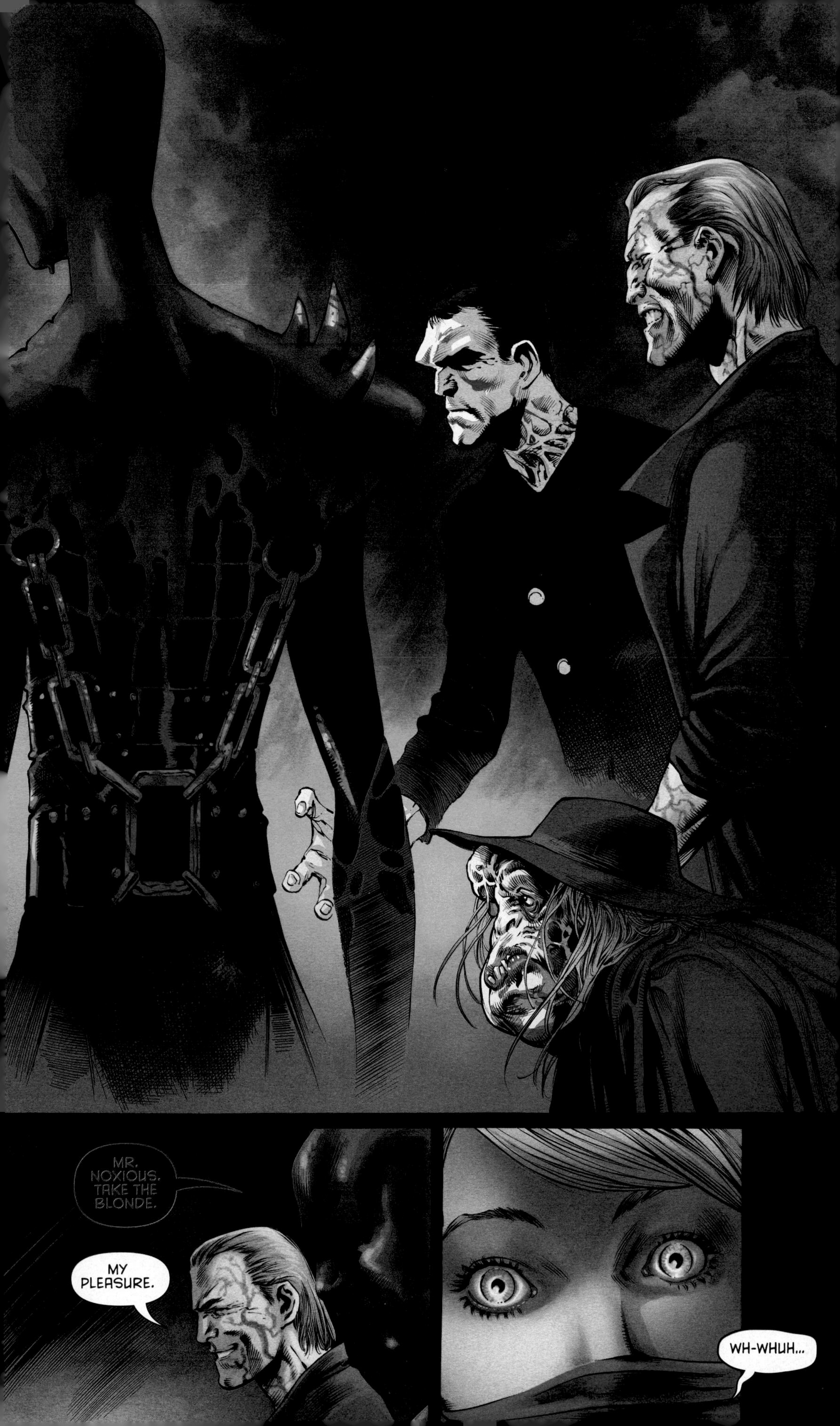
MR. NOXIOUS. TAKE THE BLONDE.
MY PLEASURE.
WH-WHUH...

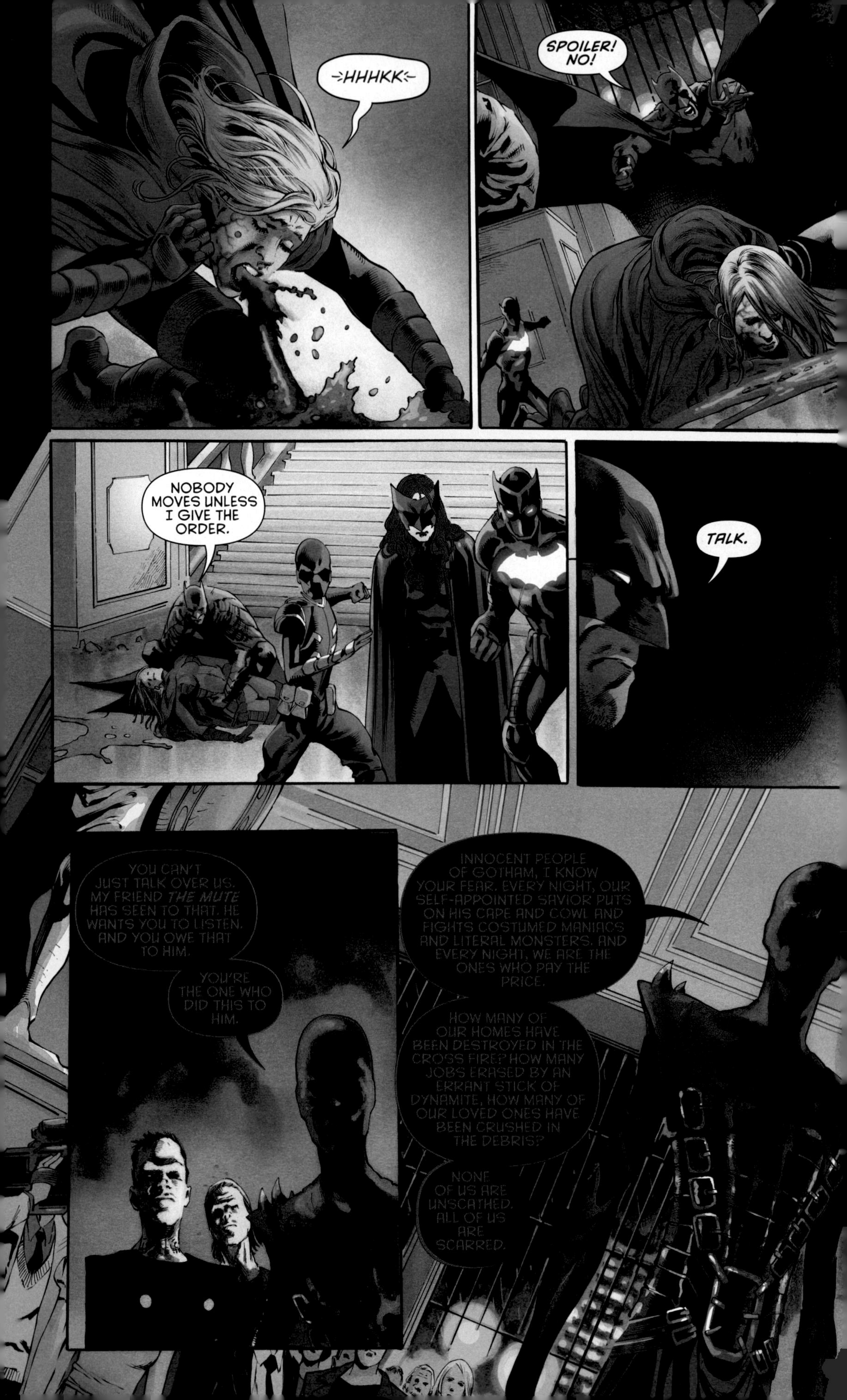

-HHHKK-
SPOILER! NO!
NOBODY MOVES UNLESS I GIVE THE ORDER.
TALK.
YOU CAN'T JUST TALK OVER US. MY FRIEND *THE MUTE* HAS SEEN TO THAT. HE WANTS YOU TO LISTEN. AND YOU OWE THAT TO HIM.
YOU'RE THE ONE WHO DID THIS TO HIM.
INNOCENT PEOPLE OF GOTHAM, I KNOW YOUR FEAR. EVERY NIGHT, OUR SELF-APPOINTED SAVIOR PUTS ON HIS CAPE AND COWL AND FIGHTS COSTUMED MANIACS AND LITERAL MONSTERS. AND EVERY NIGHT, WE ARE THE ONES WHO PAY THE PRICE.
HOW MANY OF OUR HOMES HAVE BEEN DESTROYED IN THE CROSS FIRE? HOW MANY JOBS ERASED BY AN ERRANT STICK OF DYNAMITE, HOW MANY OF OUR LOVED ONES HAVE BEEN CRUSHED IN THE DEBRIS?
NONE OF US ARE UNSCATHED. ALL OF US ARE SCARRED.

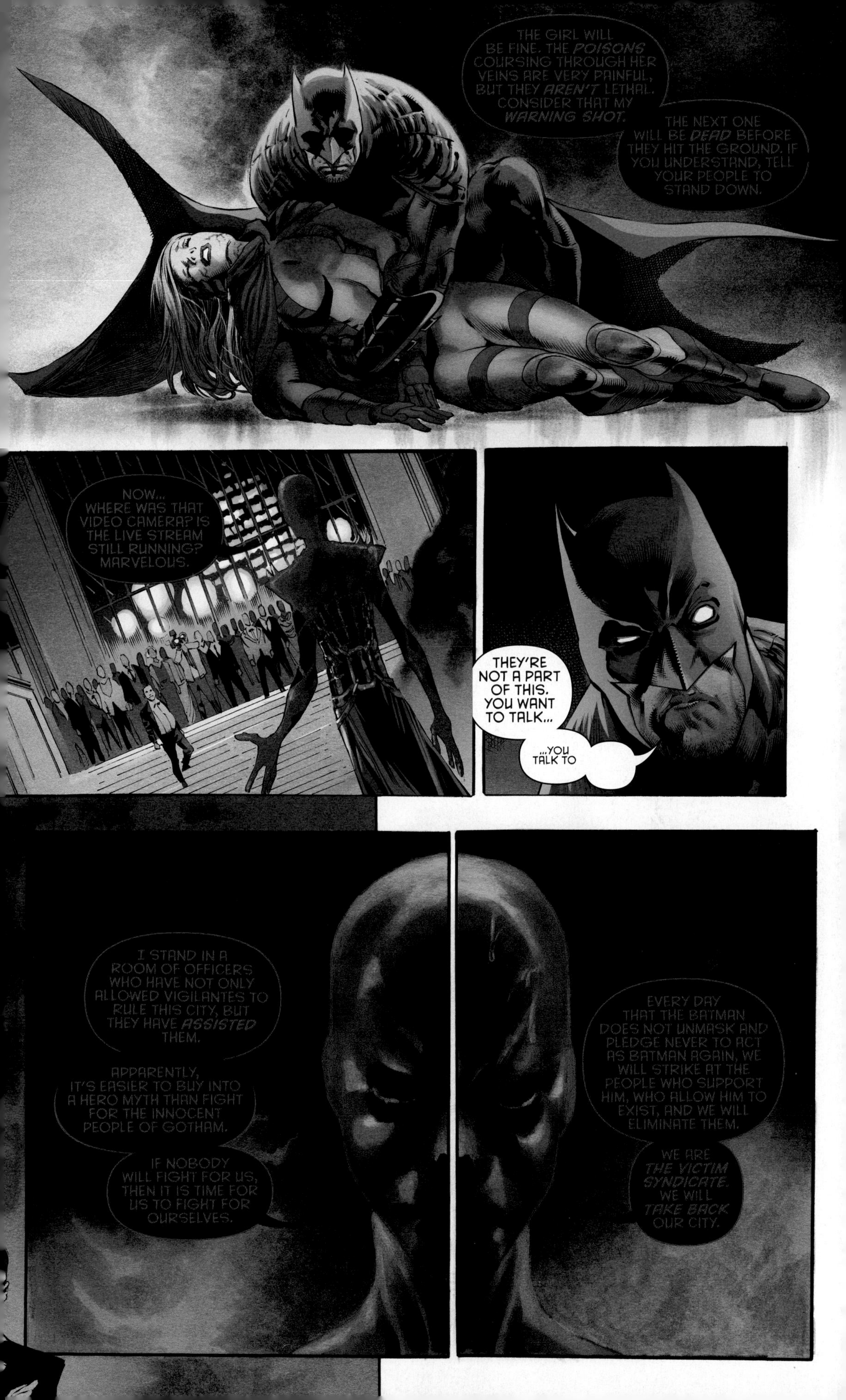
THE GIRL WILL BE FINE. THE POISONS COURSING THROUGH HER VEINS ARE VERY PAINFUL, BUT THEY AREN'T LETHAL. CONSIDER THAT MY WARNING SHOT.
THE NEXT ONE WILL BE DEAD BEFORE THEY HIT THE GROUND. IF YOU UNDERSTAND, TELL YOUR PEOPLE TO STAND DOWN.
NOW... WHERE WAS THAT VIDEO CAMERA? IS THE LIVE STREAM STILL RUNNING? MARVELOUS.
THEY'RE NOT A PART OF THIS. YOU WANT TO TALK...
...YOU TALK TO
I STAND IN A ROOM OF OFFICERS WHO HAVE NOT ONLY ALLOWED VIGILANTES TO RULE THIS CITY, BUT THEY HAVE ASSISTED THEM.
APPARENTLY, IT'S EASIER TO BUY INTO A HERO MYTH THAN FIGHT FOR THE INNOCENT PEOPLE OF GOTHAM.
IF NOBODY WILL FIGHT FOR US, THEN IT IS TIME FOR US TO FIGHT FOR OURSELVES.
EVERY DAY THAT THE BATMAN DOES NOT UNMASK AND PLEDGE NEVER TO ACT AS BATMAN AGAIN, WE WILL STRIKE AT THE PEOPLE WHO SUPPORT HIM, WHO ALLOW HIM TO EXIST, AND WE WILL ELIMINATE THEM.
WE ARE THE VICTIM SYNDICATE. WE WILL TAKE BACK OUR CITY.

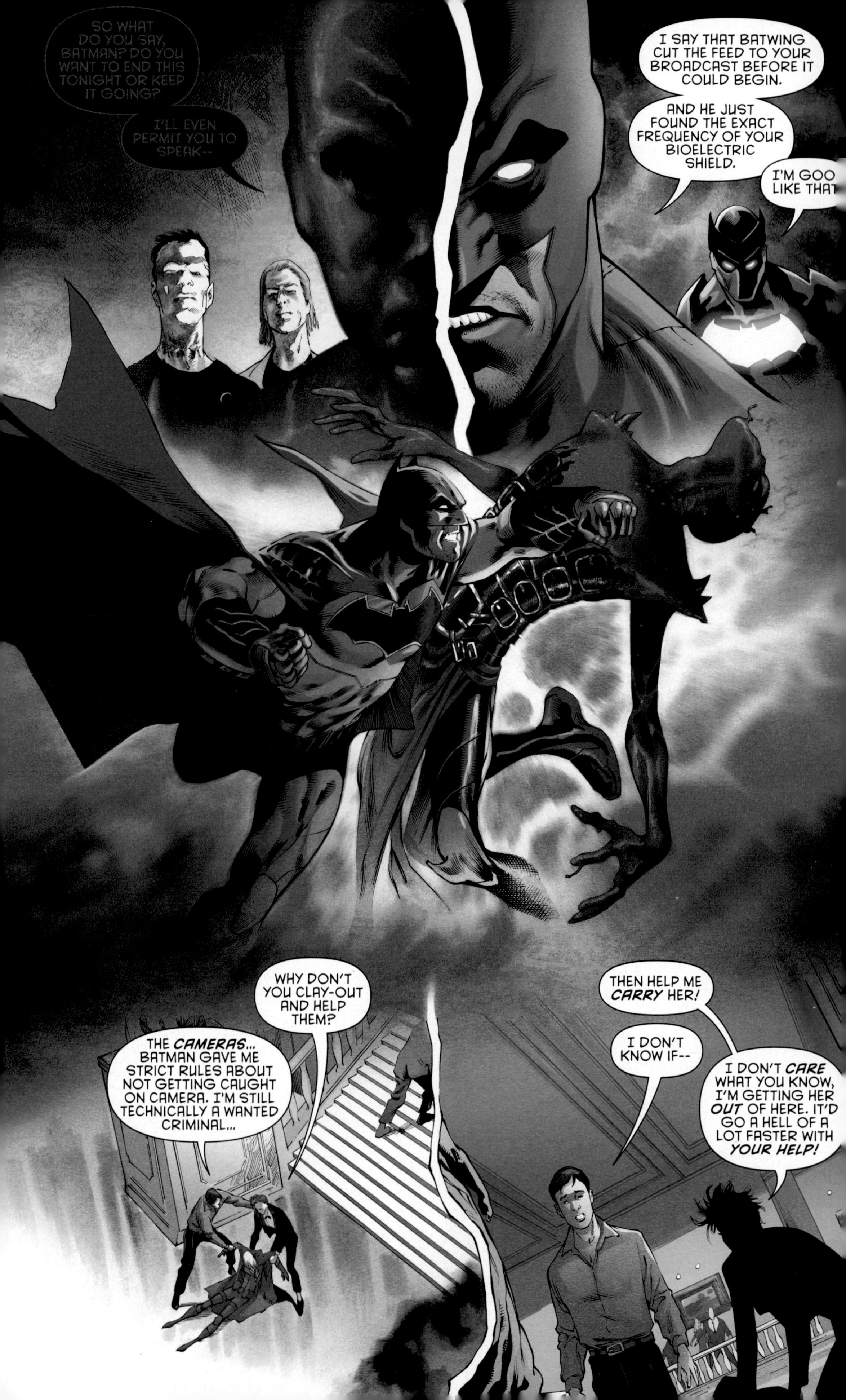
SO WHAT DO YOU SAY, BATMAN? DO YOU WANT TO END THIS TONIGHT OR KEEP IT GOING?
I'LL EVEN PERMIT YOU TO SPEAK--
I SAY THAT BATWING CUT THE FEED TO YOUR BROADCAST BEFORE IT COULD BEGIN.
AND HE JUST FOUND THE EXACT FREQUENCY OF YOUR BIOELECTRIC SHIELD.
I'M GOO LIKE THAT
WHY DON'T YOU CLAY-OUT AND HELP THEM?
THE CAMERAS... BATMAN GAVE ME STRICT RULES ABOUT NOT GETTING CAUGHT ON CAMERA. I'M STILL TECHNICALLY A WANTED CRIMINAL...
THEN HELP ME CARRY HER!
I DON'T KNOW IF--
I DON'T CARE WHAT YOU KNOW, I'M GETTING HER OUT OF HERE. IT'D GO A HELL OF A LOT FASTER WITH YOUR HELP!

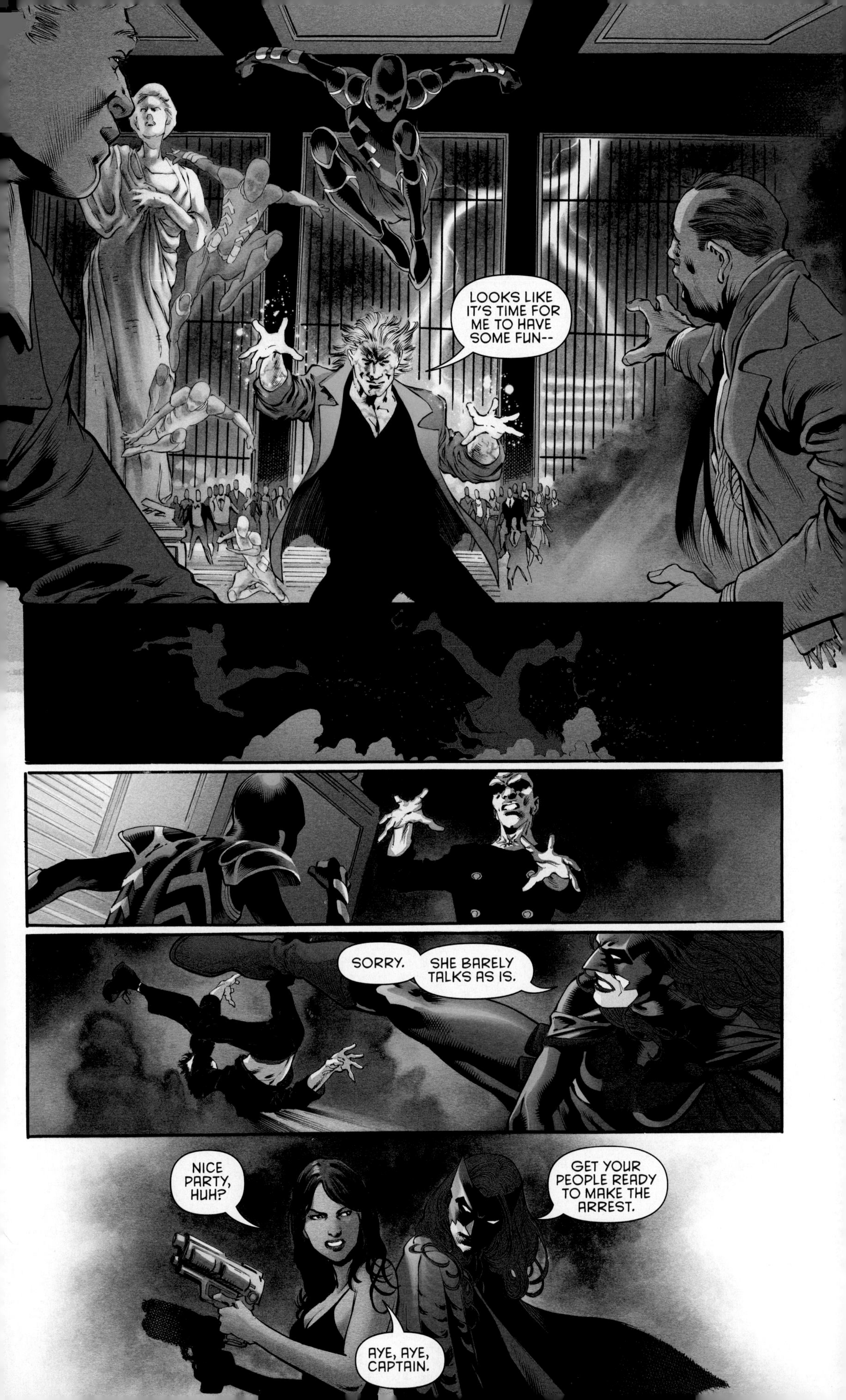
LOOKS LIKE IT'S TIME FOR ME TO HAVE SOME FUN--
SORRY.
SHE BARELY TALKS AS IS.
NICE PARTY, HUH?
GET YOUR PEOPLE READY TO MAKE THE ARREST.
AYE, AYE, CAPTAIN.

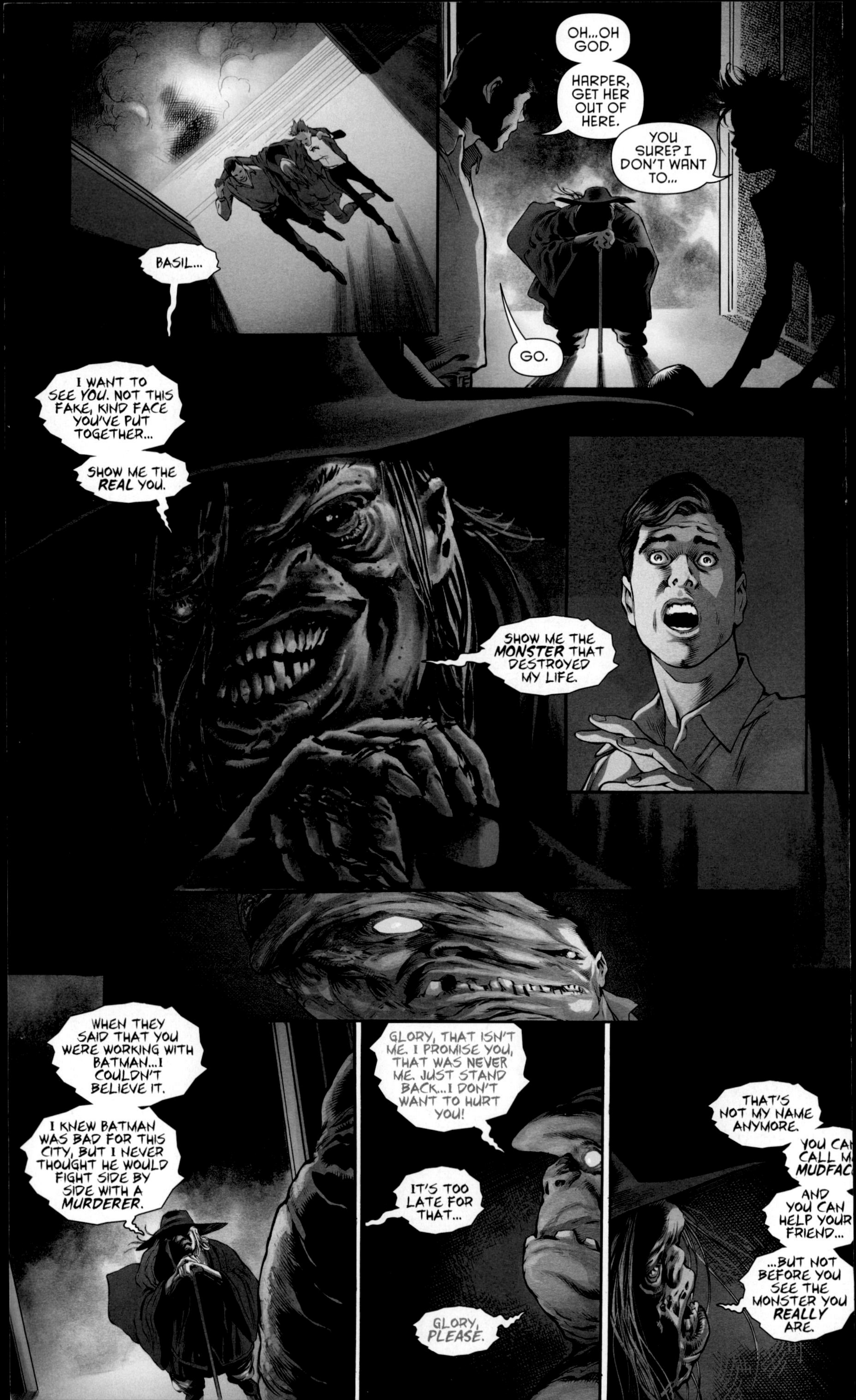

BASIL...
OH...OH GOD.
HARPER, GET HER OUT OF HERE.
YOU SURE? I DON'T WANT TO...
GO.
I WANT TO SEE YOU. NOT THIS FAKE, KIND FACE YOU'VE PUT TOGETHER...
SHOW ME THE REAL YOU.
SHOW ME THE MONSTER THAT DESTROYED MY LIFE.
WHEN THEY SAID THAT YOU WERE WORKING WITH BATMAN...I COULDN'T BELIEVE IT.
I KNEW BATMAN WAS BAD FOR THIS CITY, BUT I NEVER THOUGHT HE WOULD FIGHT SIDE BY SIDE WITH A MURDERER.
GLORY, THAT ISN'T ME. I PROMISE YOU, THAT WAS NEVER ME. JUST STAND BACK...I DON'T WANT TO HURT YOU!
IT'S TOO LATE FOR THAT...
GLORY, PLEASE.
THAT'S NOT MY NAME ANYMORE.
AND YOU CAN HELP YOUR FRIEND...
...BUT NOT BEFORE YOU SEE THE MONSTER YOU REALLY ARE.

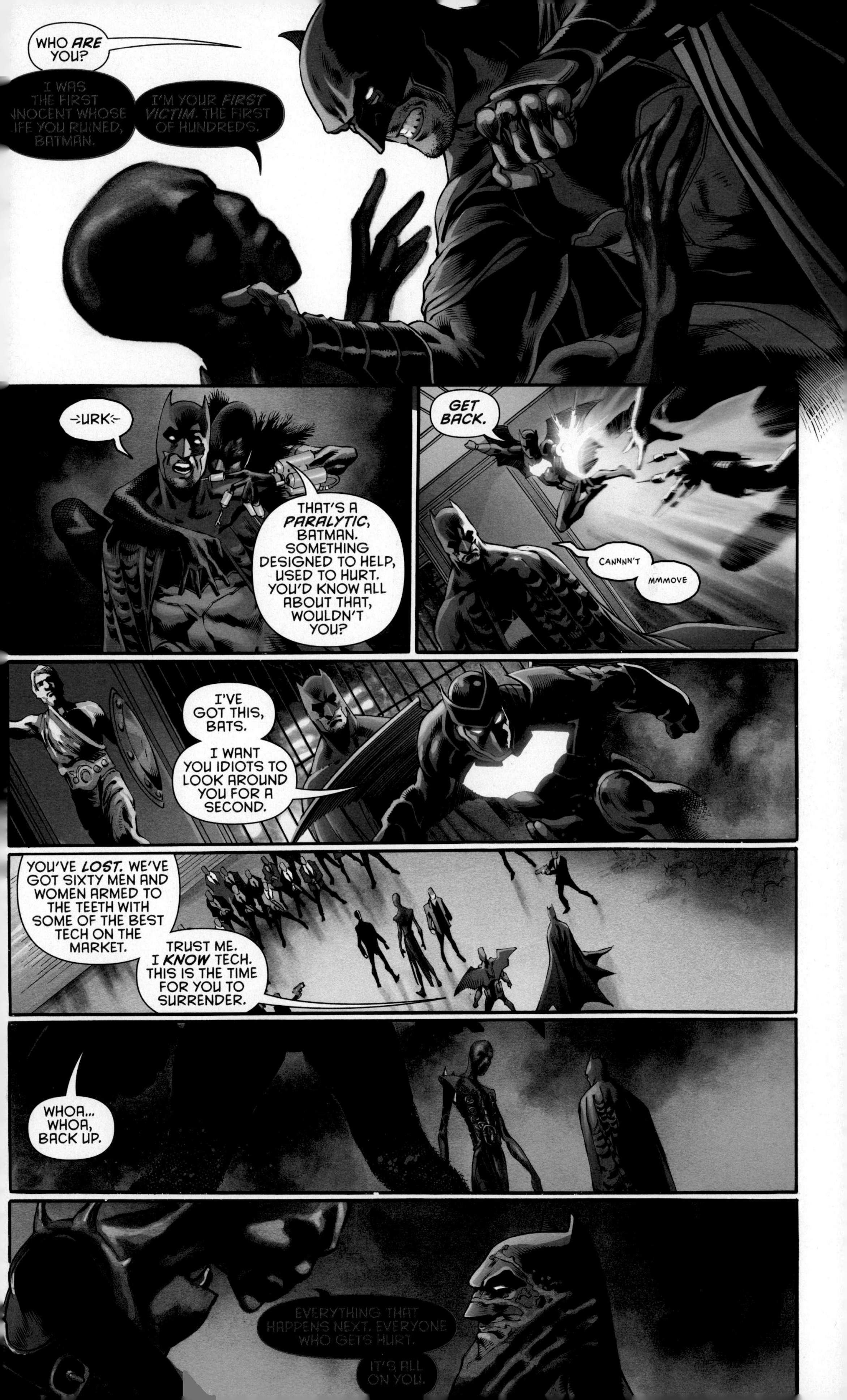
WHO *ARE* YOU?
I WAS THE FIRST NNOCENT WHOSE IFE YOU RUINED, BATMAN.
I'M YOUR *FIRST VICTIM.* THE FIRST OF HUNDREDS.
URK
THAT'S A *PARALYTIC,* BATMAN. SOMETHING DESIGNED TO HELP, USED TO HURT. YOU'D KNOW ALL ABOUT THAT, WOULDN'T YOU?
GET BACK.
CANNNN'T
MMMOVE
I'VE GOT THIS, BATS.
I WANT YOU IDIOTS TO LOOK AROUND YOU FOR A SECOND.
YOU'VE *LOST.* WE'VE GOT SIXTY MEN AND WOMEN ARMED TO THE TEETH WITH SOME OF THE BEST TECH ON THE MARKET.
TRUST ME. I *KNOW* TECH. THIS IS THE TIME FOR YOU TO SURRENDER.
WHOA... WHOA, BACK UP.
EVERYTHING THAT HAPPENS NEXT. EVERYONE WHO GETS HURT.
IT'S ALL ON YOU.

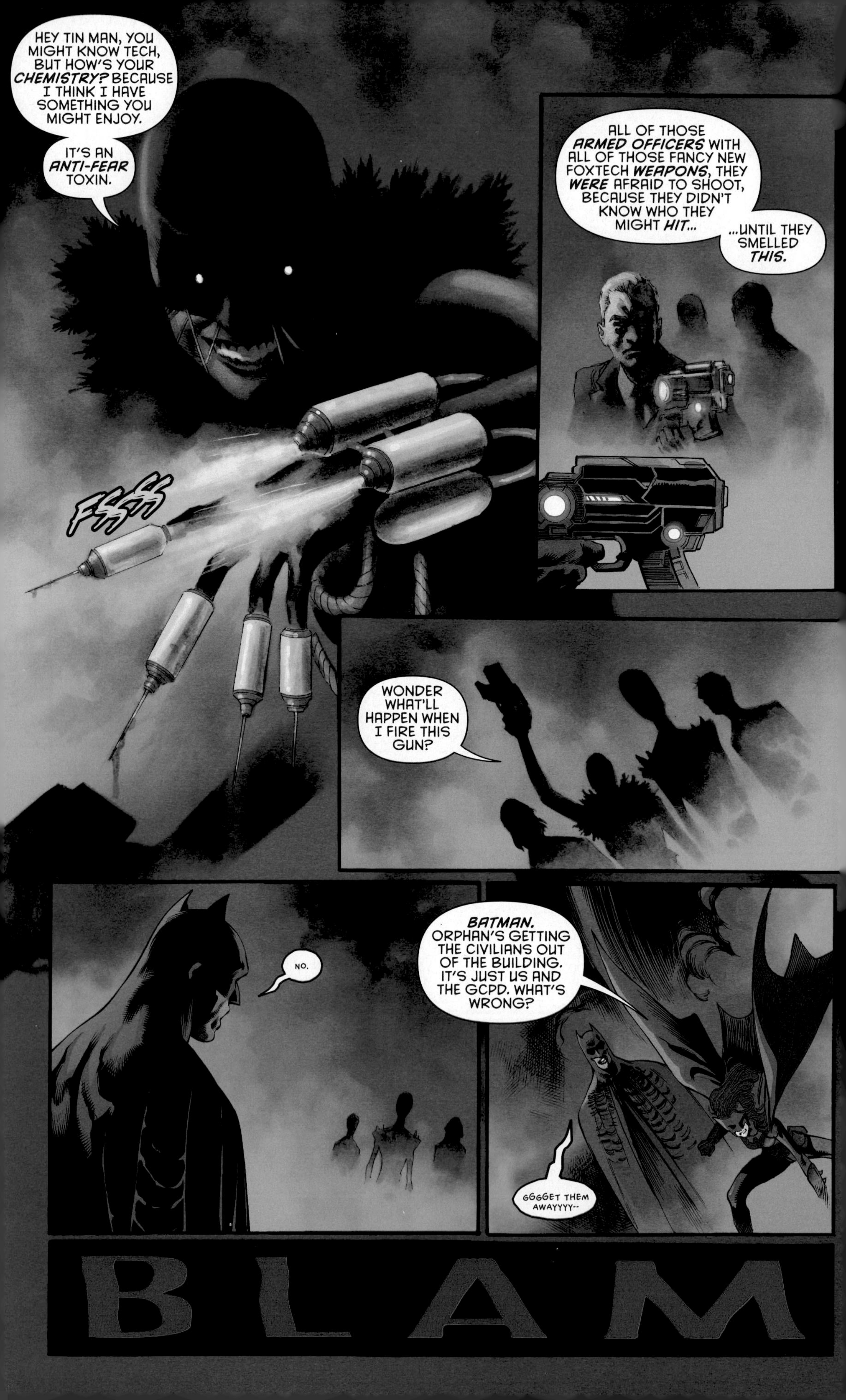
HEY TIN MAN, YOU MIGHT KNOW TECH, BUT HOW'S YOUR *CHEMISTRY?* BECAUSE I THINK I HAVE SOMETHING YOU MIGHT ENJOY.
IT'S AN *ANTI-FEAR* TOXIN.
FSSS
ALL OF THOSE *ARMED OFFICERS* WITH ALL OF THOSE FANCY NEW FOXTECH *WEAPONS*, THEY *WERE* AFRAID TO SHOOT, BECAUSE THEY DIDN'T KNOW WHO THEY MIGHT *HIT*...
...UNTIL THEY SMELLED *THIS.*
WONDER WHAT'LL HAPPEN WHEN I FIRE THIS GUN?
NO.
BATMAN. ORPHAN'S GETTING THE CIVILIANS OUT OF THE BUILDING. IT'S JUST US AND THE GCPD. WHAT'S WRONG?
GGGGET THEM AWAYYYY--
BLAM

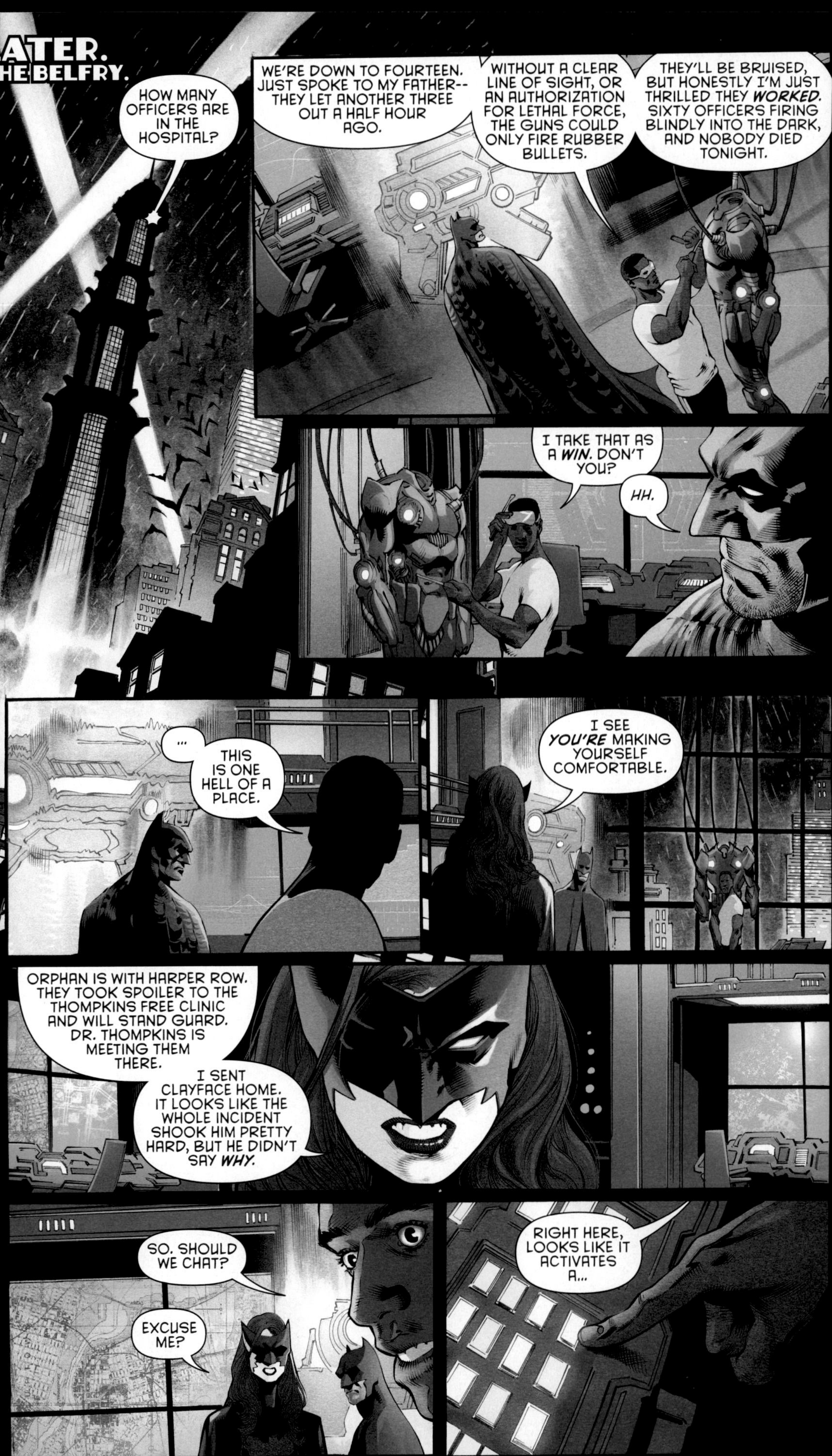
LATER.
THE BELFRY.
HOW MANY OFFICERS ARE IN THE HOSPITAL?
WE'RE DOWN TO FOURTEEN. JUST SPOKE TO MY FATHER-- THEY LET ANOTHER THREE OUT A HALF HOUR AGO.
WITHOUT A CLEAR LINE OF SIGHT, OR AN AUTHORIZATION FOR LETHAL FORCE, THE GUNS COULD ONLY FIRE RUBBER BULLETS.
THEY'LL BE BRUISED, BUT HONESTLY I'M JUST THRILLED THEY *WORKED*. SIXTY OFFICERS FIRING BLINDLY INTO THE DARK, AND NOBODY DIED TONIGHT.
I TAKE THAT AS A *WIN*. DON'T YOU?
HH.
...
THIS IS ONE HELL OF A PLACE.
I SEE *YOU'RE* MAKING YOURSELF COMFORTABLE.
ORPHAN IS WITH HARPER ROW. THEY TOOK SPOILER TO THE THOMPKINS FREE CLINIC AND WILL STAND GUARD. DR. THOMPKINS IS MEETING THEM THERE.
I SENT CLAYFACE HOME. IT LOOKS LIKE THE WHOLE INCIDENT SHOOK HIM PRETTY HARD, BUT HE DIDN'T SAY *WHY*.
SO. SHOULD WE CHAT?
EXCUSE ME?
RIGHT HERE, LOOKS LIKE IT ACTIVATES A...

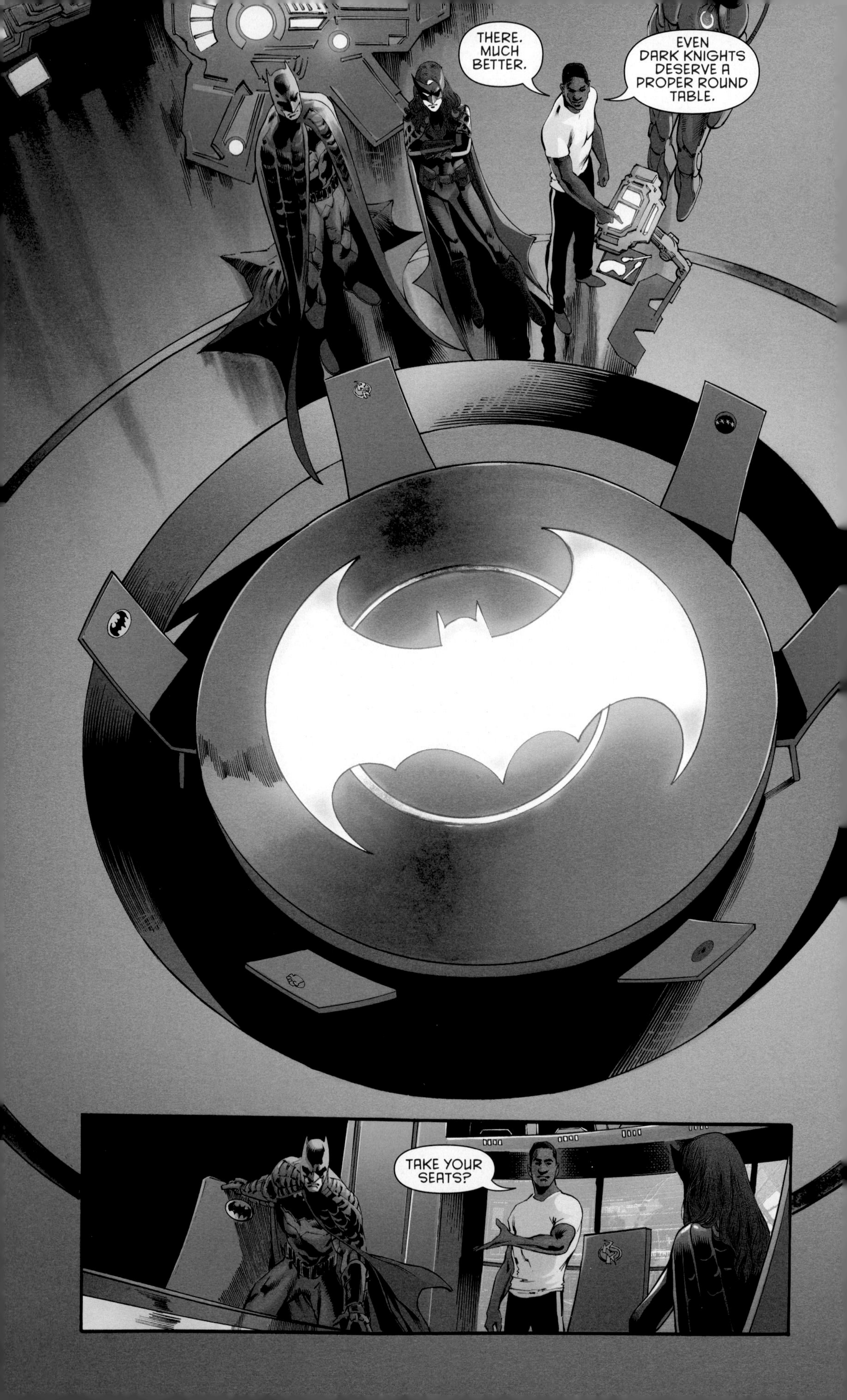
THERE. MUCH BETTER.
EVEN DARK KNIGHTS DESERVE A PROPER ROUND TABLE.
TAKE YOUR SEATS?

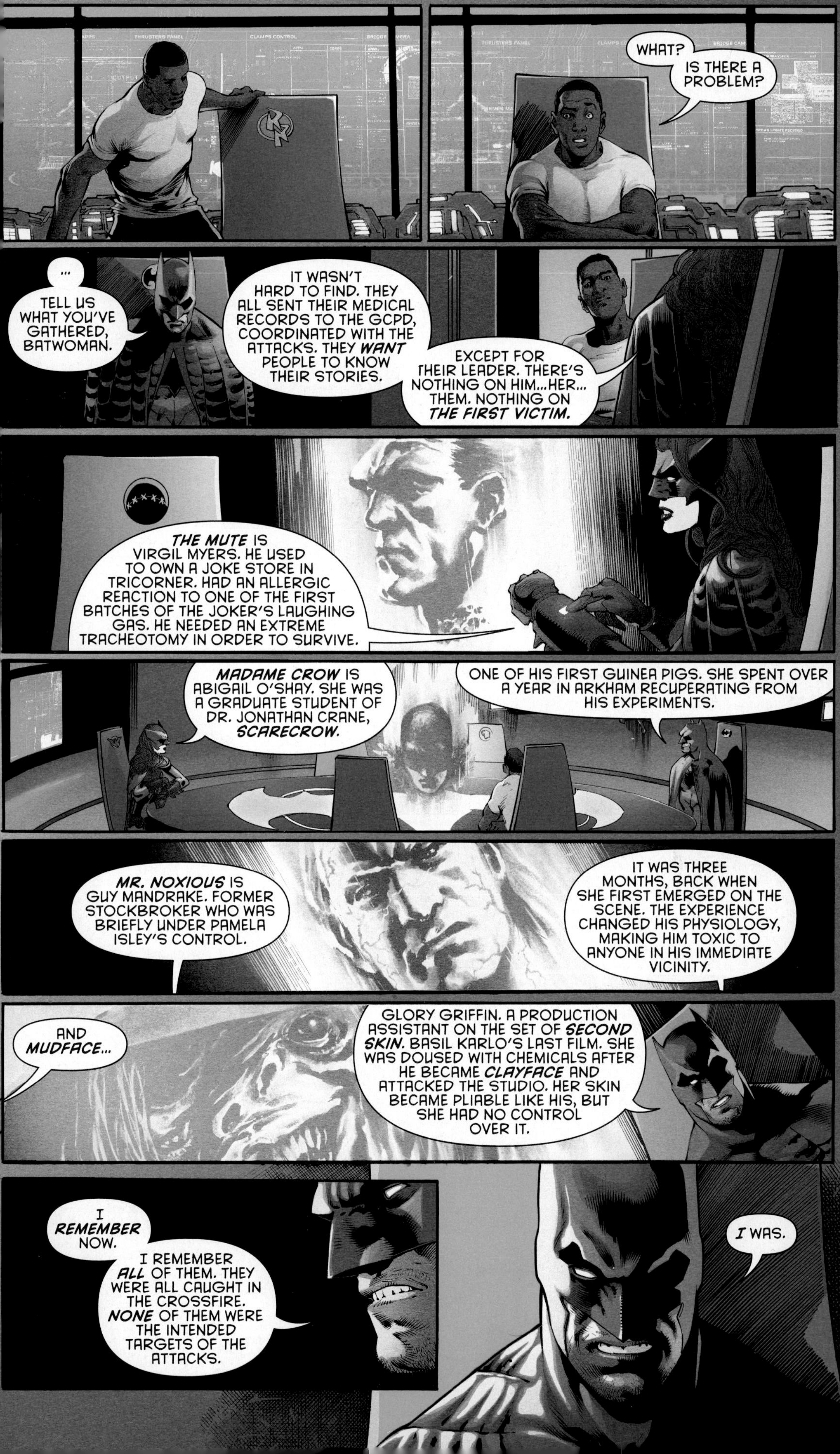
WHAT?
IS THERE A PROBLEM?
...
TELL US WHAT YOU'VE GATHERED, BATWOMAN.
IT WASN'T HARD TO FIND. THEY ALL SENT THEIR MEDICAL RECORDS TO THE GCPD, COORDINATED WITH THE ATTACKS. THEY WANT PEOPLE TO KNOW THEIR STORIES.
EXCEPT FOR THEIR LEADER. THERE'S NOTHING ON HIM...HER... THEM. NOTHING ON THE FIRST VICTIM.
THE MUTE IS VIRGIL MYERS. HE USED TO OWN A JOKE STORE IN TRICORNER. HAD AN ALLERGIC REACTION TO ONE OF THE FIRST BATCHES OF THE JOKER'S LAUGHING GAS. HE NEEDED AN EXTREME TRACHEOTOMY IN ORDER TO SURVIVE.
MADAME CROW IS ABIGAIL O'SHAY. SHE WAS A GRADUATE STUDENT OF DR. JONATHAN CRANE, SCARECROW.
ONE OF HIS FIRST GUINEA PIGS. SHE SPENT OVER A YEAR IN ARKHAM RECUPERATING FROM HIS EXPERIMENTS.
MR. NOXIOUS IS GUY MANDRAKE. FORMER STOCKBROKER WHO WAS BRIEFLY UNDER PAMELA ISLEY'S CONTROL.
IT WAS THREE MONTHS, BACK WHEN SHE FIRST EMERGED ON THE SCENE. THE EXPERIENCE CHANGED HIS PHYSIOLOGY, MAKING HIM TOXIC TO ANYONE IN HIS IMMEDIATE VICINITY.
AND MUDFACE...
GLORY GRIFFIN. A PRODUCTION ASSISTANT ON THE SET OF SECOND SKIN. BASIL KARLO'S LAST FILM. SHE WAS DOUSED WITH CHEMICALS AFTER HE BECAME CLAYFACE AND ATTACKED THE STUDIO. HER SKIN BECAME PLIABLE LIKE HIS, BUT SHE HAD NO CONTROL OVER IT.
I REMEMBER NOW.
I REMEMBER ALL OF THEM. THEY WERE ALL CAUGHT IN THE CROSSFIRE. NONE OF THEM WERE THE INTENDED TARGETS OF THE ATTACKS.
I WAS.

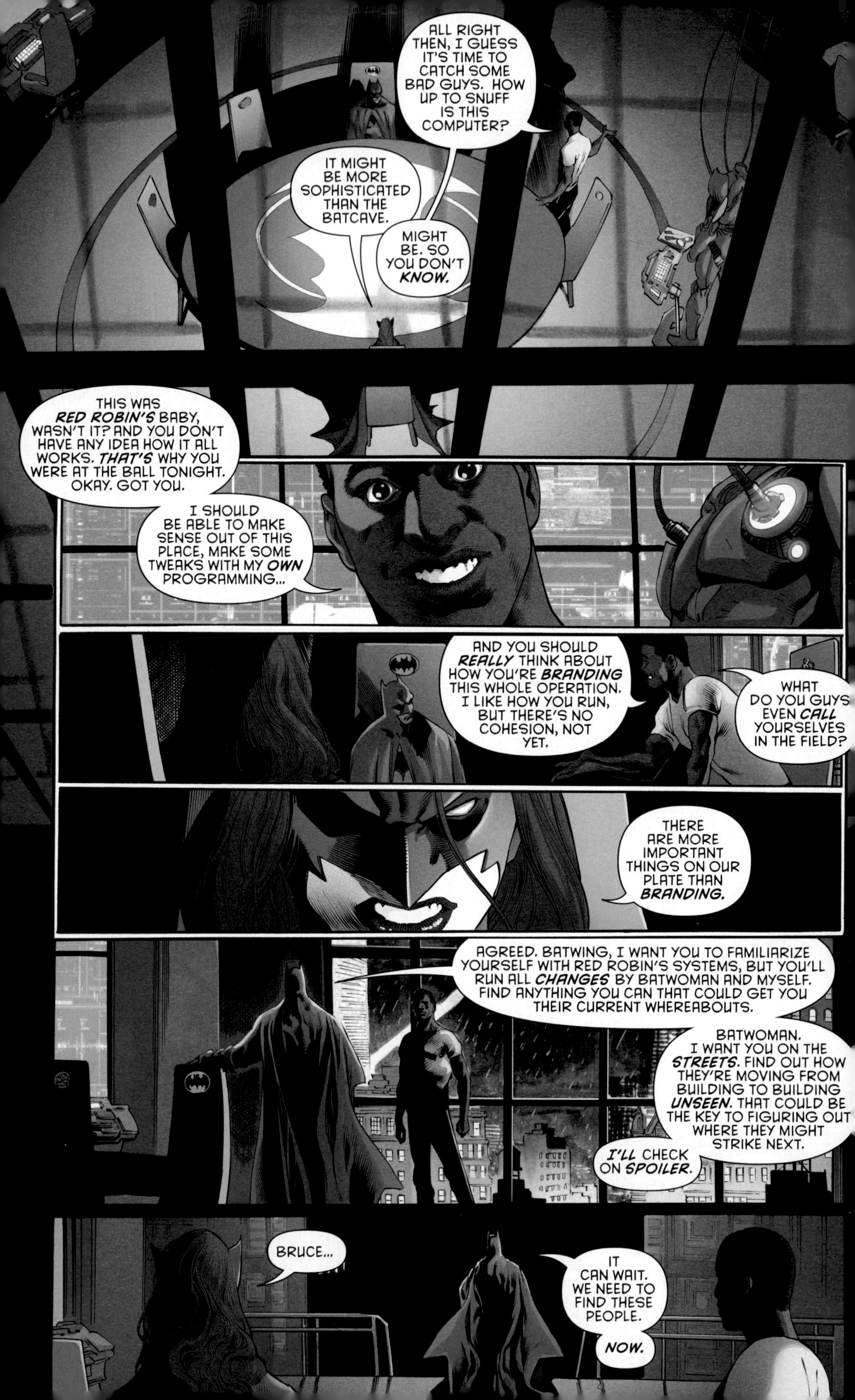
ALL RIGHT THEN, I GUESS IT'S TIME TO CATCH SOME BAD GUYS. HOW UP TO SNUFF IS THIS COMPUTER?
IT MIGHT BE MORE SOPHISTICATED THAN THE BATCAVE.
MIGHT BE. SO YOU DON'T ***KNOW.***
THIS WAS ***RED ROBIN'S*** BABY, WASN'T IT? AND YOU DON'T HAVE ANY IDEA HOW IT ALL WORKS. ***THAT'S*** WHY YOU WERE AT THE BALL TONIGHT. OKAY. GOT YOU.
I SHOULD BE ABLE TO MAKE SENSE OUT OF THIS PLACE, MAKE SOME TWEAKS WITH MY ***OWN*** PROGRAMMING...
AND YOU SHOULD ***REALLY*** THINK ABOUT HOW YOU'RE ***BRANDING*** THIS WHOLE OPERATION. I LIKE HOW YOU RUN, BUT THERE'S NO COHESION, NOT YET.
WHAT DO YOU GUYS EVEN ***CALL*** YOURSELVES IN THE FIELD?
THERE ARE MORE IMPORTANT THINGS ON OUR PLATE THAN ***BRANDING.***
AGREED. BATWING, I WANT YOU TO FAMILIARIZE YOURSELF WITH RED ROBIN'S SYSTEMS, BUT YOU'LL RUN ALL ***CHANGES*** BY BATWOMAN AND MYSELF. FIND ANYTHING YOU CAN THAT COULD GET YOU THEIR CURRENT WHEREABOUTS.
BATWOMAN. I WANT YOU ON THE ***STREETS.*** FIND OUT HOW THEY'RE MOVING FROM BUILDING TO BUILDING ***UNSEEN.*** THAT COULD BE THE KEY TO FIGURING OUT WHERE THEY MIGHT STRIKE NEXT.
I'LL CHECK ON ***SPOILER.***
BRUCE...
IT CAN WAIT. WE NEED TO FIND THESE PEOPLE.
NOW.

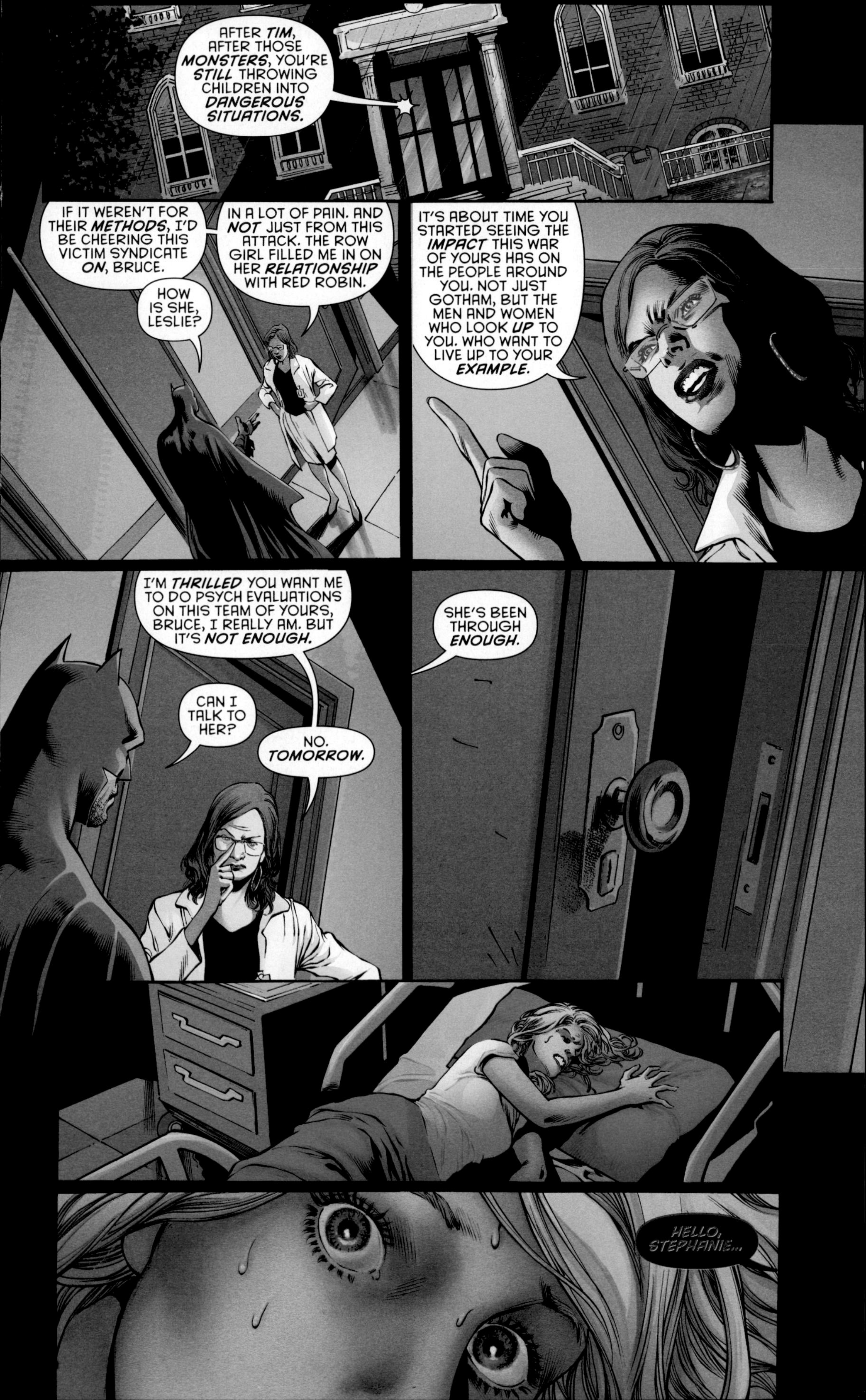
AFTER *TIM*, AFTER THOSE *MONSTERS*, YOU'RE *STILL* THROWING CHILDREN INTO *DANGEROUS SITUATIONS.*
IF IT WEREN'T FOR THEIR *METHODS*, I'D BE CHEERING THIS VICTIM SYNDICATE *ON*, BRUCE.
HOW IS SHE, LESLIE?
IN A LOT OF PAIN. AND *NOT* JUST FROM THIS ATTACK. THE ROW GIRL FILLED ME IN ON HER *RELATIONSHIP* WITH RED ROBIN.
IT'S ABOUT TIME YOU STARTED SEEING THE *IMPACT* THIS WAR OF YOURS HAS ON THE PEOPLE AROUND YOU. NOT JUST GOTHAM, BUT THE MEN AND WOMEN WHO LOOK *UP* TO YOU. WHO WANT TO LIVE UP TO YOUR *EXAMPLE*.
I'M *THRILLED* YOU WANT ME TO DO PSYCH EVALUATIONS ON THIS TEAM OF YOURS, BRUCE, I REALLY AM. BUT IT'S *NOT ENOUGH.*
CAN I TALK TO HER?
NO. *TOMORROW.*
SHE'S BEEN THROUGH *ENOUGH.*
HELLO, STEPHANIE...

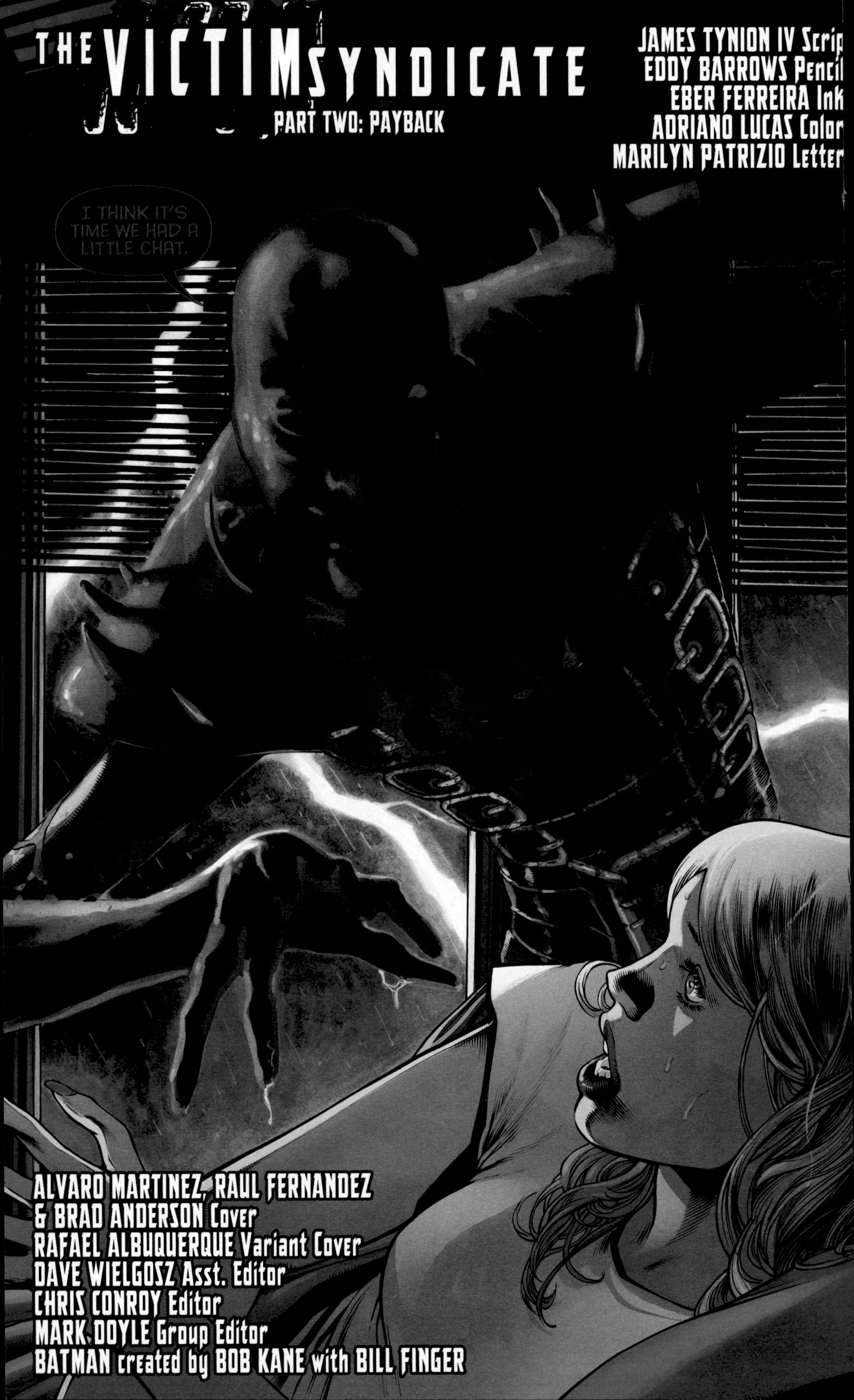
THE VICTIM SYNDICATE
PART TWO: PAYBACK
JAMES TYNION IV Scrip
EDDY BARROWS Pencil
EBER FERREIRA Ink
ADRIANO LUCAS Color
MARILYN PATRIZIO Letter
I THINK IT'S TIME WE HAD A LITTLE CHAT.
ALVARO MARTINEZ, RAUL FERNANDEZ & BRAD ANDERSON Cover
RAFAEL ALBUQUERQUE Variant Cover
DAVE WIELGOSZ Asst. Editor
CHRIS CONROY Editor
MARK DOYLE Group Editor
BATMAN created by BOB KANE with BILL FINGER

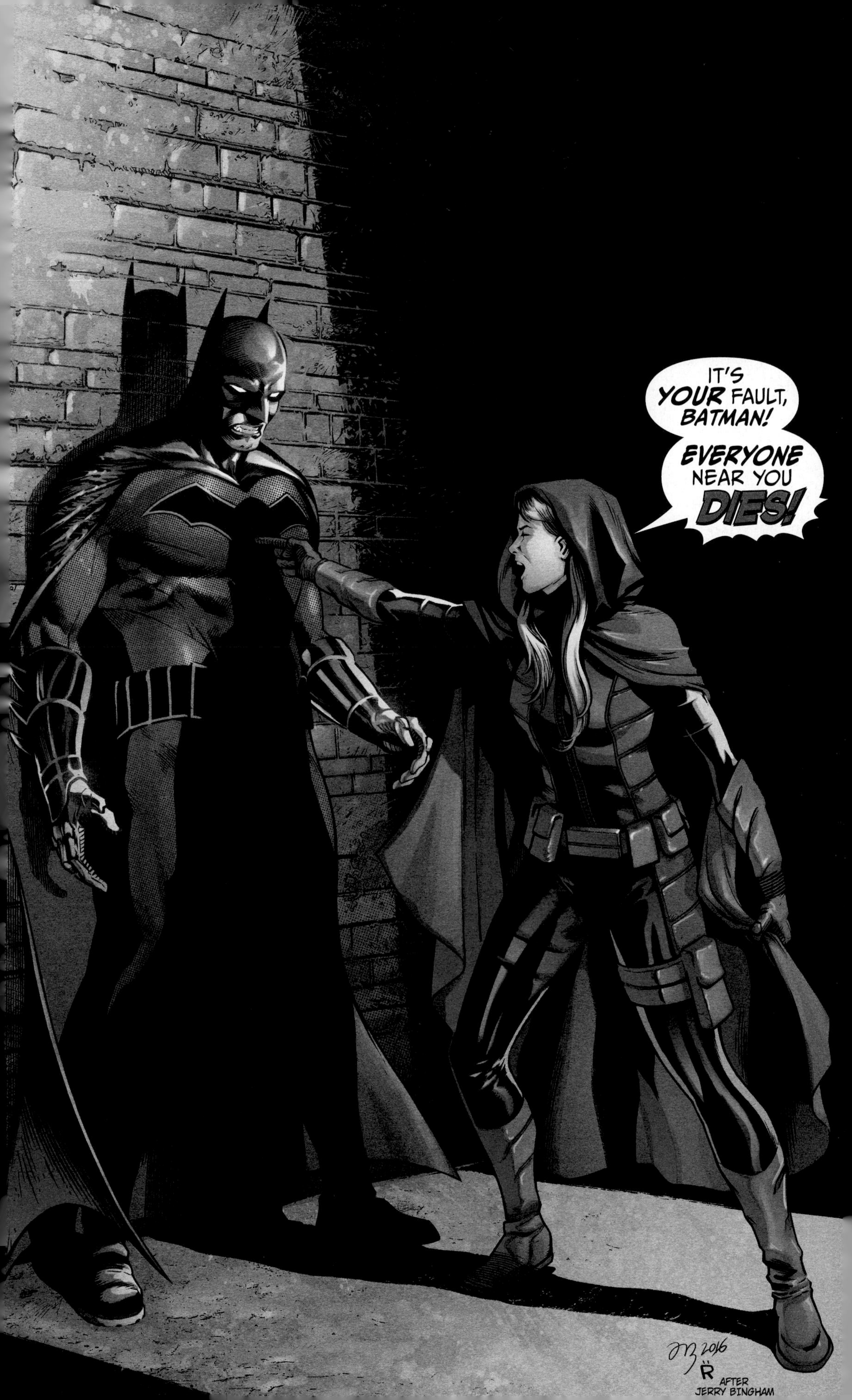
IT'S YOUR FAULT, BATMAN!
EVERYONE NEAR YOU DIES!
2016
AFTER JERRY BINGHAM

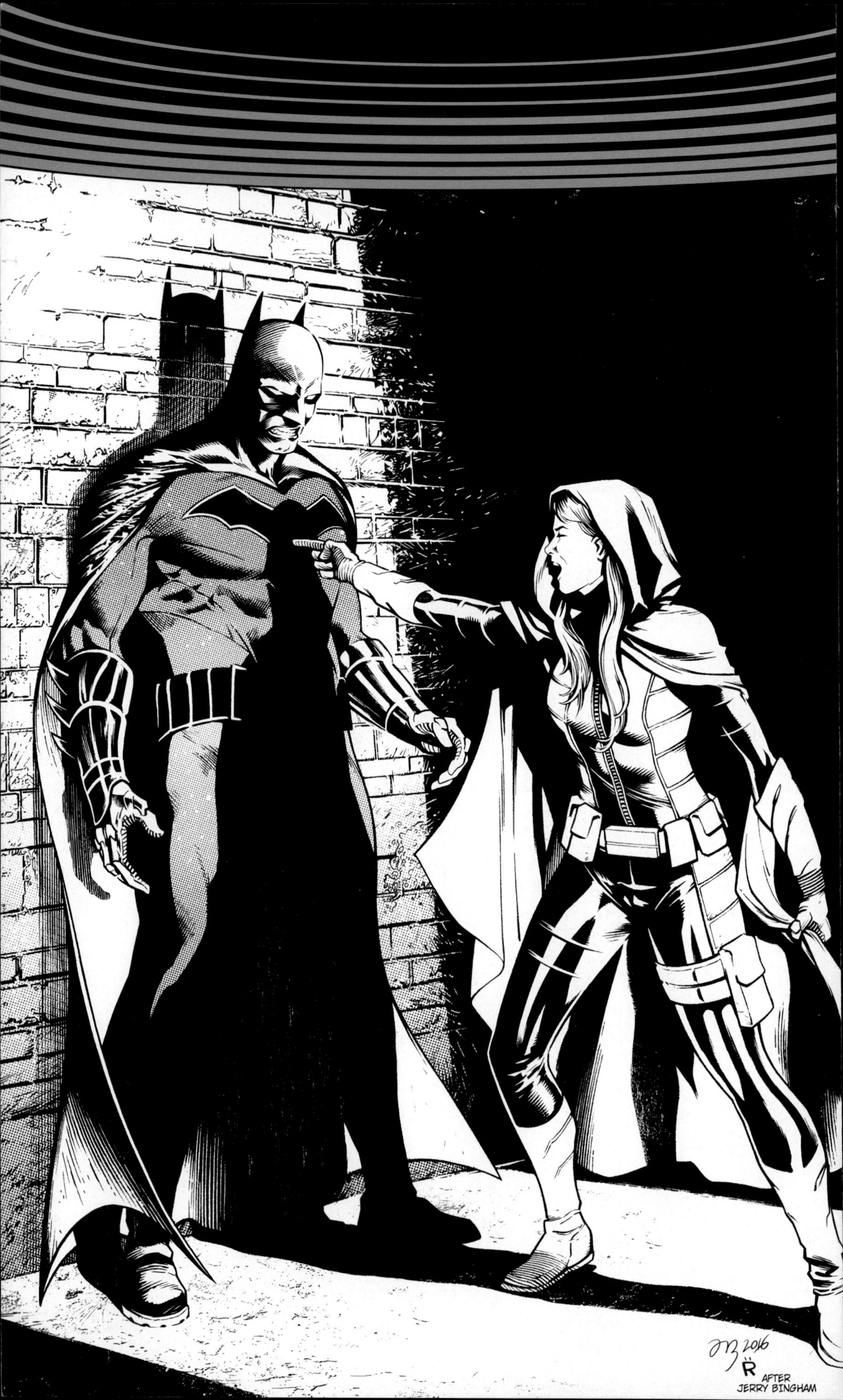
2016
AFTER
JERRY BINGHAM

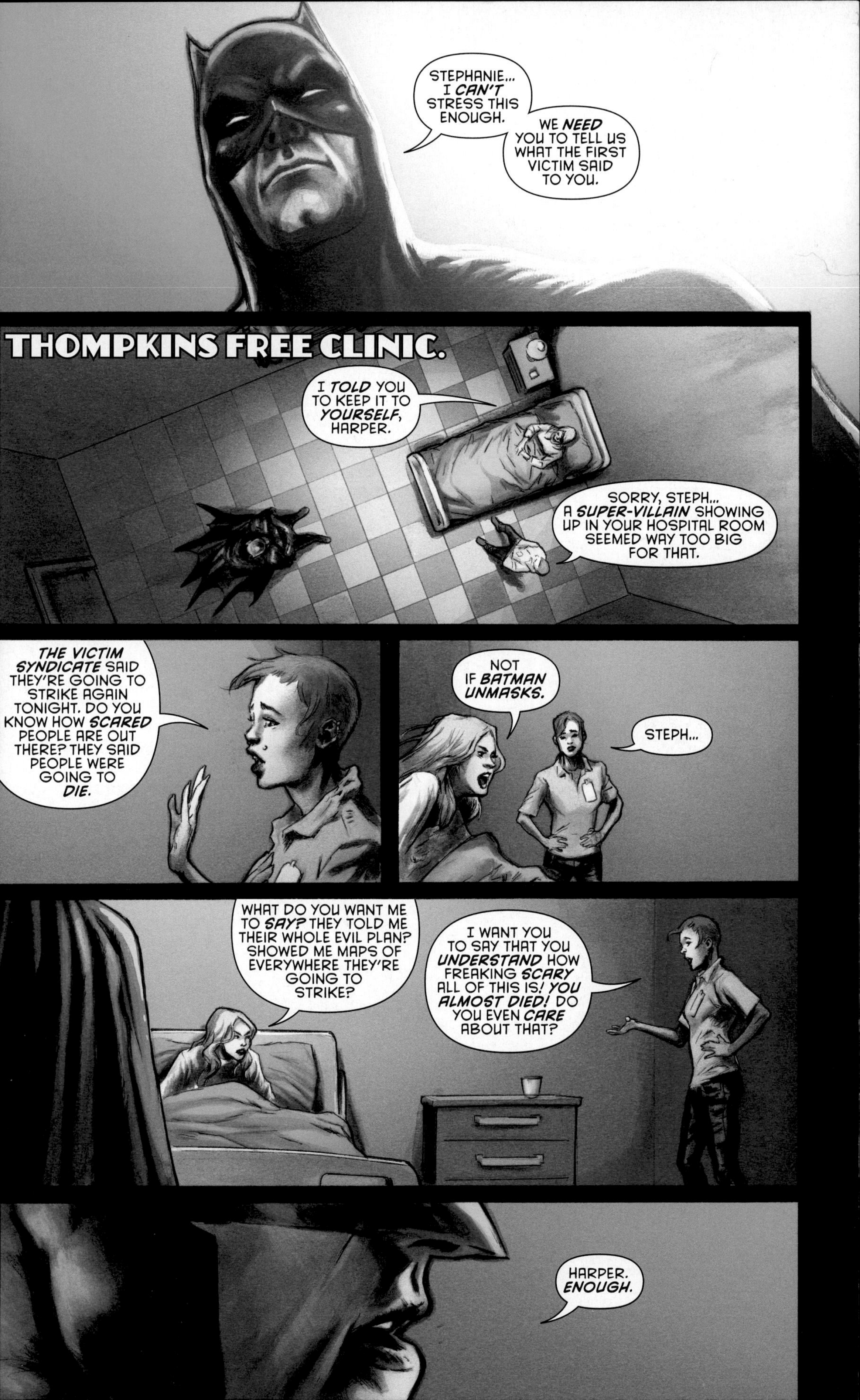

STEPHANIE... I CAN'T STRESS THIS ENOUGH.
WE NEED YOU TO TELL US WHAT THE FIRST VICTIM SAID TO YOU.
THOMPKINS FREE CLINIC.
I TOLD YOU TO KEEP IT TO YOURSELF, HARPER.
SORRY, STEPH... A SUPER-VILLAIN SHOWING UP IN YOUR HOSPITAL ROOM SEEMED WAY TOO BIG FOR THAT.
THE VICTIM SYNDICATE SAID THEY'RE GOING TO STRIKE AGAIN TONIGHT. DO YOU KNOW HOW SCARED PEOPLE ARE OUT THERE? THEY SAID PEOPLE WERE GOING TO DIE.
NOT IF BATMAN UNMASKS.
STEPH...
WHAT DO YOU WANT ME TO SAY? THEY TOLD ME THEIR WHOLE EVIL PLAN? SHOWED ME MAPS OF EVERYWHERE THEY'RE GOING TO STRIKE?
I WANT YOU TO SAY THAT YOU UNDERSTAND HOW FREAKING SCARY ALL OF THIS IS! YOU ALMOST DIED! DO YOU EVEN CARE ABOUT THAT?
HARPER. ENOUGH.

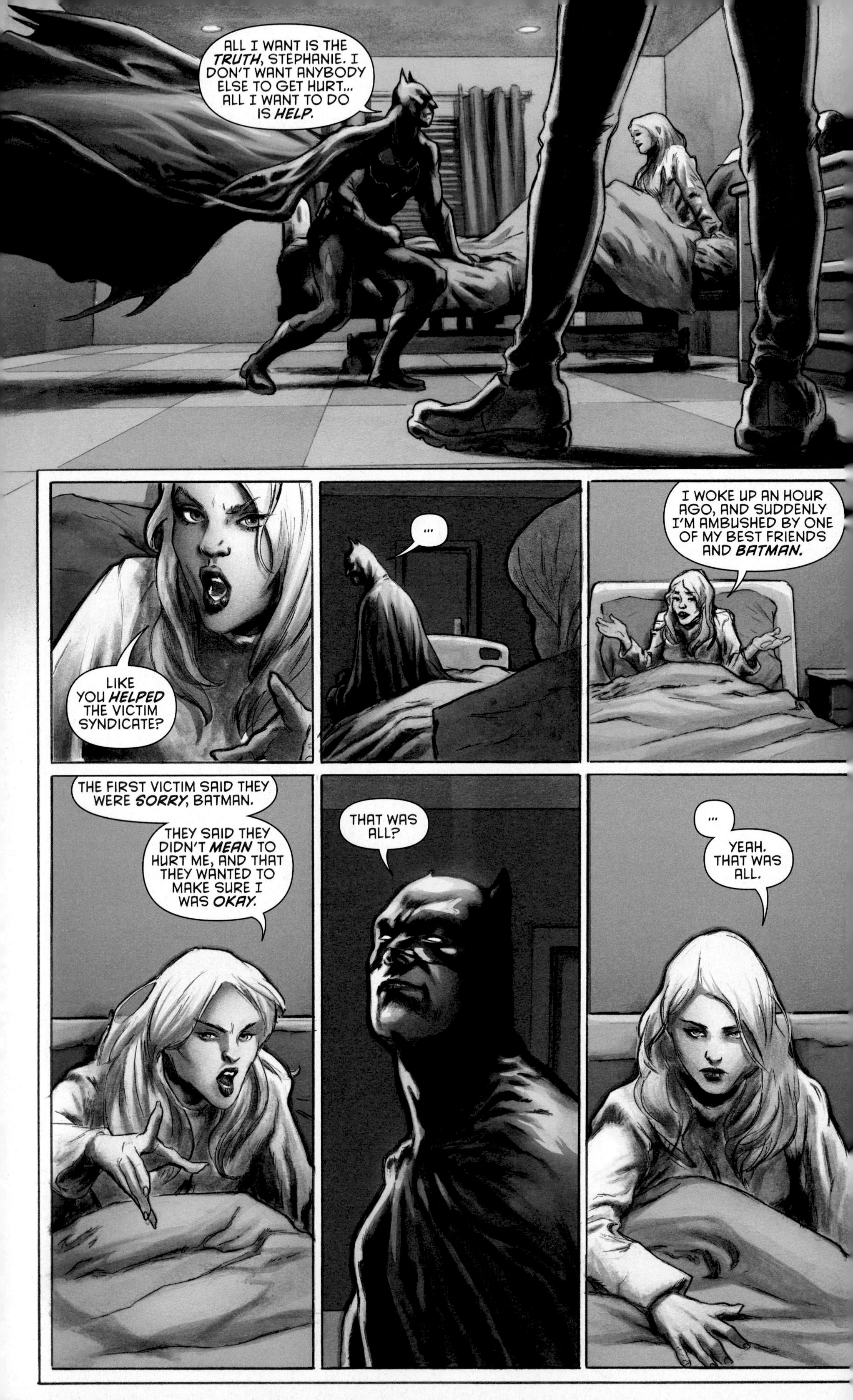
ALL I WANT IS THE TRUTH, STEPHANIE. I DON'T WANT ANYBODY ELSE TO GET HURT... ALL I WANT TO DO IS HELP.
LIKE YOU HELPED THE VICTIM SYNDICATE?
...
I WOKE UP AN HOUR AGO, AND SUDDENLY I'M AMBUSHED BY ONE OF MY BEST FRIENDS AND BATMAN.
THE FIRST VICTIM SAID THEY WERE SORRY, BATMAN.
THEY SAID THEY DIDN'T MEAN TO HURT ME, AND THAT THEY WANTED TO MAKE SURE I WAS OKAY.
THAT WAS ALL?
...
YEAH. THAT WAS ALL.

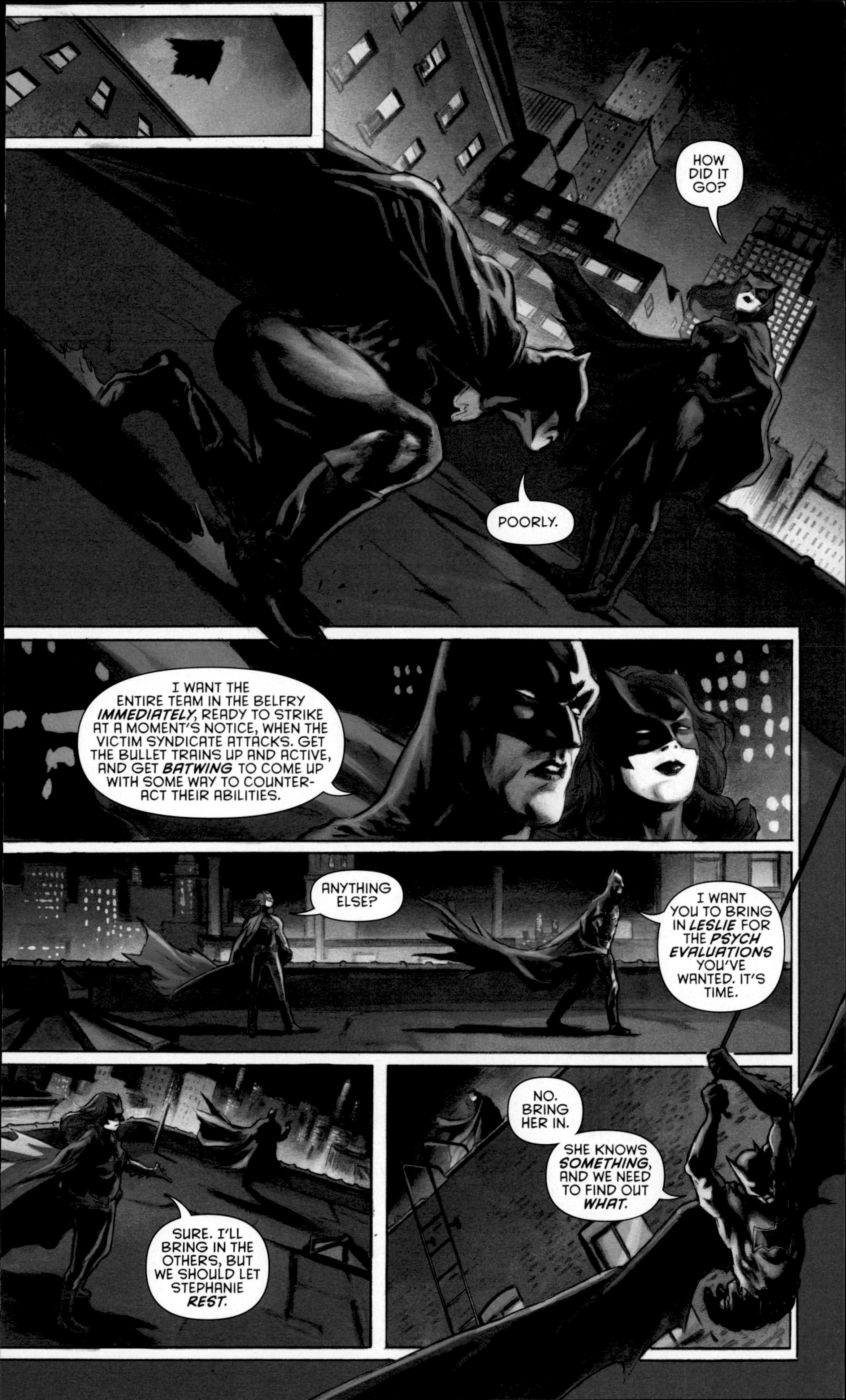

HOW DID IT GO?
POORLY.
I WANT THE ENTIRE TEAM IN THE BELFRY *IMMEDIATELY*, READY TO STRIKE AT A MOMENT'S NOTICE, WHEN THE VICTIM SYNDICATE ATTACKS. GET THE BULLET TRAINS UP AND ACTIVE, AND GET *BATWING* TO COME UP WITH SOME WAY TO COUNTER-ACT THEIR ABILITIES.
ANYTHING ELSE?
I WANT YOU TO BRING IN *LESLIE* FOR THE *PSYCH EVALUATIONS* YOU'VE WANTED. IT'S TIME.
SURE. I'LL BRING IN THE OTHERS, BUT WE SHOULD LET STEPHANIE *REST*.
NO. BRING HER IN.
SHE KNOWS *SOMETHING*, AND WE NEED TO FIND OUT *WHAT*.

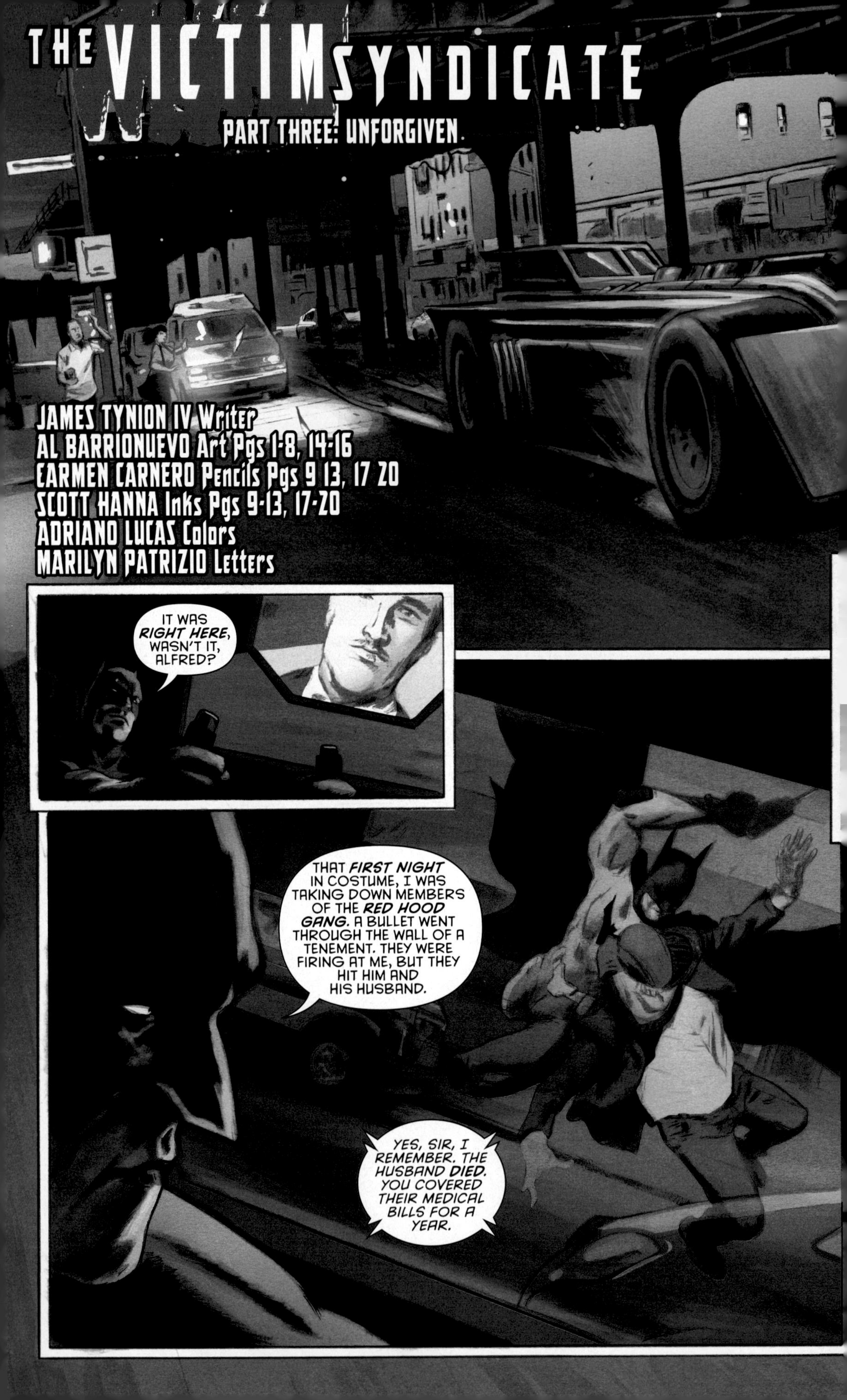
THE VICTIM SYNDICATE
PART THREE: UNFORGIVEN
JAMES TYNION IV Writer
AL BARRIONUEVO Art Pgs 1-8, 14-16
CARMEN CARNERO Pencils Pgs 9 13, 17 20
SCOTT HANNA Inks Pgs 9-13, 17-20
ADRIANO LUCAS Colors
MARILYN PATRIZIO Letters
IT WAS RIGHT HERE, WASN'T IT, ALFRED?
THAT FIRST NIGHT IN COSTUME, I WAS TAKING DOWN MEMBERS OF THE RED HOOD GANG. A BULLET WENT THROUGH THE WALL OF A TENEMENT. THEY WERE FIRING AT ME, BUT THEY HIT HIM AND HIS HUSBAND.
YES, SIR, I REMEMBER. THE HUSBAND DIED. YOU COVERED THEIR MEDICAL BILLS FOR A YEAR.

ALVARO MARTINEZ, RAUL FERNANDEZ,
BRAD ANDERSON Cover
RAFAEL ALBUQUERQUE Variant Cover
DAVE WIELGOSZ Asst. Editor
CHRIS CONROY Editor
MARK DOYLE Group Editor
BATMAN CREATED BY BOB KANE WITH BILL FINGER

THAT WAS THE *SECOND* NIGHT, I. THE WHOLE UNFORTUNATE AIR WITH THAT TY BUS. THE RST NIGHT WAS MORE *INTIMATE*, I SEEM TO REMEMBER.

DID ANYONE GET HURT?

FORGIVE ME, SIR. I DON'T REMEMBER.

I USED TO KNOW *ALL* THEIR NAMES.

I THOUGHT I COULD *ALWAYS* REMEMBER THE INNOCENT PEOPLE WHO GOT HURT IN THIS WAR.

BUT I *DON'T* REMEMBER THEIR NAMES, ALFRED. ANY *ONE* OF THEM COULD BE THE FIRST VICTIM. ANY ONE OF THEM.

SIR, MIGHT I ASK A QUESTION?

WHAT DO YOU HOPE TO *GAIN* FROM RIPPING OPEN THESE OLD WOUNDS? ARE YOU WORRIED THERE'S A KERNEL OF *TRUTH* TO WHAT THIS PERSON'S SAYING? THAT PERHAPS THIS CITY WOULD BE SAFER *WITHOUT* A BATMAN?

OR IS ALL OF THIS ABOUT MASTER TIMOTHY?

I *DON'T* KNOW, ALFRED.

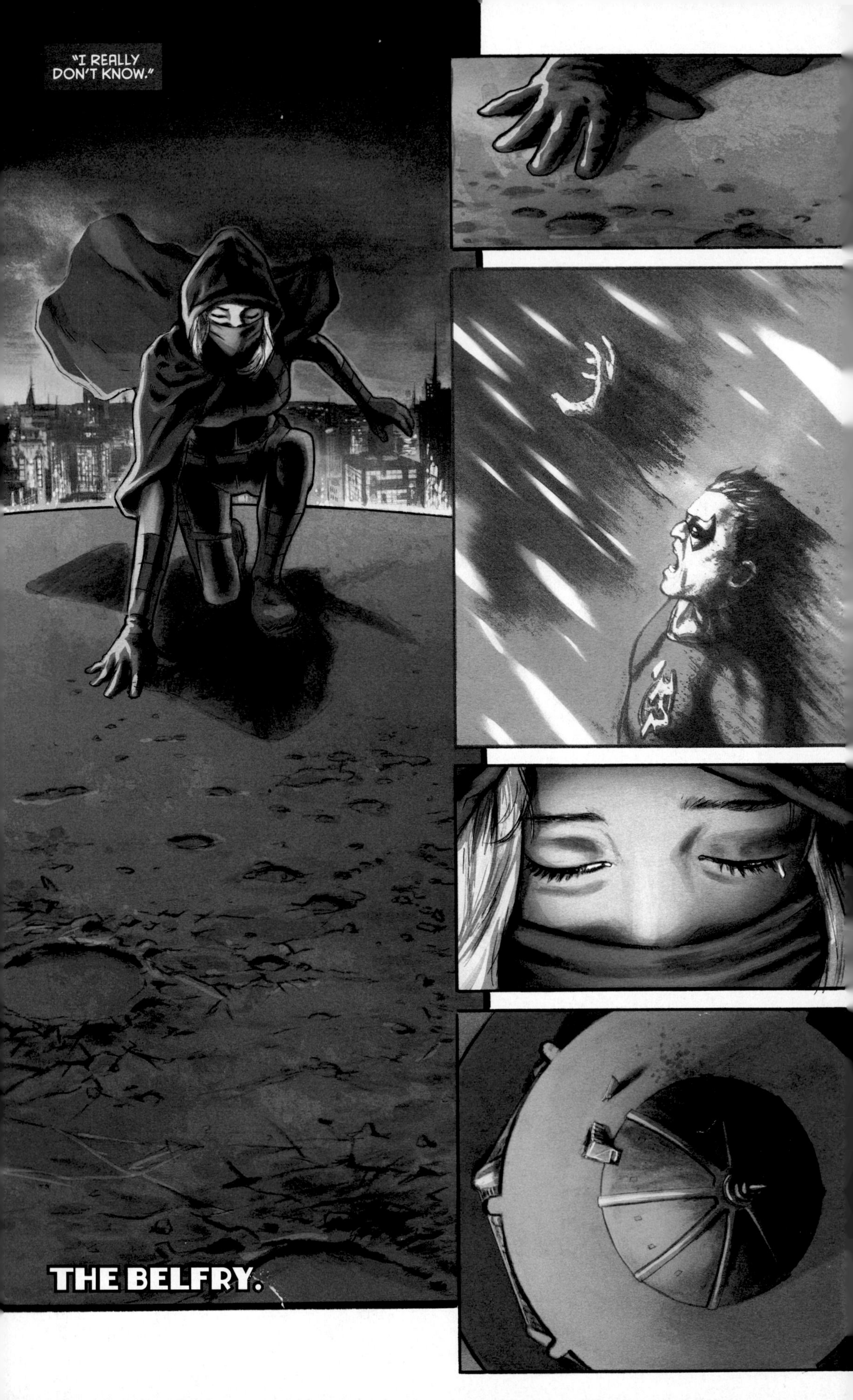
"I REALLY DON'T KNOW."
THE BELFRY.

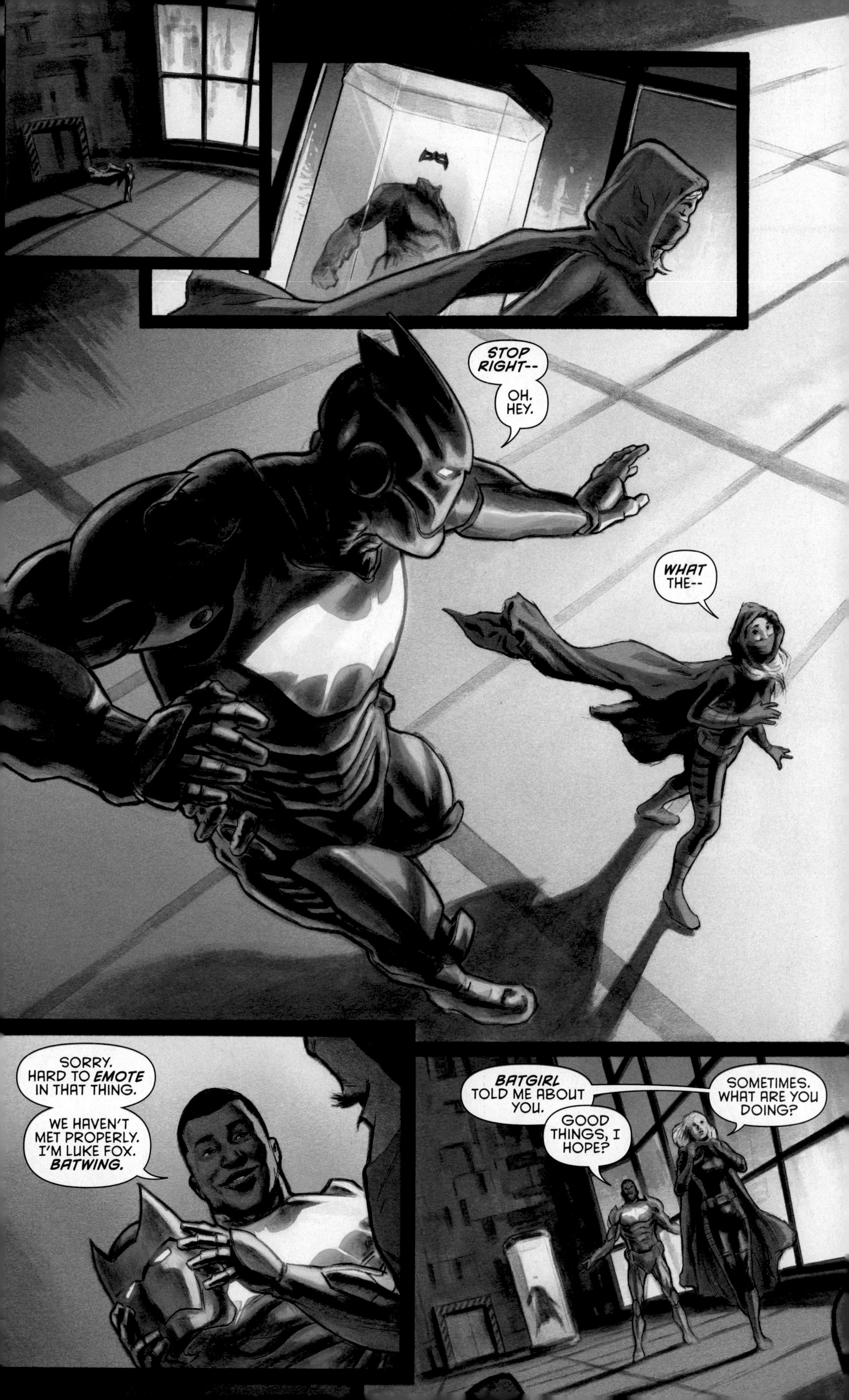
STOP RIGHT--
OH. HEY.
WHAT THE--
SORRY. HARD TO EMOTE IN THAT THING.
WE HAVEN'T MET PROPERLY. I'M LUKE FOX. BATWING.
BATGIRL TOLD ME ABOUT YOU.
GOOD THINGS, I HOPE?
SOMETIMES. WHAT ARE YOU DOING?

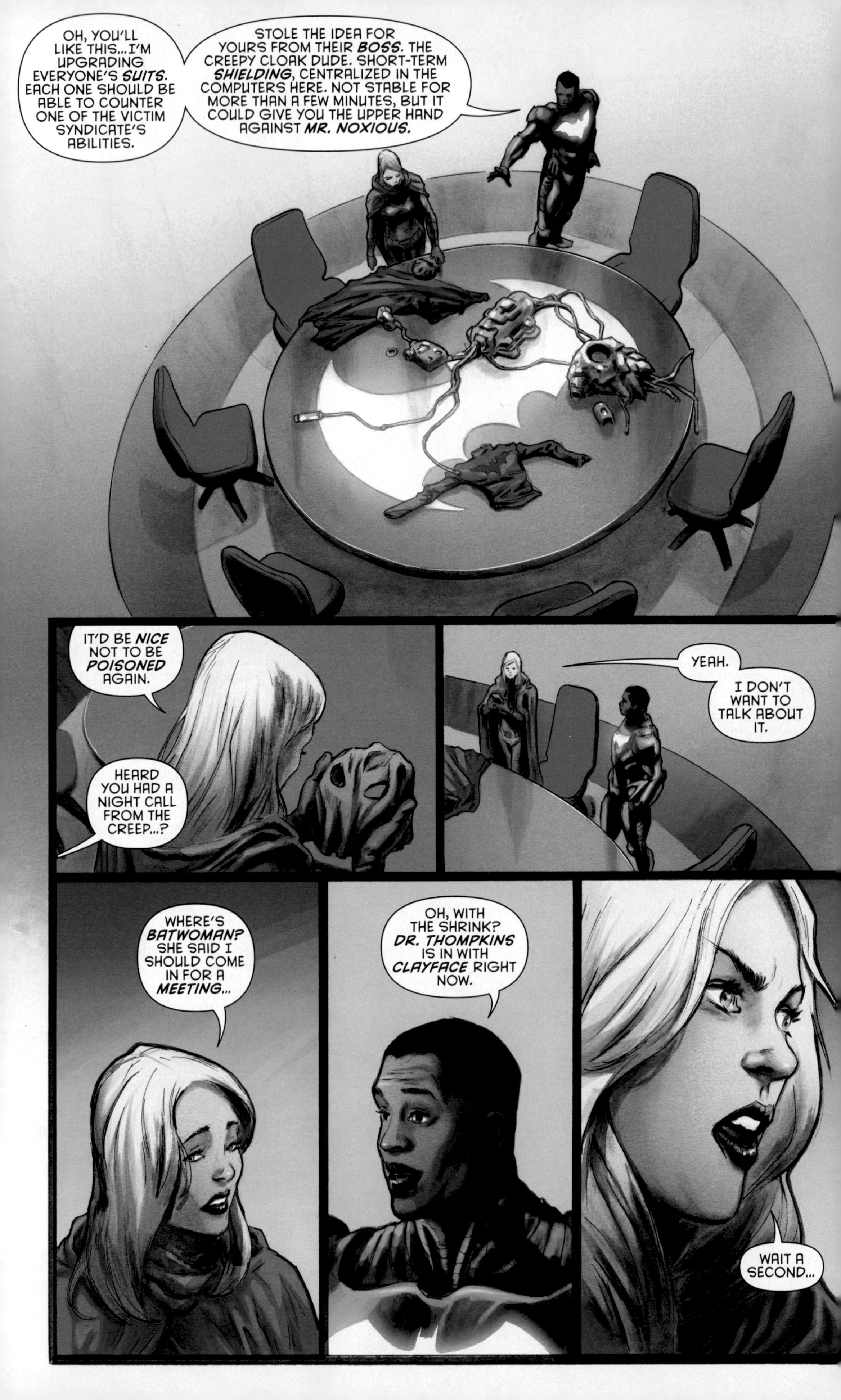

OH, YOU'LL LIKE THIS...I'M UPGRADING EVERYONE'S *SUITS.* EACH ONE SHOULD BE ABLE TO COUNTER ONE OF THE VICTIM SYNDICATE'S ABILITIES.
STOLE THE IDEA FOR YOURS FROM THEIR *BOSS.* THE CREEPY CLOAK DUDE. SHORT-TERM *SHIELDING,* CENTRALIZED IN THE COMPUTERS HERE. NOT STABLE FOR MORE THAN A FEW MINUTES, BUT IT COULD GIVE YOU THE UPPER HAND AGAINST *MR. NOXIOUS.*
IT'D BE *NICE* NOT TO BE *POISONED* AGAIN.
HEARD YOU HAD A NIGHT CALL FROM THE CREEP...?
YEAH.
I DON'T WANT TO TALK ABOUT IT.
WHERE'S *BATWOMAN?* SHE SAID I SHOULD COME IN FOR A *MEETING...*
OH, WITH THE SHRINK? *DR. THOMPKINS* IS IN WITH *CLAYFACE* RIGHT NOW.
WAIT A SECOND...

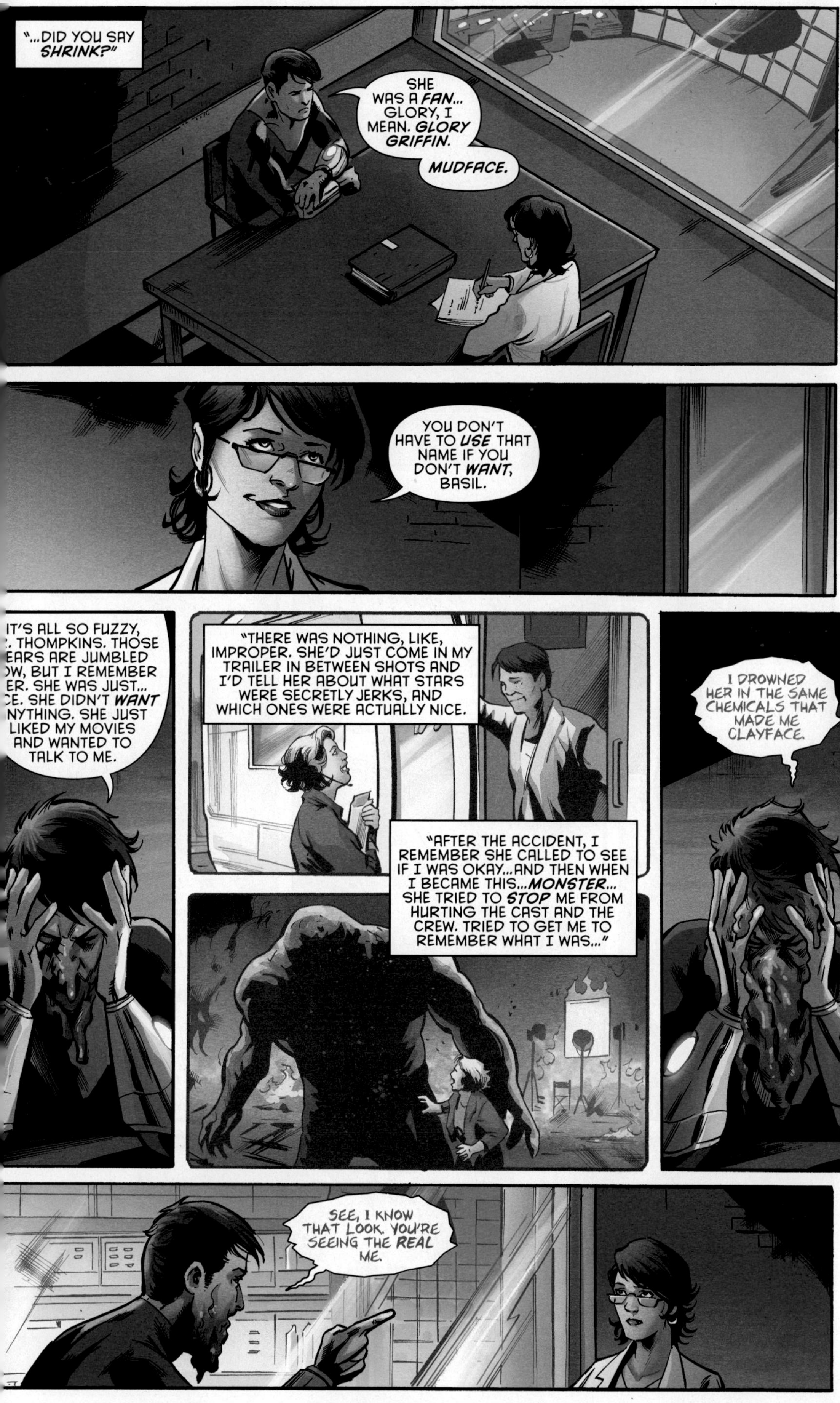
"...DID YOU SAY SHRINK?"
SHE WAS A FAN... GLORY, I MEAN. GLORY GRIFFIN.
MUDFACE.
YOU DON'T HAVE TO USE THAT NAME IF YOU DON'T WANT, BASIL.
IT'S ALL SO FUZZY, . THOMPKINS. THOSE EARS ARE JUMBLED OW, BUT I REMEMBER ER. SHE WAS JUST... CE. SHE DIDN'T WANT NYTHING. SHE JUST LIKED MY MOVIES AND WANTED TO TALK TO ME.
"THERE WAS NOTHING, LIKE, IMPROPER. SHE'D JUST COME IN MY TRAILER IN BETWEEN SHOTS AND I'D TELL HER ABOUT WHAT STARS WERE SECRETLY JERKS, AND WHICH ONES WERE ACTUALLY NICE.
"AFTER THE ACCIDENT, I REMEMBER SHE CALLED TO SEE IF I WAS OKAY...AND THEN WHEN I BECAME THIS...MONSTER... SHE TRIED TO STOP ME FROM HURTING THE CAST AND THE CREW. TRIED TO GET ME TO REMEMBER WHAT I WAS..."
I DROWNED HER IN THE SAME CHEMICALS THAT MADE ME CLAYFACE.
SEE, I KNOW THAT LOOK. YOU'RE SEEING THE REAL ME.

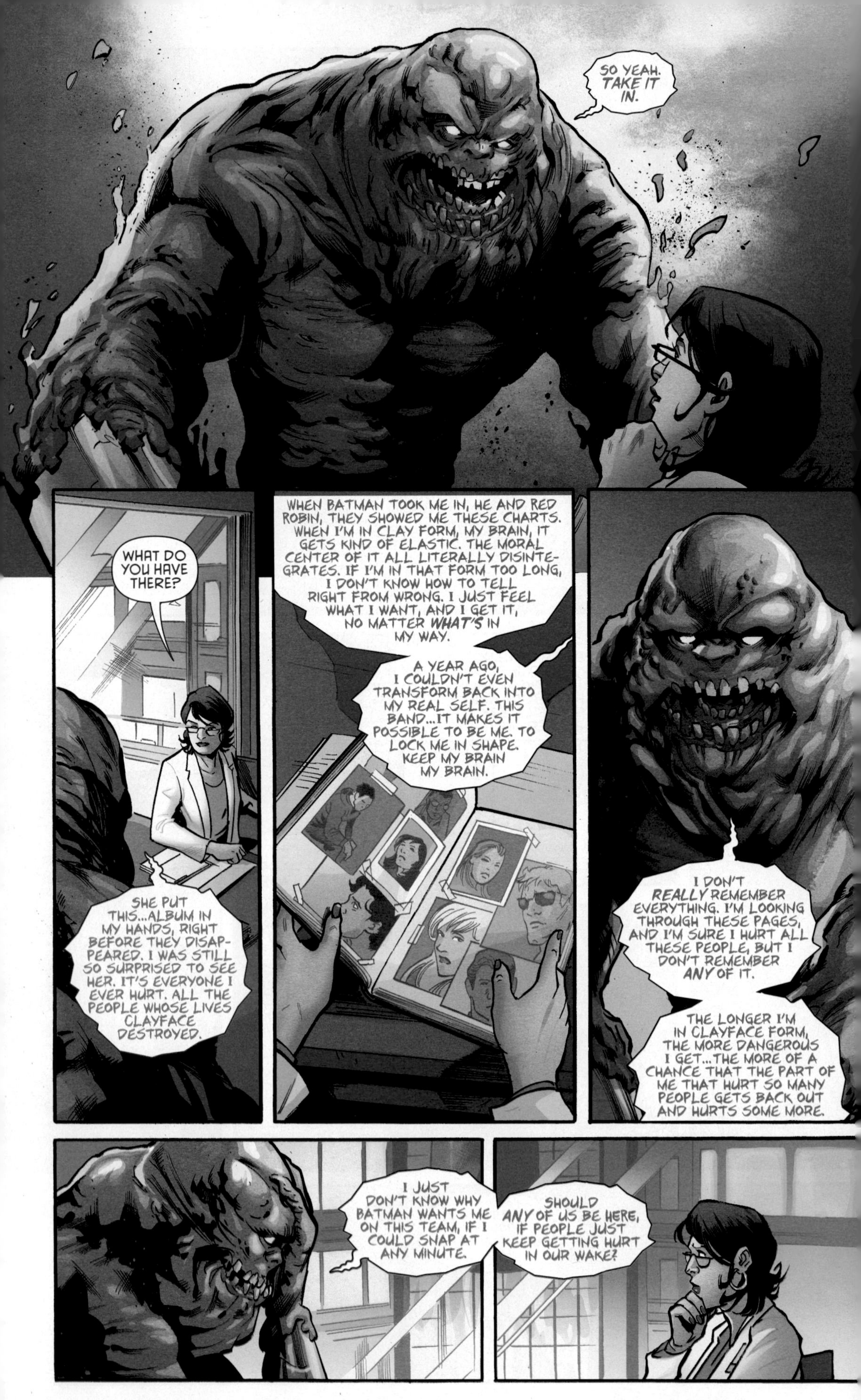
SO YEAH. TAKE IT IN.
WHAT DO YOU HAVE THERE?
SHE PUT THIS...ALBUM IN MY HANDS, RIGHT BEFORE THEY DISAPPEARED. I WAS STILL SO SURPRISED TO SEE HER. IT'S EVERYONE I EVER HURT. ALL THE PEOPLE WHOSE LIVES CLAYFACE DESTROYED.
WHEN BATMAN TOOK ME IN, HE AND RED ROBIN, THEY SHOWED ME THESE CHARTS. WHEN I'M IN CLAY FORM, MY BRAIN, IT GETS KIND OF ELASTIC. THE MORAL CENTER OF IT ALL LITERALLY DISINTEGRATES. IF I'M IN THAT FORM TOO LONG, I DON'T KNOW HOW TO TELL RIGHT FROM WRONG. I JUST FEEL WHAT I WANT, AND I GET IT, NO MATTER WHAT'S IN MY WAY.
A YEAR AGO, I COULDN'T EVEN TRANSFORM BACK INTO MY REAL SELF. THIS BAND...IT MAKES IT POSSIBLE TO BE ME. TO LOCK ME IN SHAPE. KEEP MY BRAIN MY BRAIN.
I DON'T REALLY REMEMBER EVERYTHING. I'M LOOKING THROUGH THESE PAGES, AND I'M SURE I HURT ALL THESE PEOPLE, BUT I DON'T REMEMBER ANY OF IT.
THE LONGER I'M IN CLAYFACE FORM, THE MORE DANGEROUS I GET...THE MORE OF A CHANCE THAT THE PART OF ME THAT HURT SO MANY PEOPLE GETS BACK OUT AND HURTS SOME MORE.
I JUST DON'T KNOW WHY BATMAN WANTS ME ON THIS TEAM, IF I COULD SNAP AT ANY MINUTE.
SHOULD ANY OF US BE HERE, IF PEOPLE JUST KEEP GETTING HURT IN OUR WAKE?

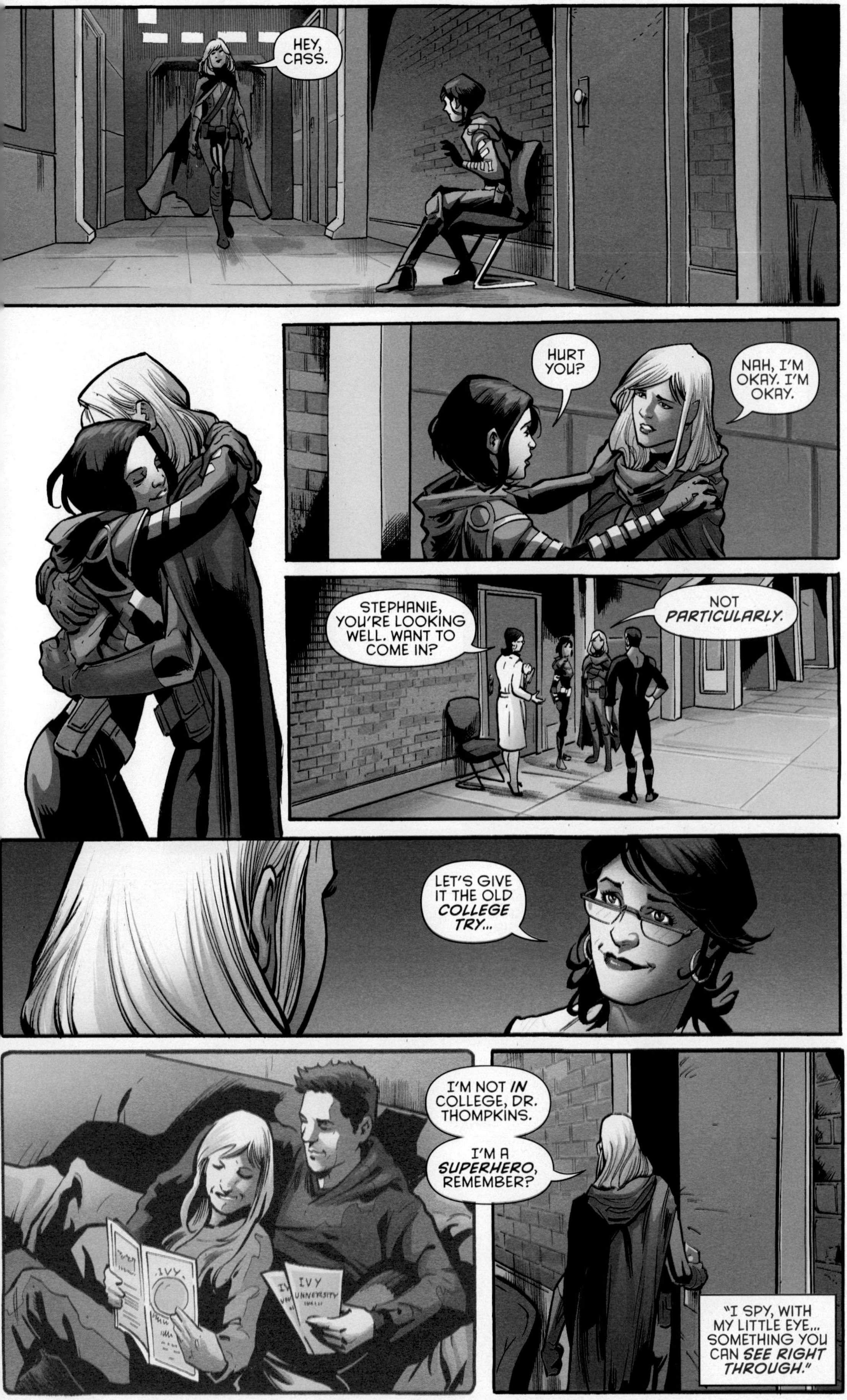
HEY, CASS.
HURT YOU?
NAH, I'M OKAY. I'M OKAY.
STEPHANIE, YOU'RE LOOKING WELL. WANT TO COME IN?
NOT *PARTICULARLY.*
LET'S GIVE IT THE OLD *COLLEGE TRY...*
I'M NOT *IN* COLLEGE, DR. THOMPKINS.
I'M A *SUPERHERO,* REMEMBER?
"I SPY, WITH MY LITTLE EYE... SOMETHING YOU CAN *SEE RIGHT THROUGH.*"

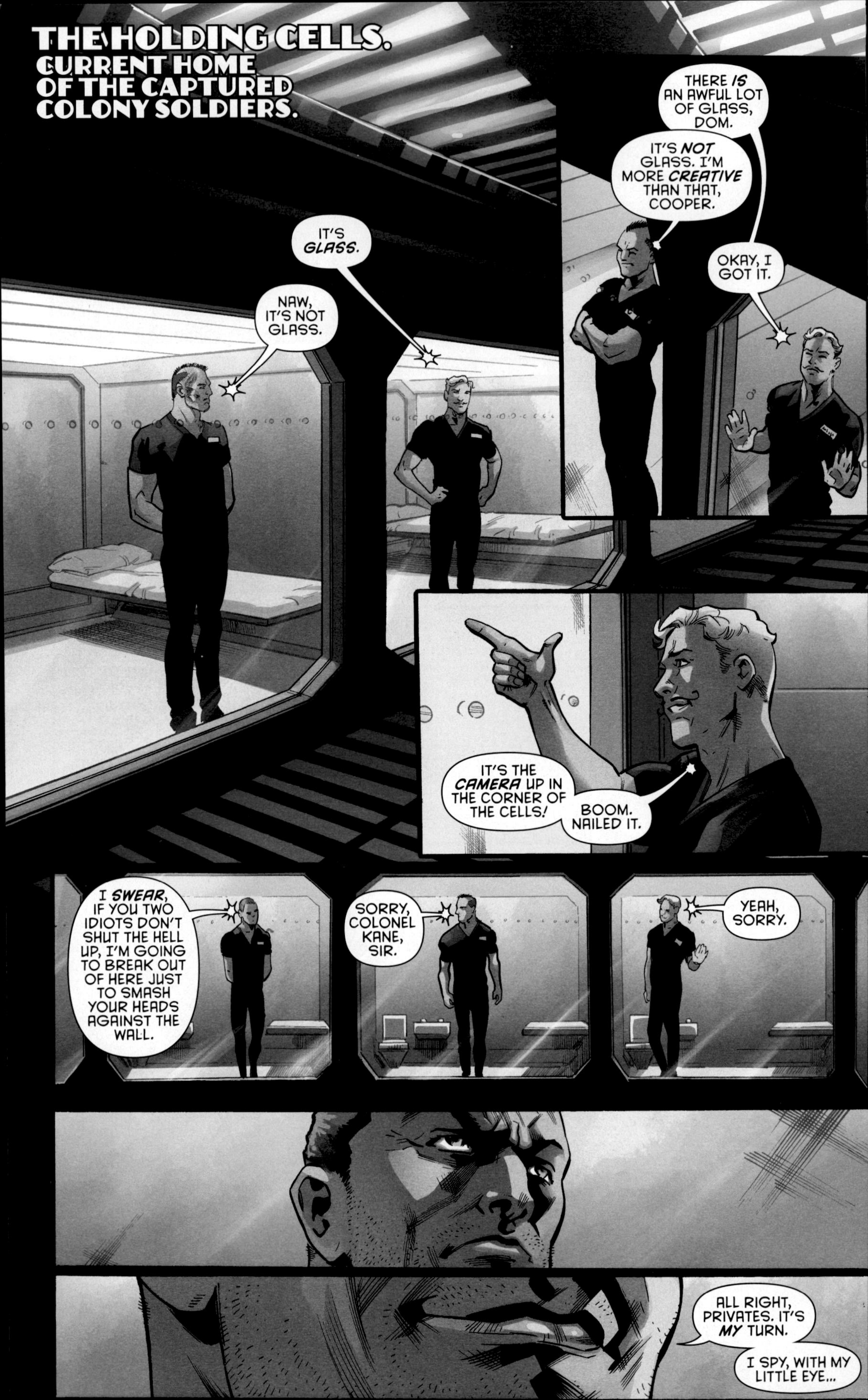
THE HOLDING CELLS. CURRENT HOME OF THE CAPTURED COLONY SOLDIERS.
IT'S GLASS.
NAW, IT'S NOT GLASS.
THERE IS AN AWFUL LOT OF GLASS, DOM.
IT'S NOT GLASS. I'M MORE CREATIVE THAN THAT, COOPER.
OKAY, I GOT IT.
IT'S THE CAMERA UP IN THE CORNER OF THE CELLS!
BOOM. NAILED IT.
I SWEAR, IF YOU TWO IDIOTS DON'T SHUT THE HELL UP, I'M GOING TO BREAK OUT OF HERE JUST TO SMASH YOUR HEADS AGAINST THE WALL.
SORRY, COLONEL KANE, SIR.
YEAH, SORRY.
ALL RIGHT, PRIVATES. IT'S MY TURN.
I SPY, WITH MY LITTLE EYE...

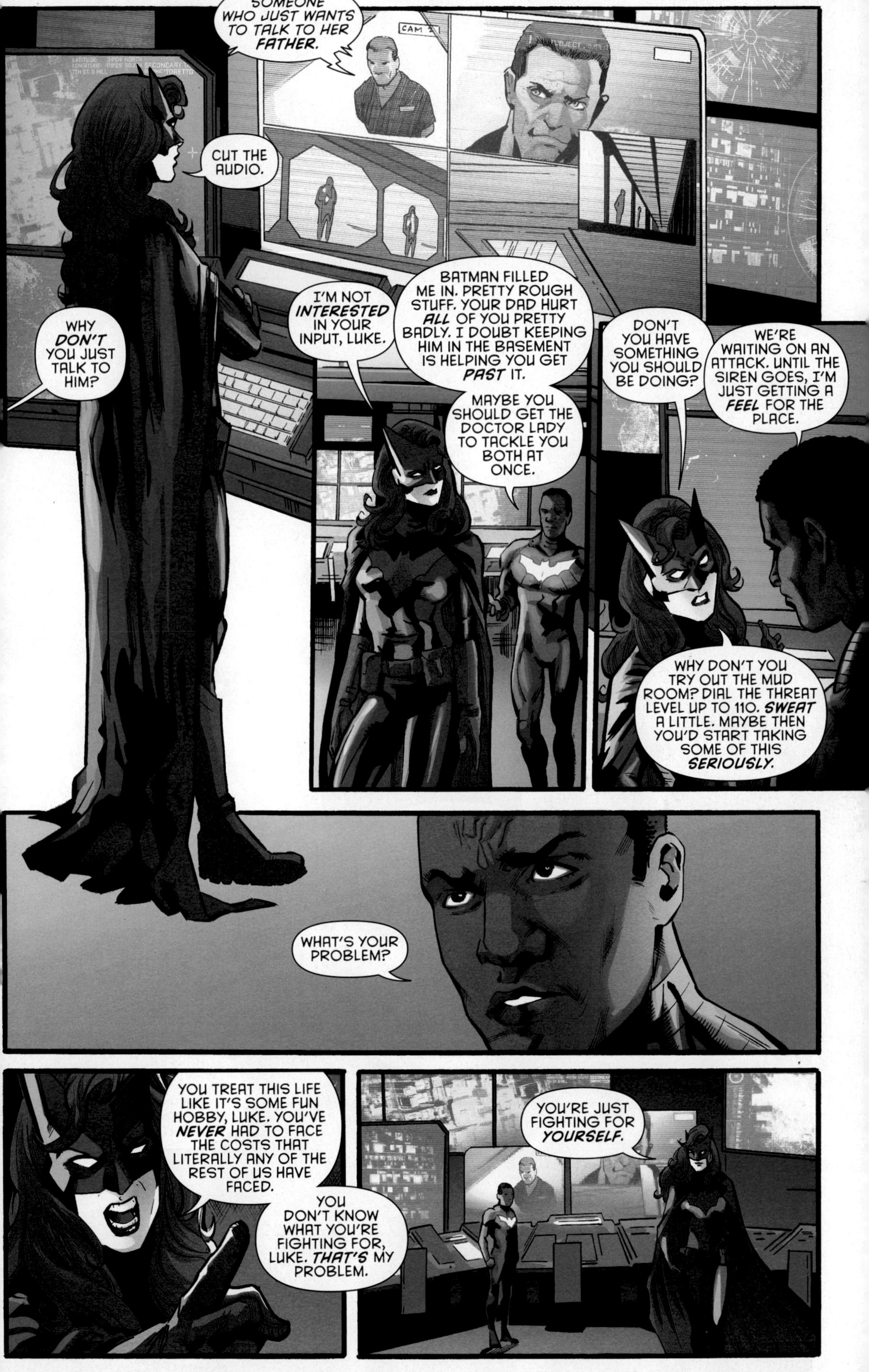
SOMEONE WHO JUST WANTS TO TALK TO HER FATHER.
CAM 2
CUT THE AUDIO.
WHY DON'T YOU JUST TALK TO HIM?
I'M NOT INTERESTED IN YOUR INPUT, LUKE.
BATMAN FILLED ME IN. PRETTY ROUGH STUFF. YOUR DAD HURT ALL OF YOU PRETTY BADLY. I DOUBT KEEPING HIM IN THE BASEMENT IS HELPING YOU GET PAST IT.
MAYBE YOU SHOULD GET THE DOCTOR LADY TO TACKLE YOU BOTH AT ONCE.
DON'T YOU HAVE SOMETHING YOU SHOULD BE DOING?
WE'RE WAITING ON AN ATTACK. UNTIL THE SIREN GOES, I'M JUST GETTING A FEEL FOR THE PLACE.
WHY DON'T YOU TRY OUT THE MUD ROOM? DIAL THE THREAT LEVEL UP TO 110. SWEAT A LITTLE. MAYBE THEN YOU'D START TAKING SOME OF THIS SERIOUSLY.
WHAT'S YOUR PROBLEM?
YOU TREAT THIS LIFE LIKE IT'S SOME FUN HOBBY, LUKE. YOU'VE NEVER HAD TO FACE THE COSTS THAT LITERALLY ANY OF THE REST OF US HAVE FACED.
YOU DON'T KNOW WHAT YOU'RE FIGHTING FOR, LUKE. THAT'S MY PROBLEM.
YOU'RE JUST FIGHTING FOR YOURSELF.

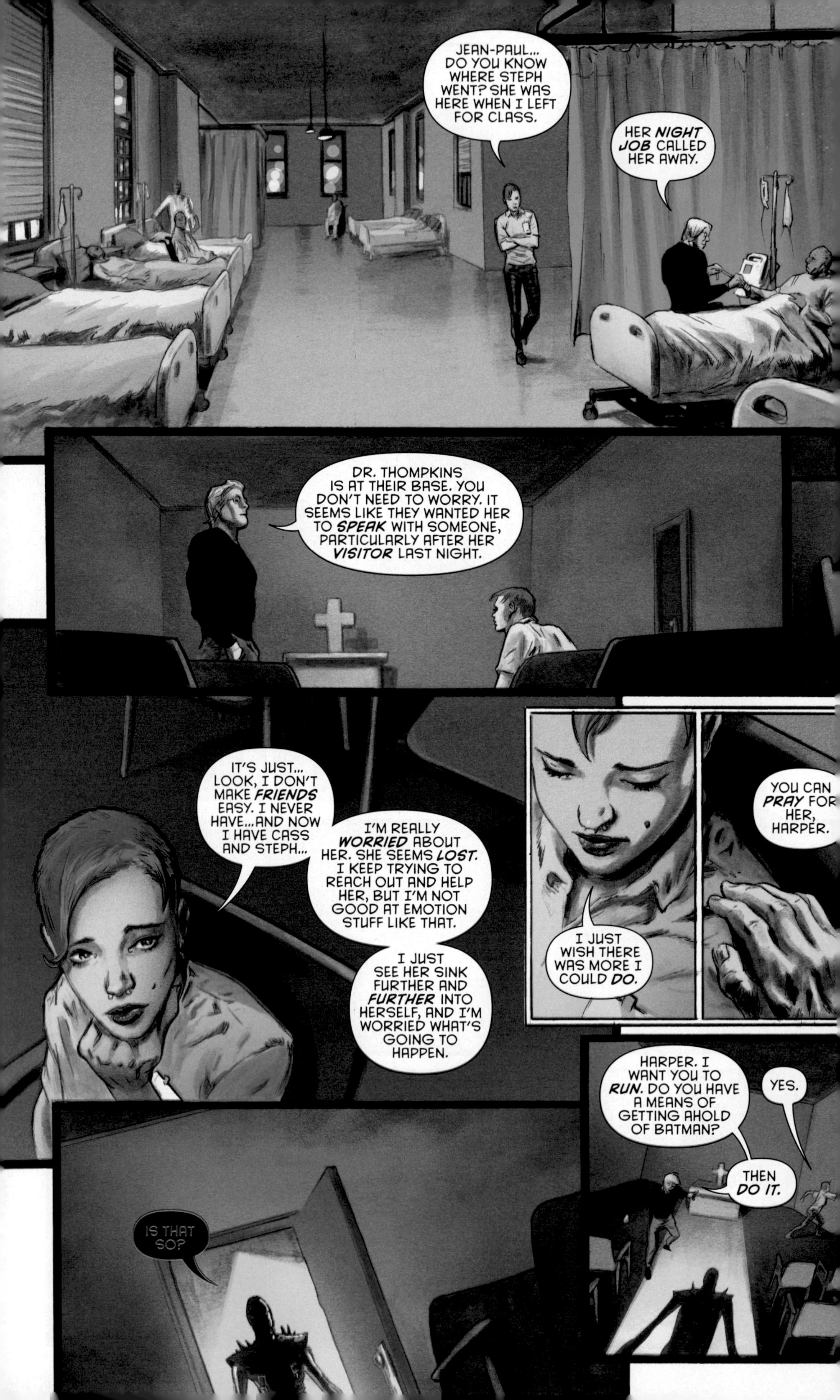

JEAN-PAUL... DO YOU KNOW WHERE STEPH WENT? SHE WAS HERE WHEN I LEFT FOR CLASS.
HER NIGHT JOB CALLED HER AWAY.
DR. THOMPKINS IS AT THEIR BASE. YOU DON'T NEED TO WORRY. IT SEEMS LIKE THEY WANTED HER TO SPEAK WITH SOMEONE, PARTICULARLY AFTER HER VISITOR LAST NIGHT.
IT'S JUST... LOOK, I DON'T MAKE FRIENDS EASY. I NEVER HAVE...AND NOW I HAVE CASS AND STEPH...
I'M REALLY WORRIED ABOUT HER. SHE SEEMS LOST. I KEEP TRYING TO REACH OUT AND HELP HER, BUT I'M NOT GOOD AT EMOTION STUFF LIKE THAT.
I JUST SEE HER SINK FURTHER AND FURTHER INTO HERSELF, AND I'M WORRIED WHAT'S GOING TO HAPPEN.
I JUST WISH THERE WAS MORE I COULD DO.
YOU CAN PRAY FOR HER, HARPER.
IS THAT SO?
HARPER. I WANT YOU TO RUN. DO YOU HAVE A MEANS OF GETTING AHOLD OF BATMAN?
YES.
THEN DO IT.

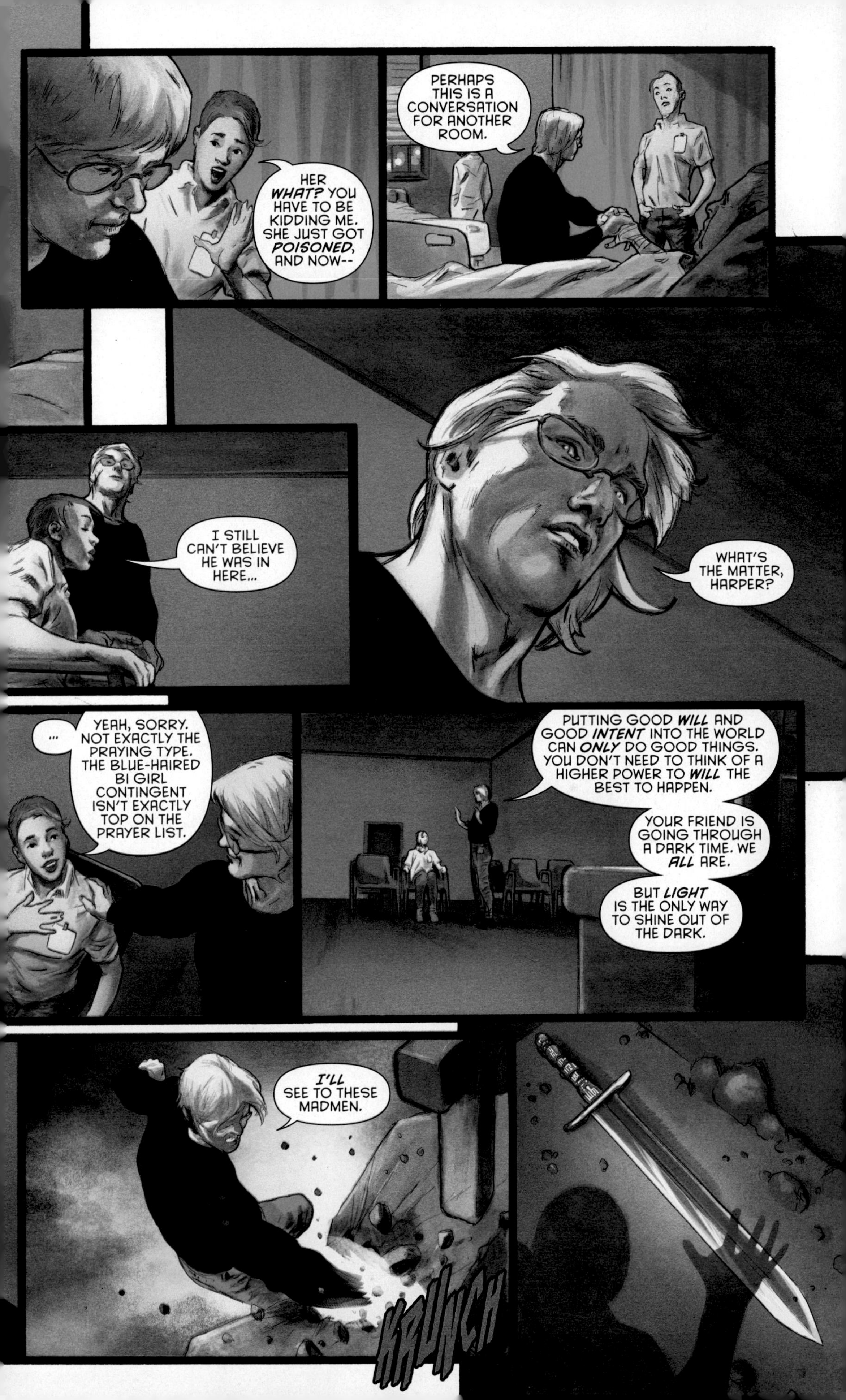
HER WHAT? YOU HAVE TO BE KIDDING ME. SHE JUST GOT POISONED, AND NOW--
PERHAPS THIS IS A CONVERSATION FOR ANOTHER ROOM.
I STILL CAN'T BELIEVE HE WAS IN HERE...
WHAT'S THE MATTER, HARPER?
...
YEAH, SORRY. NOT EXACTLY THE PRAYING TYPE. THE BLUE-HAIRED BI GIRL CONTINGENT ISN'T EXACTLY TOP ON THE PRAYER LIST.
PUTTING GOOD WILL AND GOOD INTENT INTO THE WORLD CAN ONLY DO GOOD THINGS. YOU DON'T NEED TO THINK OF A HIGHER POWER TO WILL THE BEST TO HAPPEN.
YOUR FRIEND IS GOING THROUGH A DARK TIME. WE ALL ARE.
BUT LIGHT IS THE ONLY WAY TO SHINE OUT OF THE DARK.
I'LL SEE TO THESE MADMEN.
KRUNCH

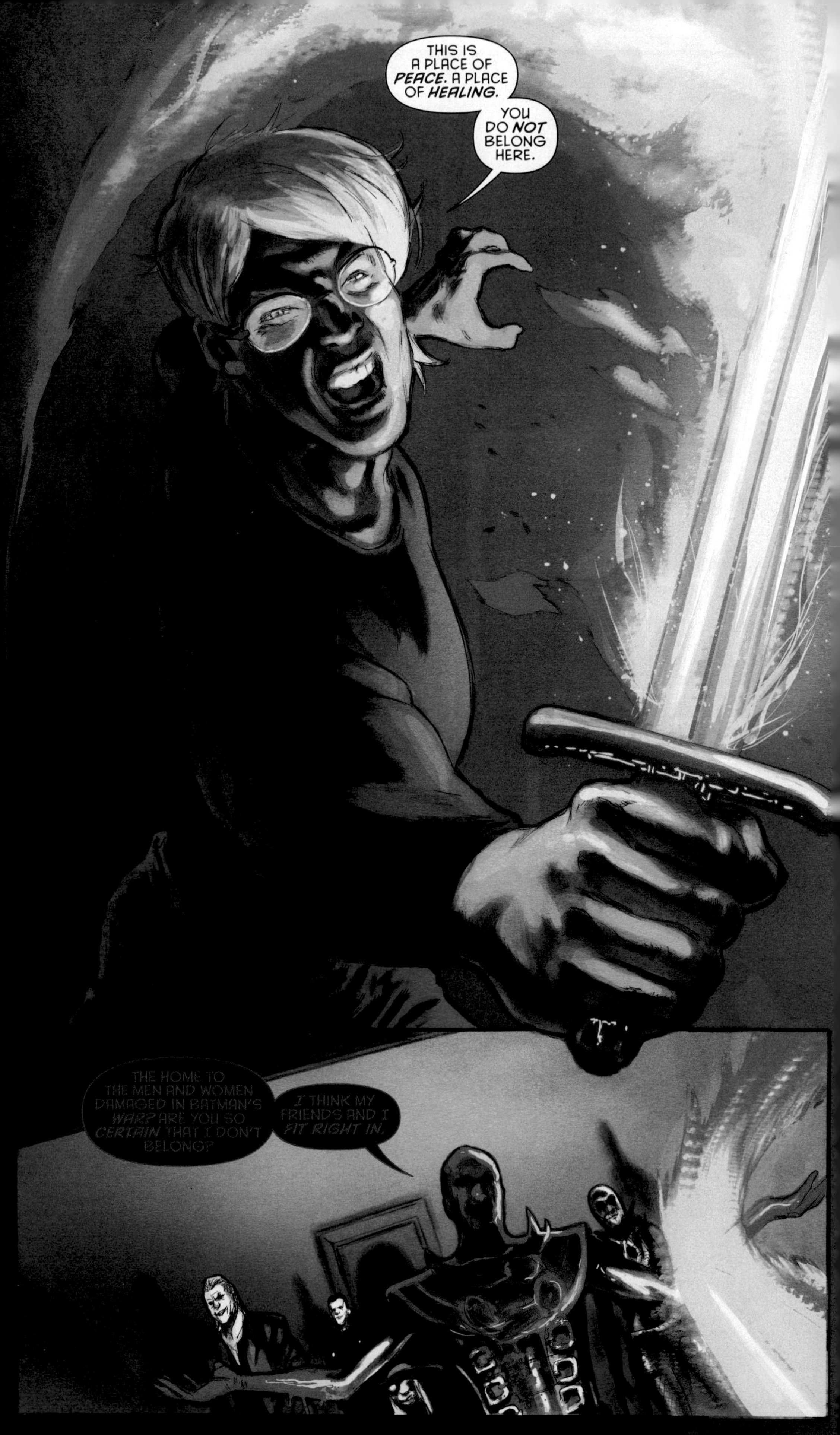
THIS IS A PLACE OF PEACE. A PLACE OF HEALING.
YOU DO NOT BELONG HERE.
THE HOME TO THE MEN AND WOMEN DAMAGED IN BATMAN'S WAR? ARE YOU SO CERTAIN THAT I DON'T BELONG?
I THINK MY FRIENDS AND I FIT RIGHT IN.

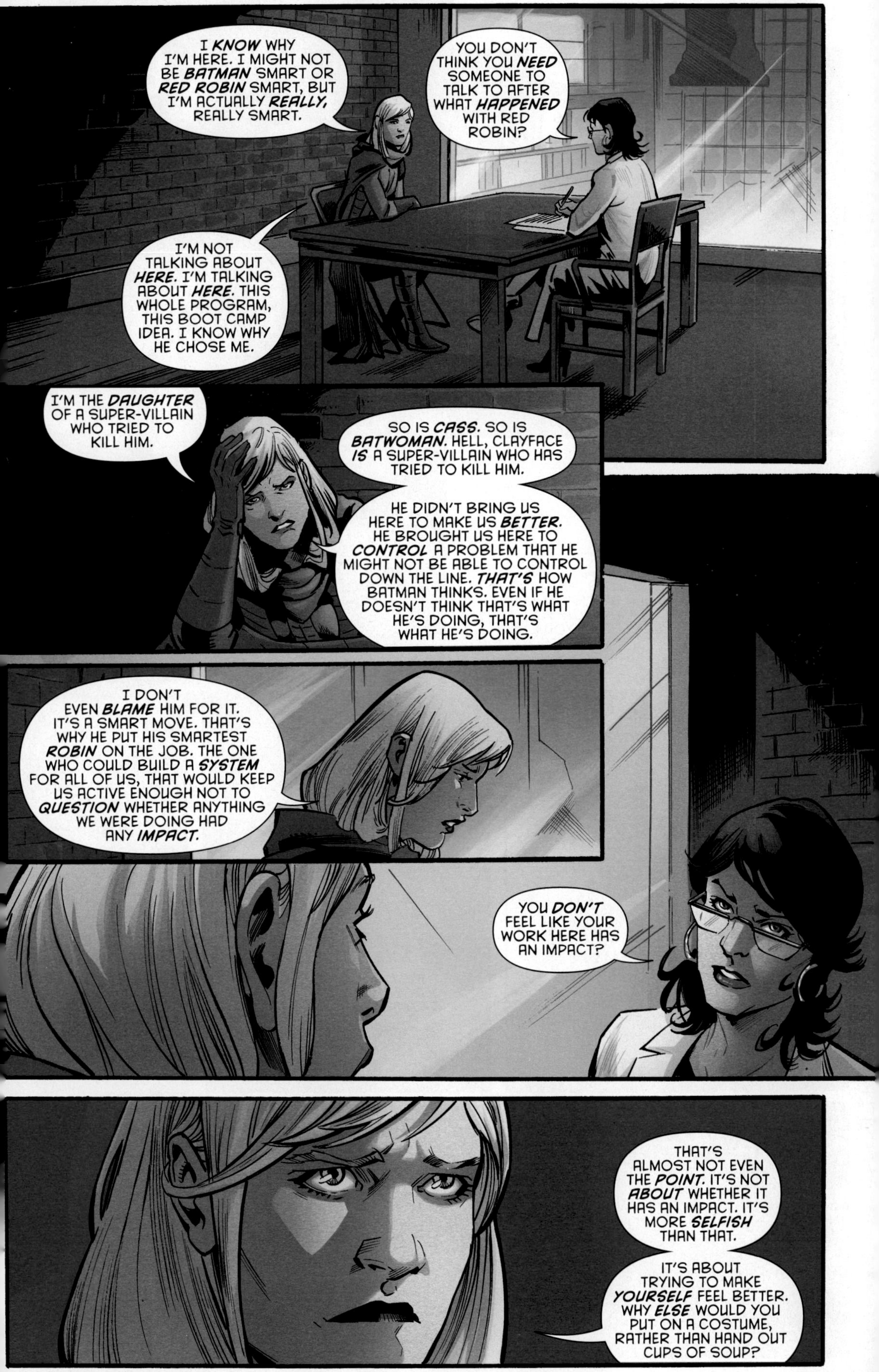

I KNOW WHY I'M HERE. I MIGHT NOT BE BATMAN SMART OR RED ROBIN SMART, BUT I'M ACTUALLY REALLY, REALLY SMART.
YOU DON'T THINK YOU NEED SOMEONE TO TALK TO AFTER WHAT HAPPENED WITH RED ROBIN?
I'M NOT TALKING ABOUT HERE. I'M TALKING ABOUT HERE. THIS WHOLE PROGRAM, THIS BOOT CAMP IDEA. I KNOW WHY HE CHOSE ME.
I'M THE DAUGHTER OF A SUPER-VILLAIN WHO TRIED TO KILL HIM.
SO IS CASS. SO IS BATWOMAN. HELL, CLAYFACE IS A SUPER-VILLAIN WHO HAS TRIED TO KILL HIM.
HE DIDN'T BRING US HERE TO MAKE US BETTER. HE BROUGHT US HERE TO CONTROL A PROBLEM THAT HE MIGHT NOT BE ABLE TO CONTROL DOWN THE LINE. THAT'S HOW BATMAN THINKS. EVEN IF HE DOESN'T THINK THAT'S WHAT HE'S DOING, THAT'S WHAT HE'S DOING.
I DON'T EVEN BLAME HIM FOR IT. IT'S A SMART MOVE. THAT'S WHY HE PUT HIS SMARTEST ROBIN ON THE JOB. THE ONE WHO COULD BUILD A SYSTEM FOR ALL OF US, THAT WOULD KEEP US ACTIVE ENOUGH NOT TO QUESTION WHETHER ANYTHING WE WERE DOING HAD ANY IMPACT.
YOU DON'T FEEL LIKE YOUR WORK HERE HAS AN IMPACT?
THAT'S ALMOST NOT EVEN THE POINT. IT'S NOT ABOUT WHETHER IT HAS AN IMPACT. IT'S MORE SELFISH THAN THAT.
IT'S ABOUT TRYING TO MAKE YOURSELF FEEL BETTER. WHY ELSE WOULD YOU PUT ON A COSTUME, RATHER THAN HAND OUT CUPS OF SOUP?

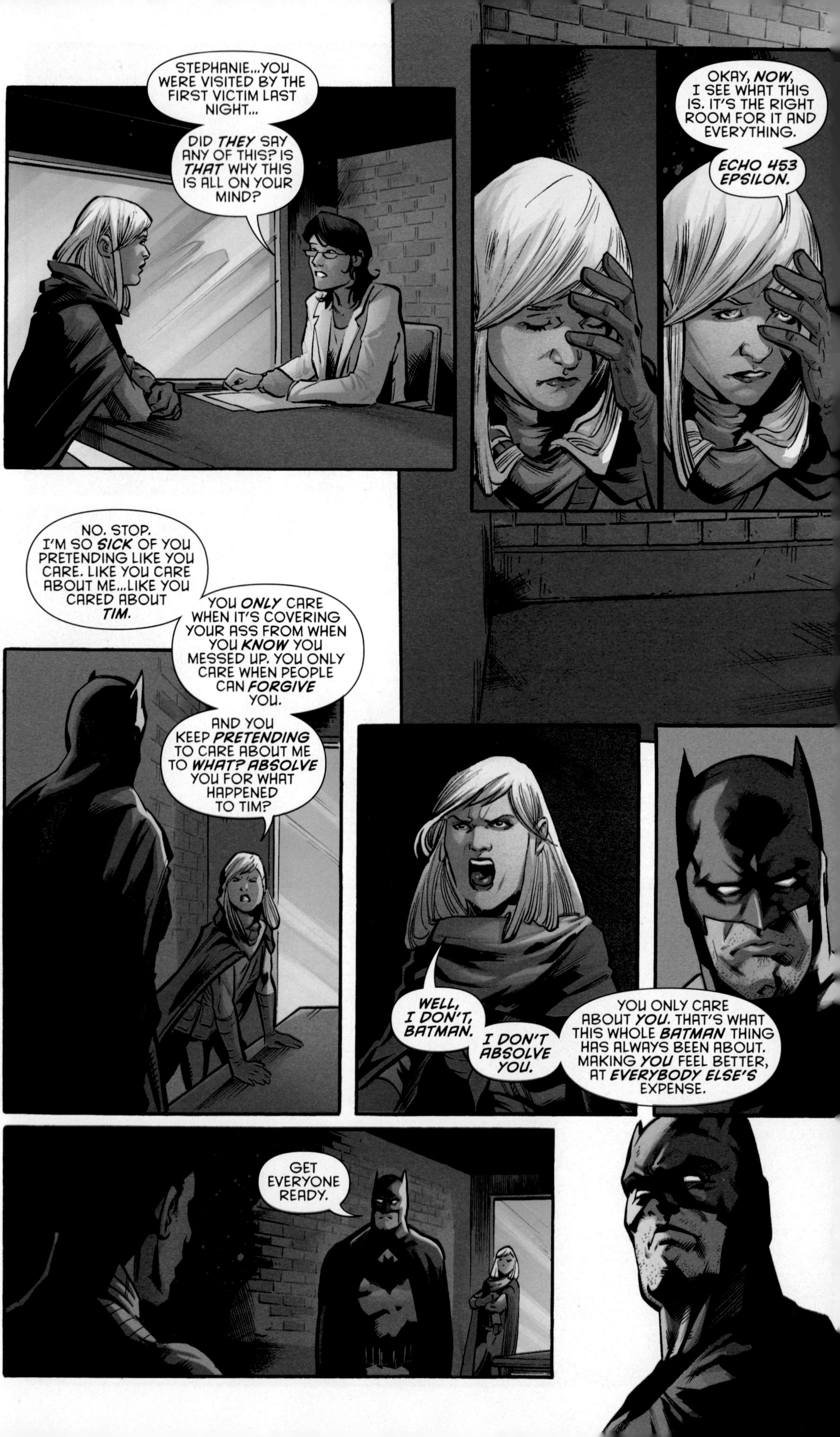
STEPHANIE...YOU WERE VISITED BY THE FIRST VICTIM LAST NIGHT...
DID THEY SAY ANY OF THIS? IS THAT WHY THIS IS ALL ON YOUR MIND?
OKAY, NOW, I SEE WHAT THIS IS. IT'S THE RIGHT ROOM FOR IT AND EVERYTHING.
ECHO 453 EPSILON.
NO. STOP. I'M SO SICK OF YOU PRETENDING LIKE YOU CARE. LIKE YOU CARE ABOUT ME...LIKE YOU CARED ABOUT TIM.
YOU ONLY CARE WHEN IT'S COVERING YOUR ASS FROM WHEN YOU KNOW YOU MESSED UP. YOU ONLY CARE WHEN PEOPLE CAN FORGIVE YOU.
AND YOU KEEP PRETENDING TO CARE ABOUT ME TO WHAT? ABSOLVE YOU FOR WHAT HAPPENED TO TIM?
WELL, I DON'T, BATMAN.
I DON'T ABSOLVE YOU.
YOU ONLY CARE ABOUT YOU. THAT'S WHAT THIS WHOLE BATMAN THING HAS ALWAYS BEEN ABOUT. MAKING YOU FEEL BETTER, AT EVERYBODY ELSE'S EXPENSE.
GET EVERYONE READY.

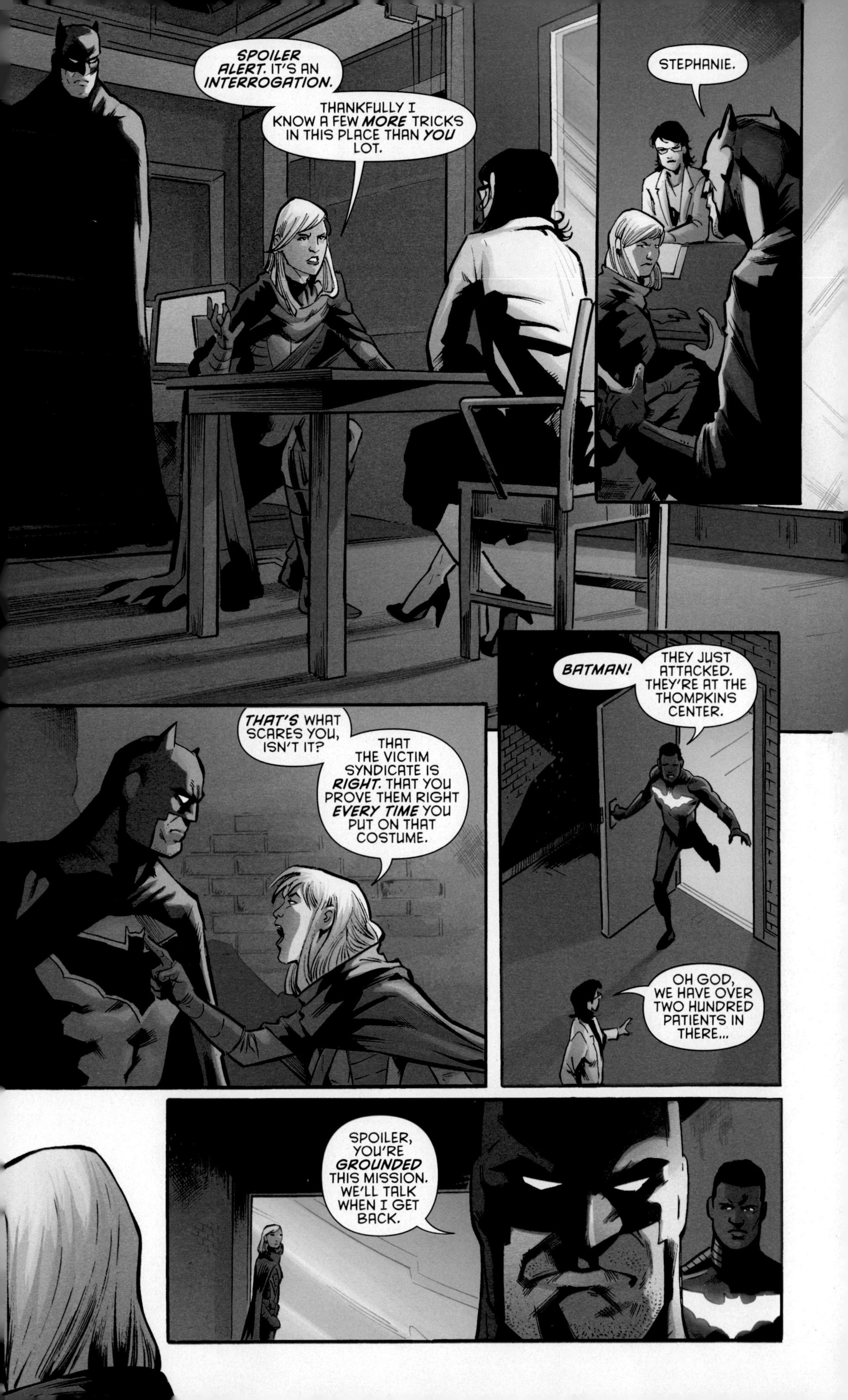
SPOILER ALERT. IT'S AN INTERROGATION.
THANKFULLY I KNOW A FEW MORE TRICKS IN THIS PLACE THAN YOU LOT.
STEPHANIE.
THAT'S WHAT SCARES YOU, ISN'T IT?
THAT THE VICTIM SYNDICATE IS RIGHT. THAT YOU PROVE THEM RIGHT EVERY TIME YOU PUT ON THAT COSTUME.
BATMAN!
THEY JUST ATTACKED. THEY'RE AT THE THOMPKINS CENTER.
OH GOD, WE HAVE OVER TWO HUNDRED PATIENTS IN THERE...
SPOILER, YOU'RE GROUNDED THIS MISSION. WE'LL TALK WHEN I GET BACK.

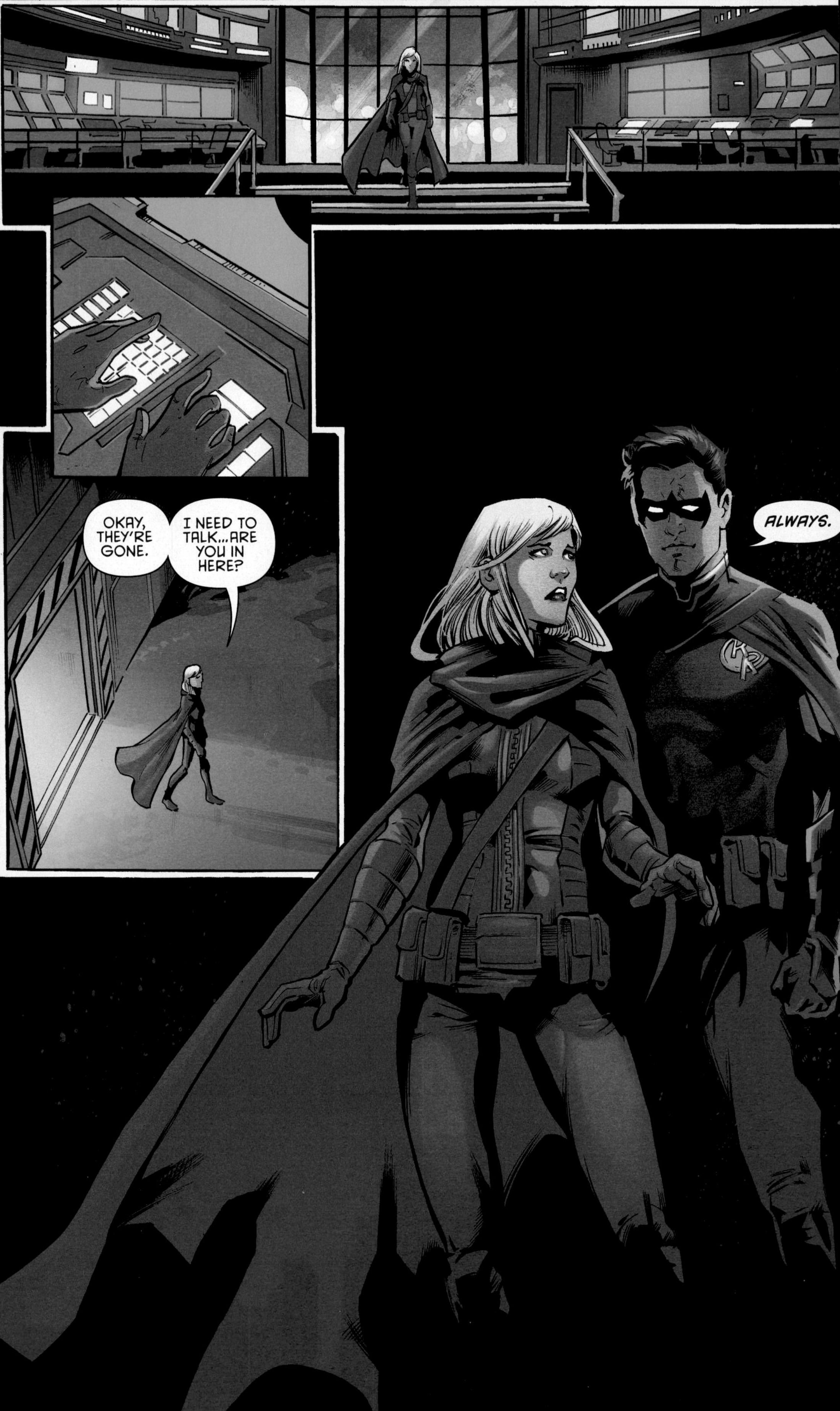
OKAY, THEY'RE GONE.
I NEED TO TALK...ARE YOU IN HERE?
ALWAYS.

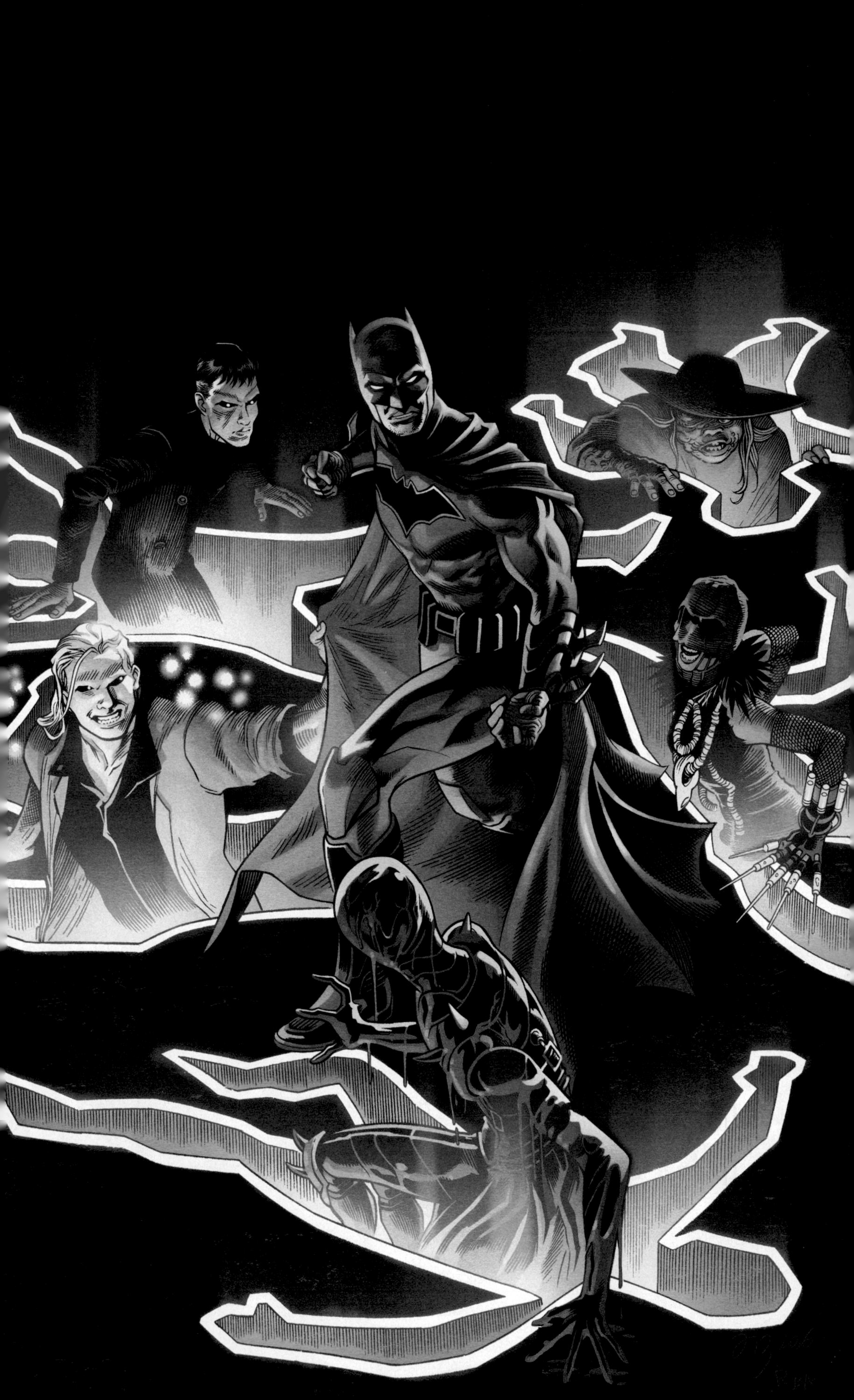

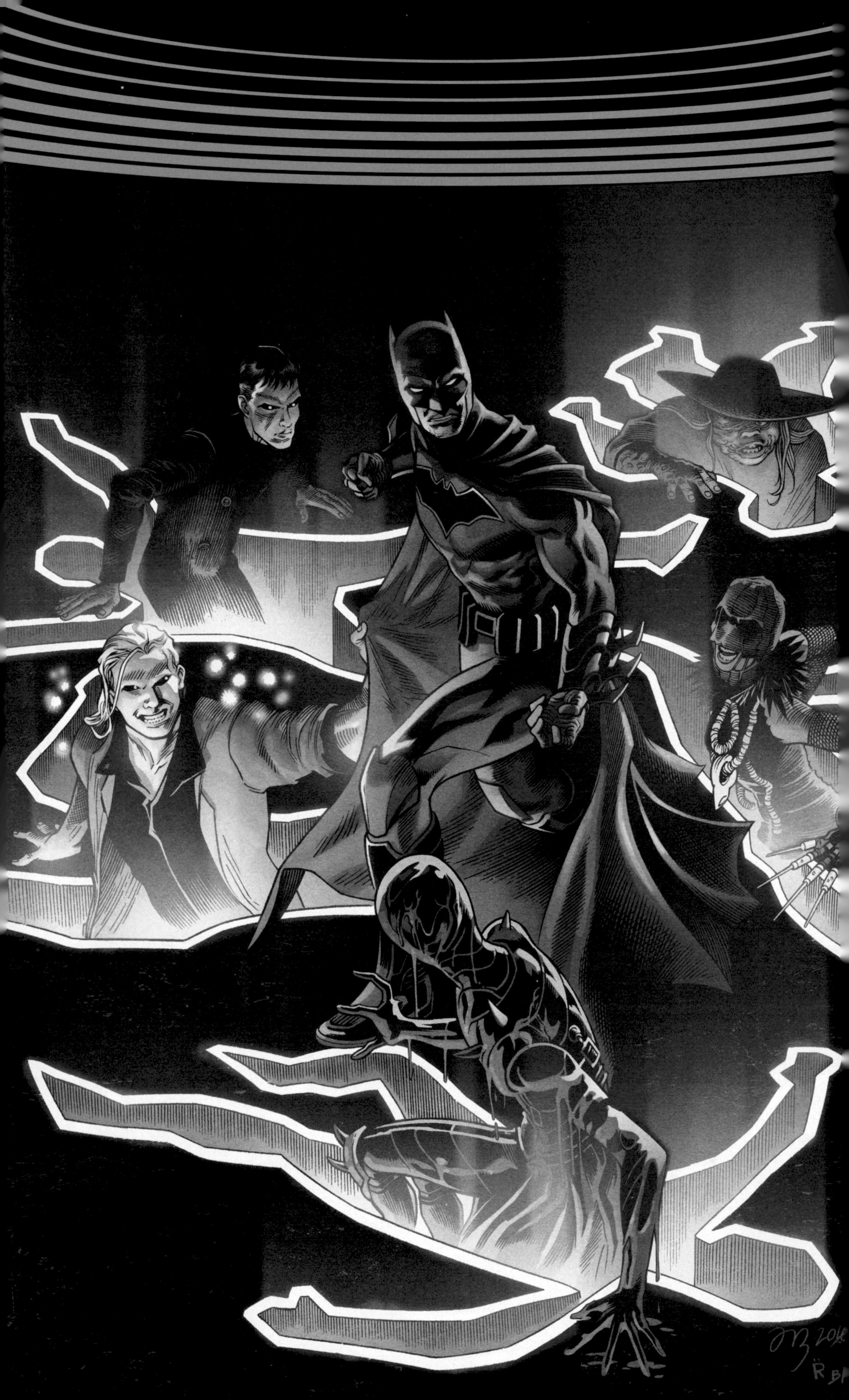

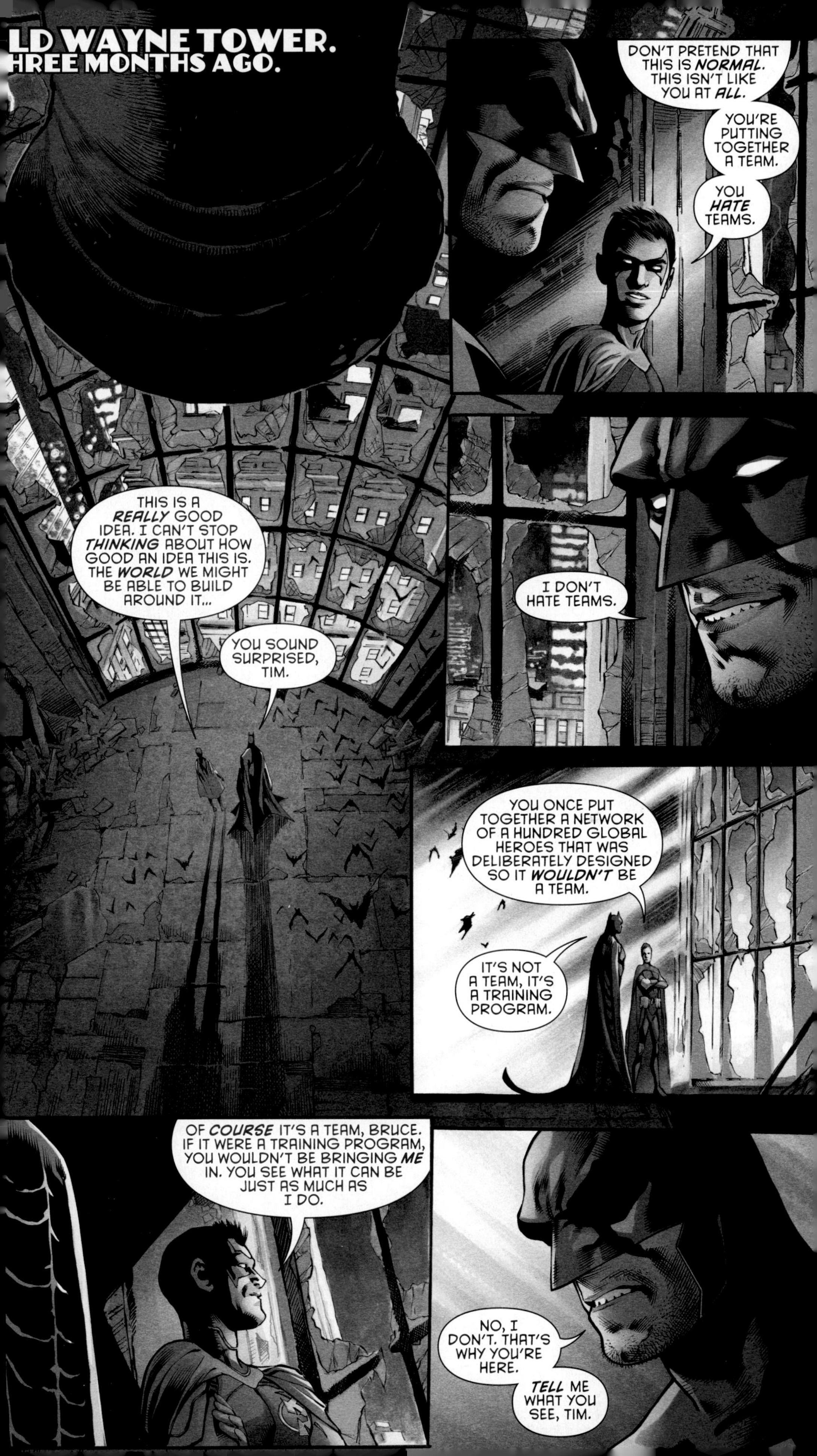

LD WAYNE TOWER.
HREE MONTHS AGO.
DON'T PRETEND THAT THIS IS NORMAL. THIS ISN'T LIKE YOU AT ALL.
YOU'RE PUTTING TOGETHER A TEAM.
YOU HATE TEAMS.
I DON'T HATE TEAMS.
THIS IS A REALLY GOOD IDEA. I CAN'T STOP THINKING ABOUT HOW GOOD AN IDEA THIS IS. THE WORLD WE MIGHT BE ABLE TO BUILD AROUND IT...
YOU SOUND SURPRISED, TIM.
YOU ONCE PUT TOGETHER A NETWORK OF A HUNDRED GLOBAL HEROES THAT WAS DELIBERATELY DESIGNED SO IT WOULDN'T BE A TEAM.
IT'S NOT A TEAM, IT'S A TRAINING PROGRAM.
OF COURSE IT'S A TEAM, BRUCE. IF IT WERE A TRAINING PROGRAM, YOU WOULDN'T BE BRINGING ME IN. YOU SEE WHAT IT CAN BE JUST AS MUCH AS I DO.
NO, I DON'T. THAT'S WHY YOU'RE HERE.
TELL ME WHAT YOU SEE, TIM.

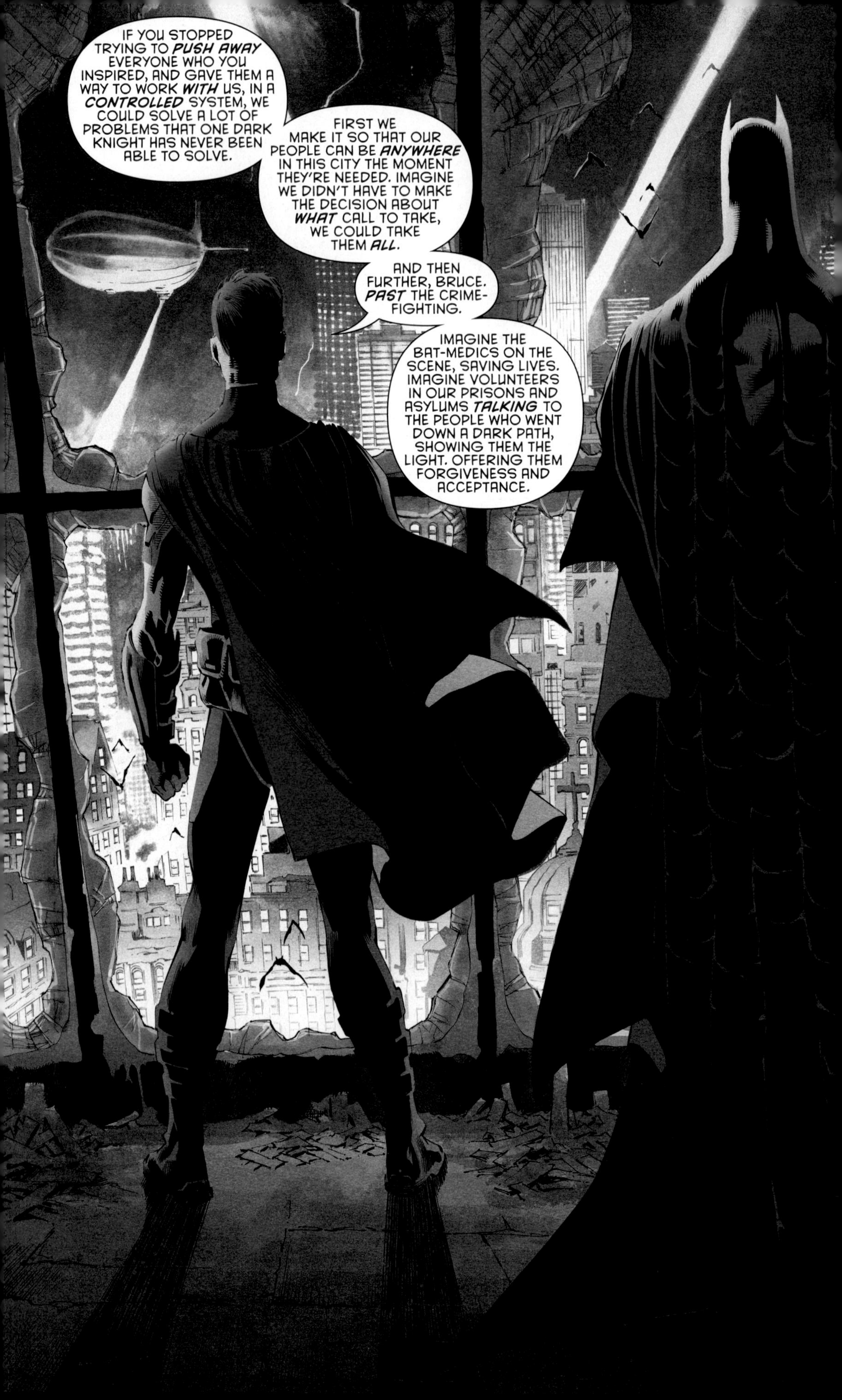
IF YOU STOPPED TRYING TO PUSH AWAY EVERYONE WHO YOU INSPIRED, AND GAVE THEM A WAY TO WORK WITH US, IN A CONTROLLED SYSTEM, WE COULD SOLVE A LOT OF PROBLEMS THAT ONE DARK KNIGHT HAS NEVER BEEN ABLE TO SOLVE.
FIRST WE MAKE IT SO THAT OUR PEOPLE CAN BE ANYWHERE IN THIS CITY THE MOMENT THEY'RE NEEDED. IMAGINE WE DIDN'T HAVE TO MAKE THE DECISION ABOUT WHAT CALL TO TAKE, WE COULD TAKE THEM ALL.
AND THEN FURTHER, BRUCE. PAST THE CRIME-FIGHTING.
IMAGINE THE BAT-MEDICS ON THE SCENE, SAVING LIVES. IMAGINE VOLUNTEERS IN OUR PRISONS AND ASYLUMS TALKING TO THE PEOPLE WHO WENT DOWN A DARK PATH, SHOWING THEM THE LIGHT. OFFERING THEM FORGIVENESS AND ACCEPTANCE.

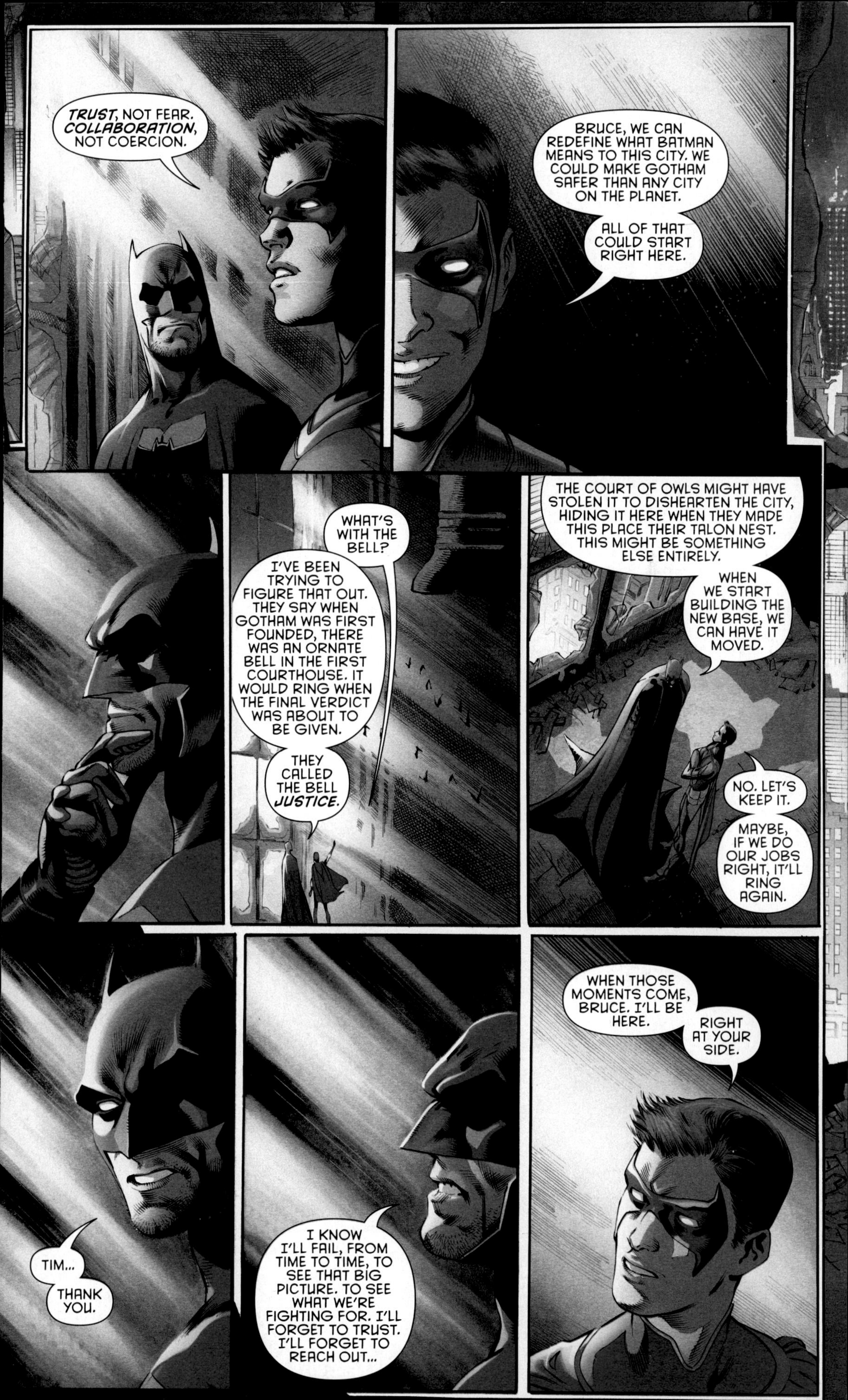
TRUST, NOT FEAR. COLLABORATION, NOT COERCION.
BRUCE, WE CAN REDEFINE WHAT BATMAN MEANS TO THIS CITY. WE COULD MAKE GOTHAM SAFER THAN ANY CITY ON THE PLANET.
ALL OF THAT COULD START RIGHT HERE.
WHAT'S WITH THE BELL?
I'VE BEEN TRYING TO FIGURE THAT OUT. THEY SAY WHEN GOTHAM WAS FIRST FOUNDED, THERE WAS AN ORNATE BELL IN THE FIRST COURTHOUSE. IT WOULD RING WHEN THE FINAL VERDICT WAS ABOUT TO BE GIVEN.
THEY CALLED THE BELL JUSTICE.
THE COURT OF OWLS MIGHT HAVE STOLEN IT TO DISHEARTEN THE CITY, HIDING IT HERE WHEN THEY MADE THIS PLACE THEIR TALON NEST. THIS MIGHT BE SOMETHING ELSE ENTIRELY.
WHEN WE START BUILDING THE NEW BASE, WE CAN HAVE IT MOVED.
NO. LET'S KEEP IT.
MAYBE, IF WE DO OUR JOBS RIGHT, IT'LL RING AGAIN.
TIM...
THANK YOU.
I KNOW I'LL FAIL, FROM TIME TO TIME, TO SEE THAT BIG PICTURE. TO SEE WHAT WE'RE FIGHTING FOR. I'LL FORGET TO TRUST. I'LL FORGET TO REACH OUT...
WHEN THOSE MOMENTS COME, BRUCE. I'LL BE HERE.
RIGHT AT YOUR SIDE.

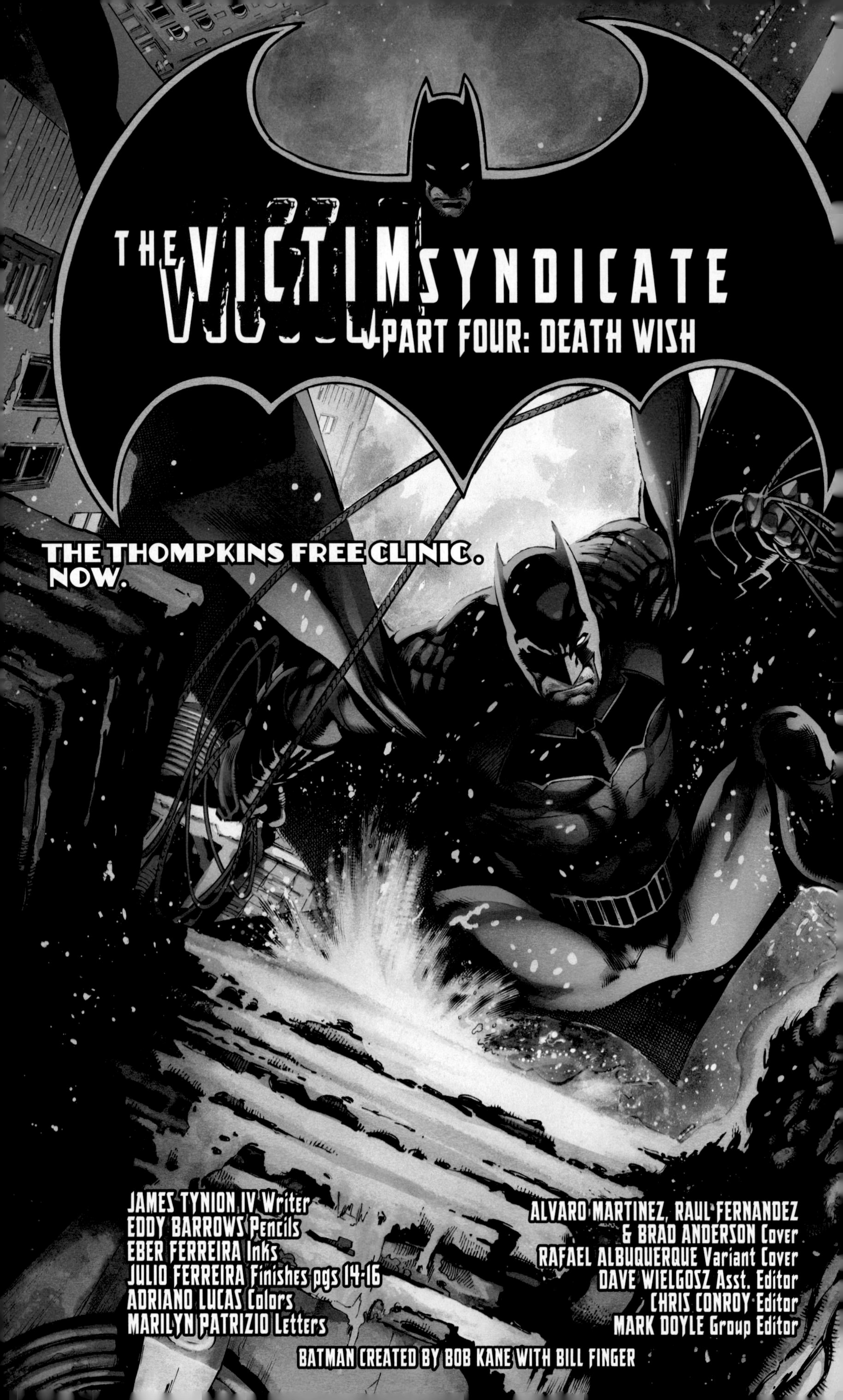
THE VICTIM SYNDICATE
PART FOUR: DEATH WISH
THE THOMPKINS FREE CLINIC. NOW.
JAMES TYNION IV Writer
EDDY BARROWS Pencils
EBER FERREIRA Inks
JULIO FERREIRA Finishes pgs 14-16
ADRIANO LUCAS Colors
MARILYN PATRIZIO Letters
ALVARO MARTINEZ, RAUL FERNANDEZ & BRAD ANDERSON Cover
RAFAEL ALBUQUERQUE Variant Cover
DAVE WIELGOSZ Asst. Editor
CHRIS CONROY Editor
MARK DOYLE Group Editor
BATMAN CREATED BY BOB KANE WITH BILL FINGER

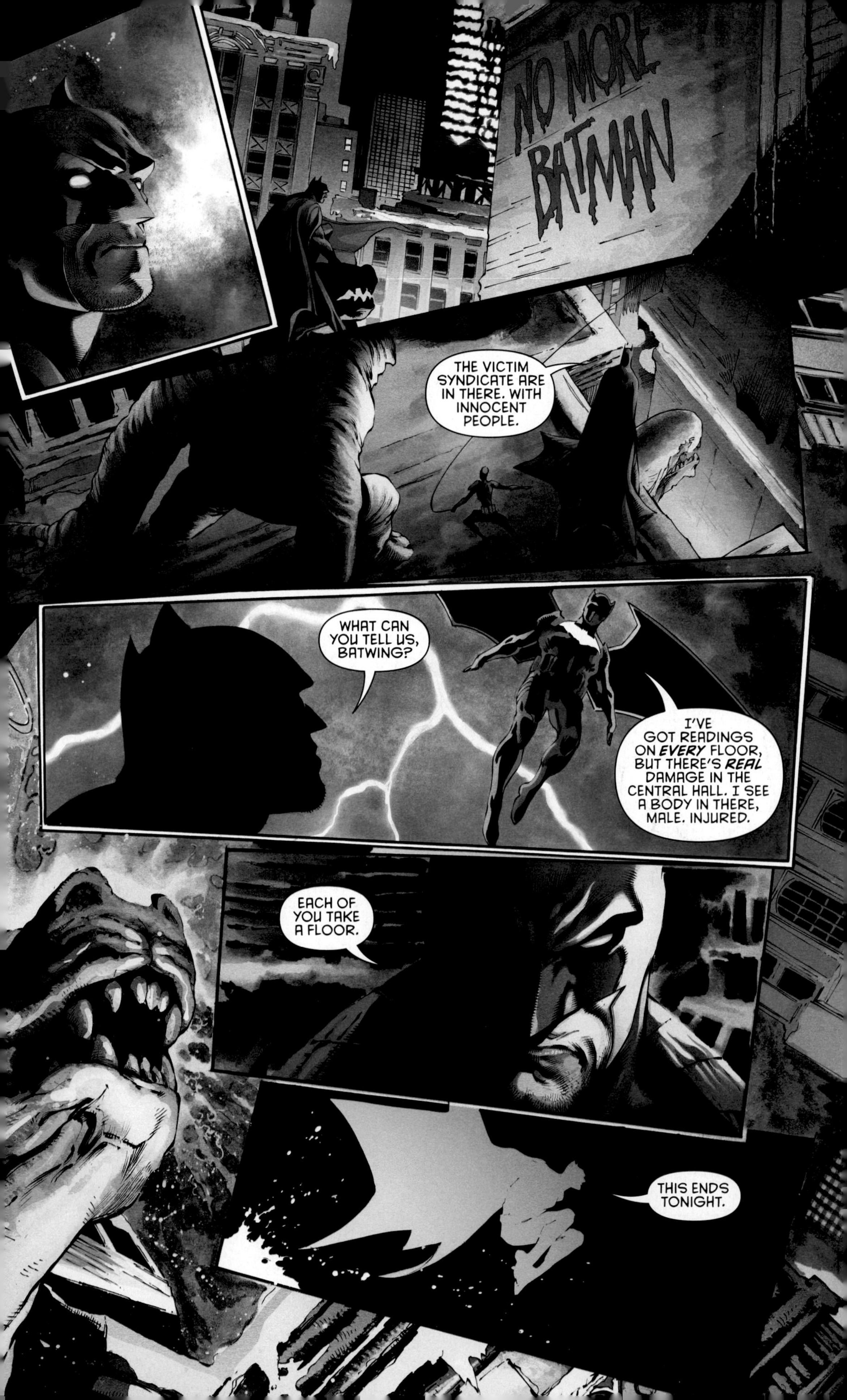
NO MORE BATMAN
THE VICTIM SYNDICATE ARE IN THERE. WITH INNOCENT PEOPLE.
WHAT CAN YOU TELL US, BATWING?
I'VE GOT READINGS ON EVERY FLOOR, BUT THERE'S REAL DAMAGE IN THE CENTRAL HALL. I SEE A BODY IN THERE, MALE. INJURED.
EACH OF YOU TAKE A FLOOR.
THIS ENDS TONIGHT.

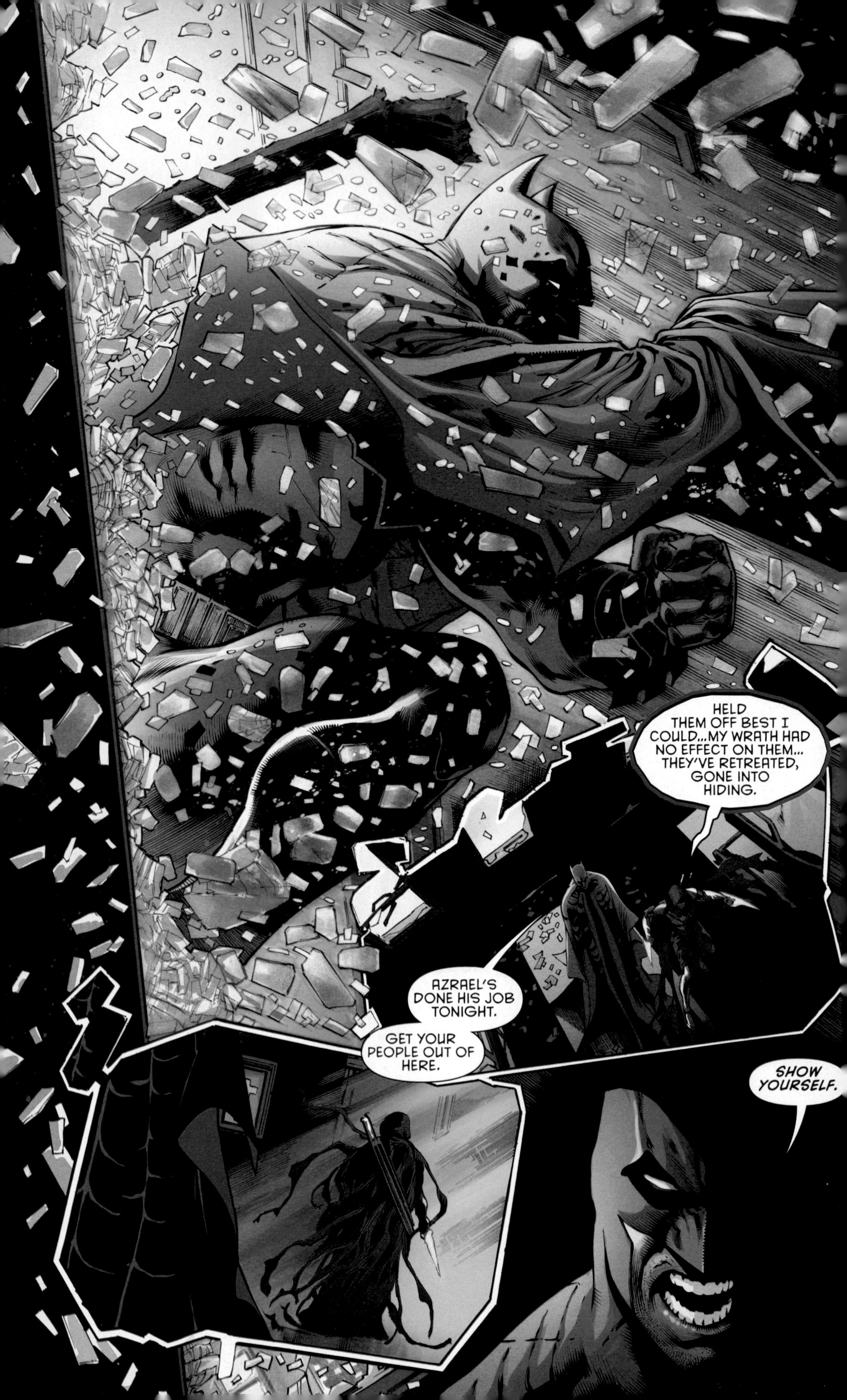
HELD THEM OFF BEST I COULD...MY WRATH HAD NO EFFECT ON THEM... THEY'VE RETREATED, GONE INTO HIDING.
AZRAEL'S DONE HIS JOB TONIGHT.
GET YOUR PEOPLE OUT OF HERE.
SHOW YOURSELF.

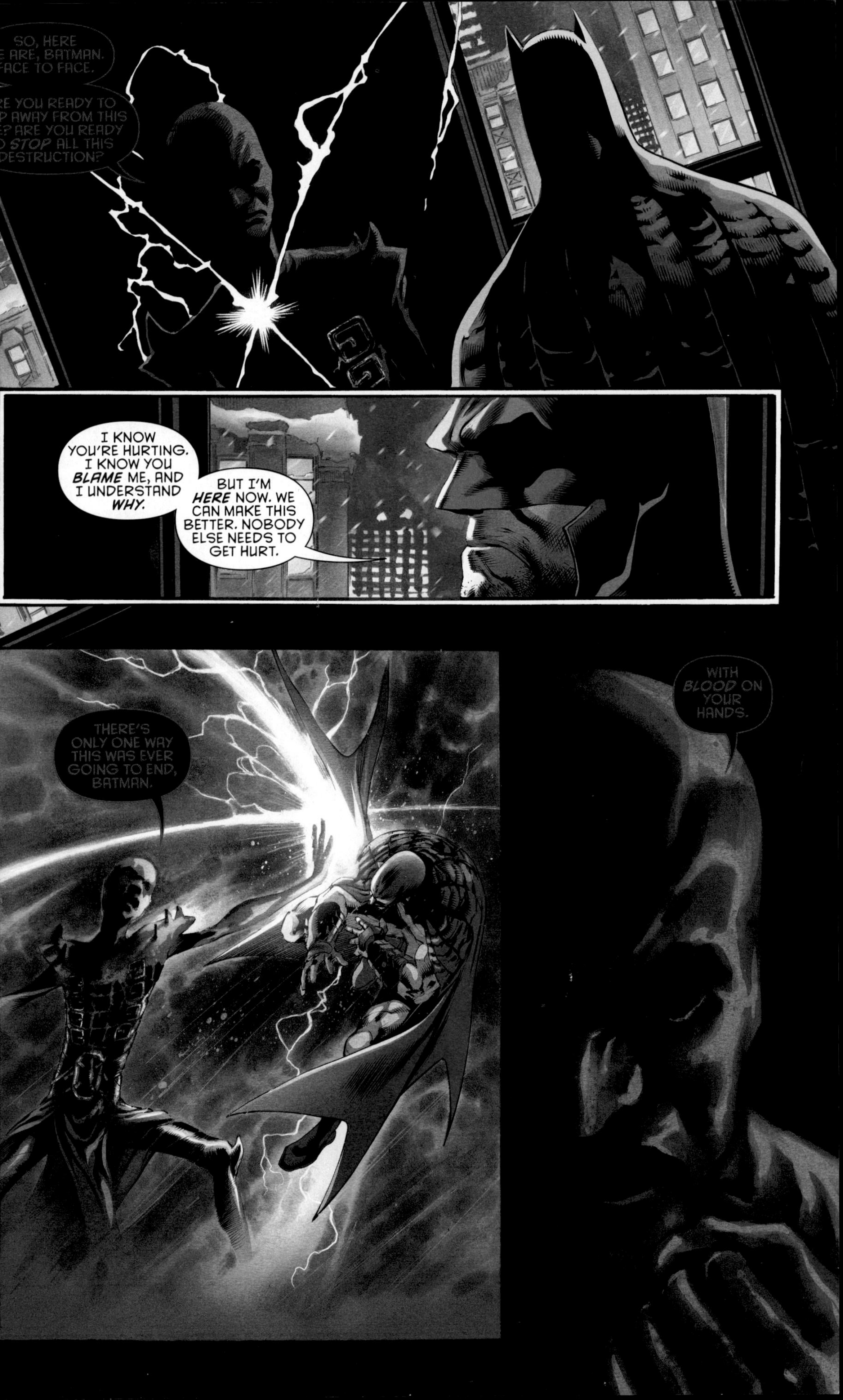
SO, HERE
E ARE, BATMAN.
FACE TO FACE.
E YOU READY TO
P AWAY FROM THIS
? ARE YOU READY
STOP ALL THIS
DESTRUCTION?
I KNOW YOU'RE HURTING. I KNOW YOU BLAME ME, AND I UNDERSTAND WHY.
BUT I'M HERE NOW. WE CAN MAKE THIS BETTER. NOBODY ELSE NEEDS TO GET HURT.
THERE'S ONLY ONE WAY THIS WAS EVER GOING TO END, BATMAN.
WITH BLOOD ON YOUR HANDS.

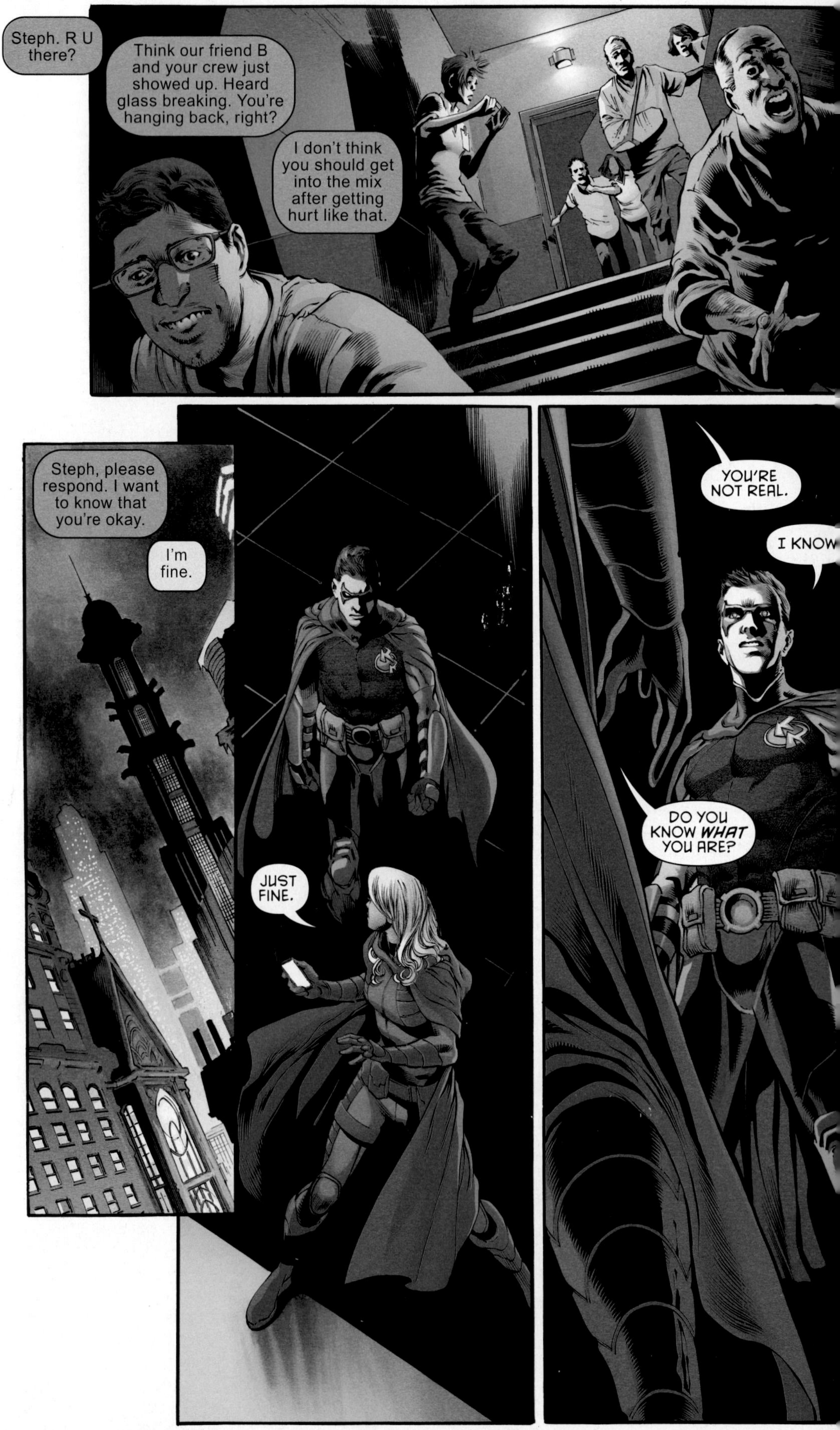

Steph. R U there?
Think our friend B and your crew just showed up. Heard glass breaking. You're hanging back, right?
I don't think you should get into the mix after getting hurt like that.
Steph, please respond. I want to know that you're okay.
I'm fine.
JUST FINE.
YOU'RE NOT REAL.
I KNOW
DO YOU KNOW *WHAT* YOU ARE?

I'm grounded, Harper.

Okay. I'm going to see if these guys need med help. I'm sure it'll all be okay.

Maybe you, me, and Cass go grab late-night pad thai later? Or just us? I want to talk to you.

I AM A LIMITED RESPONSE PROGRAM, BUILT FROM CONVERSATIONS WITH MY CREATOR, *RED ROBIN*. YOU ARE ACCESSING ME THROUGH A TRAINING PROGRAM THAT ALLOWS ME TO TAKE FORM THROUGH THE MOLECULAR-BONDING AGENT THAT COMPRISES YOUR TEAMMATE, CLAYFACE.

I KNOW YOU ARE STEPHANIE BROWN, *SPOILER*. YOU ARE THE ONLY ONE WHO CAN ACCESS THIS PROGRAM ASIDE FROM MY CREATOR.

THIS WAS A BAD IDEA.

I WAS BUILT TO *LISTEN* AND *ADAPT*, STEPHANIE. I WANT TO HEAR WHAT YOU HAVE TO SAY. I MAY NOT UNDERSTAND, BUT THROUGH CONVERSATION I MAY BE ABLE TO *LEARN*.

THIS IS ALL JUST *WRONG*. THIS ISN'T HOW IT WAS SUPPOSED TO BE AT *ALL*.

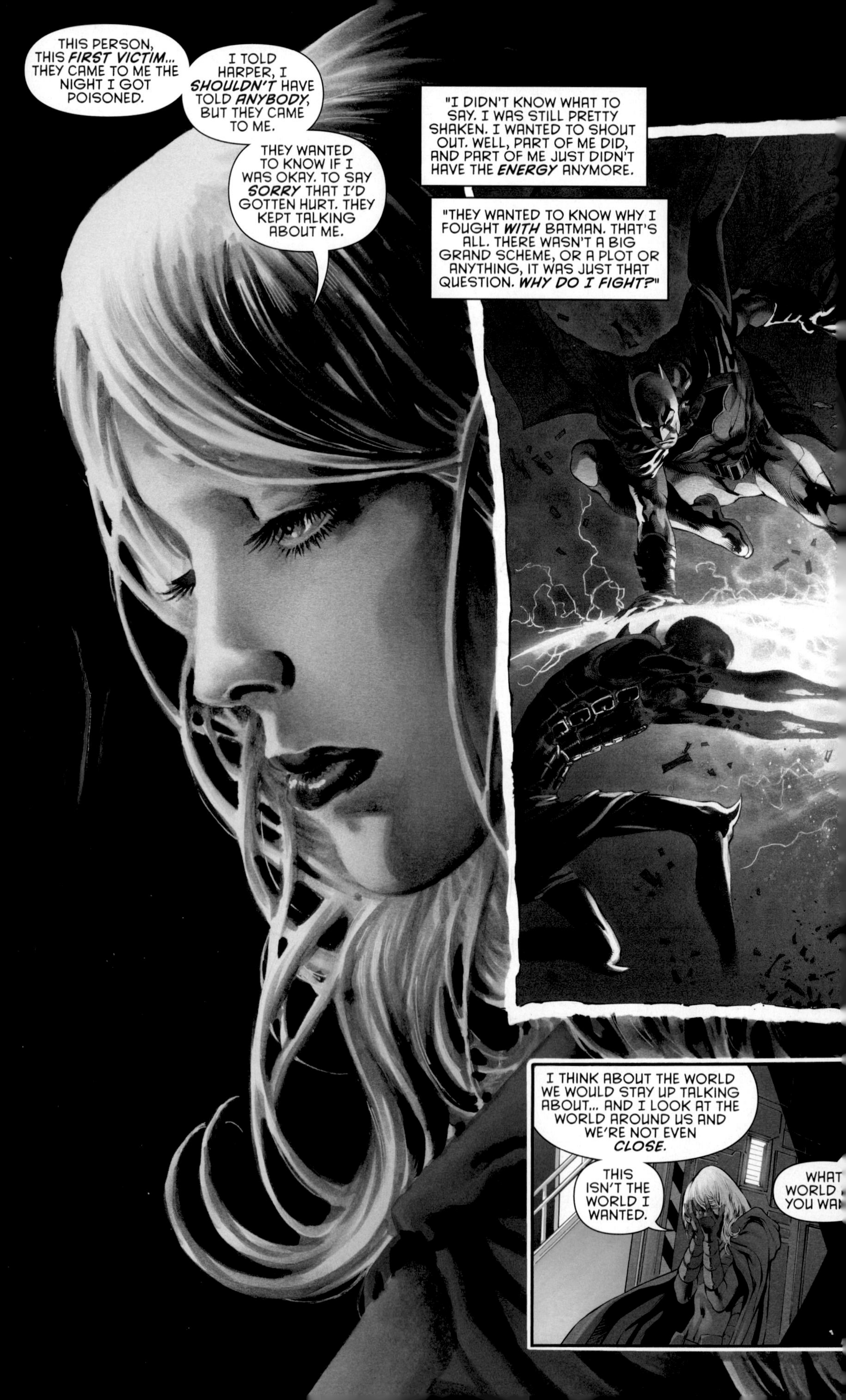

THIS PERSON, THIS FIRST VICTIM... THEY CAME TO ME THE NIGHT I GOT POISONED.
I TOLD HARPER, I SHOULDN'T HAVE TOLD ANYBODY, BUT THEY CAME TO ME.
THEY WANTED TO KNOW IF I WAS OKAY. TO SAY SORRY THAT I'D GOTTEN HURT. THEY KEPT TALKING ABOUT ME.
"I DIDN'T KNOW WHAT TO SAY. I WAS STILL PRETTY SHAKEN. I WANTED TO SHOUT OUT. WELL, PART OF ME DID, AND PART OF ME JUST DIDN'T HAVE THE ENERGY ANYMORE.
"THEY WANTED TO KNOW WHY I FOUGHT WITH BATMAN. THAT'S ALL. THERE WASN'T A BIG GRAND SCHEME, OR A PLOT OR ANYTHING, IT WAS JUST THAT QUESTION. WHY DO I FIGHT?"
I THINK ABOUT THE WORLD WE WOULD STAY UP TALKING ABOUT... AND I LOOK AT THE WORLD AROUND US AND WE'RE NOT EVEN CLOSE.
THIS ISN'T THE WORLD I WANTED.

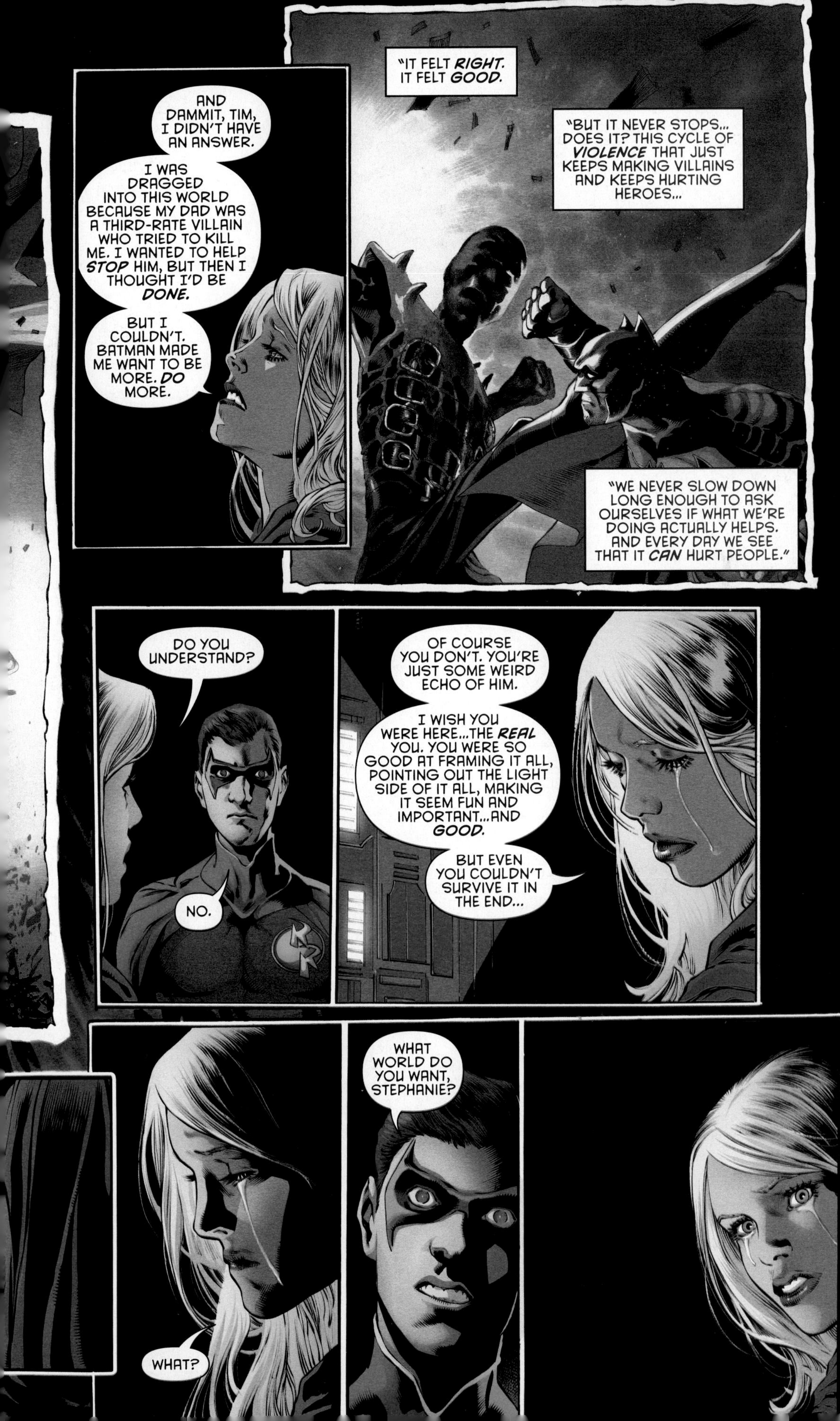
AND DAMMIT, TIM, I DIDN'T HAVE AN ANSWER.
I WAS DRAGGED INTO THIS WORLD BECAUSE MY DAD WAS A THIRD-RATE VILLAIN WHO TRIED TO KILL ME. I WANTED TO HELP STOP HIM, BUT THEN I THOUGHT I'D BE DONE.
BUT I COULDN'T. BATMAN MADE ME WANT TO BE MORE. DO MORE.
"IT FELT RIGHT. IT FELT GOOD.
"BUT IT NEVER STOPS... DOES IT? THIS CYCLE OF VIOLENCE THAT JUST KEEPS MAKING VILLAINS AND KEEPS HURTING HEROES...
"WE NEVER SLOW DOWN LONG ENOUGH TO ASK OURSELVES IF WHAT WE'RE DOING ACTUALLY HELPS. AND EVERY DAY WE SEE THAT IT CAN HURT PEOPLE."
DO YOU UNDERSTAND?
NO.
OF COURSE YOU DON'T. YOU'RE JUST SOME WEIRD ECHO OF HIM.
I WISH YOU WERE HERE...THE REAL YOU. YOU WERE SO GOOD AT FRAMING IT ALL, POINTING OUT THE LIGHT SIDE OF IT ALL, MAKING IT SEEM FUN AND IMPORTANT...AND GOOD.
BUT EVEN YOU COULDN'T SURVIVE IT IN THE END...
WHAT WORLD DO YOU WANT, STEPHANIE?
WHAT?

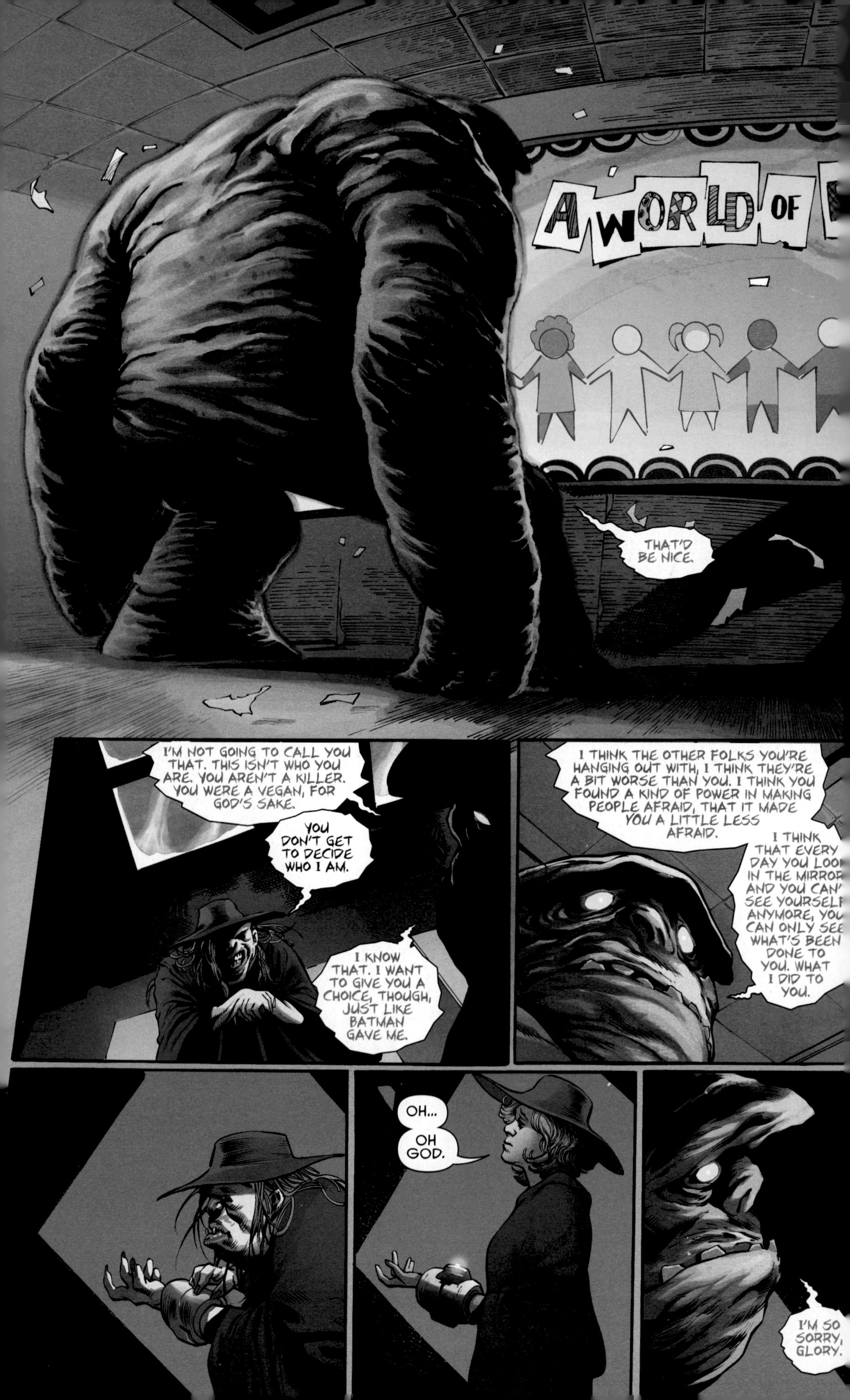
A WORLD OF
THAT'D BE NICE.
I'M NOT GOING TO CALL YOU THAT. THIS ISN'T WHO YOU ARE. YOU AREN'T A KILLER. YOU WERE A VEGAN, FOR GOD'S SAKE.
YOU DON'T GET TO DECIDE WHO I AM.
I KNOW THAT. I WANT TO GIVE YOU A CHOICE, THOUGH, JUST LIKE BATMAN GAVE ME.
I THINK THE OTHER FOLKS YOU'RE HANGING OUT WITH, I THINK THEY'RE A BIT WORSE THAN YOU. I THINK YOU FOUND A KIND OF POWER IN MAKING PEOPLE AFRAID, THAT IT MADE YOU A LITTLE LESS AFRAID.
I THINK THAT EVERY DAY YOU LOOK IN THE MIRROR AND YOU CAN'T SEE YOURSELF ANYMORE, YOU CAN ONLY SEE WHAT'S BEEN DONE TO YOU. WHAT I DID TO YOU.
OH...
OH GOD.
I'M SO SORRY, GLORY.

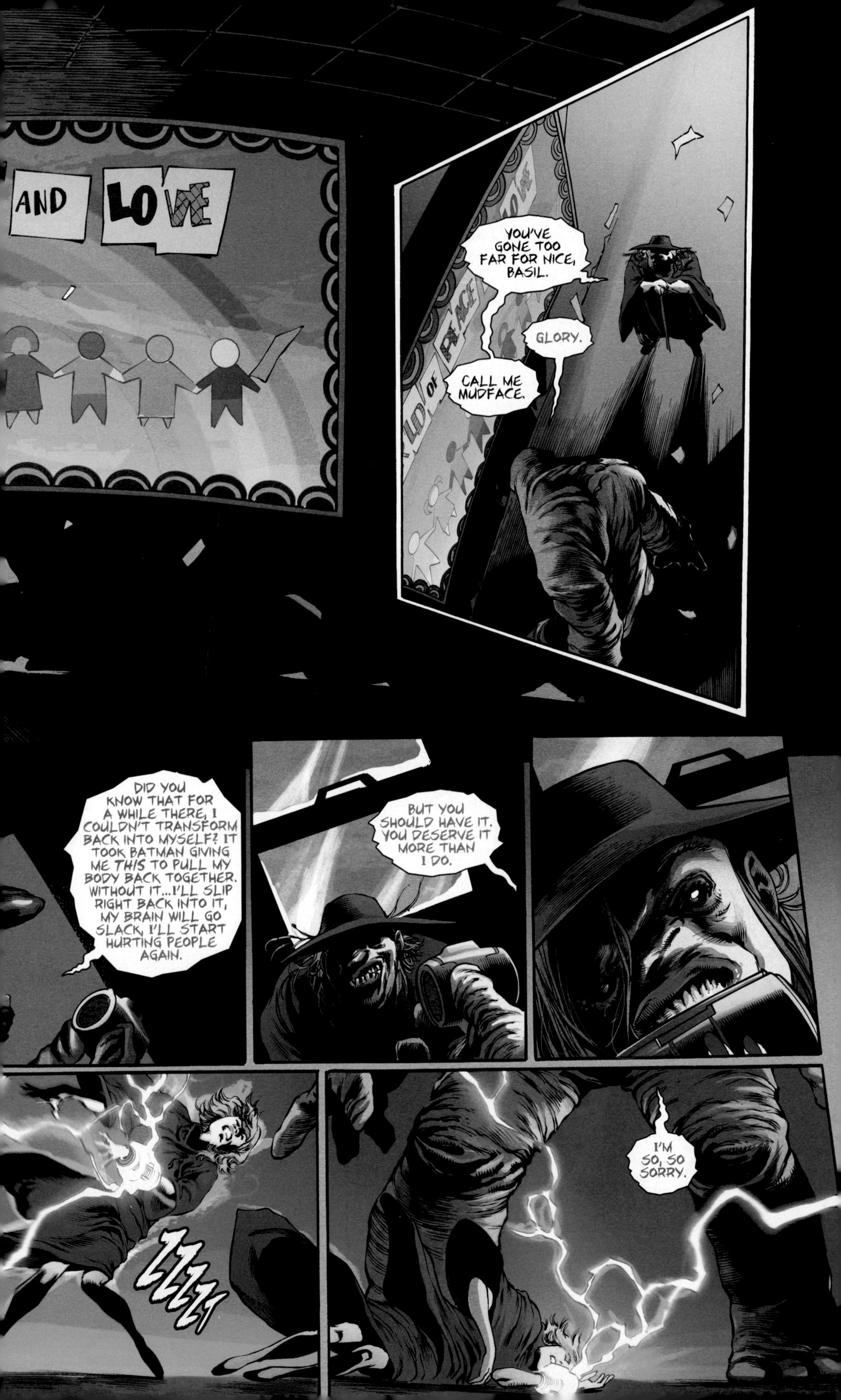
AND LOVE
YOU'VE GONE TOO FAR FOR NICE, BASIL.
GLORY.
CALL ME MUDFACE.
DID YOU KNOW THAT FOR A WHILE THERE, I COULDN'T TRANSFORM BACK INTO MYSELF? IT TOOK BATMAN GIVING ME *THIS* TO PULL MY BODY BACK TOGETHER. WITHOUT IT...I'LL SLIP RIGHT BACK INTO IT, MY BRAIN WILL GO SLACK, I'LL START HURTING PEOPLE AGAIN.
BUT YOU SHOULD HAVE IT. YOU DESERVE IT MORE THAN I DO.
ZZZZT
I'M SO, SO SORRY.

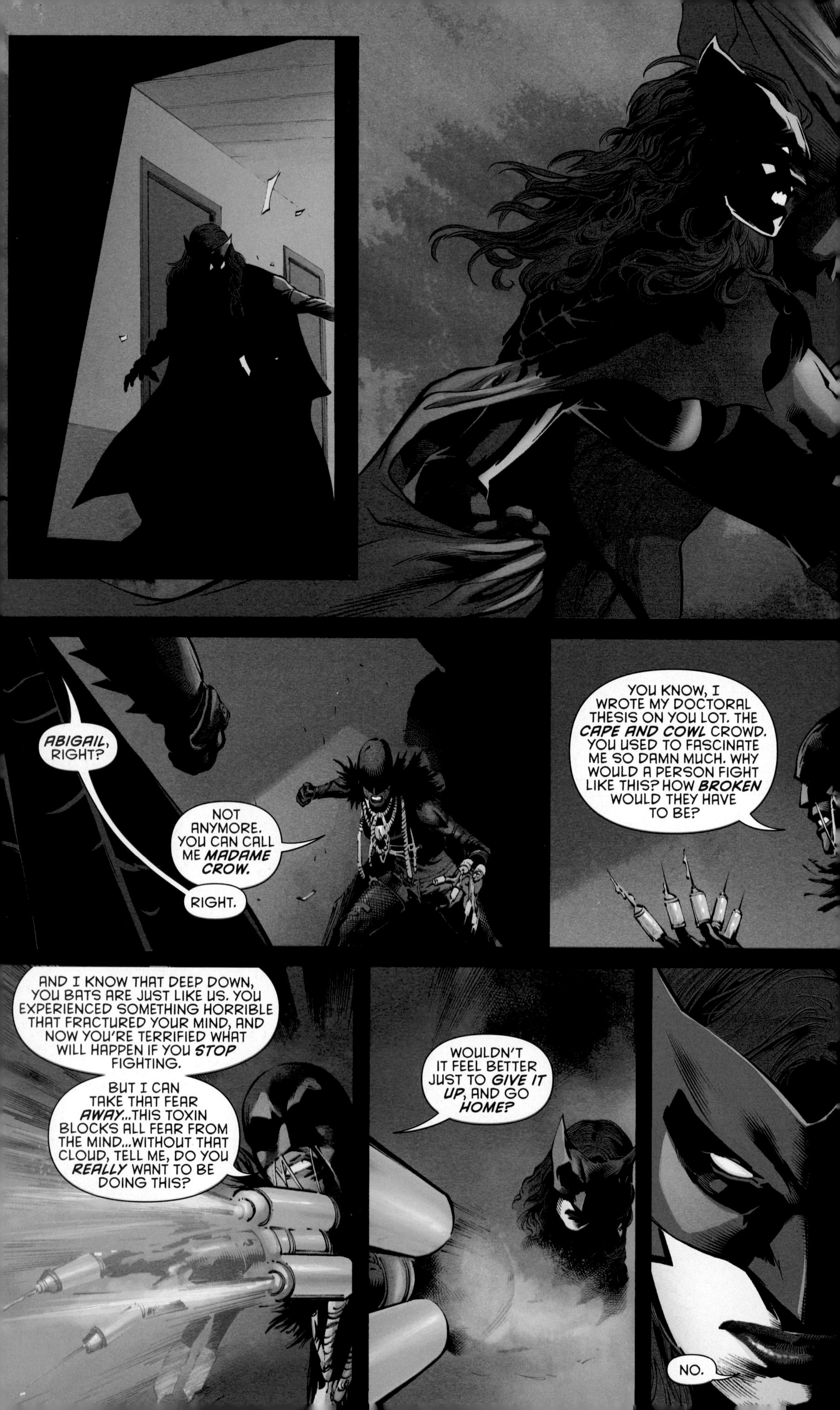
ABIGAIL, RIGHT?
NOT ANYMORE. YOU CAN CALL ME MADAME CROW.
RIGHT.
YOU KNOW, I WROTE MY DOCTORAL THESIS ON YOU LOT. THE CAPE AND COWL CROWD. YOU USED TO FASCINATE ME SO DAMN MUCH. WHY WOULD A PERSON FIGHT LIKE THIS? HOW BROKEN WOULD THEY HAVE TO BE?
AND I KNOW THAT DEEP DOWN, YOU BATS ARE JUST LIKE US. YOU EXPERIENCED SOMETHING HORRIBLE THAT FRACTURED YOUR MIND, AND NOW YOU'RE TERRIFIED WHAT WILL HAPPEN IF YOU STOP FIGHTING.
BUT I CAN TAKE THAT FEAR AWAY...THIS TOXIN BLOCKS ALL FEAR FROM THE MIND...WITHOUT THAT CLOUD, TELL ME, DO YOU REALLY WANT TO BE DOING THIS?
WOULDN'T IT FEEL BETTER JUST TO GIVE IT UP, AND GO HOME?
NO.

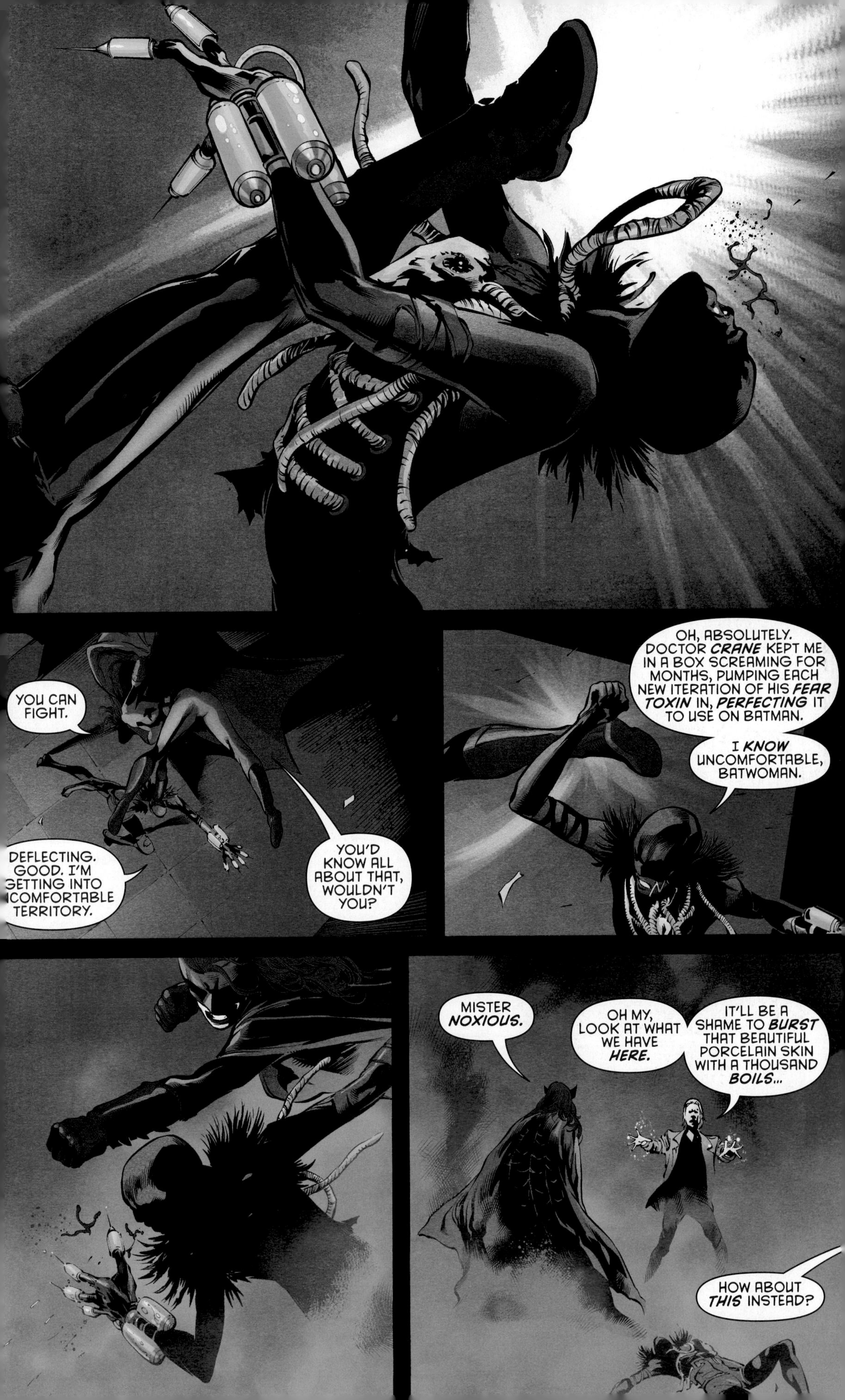

YOU CAN FIGHT.
YOU'D KNOW ALL ABOUT THAT, WOULDN'T YOU?
DEFLECTING. GOOD. I'M GETTING INTO COMFORTABLE TERRITORY.
OH, ABSOLUTELY. DOCTOR CRANE KEPT ME IN A BOX SCREAMING FOR MONTHS, PUMPING EACH NEW ITERATION OF HIS FEAR TOXIN IN, PERFECTING IT TO USE ON BATMAN.
I KNOW UNCOMFORTABLE, BATWOMAN.
MISTER NOXIOUS.
OH MY, LOOK AT WHAT WE HAVE HERE.
IT'LL BE A SHAME TO BURST THAT BEAUTIFUL PORCELAIN SKIN WITH A THOUSAND BOILS...
HOW ABOUT THIS INSTEAD?

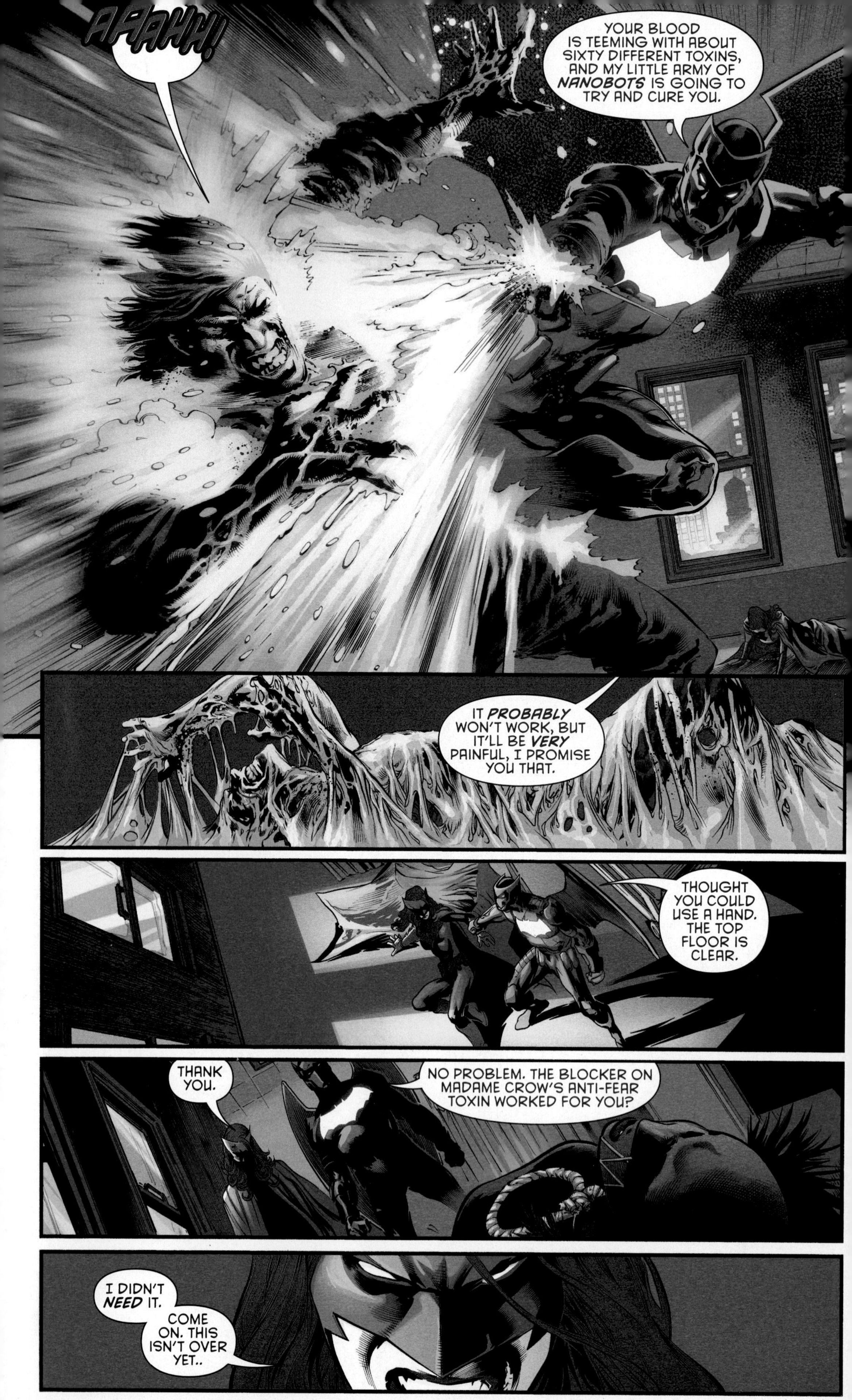
AAAHH!
YOUR BLOOD IS TEEMING WITH ABOUT SIXTY DIFFERENT TOXINS, AND MY LITTLE ARMY OF *NANOBOTS* IS GOING TO TRY AND CURE YOU.
IT *PROBABLY* WON'T WORK, BUT IT'LL BE *VERY* PAINFUL, I PROMISE YOU THAT.
THOUGHT YOU COULD USE A HAND. THE TOP FLOOR IS CLEAR.
THANK YOU.
NO PROBLEM. THE BLOCKER ON MADAME CROW'S ANTI-FEAR TOXIN WORKED FOR YOU?
I DIDN'T *NEED* IT.
COME ON. THIS ISN'T OVER YET..

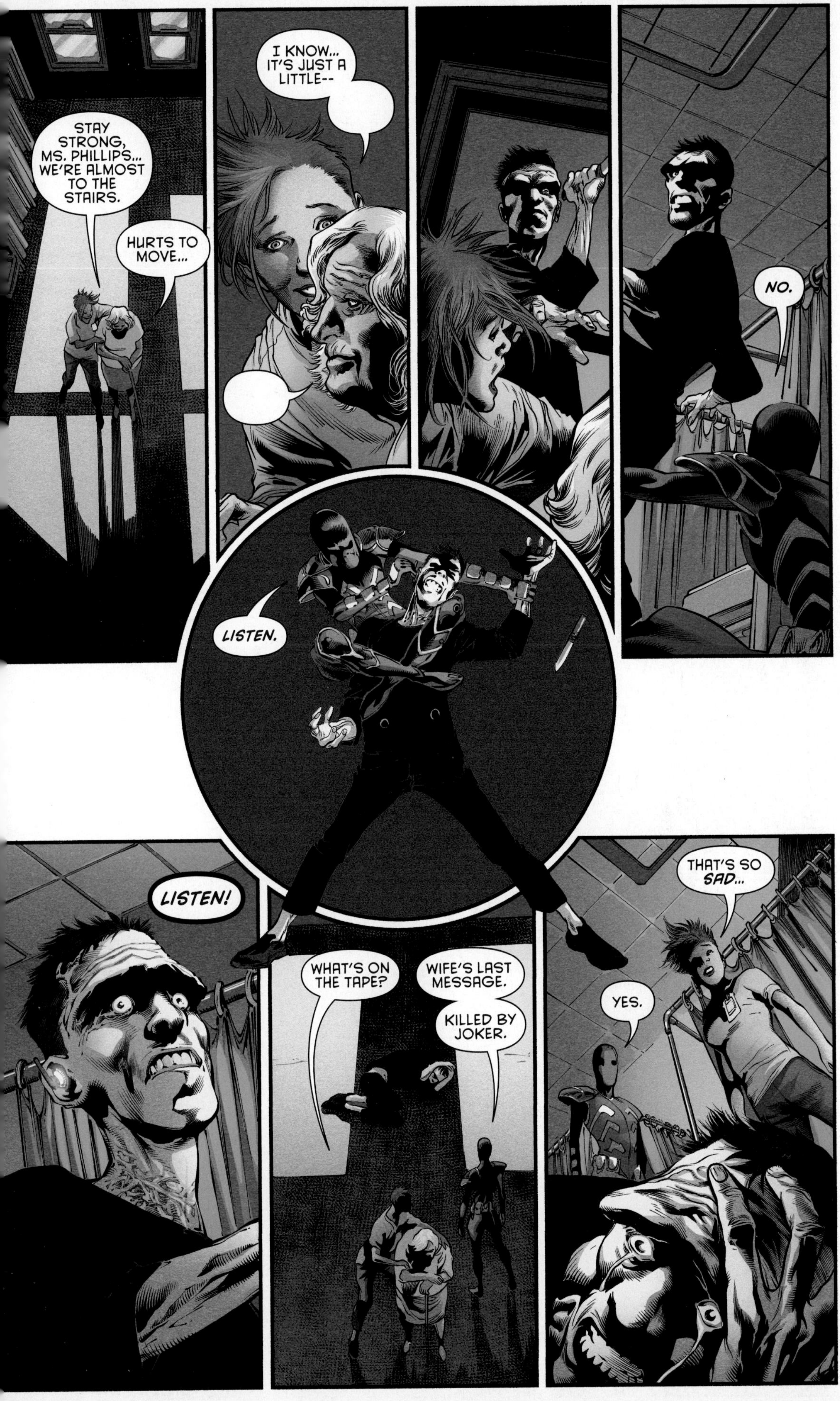
STAY STRONG, MS. PHILLIPS... WE'RE ALMOST TO THE STAIRS.
HURTS TO MOVE...
I KNOW... IT'S JUST A LITTLE--
NO.
LISTEN.
LISTEN!
WHAT'S ON THE TAPE?
WIFE'S LAST MESSAGE.
KILLED BY JOKER.
THAT'S SO SAD...
YES.

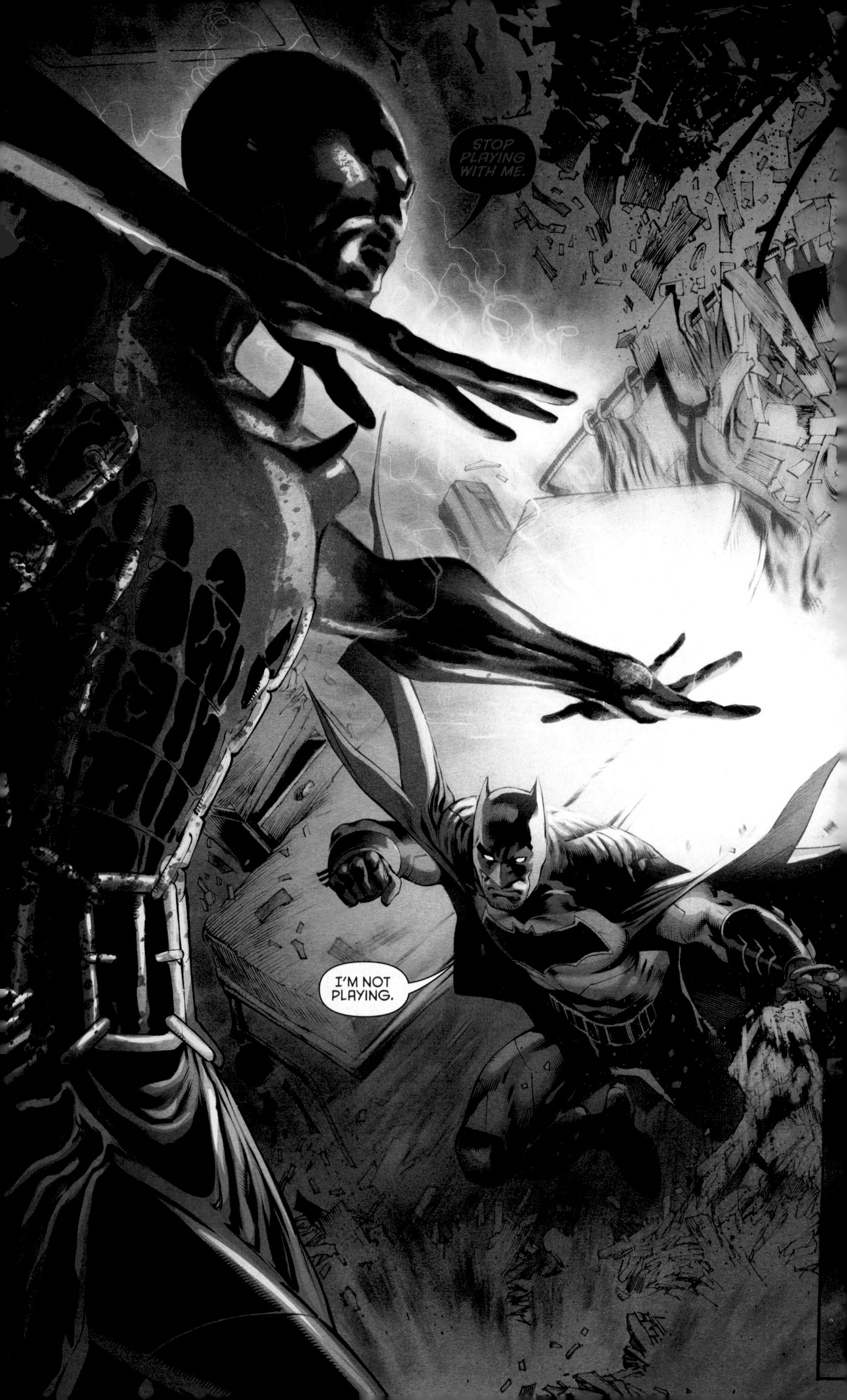
STOP PLAYING WITH ME.
I'M NOT PLAYING.

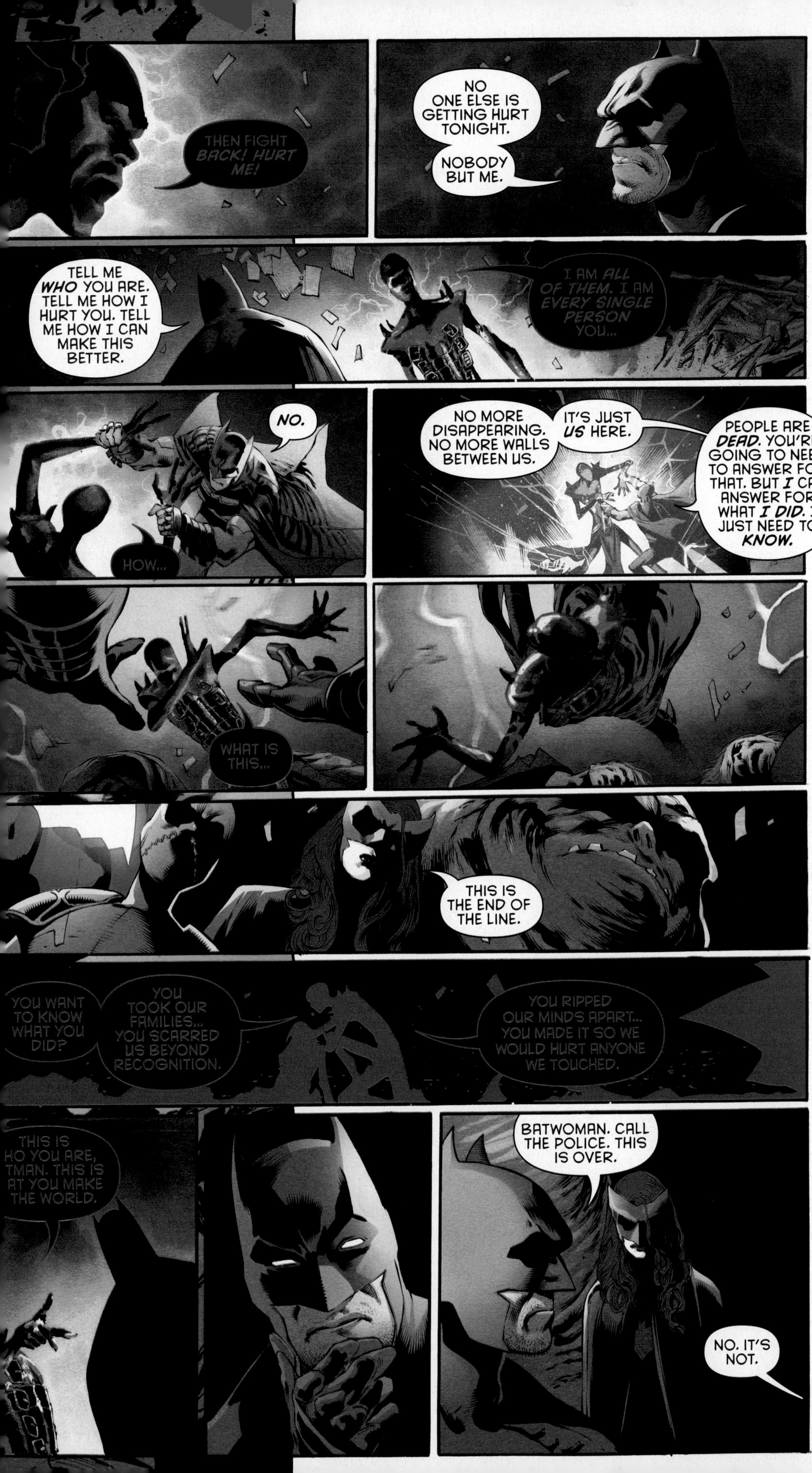
THEN FIGHT BACK! HURT ME!
NO ONE ELSE IS GETTING HURT TONIGHT.
NOBODY BUT ME.
TELL ME WHO YOU ARE. TELL ME HOW I HURT YOU. TELL ME HOW I CAN MAKE THIS BETTER.
I AM ALL OF THEM. I AM EVERY SINGLE PERSON YOU...
NO.
HOW...
NO MORE DISAPPEARING. NO MORE WALLS BETWEEN US.
IT'S JUST US HERE.
PEOPLE ARE DEAD. YOU'RE GOING TO NEED TO ANSWER FOR THAT. BUT I CAN ANSWER FOR WHAT I DID. I JUST NEED TO KNOW.
WHAT IS THIS...
THIS IS THE END OF THE LINE.
YOU WANT TO KNOW WHAT YOU DID?
YOU TOOK OUR FAMILIES... YOU SCARRED US BEYOND RECOGNITION.
YOU RIPPED OUR MINDS APART... YOU MADE IT SO WE WOULD HURT ANYONE WE TOUCHED.
THIS IS HO YOU ARE, TMAN. THIS IS AT YOU MAKE THE WORLD.
BATWOMAN. CALL THE POLICE. THIS IS OVER.
NO. IT'S NOT.

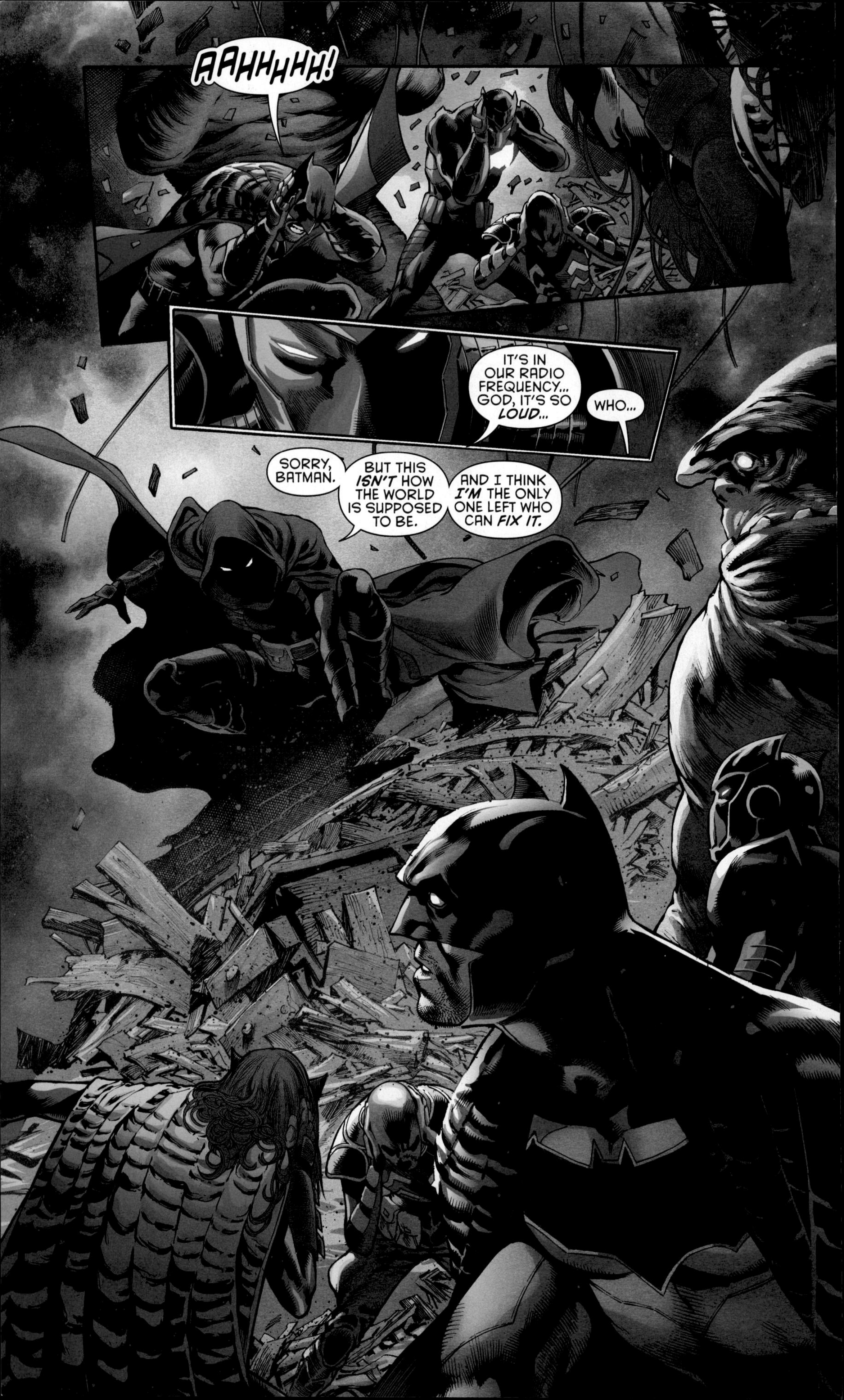
AAHHHHH!
IT'S IN OUR RADIO FREQUENCY... GOD, IT'S SO LOUD...
WHO...
SORRY, BATMAN.
BUT THIS ISN'T HOW THE WORLD IS SUPPOSED TO BE.
AND I THINK I'M THE ONLY ONE LEFT WHO CAN FIX IT.

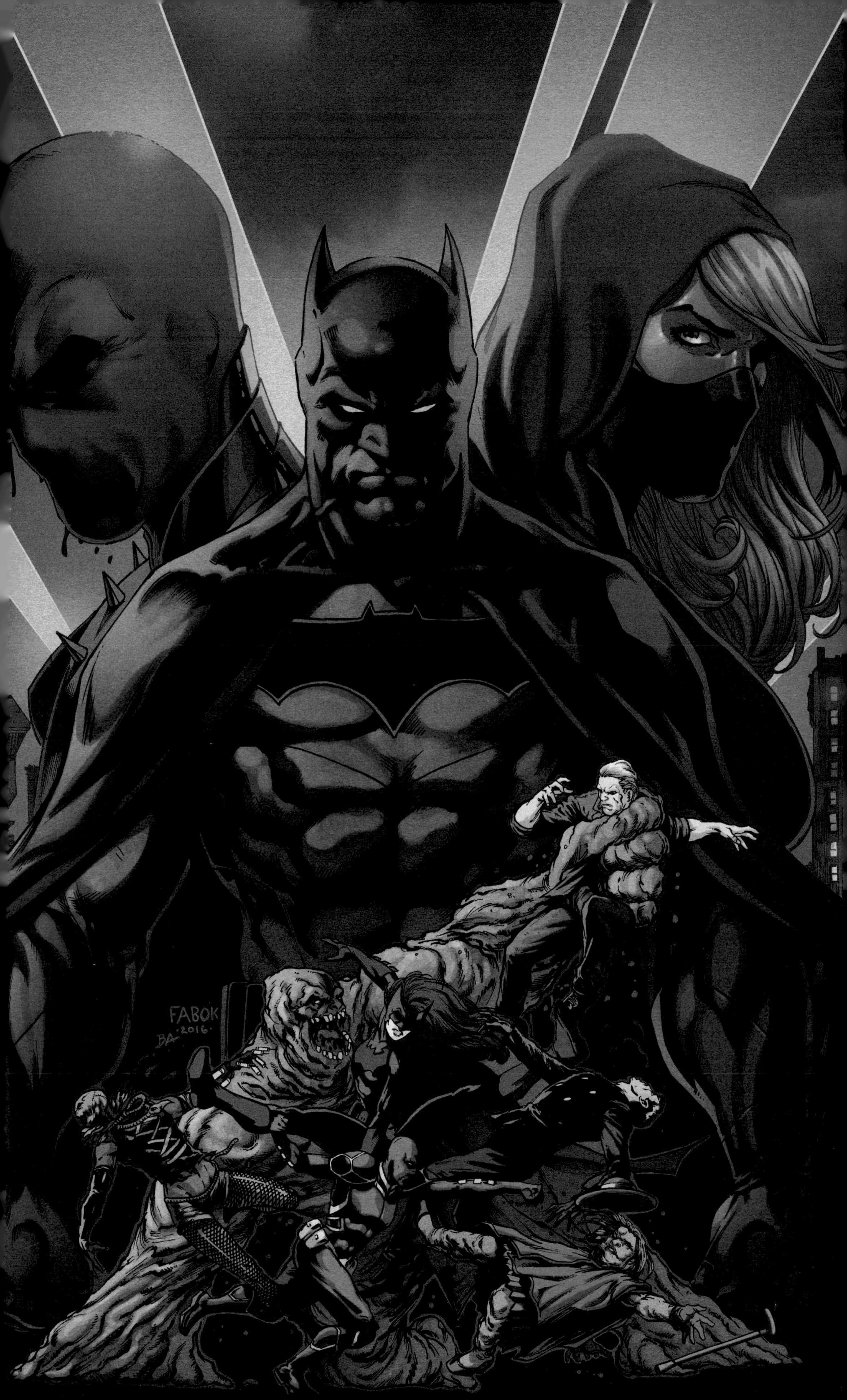
FABOK
·2016·
BA

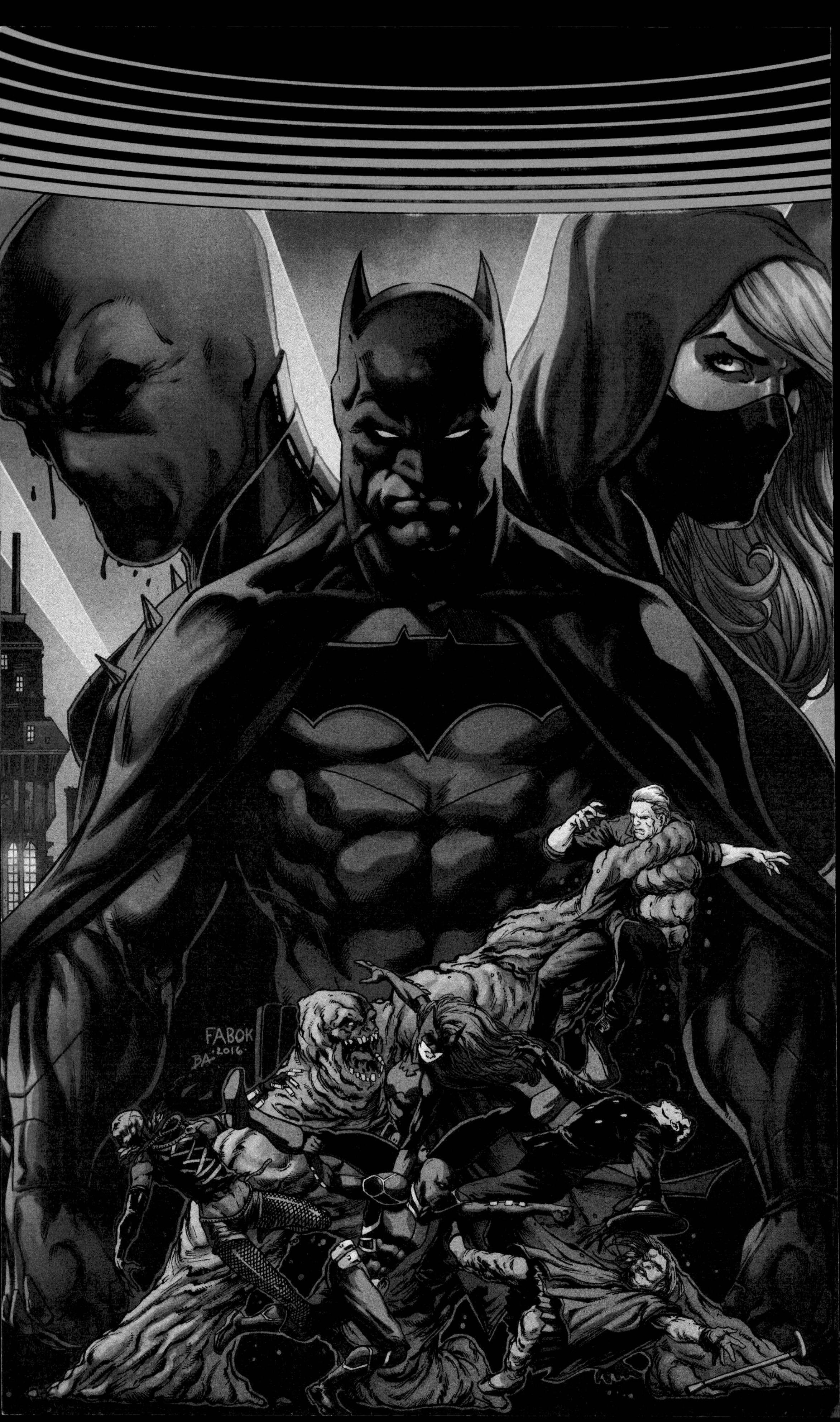
FABOK
BA 2016

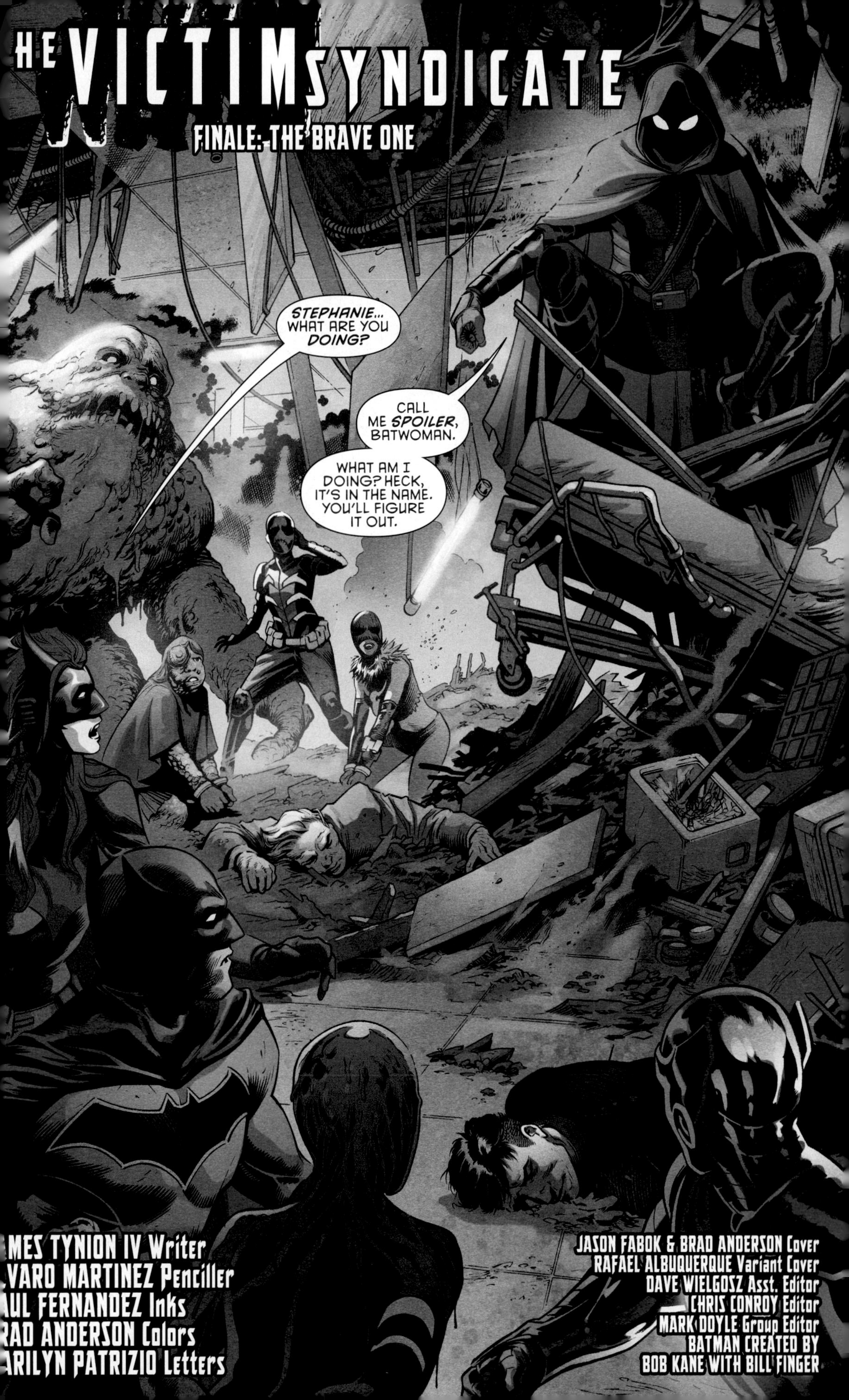

HE VICTIM SYNDICATE
FINALE: THE BRAVE ONE
STEPHANIE... WHAT ARE YOU DOING?
CALL ME SPOILER, BATWOMAN.
WHAT AM I DOING? HECK, IT'S IN THE NAME. YOU'LL FIGURE IT OUT.
MES TYNION IV Writer
VARO MARTINEZ Penciller
AUL FERNANDEZ Inks
RAD ANDERSON Colors
ARILYN PATRIZIO Letters
JASON FABOK & BRAD ANDERSON Cover
RAFAEL ALBUQUERQUE Variant Cover
DAVE WIELGOSZ Asst. Editor
CHRIS CONROY Editor
MARK DOYLE Group Editor
BATMAN CREATED BY
BOB KANE WITH BILL FINGER

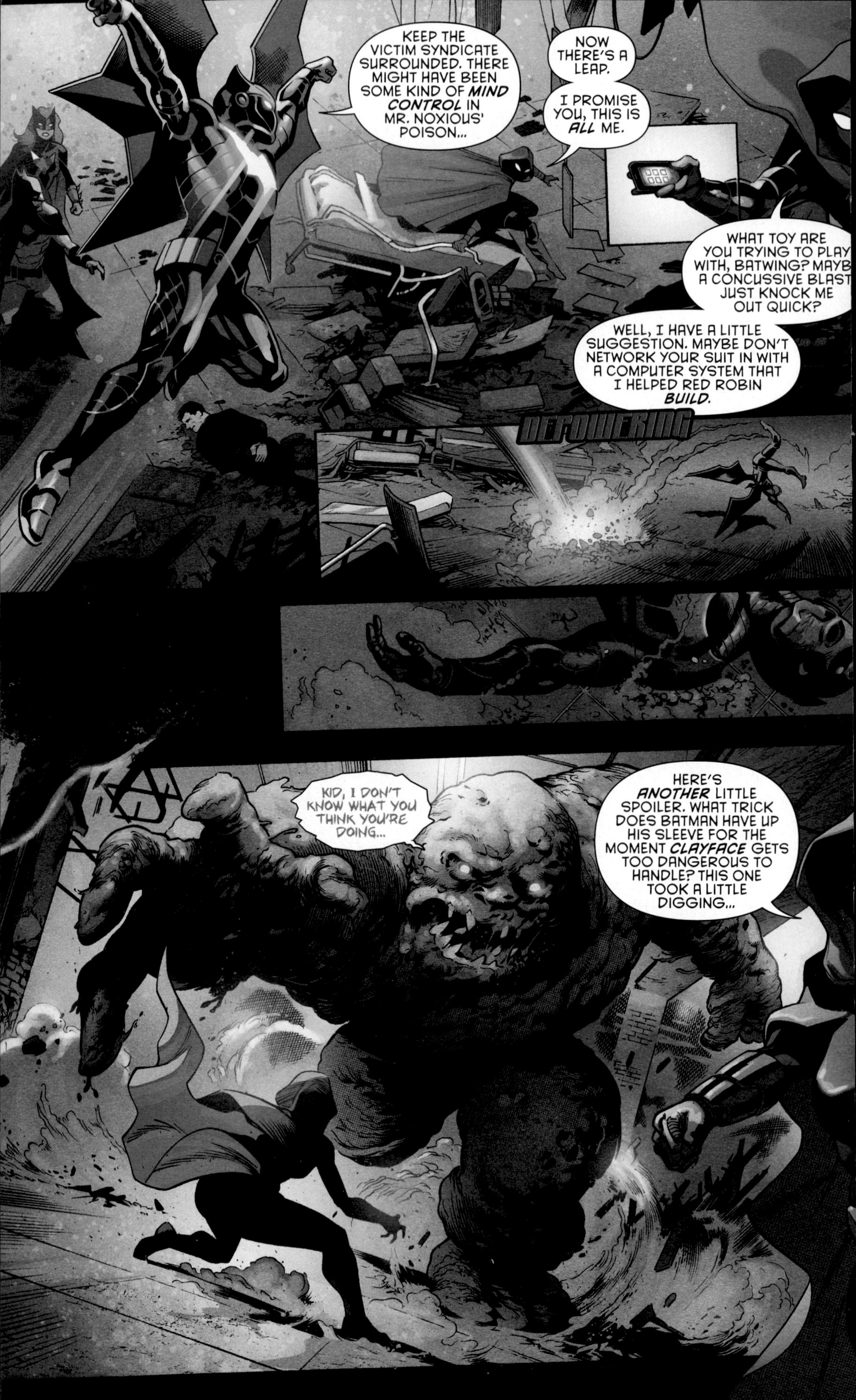
KEEP THE VICTIM SYNDICATE SURROUNDED. THERE MIGHT HAVE BEEN SOME KIND OF MIND CONTROL IN MR. NOXIOUS' POISON...
NOW THERE'S A LEAP.
I PROMISE YOU, THIS IS ALL ME.
WHAT TOY ARE YOU TRYING TO PLAY WITH, BATWING? MAYB A CONCUSSIVE BLAST JUST KNOCK ME OUT QUICK?
WELL, I HAVE A LITTLE SUGGESTION. MAYBE DON'T NETWORK YOUR SUIT IN WITH A COMPUTER SYSTEM THAT I HELPED RED ROBIN BUILD.
DEPOWERING
KID, I DON'T KNOW WHAT YOU THINK YOU'RE DOING...
HERE'S ANOTHER LITTLE SPOILER. WHAT TRICK DOES BATMAN HAVE UP HIS SLEEVE FOR THE MOMENT CLAYFACE GETS TOO DANGEROUS TO HANDLE? THIS ONE TOOK A LITTLE DIGGING...

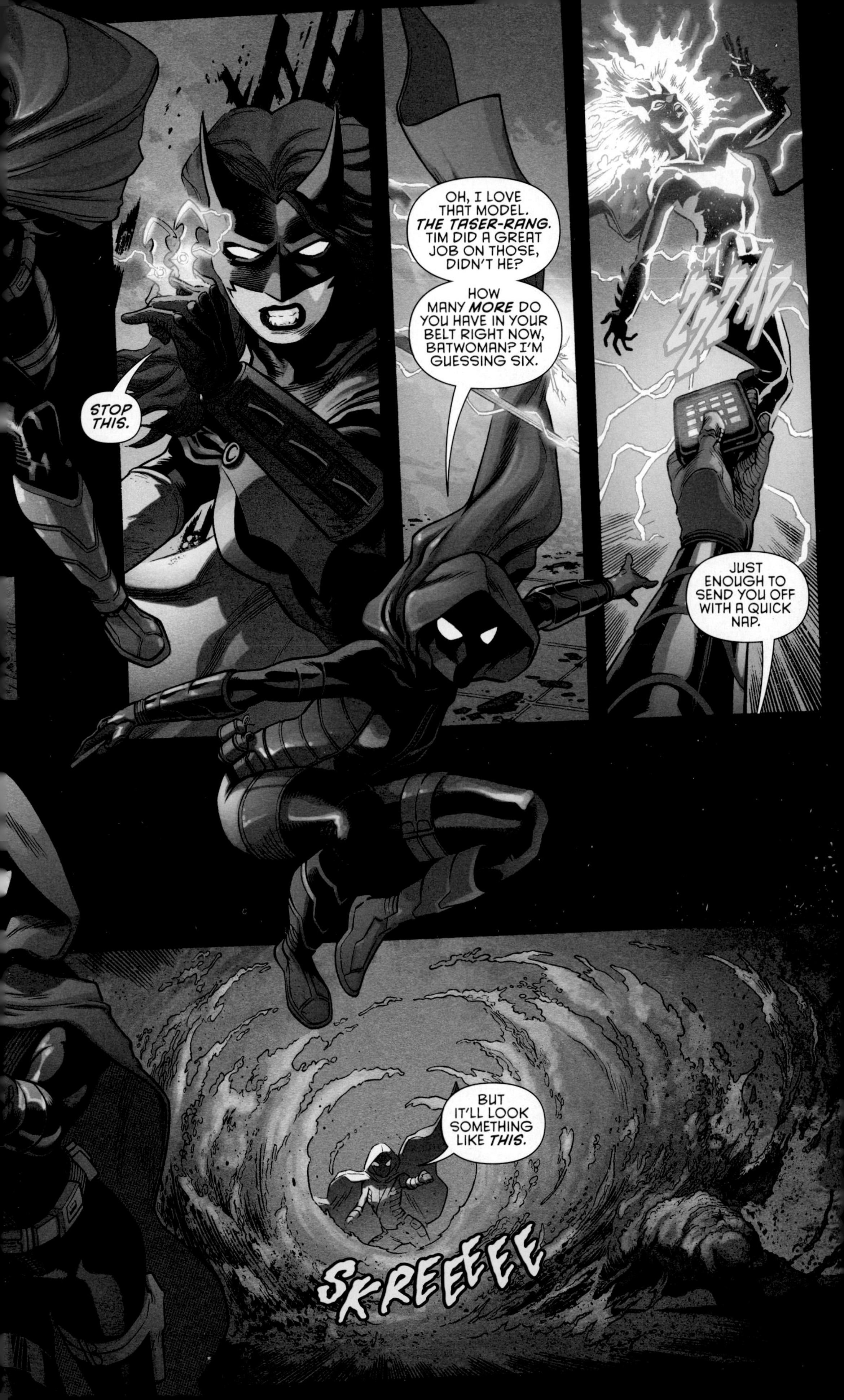
STOP THIS.
OH, I LOVE THAT MODEL. THE TASER-RANG. TIM DID A GREAT JOB ON THOSE, DIDN'T HE?
HOW MANY MORE DO YOU HAVE IN YOUR BELT RIGHT NOW, BATWOMAN? I'M GUESSING SIX.
ZZZAP
JUST ENOUGH TO SEND YOU OFF WITH A QUICK NAP.
BUT IT'LL LOOK SOMETHING LIKE THIS.
SKREEEEE

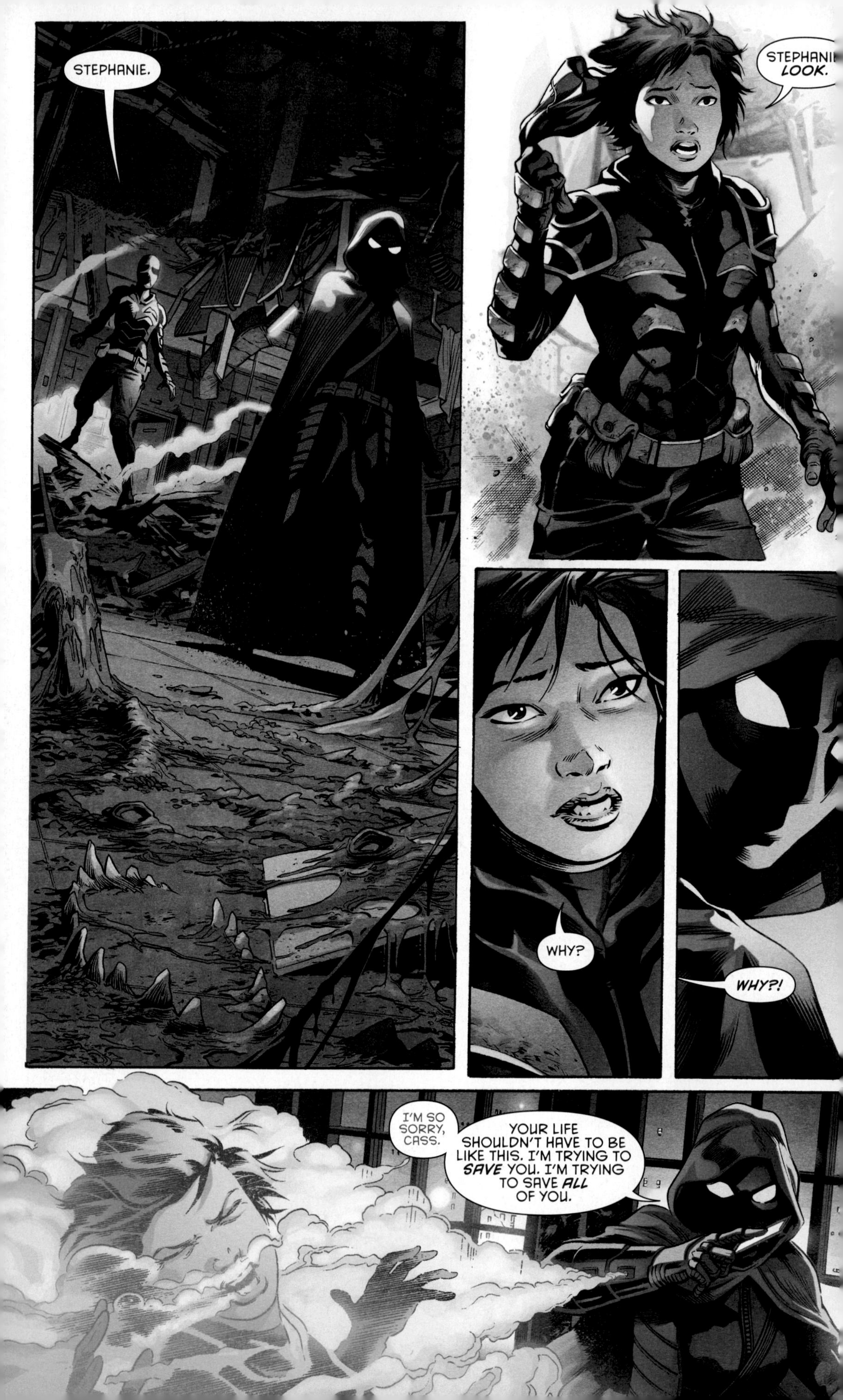
STEPHANIE.
STEPHANIE
LOOK.
WHY?
WHY?!
I'M SO SORRY, CASS.
YOUR LIFE SHOULDN'T HAVE TO BE LIKE THIS. I'M TRYING TO SAVE YOU. I'M TRYING TO SAVE ALL OF YOU.

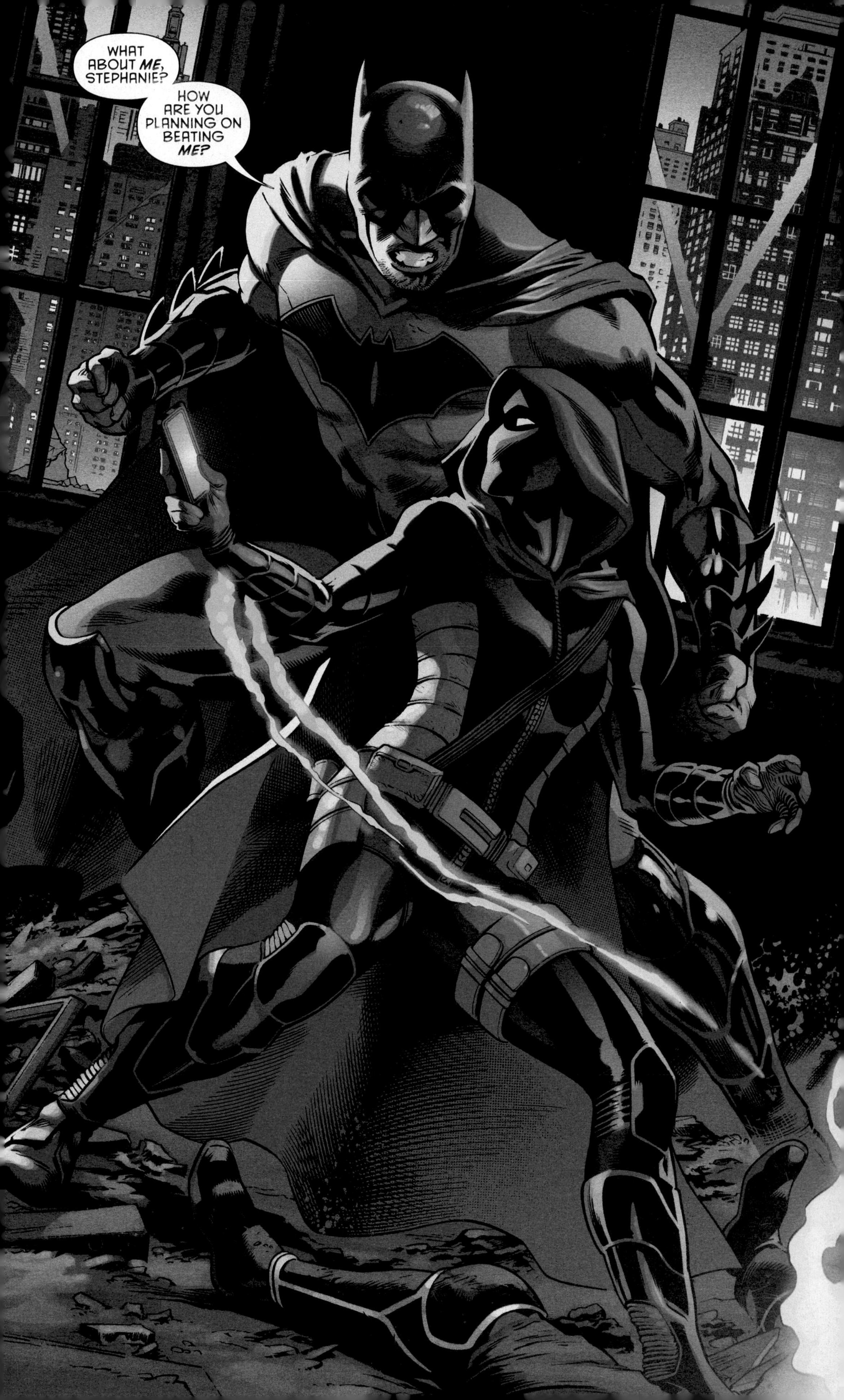

WHAT ABOUT *ME*, STEPHANIE?
HOW ARE YOU PLANNING ON BEATING *ME*?

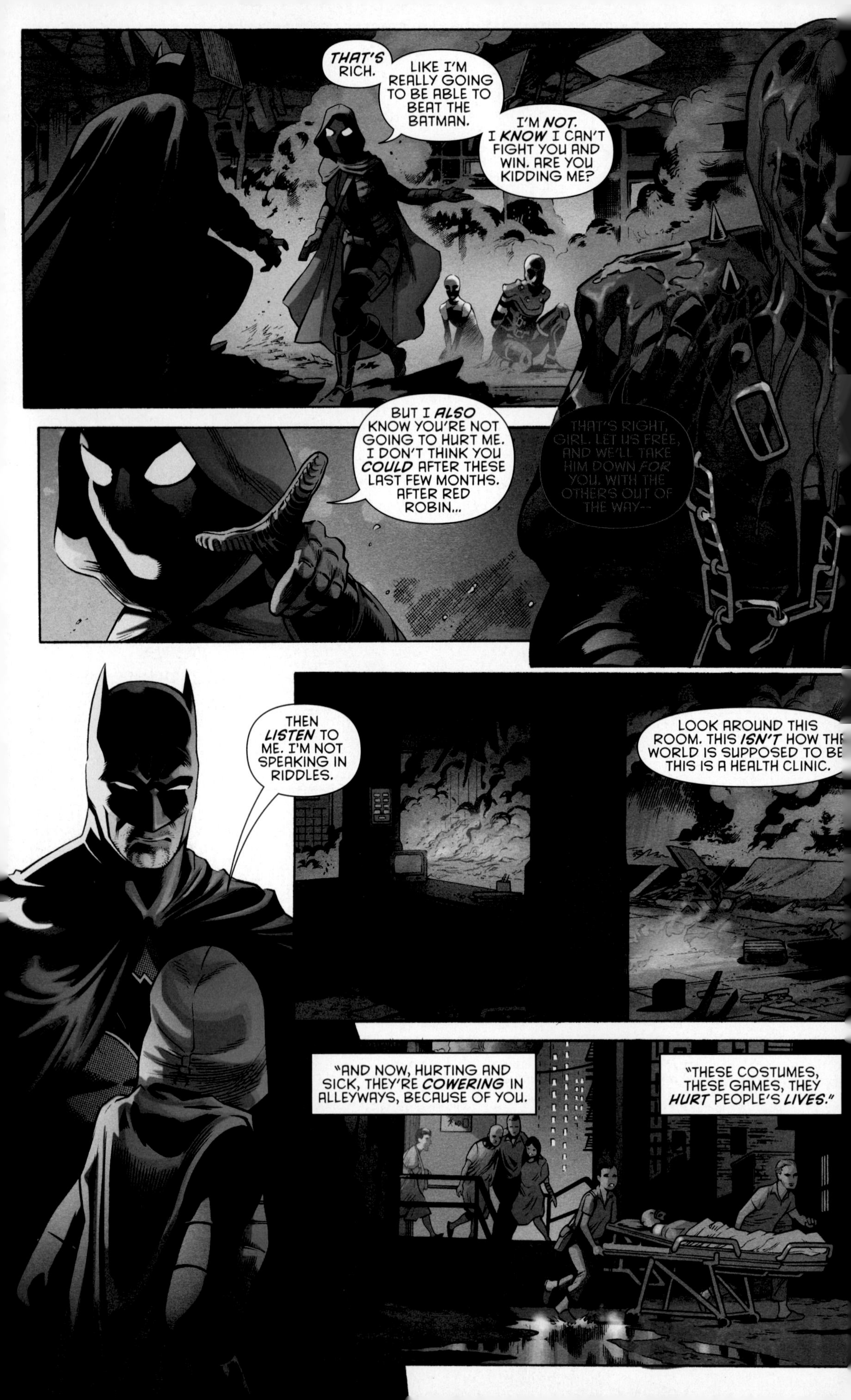
THAT'S RICH.
LIKE I'M REALLY GOING TO BE ABLE TO BEAT THE BATMAN.
I'M NOT. I KNOW I CAN'T FIGHT YOU AND WIN. ARE YOU KIDDING ME?
BUT I ALSO KNOW YOU'RE NOT GOING TO HURT ME. I DON'T THINK YOU COULD AFTER THESE LAST FEW MONTHS. AFTER RED ROBIN...
THAT'S RIGHT, GIRL. LET US FREE, AND WE'LL TAKE HIM DOWN FOR YOU. WITH THE OTHERS OUT OF THE WAY--
THEN LISTEN TO ME. I'M NOT SPEAKING IN RIDDLES.
LOOK AROUND THIS ROOM. THIS ISN'T HOW THE WORLD IS SUPPOSED TO BE. THIS IS A HEALTH CLINIC.
"AND NOW, HURTING AND SICK, THEY'RE COWERING IN ALLEYWAYS, BECAUSE OF YOU.
"THESE COSTUMES, THESE GAMES, THEY HURT PEOPLE'S LIVES."

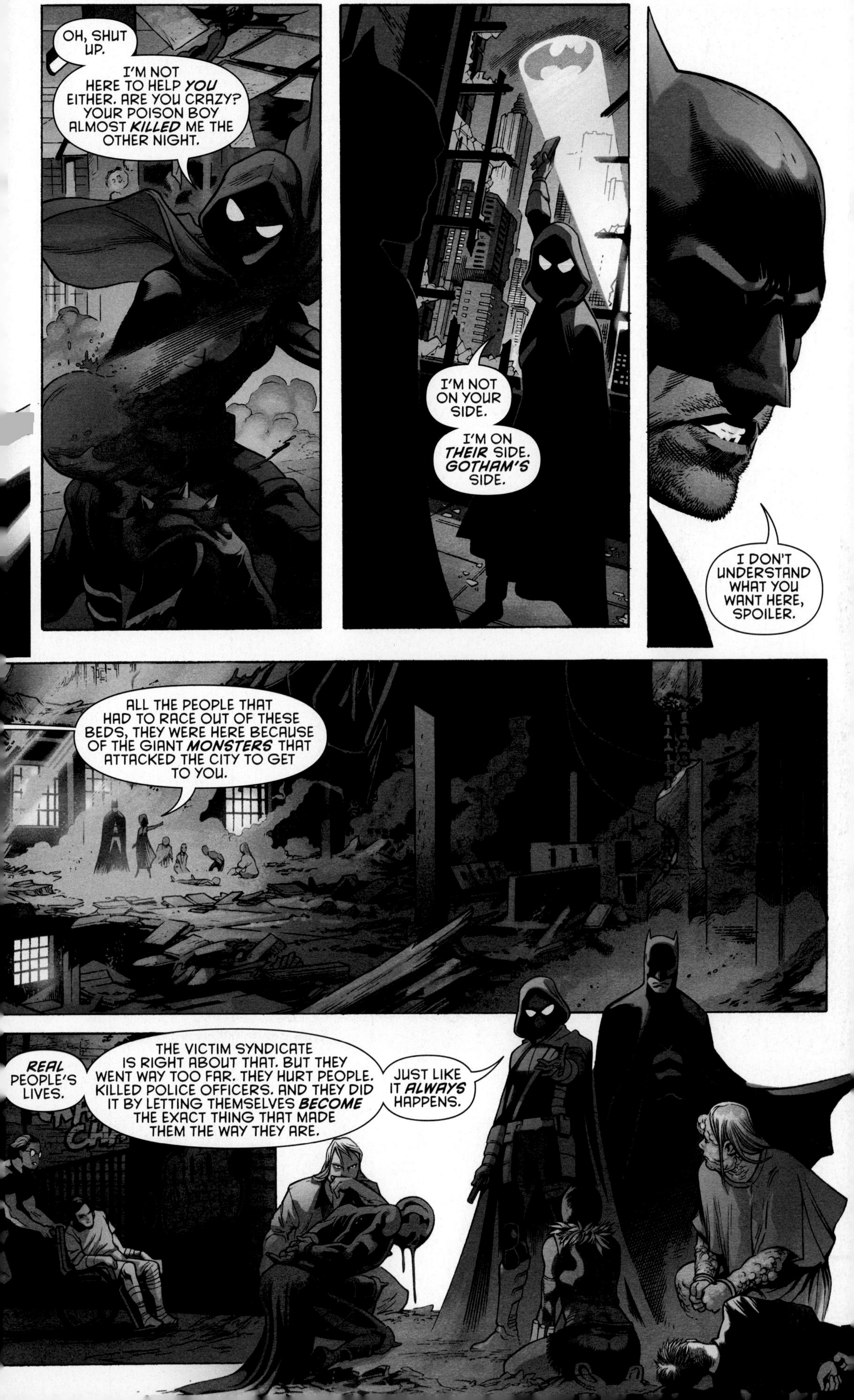

OH, SHUT UP.
I'M NOT HERE TO HELP YOU EITHER. ARE YOU CRAZY? YOUR POISON BOY ALMOST KILLED ME THE OTHER NIGHT.
I'M NOT ON YOUR SIDE.
I'M ON THEIR SIDE. GOTHAM'S SIDE.
I DON'T UNDERSTAND WHAT YOU WANT HERE, SPOILER.
ALL THE PEOPLE THAT HAD TO RACE OUT OF THESE BEDS, THEY WERE HERE BECAUSE OF THE GIANT MONSTERS THAT ATTACKED THE CITY TO GET TO YOU.
REAL PEOPLE'S LIVES.
THE VICTIM SYNDICATE IS RIGHT ABOUT THAT. BUT THEY WENT WAY TOO FAR. THEY HURT PEOPLE. KILLED POLICE OFFICERS. AND THEY DID IT BY LETTING THEMSELVES BECOME THE EXACT THING THAT MADE THEM THE WAY THEY ARE.
JUST LIKE IT ALWAYS HAPPENS.

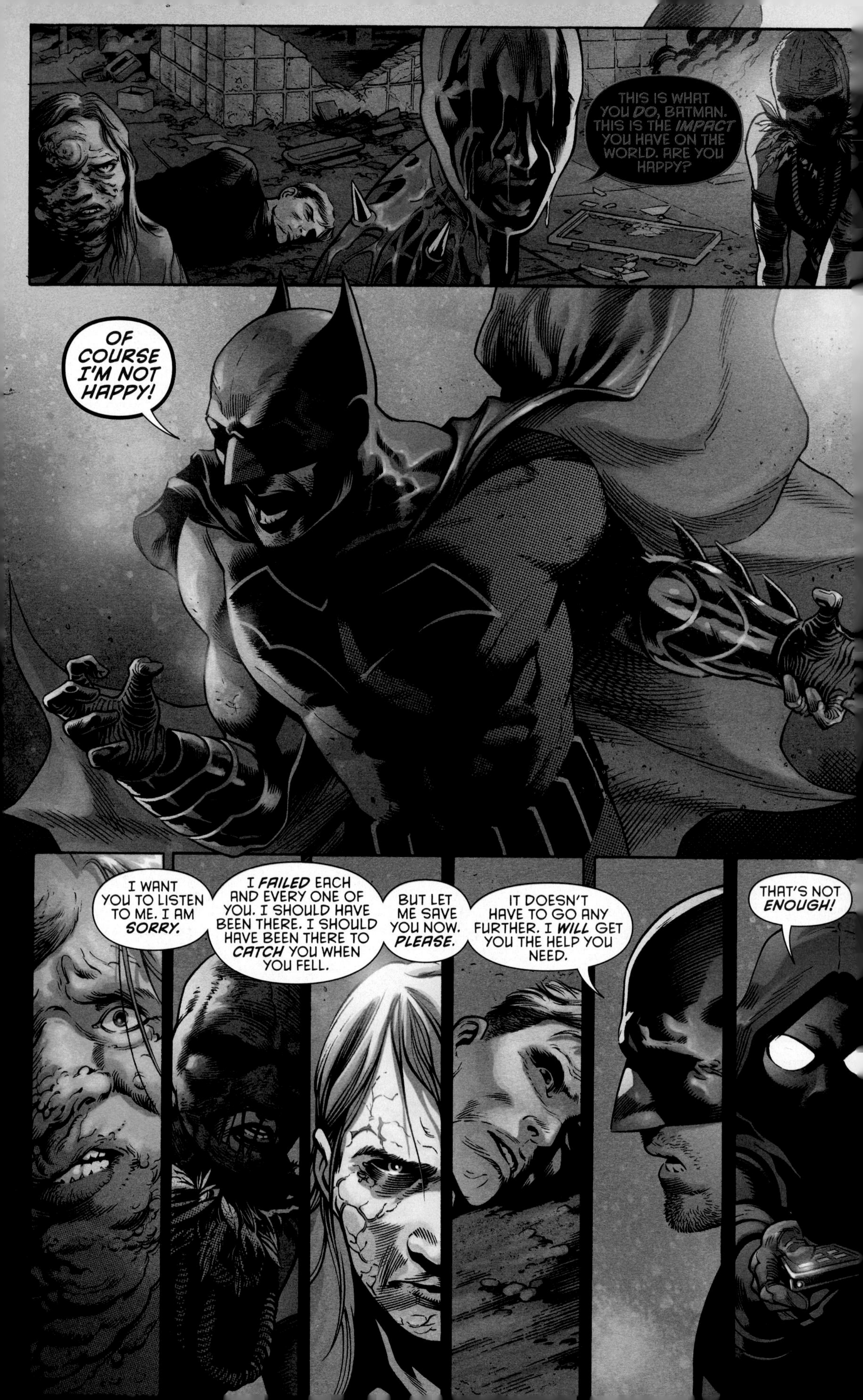
THIS IS WHAT YOU DO, BATMAN. THIS IS THE IMPACT YOU HAVE ON THE WORLD. ARE YOU HAPPY?
OF COURSE I'M NOT HAPPY!
I WANT YOU TO LISTEN TO ME. I AM SORRY.
I FAILED EACH AND EVERY ONE OF YOU. I SHOULD HAVE BEEN THERE. I SHOULD HAVE BEEN THERE TO CATCH YOU WHEN YOU FELL.
BUT LET ME SAVE YOU NOW. PLEASE.
IT DOESN'T HAVE TO GO ANY FURTHER. I WILL GET YOU THE HELP YOU NEED.
THAT'S NOT ENOUGH!

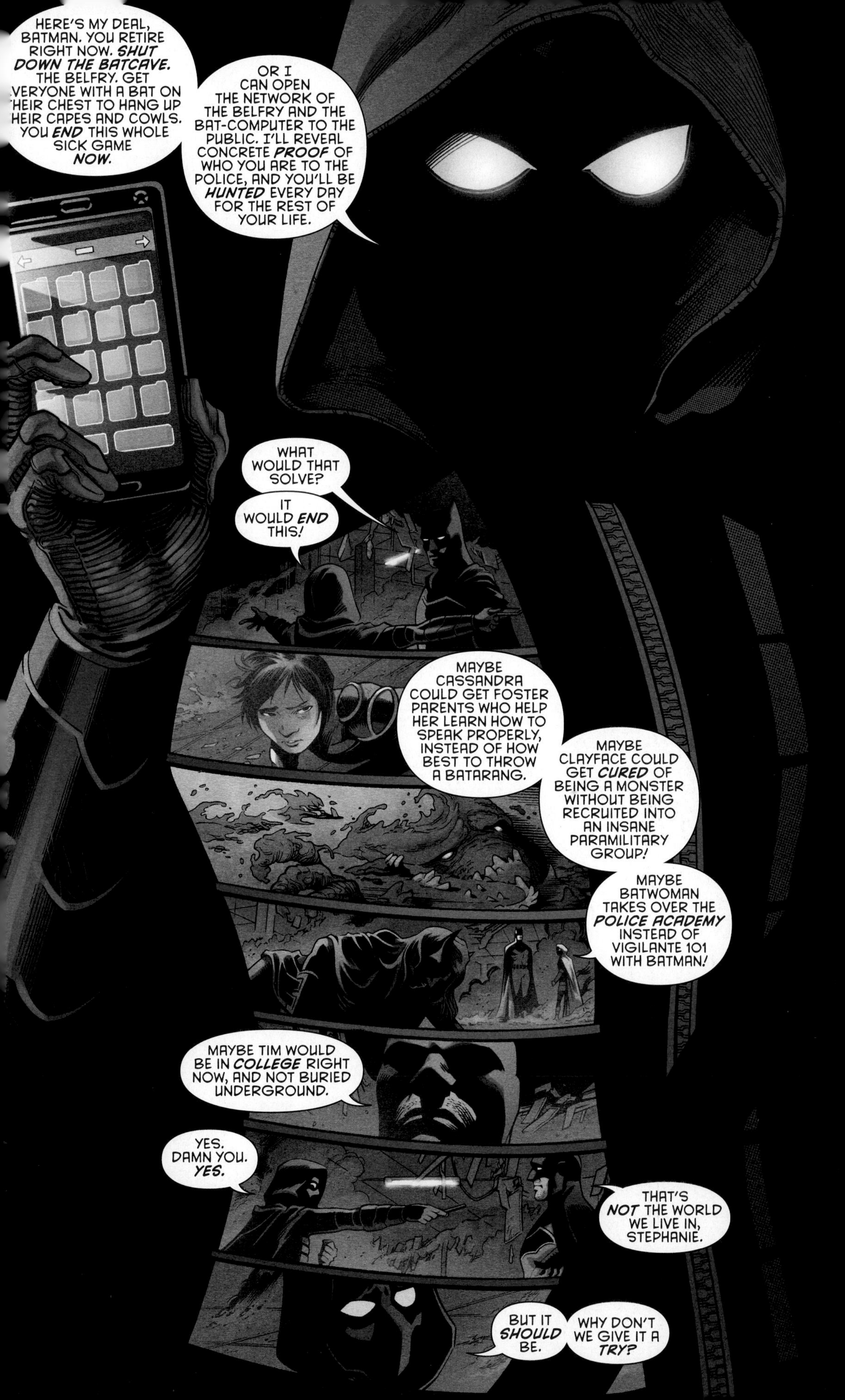

HERE'S MY DEAL, BATMAN. YOU RETIRE RIGHT NOW. SHUT DOWN THE BATCAVE. THE BELFRY. GET EVERYONE WITH A BAT ON THEIR CHEST TO HANG UP THEIR CAPES AND COWLS. YOU END THIS WHOLE SICK GAME NOW.
OR I CAN OPEN THE NETWORK OF THE BELFRY AND THE BAT-COMPUTER TO THE PUBLIC. I'LL REVEAL CONCRETE PROOF OF WHO YOU ARE TO THE POLICE, AND YOU'LL BE HUNTED EVERY DAY FOR THE REST OF YOUR LIFE.
WHAT WOULD THAT SOLVE?
IT WOULD END THIS!
MAYBE CASSANDRA COULD GET FOSTER PARENTS WHO HELP HER LEARN HOW TO SPEAK PROPERLY, INSTEAD OF HOW BEST TO THROW A BATARANG.
MAYBE CLAYFACE COULD GET CURED OF BEING A MONSTER WITHOUT BEING RECRUITED INTO AN INSANE PARAMILITARY GROUP!
MAYBE BATWOMAN TAKES OVER THE POLICE ACADEMY INSTEAD OF VIGILANTE 101 WITH BATMAN!
MAYBE TIM WOULD BE IN COLLEGE RIGHT NOW, AND NOT BURIED UNDERGROUND.
YES. DAMN YOU. YES.
THAT'S NOT THE WORLD WE LIVE IN, STEPHANIE.
BUT IT SHOULD BE.
WHY DON'T WE GIVE IT A TRY?

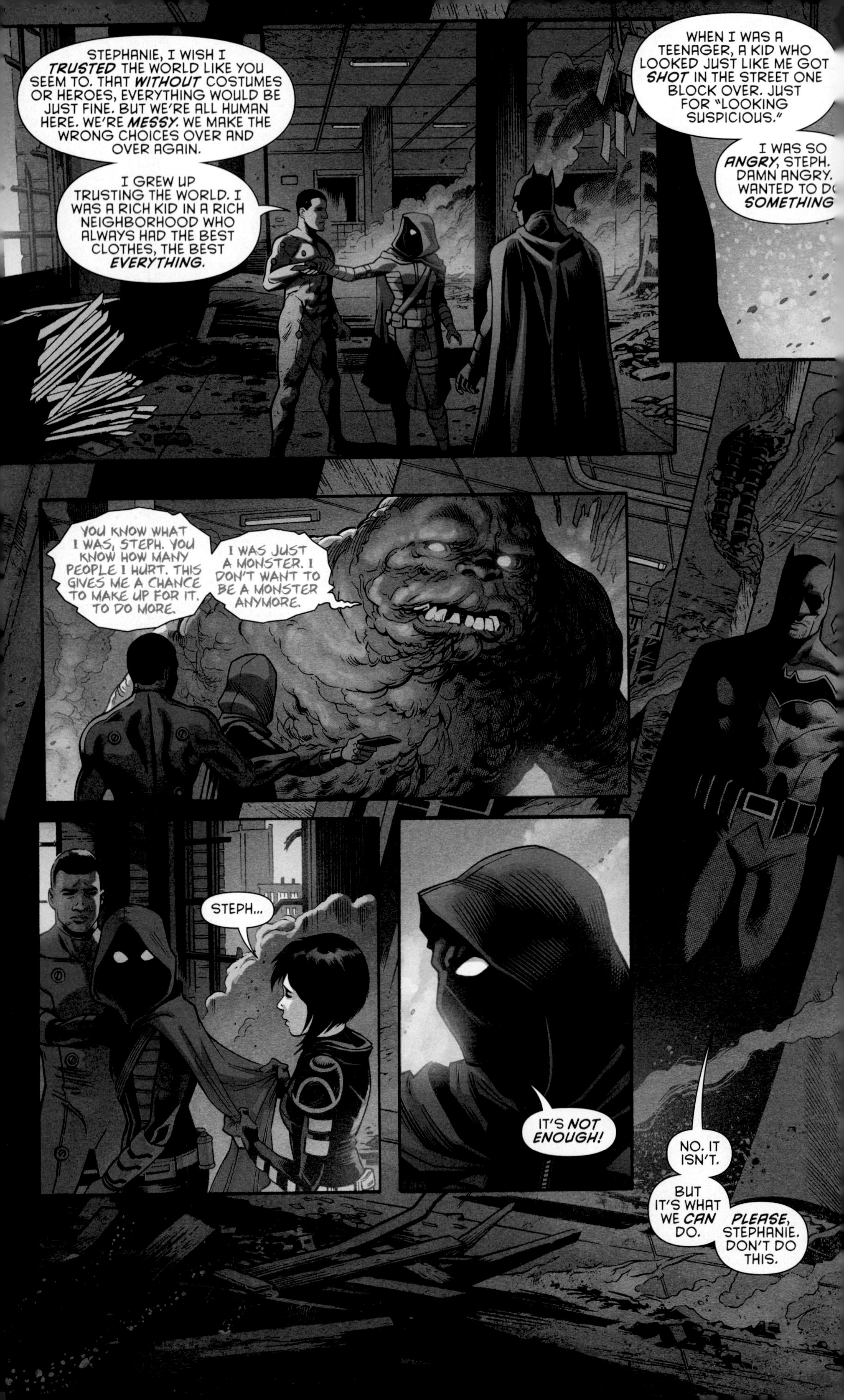
STEPHANIE, I WISH I TRUSTED THE WORLD LIKE YOU SEEM TO. THAT WITHOUT COSTUMES OR HEROES, EVERYTHING WOULD BE JUST FINE. BUT WE'RE ALL HUMAN HERE. WE'RE MESSY. WE MAKE THE WRONG CHOICES OVER AND OVER AGAIN.
I GREW UP TRUSTING THE WORLD. I WAS A RICH KID IN A RICH NEIGHBORHOOD WHO ALWAYS HAD THE BEST CLOTHES, THE BEST EVERYTHING.
WHEN I WAS A TEENAGER, A KID WHO LOOKED JUST LIKE ME GOT SHOT IN THE STREET ONE BLOCK OVER. JUST FOR "LOOKING SUSPICIOUS."
I WAS SO ANGRY, STEPH. DAMN ANGRY. WANTED TO DO SOMETHING
YOU KNOW WHAT I WAS, STEPH. YOU KNOW HOW MANY PEOPLE I HURT. THIS GIVES ME A CHANCE TO MAKE UP FOR IT. TO DO MORE.
I WAS JUST A MONSTER. I DON'T WANT TO BE A MONSTER ANYMORE.
STEPH...
IT'S NOT ENOUGH!
NO. IT ISN'T.
BUT IT'S WHAT WE CAN DO.
PLEASE, STEPHANIE. DON'T DO THIS.

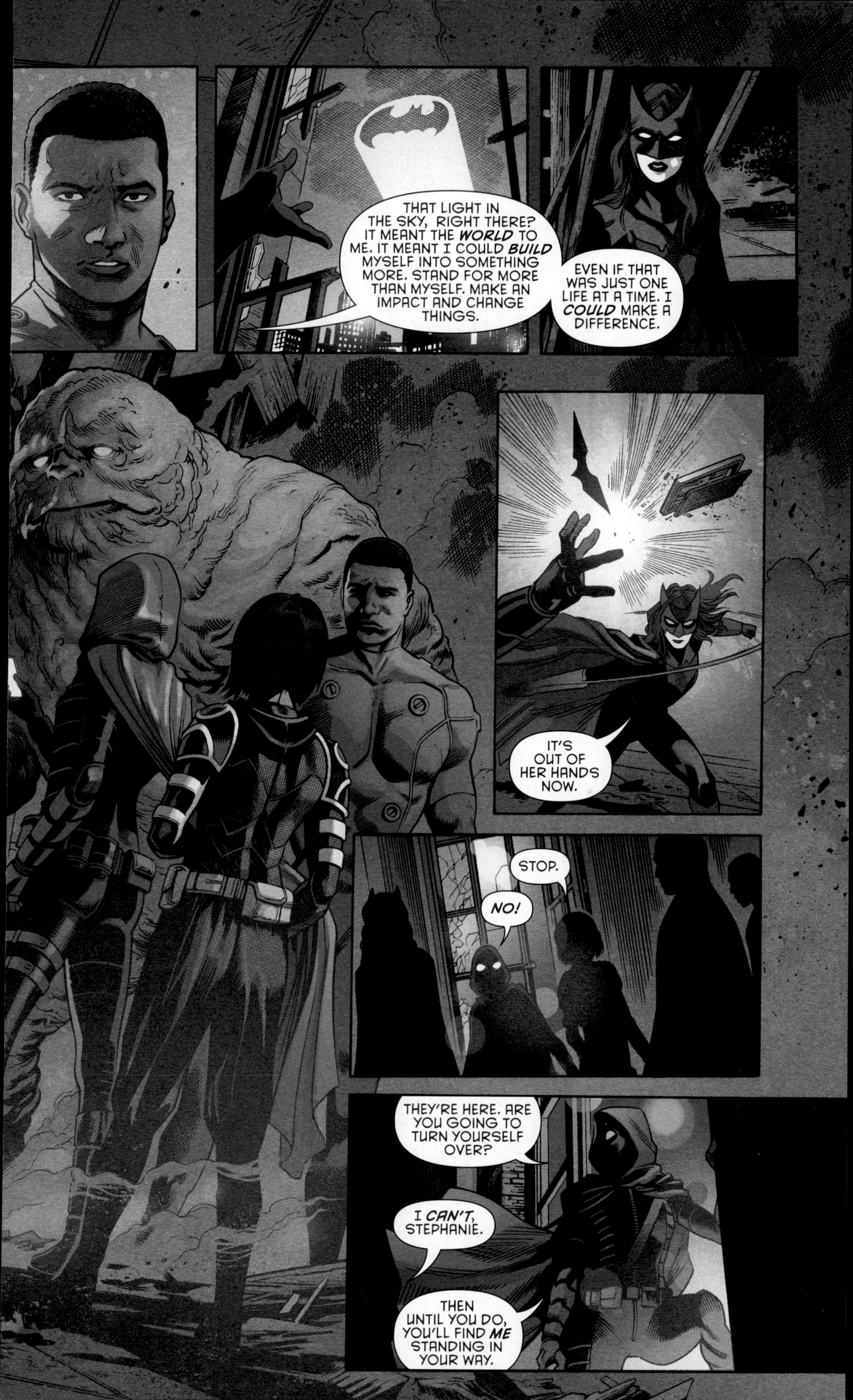
THAT LIGHT IN THE SKY, RIGHT THERE? IT MEANT THE *WORLD* TO ME. IT MEANT I COULD *BUILD* MYSELF INTO SOMETHING MORE. STAND FOR MORE THAN MYSELF. MAKE AN IMPACT AND CHANGE THINGS.
EVEN IF THAT WAS JUST ONE LIFE AT A TIME. I *COULD* MAKE A DIFFERENCE.
IT'S OUT OF HER HANDS NOW.
STOP.
NO!
THEY'RE HERE. ARE YOU GOING TO TURN YOURSELF OVER?
I *CAN'T*, STEPHANIE.
THEN UNTIL YOU DO, YOU'LL FIND *ME* STANDING IN YOUR WAY.

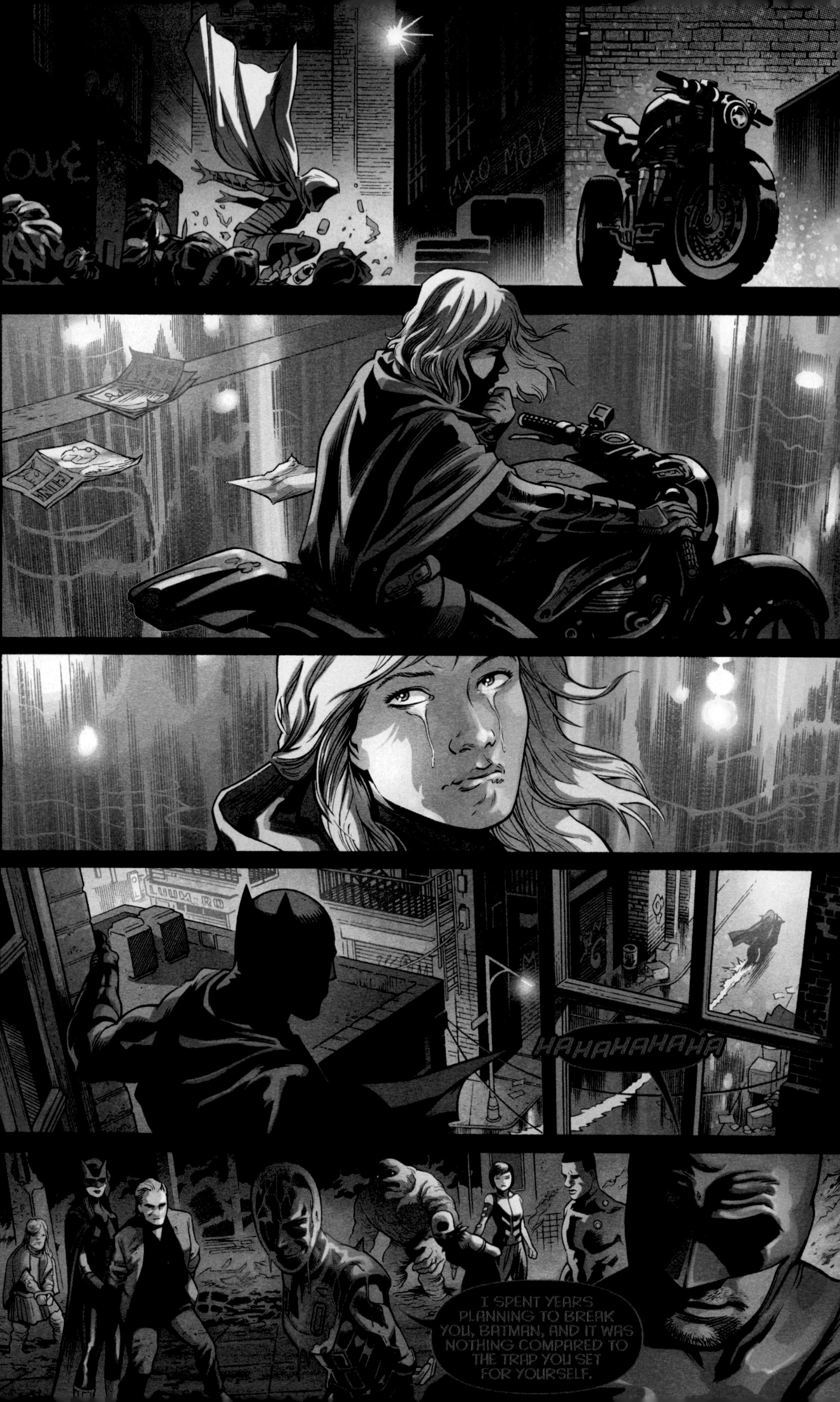
HAHAHAHAHAHA
I SPENT YEARS PLANNING TO BREAK YOU, BATMAN, AND IT WAS NOTHING COMPARED TO THE TRAP YOU SET FOR YOURSELF.

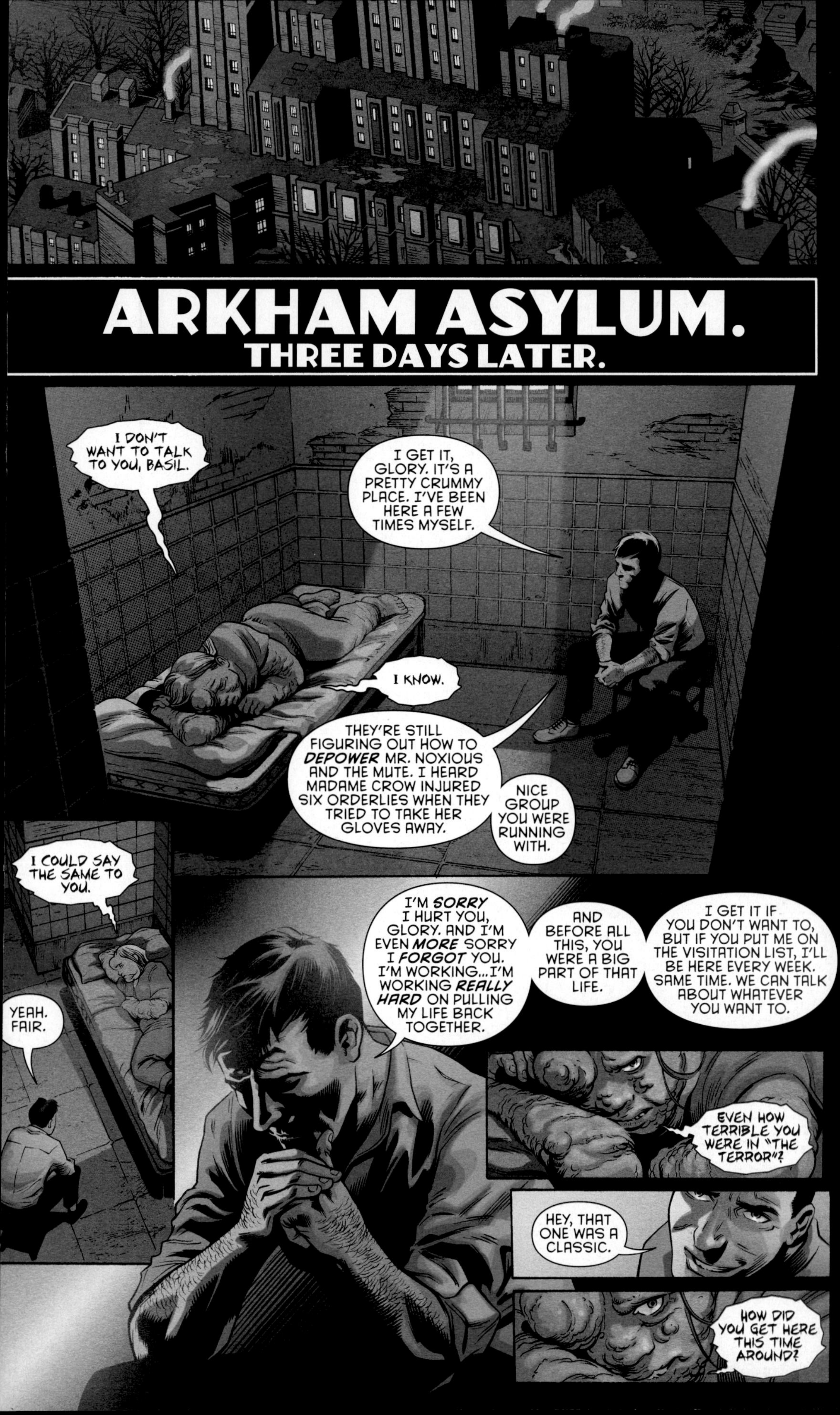
ARKHAM ASYLUM.
THREE DAYS LATER.
I DON'T WANT TO TALK TO YOU, BASIL.
I GET IT, GLORY. IT'S A PRETTY CRUMMY PLACE. I'VE BEEN HERE A FEW TIMES MYSELF.
I KNOW.
THEY'RE STILL FIGURING OUT HOW TO DEPOWER MR. NOXIOUS AND THE MUTE. I HEARD MADAME CROW INJURED SIX ORDERLIES WHEN THEY TRIED TO TAKE HER GLOVES AWAY.
NICE GROUP YOU WERE RUNNING WITH.
I COULD SAY THE SAME TO YOU.
YEAH. FAIR.
I'M SORRY I HURT YOU, GLORY. AND I'M EVEN MORE SORRY I FORGOT YOU. I'M WORKING...I'M WORKING REALLY HARD ON PULLING MY LIFE BACK TOGETHER.
AND BEFORE ALL THIS, YOU WERE A BIG PART OF THAT LIFE.
I GET IT IF YOU DON'T WANT TO, BUT IF YOU PUT ME ON THE VISITATION LIST, I'LL BE HERE EVERY WEEK. SAME TIME. WE CAN TALK ABOUT WHATEVER YOU WANT TO.
EVEN HOW TERRIBLE YOU WERE IN "THE TERROR"?
HEY, THAT ONE WAS A CLASSIC.
HOW DID YOU GET HERE THIS TIME AROUND?

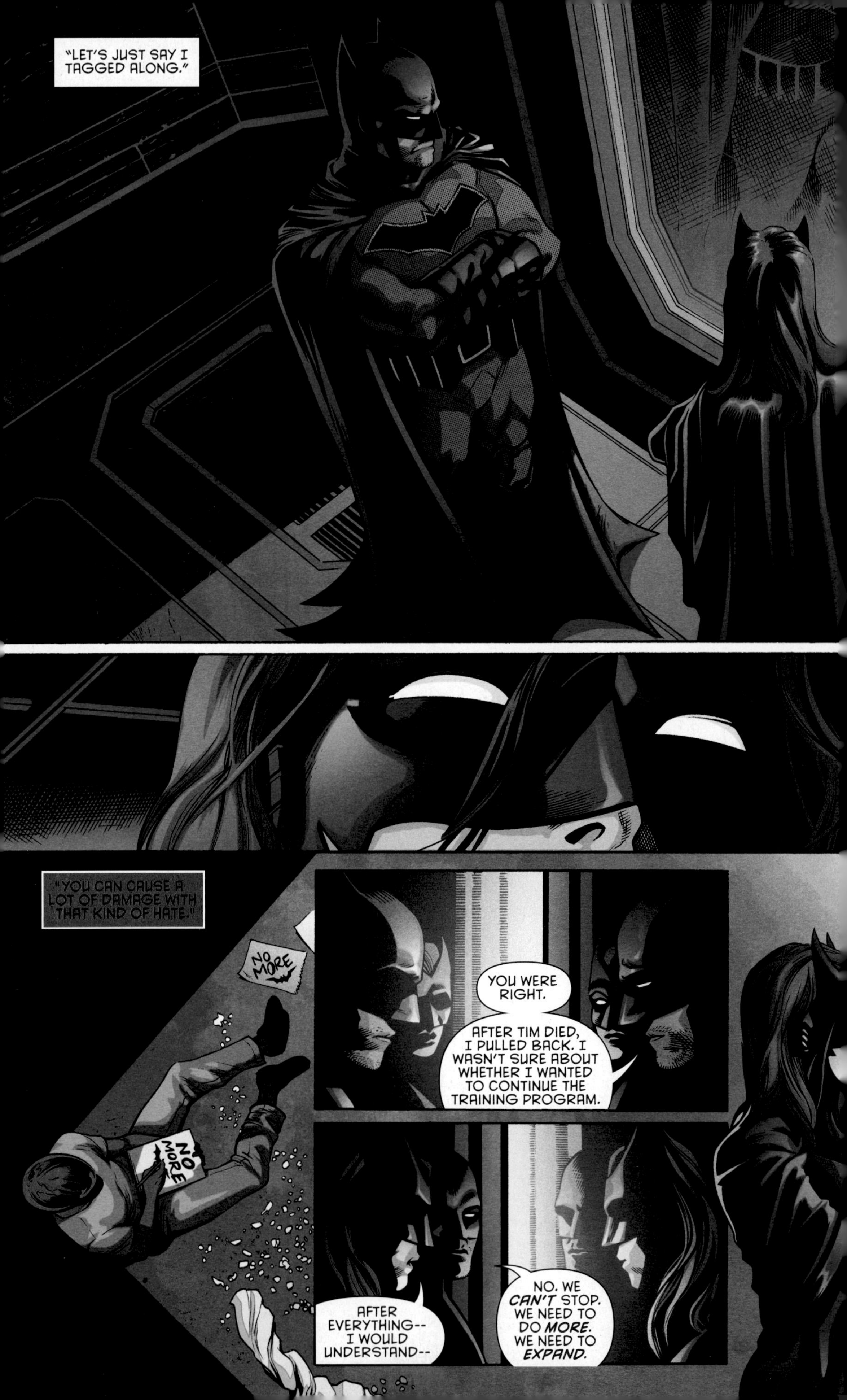
"LET'S JUST SAY I TAGGED ALONG."
"YOU CAN CAUSE A LOT OF DAMAGE WITH THAT KIND OF HATE."
NO MORE
YOU WERE RIGHT.
AFTER TIM DIED, I PULLED BACK. I WASN'T SURE ABOUT WHETHER I WANTED TO CONTINUE THE TRAINING PROGRAM.
NO MORE
AFTER EVERYTHING-- I WOULD UNDERSTAND--
NO. WE *CAN'T* STOP. WE NEED TO DO *MORE.* WE NEED TO *EXPAND.*

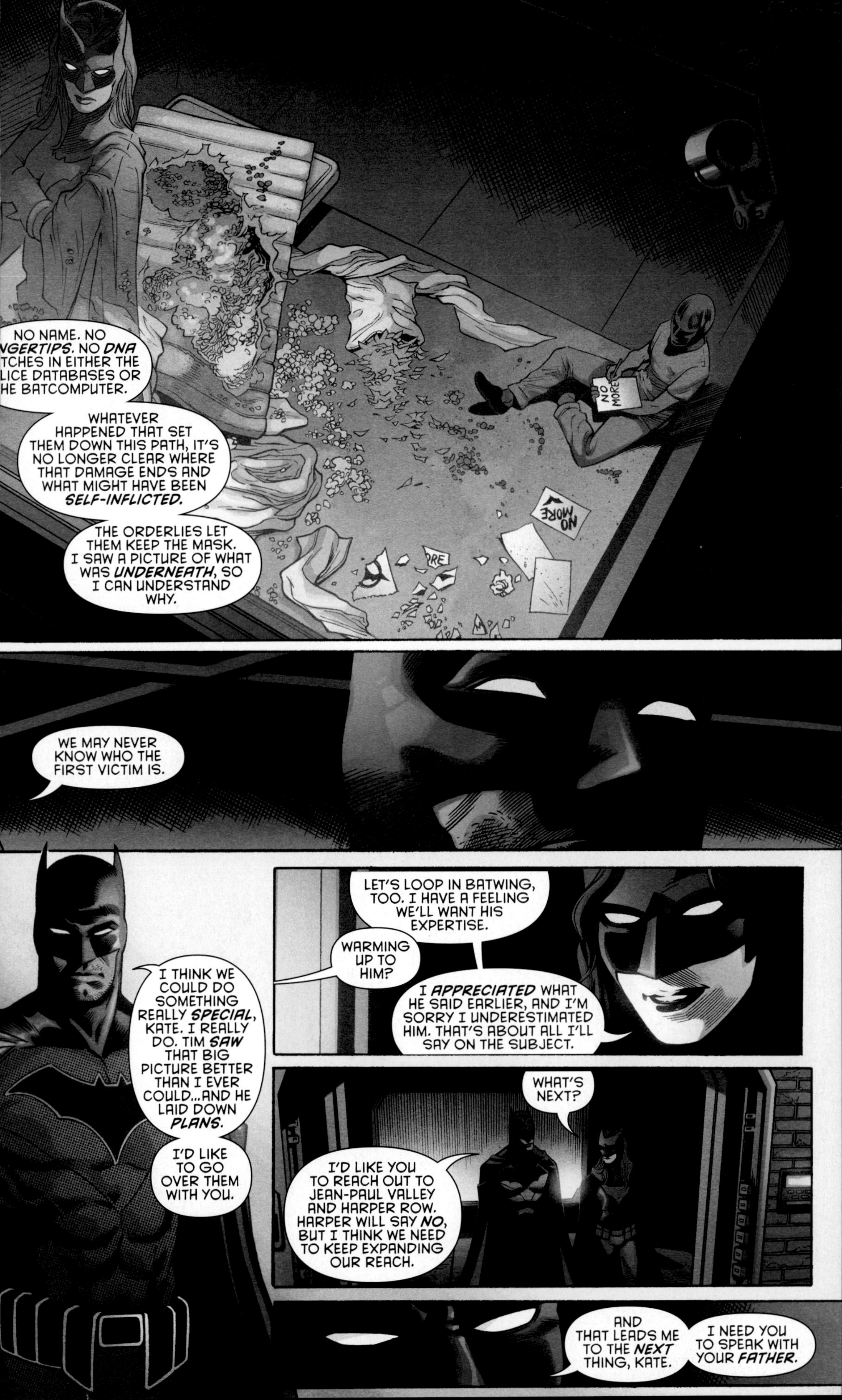
NO NAME. NO
NGERTIPS. NO DNA
TCHES IN EITHER THE
LICE DATABASES OR
HE BATCOMPUTER.
WHATEVER HAPPENED THAT SET THEM DOWN THIS PATH, IT'S NO LONGER CLEAR WHERE THAT DAMAGE ENDS AND WHAT MIGHT HAVE BEEN SELF-INFLICTED.
THE ORDERLIES LET THEM KEEP THE MASK. I SAW A PICTURE OF WHAT WAS UNDERNEATH, SO I CAN UNDERSTAND WHY.
NO MORE
NO MORE
WE MAY NEVER KNOW WHO THE FIRST VICTIM IS.
I THINK WE COULD DO SOMETHING REALLY SPECIAL, KATE. I REALLY DO. TIM SAW THAT BIG PICTURE BETTER THAN I EVER COULD...AND HE LAID DOWN PLANS.
I'D LIKE TO GO OVER THEM WITH YOU.
LET'S LOOP IN BATWING, TOO. I HAVE A FEELING WE'LL WANT HIS EXPERTISE.
WARMING UP TO HIM?
I APPRECIATED WHAT HE SAID EARLIER, AND I'M SORRY I UNDERESTIMATED HIM. THAT'S ABOUT ALL I'LL SAY ON THE SUBJECT.
WHAT'S NEXT?
I'D LIKE YOU TO REACH OUT TO JEAN-PAUL VALLEY AND HARPER ROW. HARPER WILL SAY NO, BUT I THINK WE NEED TO KEEP EXPANDING OUR REACH.
AND THAT LEADS ME TO THE NEXT THING, KATE.
I NEED YOU TO SPEAK WITH YOUR FATHER.

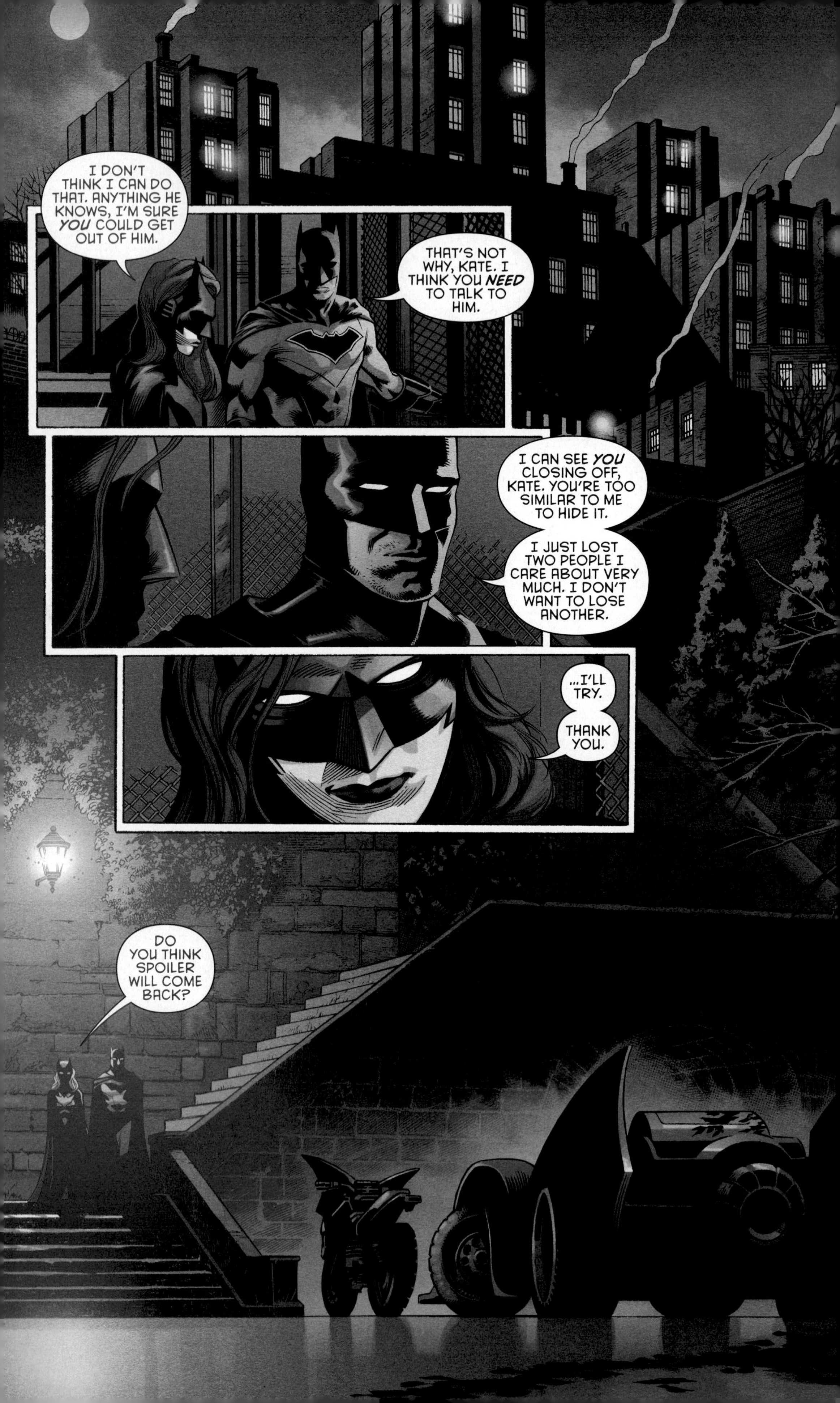
I DON'T THINK I CAN DO THAT. ANYTHING HE KNOWS, I'M SURE *YOU* COULD GET OUT OF HIM.
THAT'S NOT WHY, KATE. I THINK YOU ***NEED*** TO TALK TO HIM.
I CAN SEE *YOU* CLOSING OFF, KATE. YOU'RE TOO SIMILAR TO ME TO HIDE IT.
I JUST LOST TWO PEOPLE I CARE ABOUT VERY MUCH. I DON'T WANT TO LOSE ANOTHER.
...I'LL TRY.
THANK YOU.
DO YOU THINK SPOILER WILL COME BACK?

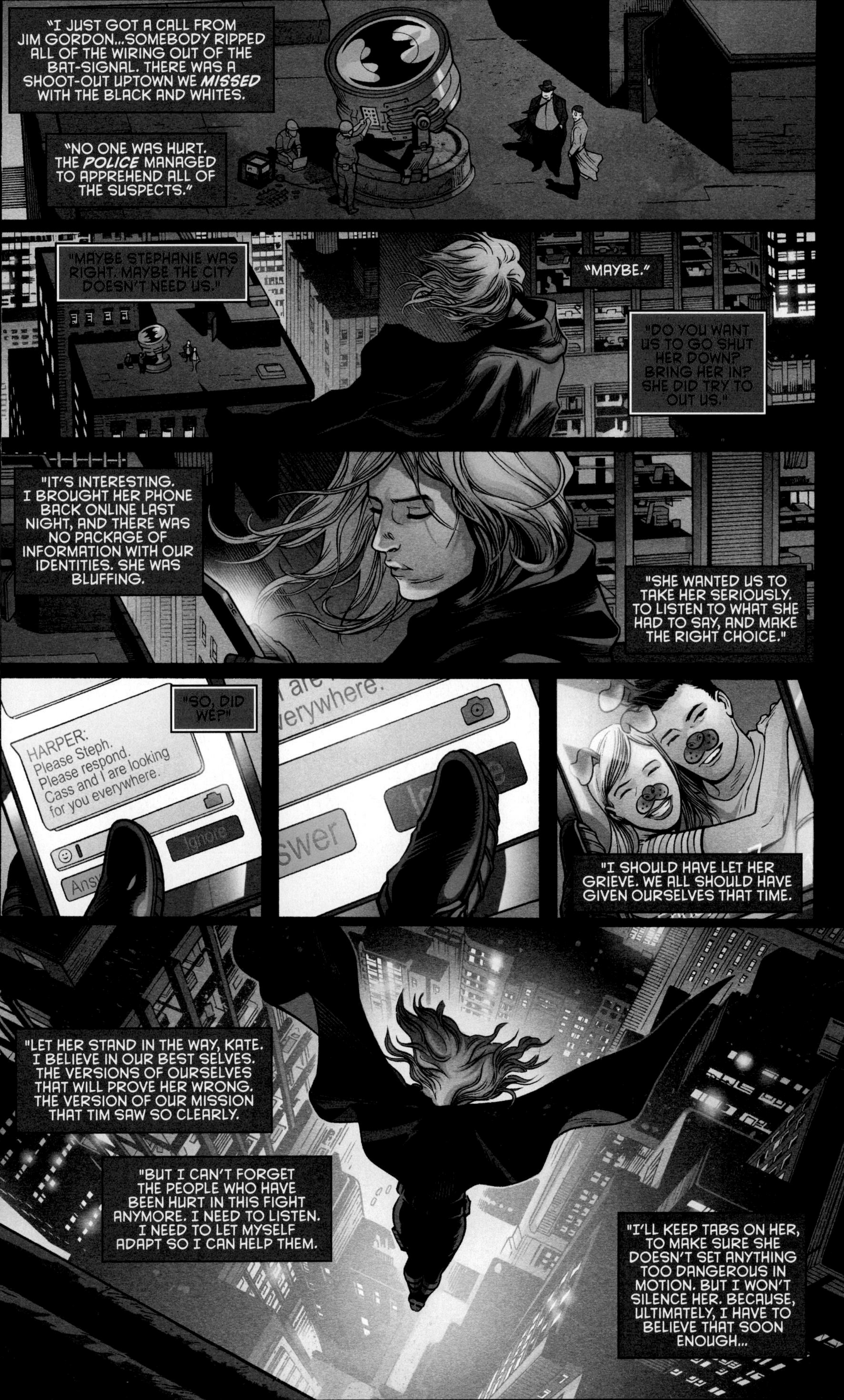
"I JUST GOT A CALL FROM JIM GORDON...SOMEBODY RIPPED ALL OF THE WIRING OUT OF THE BAT-SIGNAL. THERE WAS A SHOOT-OUT UPTOWN WE MISSED WITH THE BLACK AND WHITES.
"NO ONE WAS HURT. THE POLICE MANAGED TO APPREHEND ALL OF THE SUSPECTS."
"MAYBE STEPHANIE WAS RIGHT. MAYBE THE CITY DOESN'T NEED US."
"MAYBE."
"DO YOU WANT US TO GO SHUT HER DOWN? BRING HER IN? SHE DID TRY TO OUT US."
"IT'S INTERESTING. I BROUGHT HER PHONE BACK ONLINE LAST NIGHT, AND THERE WAS NO PACKAGE OF INFORMATION WITH OUR IDENTITIES. SHE WAS BLUFFING.
"SHE WANTED US TO TAKE HER SERIOUSLY. TO LISTEN TO WHAT SHE HAD TO SAY, AND MAKE THE RIGHT CHOICE."
"SO, DID WE?"
HARPER:
Please Steph.
Please respond.
Cass and I are looking
for you everywhere.
Ignore
"I SHOULD HAVE LET HER GRIEVE. WE ALL SHOULD HAVE GIVEN OURSELVES THAT TIME.
"LET HER STAND IN THE WAY, KATE. I BELIEVE IN OUR BEST SELVES. THE VERSIONS OF OURSELVES THAT WILL PROVE HER WRONG. THE VERSION OF OUR MISSION THAT TIM SAW SO CLEARLY.
"BUT I CAN'T FORGET THE PEOPLE WHO HAVE BEEN HURT IN THIS FIGHT ANYMORE. I NEED TO LISTEN. I NEED TO LET MYSELF ADAPT SO I CAN HELP THEM.
"I'LL KEEP TABS ON HER, TO MAKE SURE SHE DOESN'T SET ANYTHING TOO DANGEROUS IN MOTION. BUT I WON'T SILENCE HER. BECAUSE, ULTIMATELY, I HAVE TO BELIEVE THAT SOON ENOUGH...

"WE'LL ALL BE FIGHTING TOGETHER AGAIN."

VERY FAR AWAY...

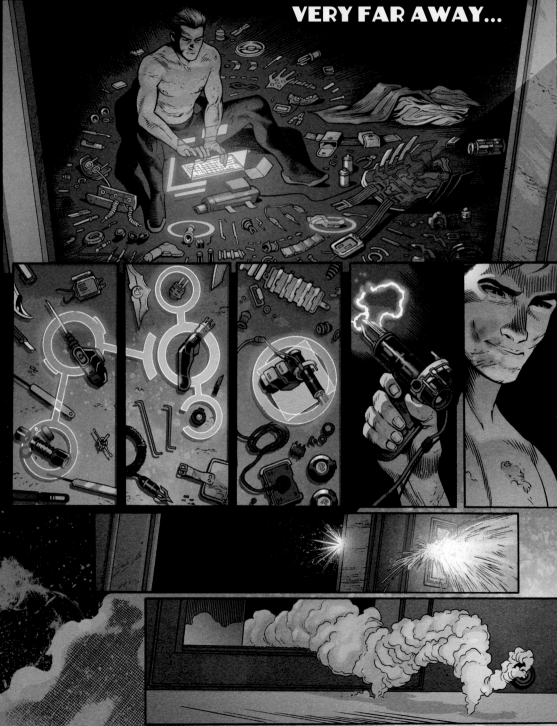

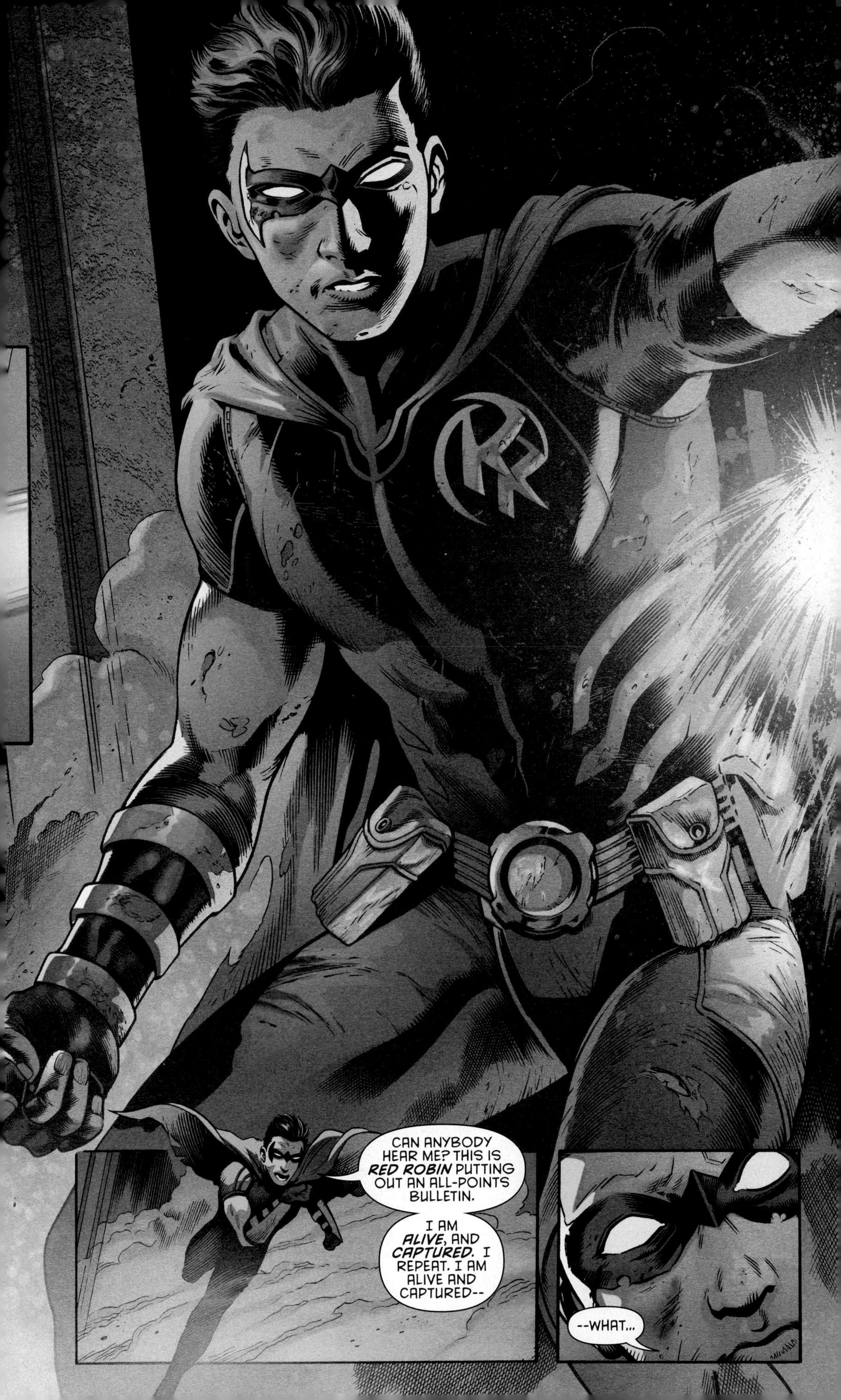

CAN ANYBODY HEAR ME? THIS IS RED ROBIN PUTTING OUT AN ALL-POINTS BULLETIN.
I AM ALIVE, AND CAPTURED. I REPEAT. I AM ALIVE AND CAPTURED--
--WHAT...

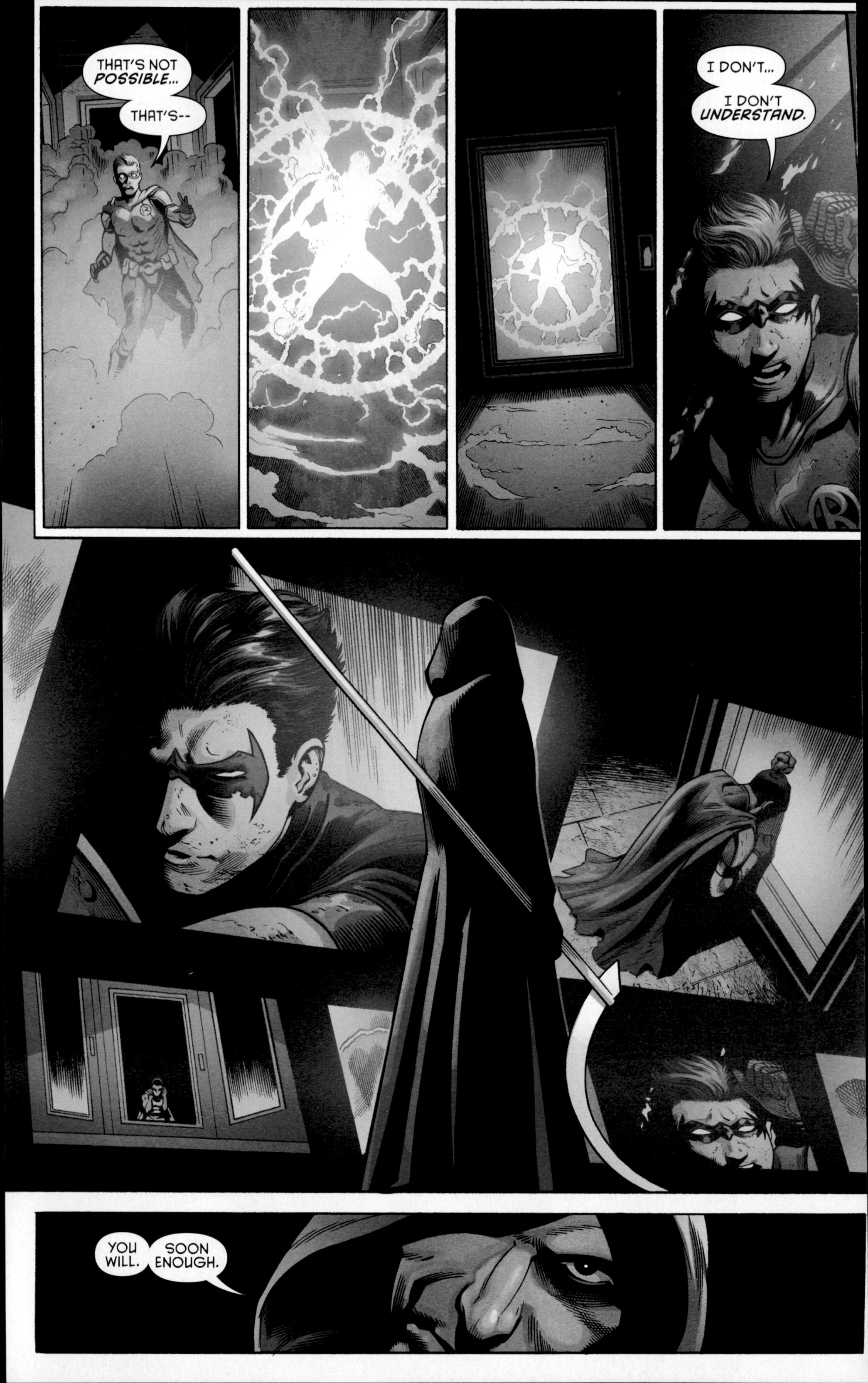
THAT'S NOT *POSSIBLE*...
THAT'S--
I DON'T...
I DON'T *UNDERSTAND*.
YOU WILL.
SOON ENOUGH.

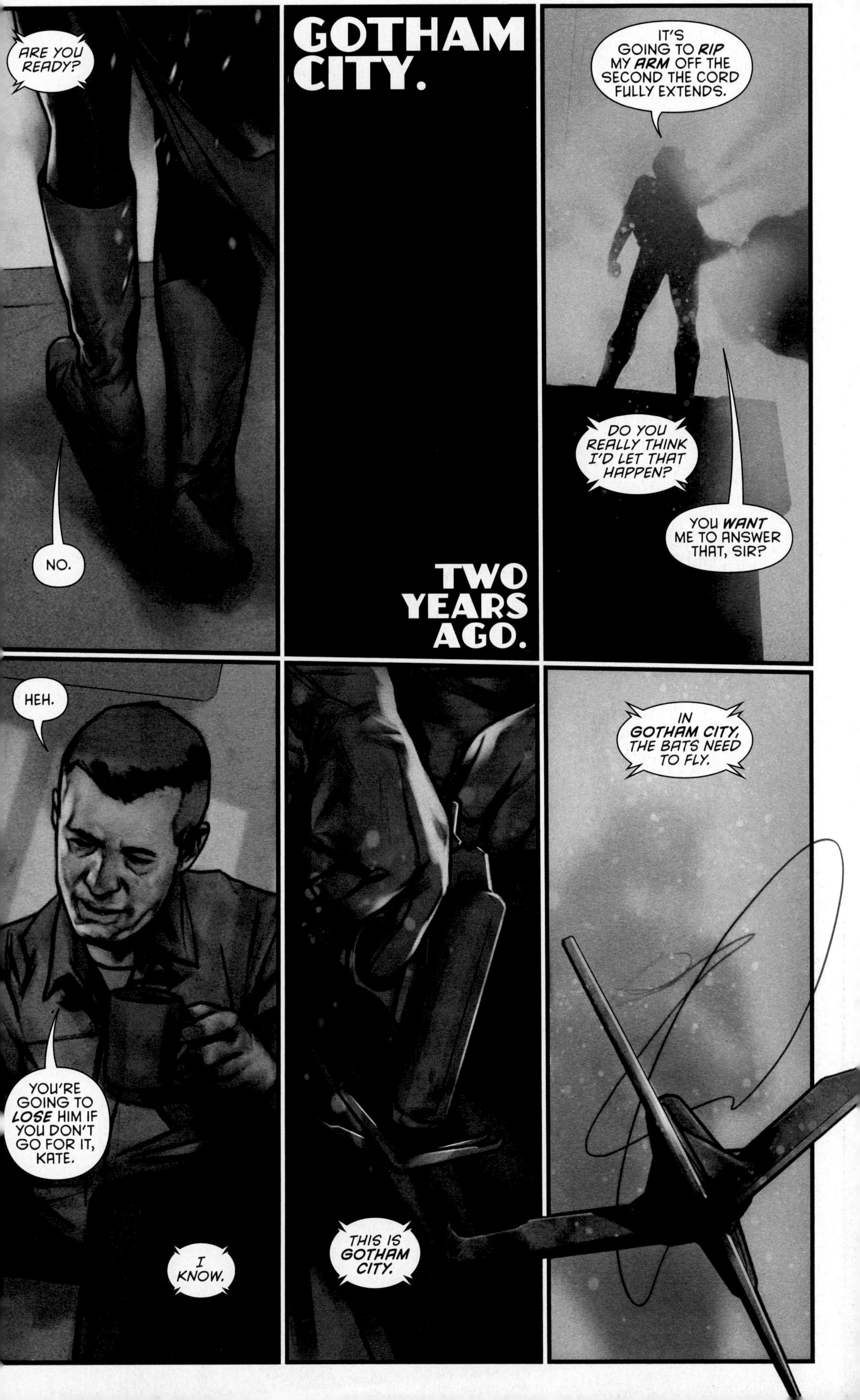
ARE YOU READY?
NO.
GOTHAM CITY.
TWO YEARS AGO.
IT'S GOING TO RIP MY ARM OFF THE SECOND THE CORD FULLY EXTENDS.
DO YOU REALLY THINK I'D LET THAT HAPPEN?
YOU WANT ME TO ANSWER THAT, SIR?
HEH.
YOU'RE GOING TO LOSE HIM IF YOU DON'T GO FOR IT, KATE.
I KNOW.
THIS IS GOTHAM CITY.
IN GOTHAM CITY, THE BATS NEED TO FLY.

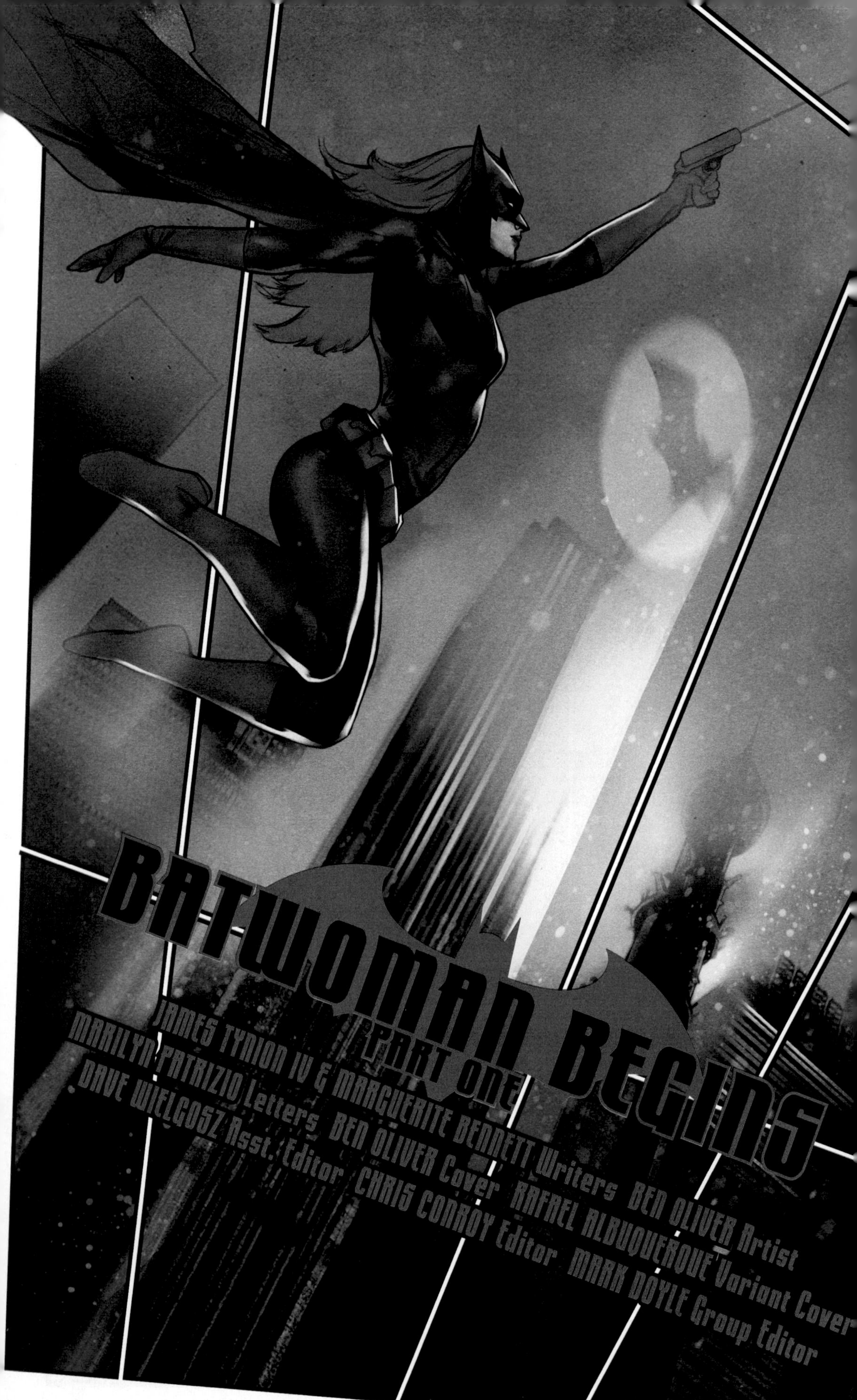
BATWOMAN BEGINS
PART ONE
JAMES TYNION IV & MARGUERITE BENNETT Writers BEN OLIVER Artist
MARILYN PATRIZIO Letters BEN OLIVER Cover RAFAEL ALBUQUERQUE Variant Cover
DAVE WIELGOSZ Asst. Editor CHRIS CONROY Editor MARK DOYLE Group Editor

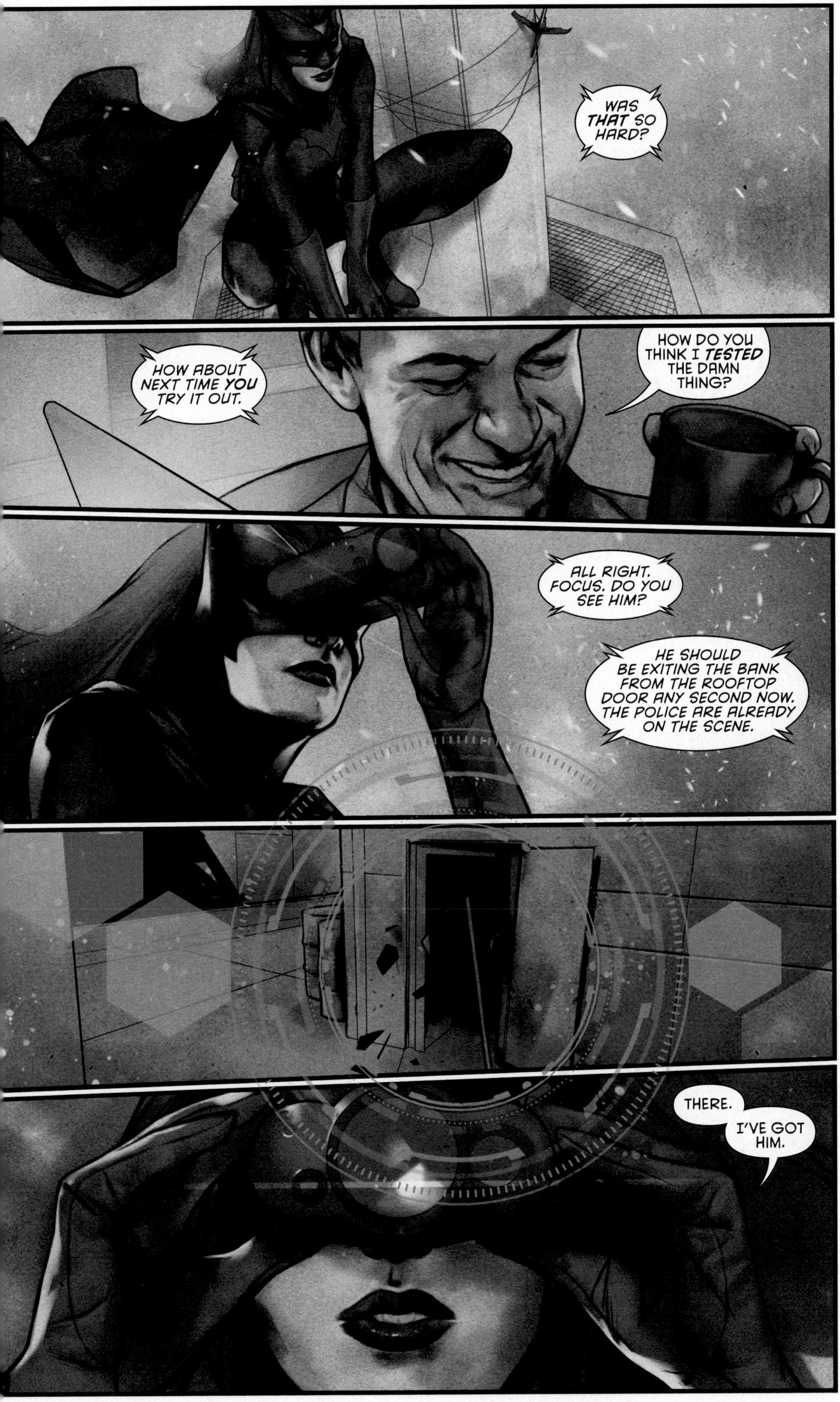
WAS THAT SO HARD?
HOW ABOUT NEXT TIME YOU TRY IT OUT.
HOW DO YOU THINK I TESTED THE DAMN THING?
ALL RIGHT. FOCUS. DO YOU SEE HIM?
HE SHOULD BE EXITING THE BANK FROM THE ROOFTOP DOOR ANY SECOND NOW. THE POLICE ARE ALREADY ON THE SCENE.
THERE.
I'VE GOT HIM.

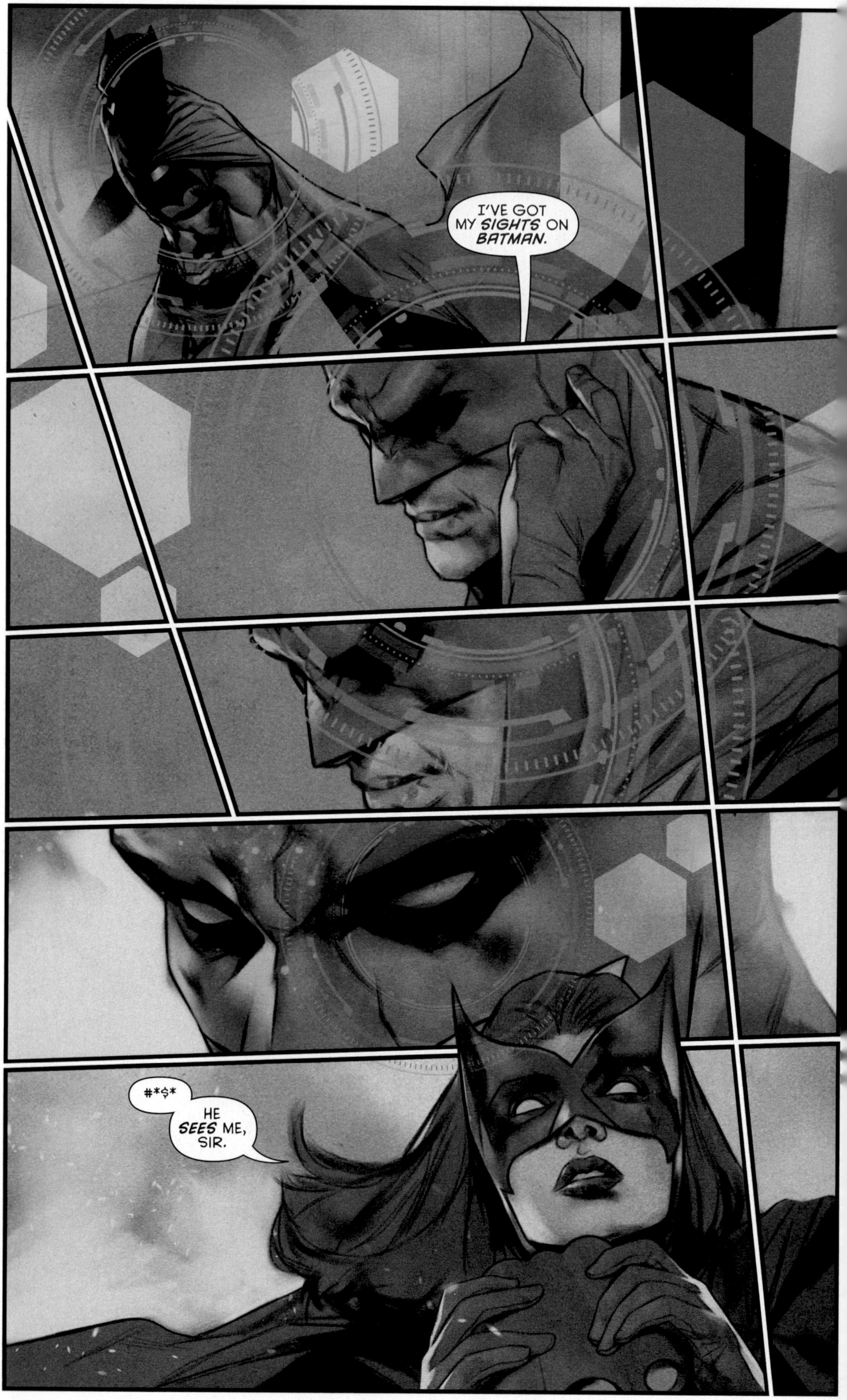
I'VE GOT MY SIGHTS ON BATMAN.
#*$*
HE SEES ME, SIR.

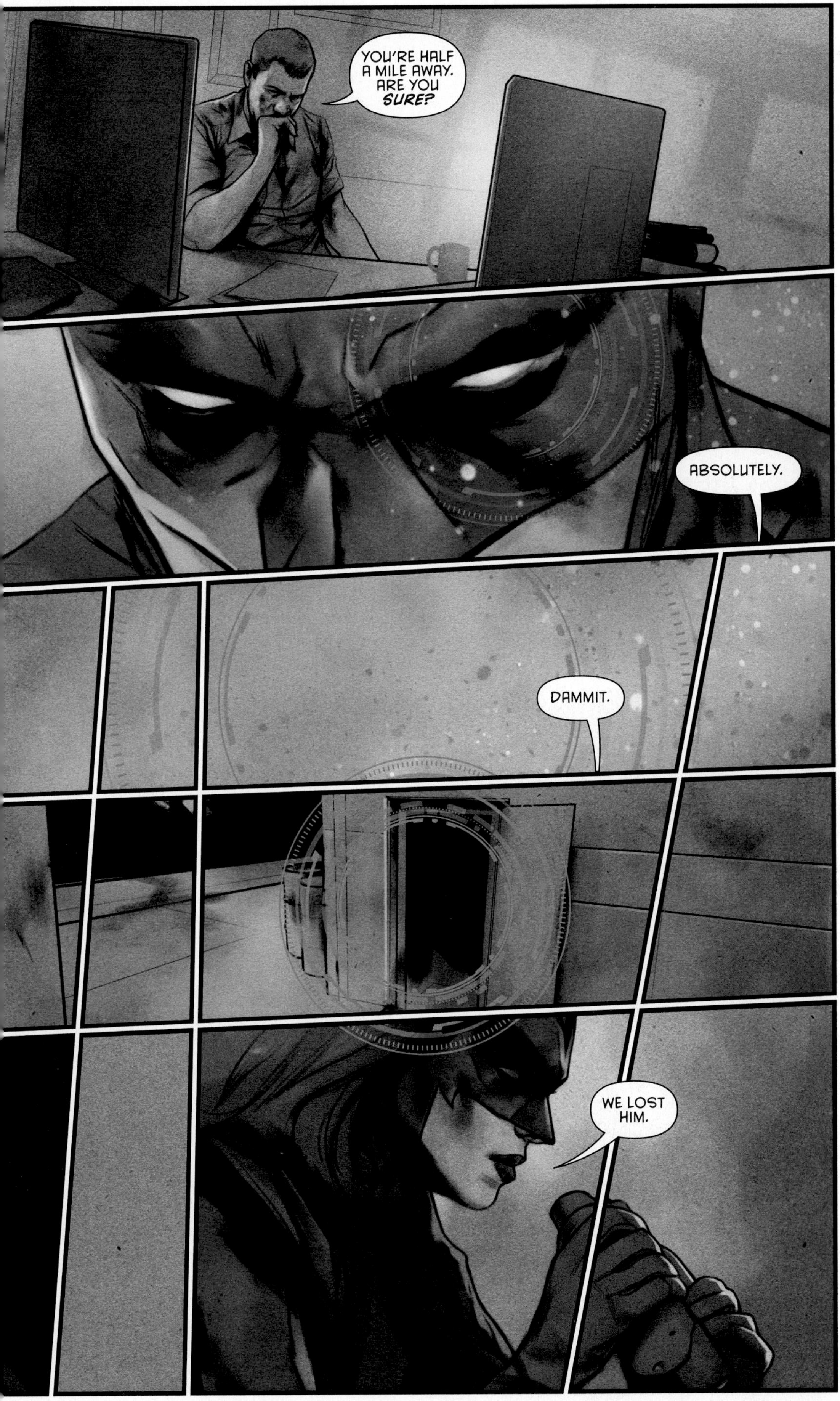
YOU'RE HALF A MILE AWAY. ARE YOU *SURE?*
ABSOLUTELY.
DAMMIT.
WE LOST HIM.

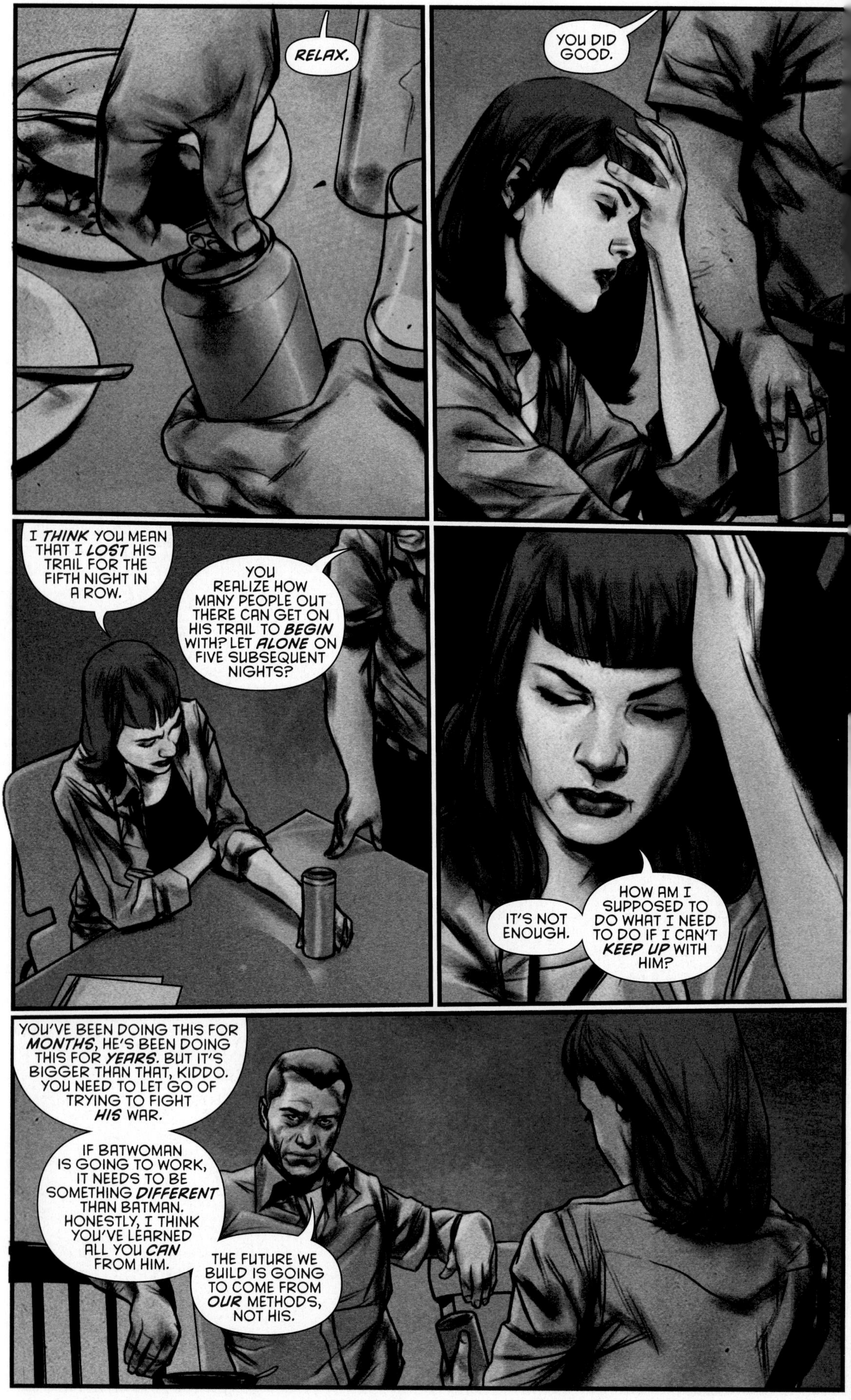
RELAX.
YOU DID GOOD.
I THINK YOU MEAN THAT I LOST HIS TRAIL FOR THE FIFTH NIGHT IN A ROW.
YOU REALIZE HOW MANY PEOPLE OUT THERE CAN GET ON HIS TRAIL TO BEGIN WITH? LET ALONE ON FIVE SUBSEQUENT NIGHTS?
IT'S NOT ENOUGH.
HOW AM I SUPPOSED TO DO WHAT I NEED TO DO IF I CAN'T KEEP UP WITH HIM?
YOU'VE BEEN DOING THIS FOR MONTHS, HE'S BEEN DOING THIS FOR YEARS. BUT IT'S BIGGER THAN THAT, KIDDO. YOU NEED TO LET GO OF TRYING TO FIGHT HIS WAR.
IF BATWOMAN IS GOING TO WORK, IT NEEDS TO BE SOMETHING DIFFERENT THAN BATMAN. HONESTLY, I THINK YOU'VE LEARNED ALL YOU CAN FROM HIM.
THE FUTURE WE BUILD IS GOING TO COME FROM OUR METHODS, NOT HIS.

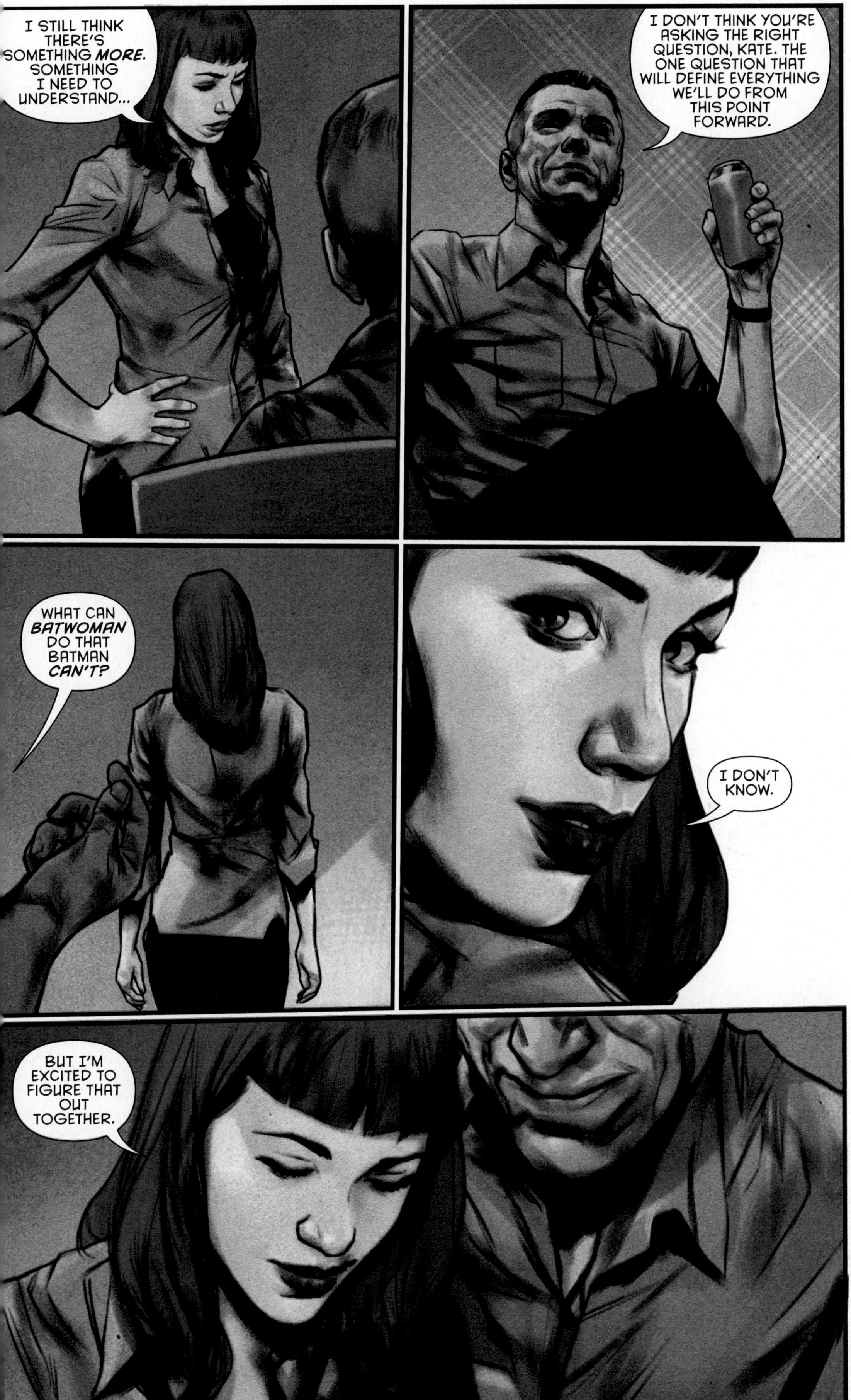
I STILL THINK THERE'S SOMETHING *MORE*. SOMETHING I NEED TO UNDERSTAND...
I DON'T THINK YOU'RE ASKING THE RIGHT QUESTION, KATE. THE ONE QUESTION THAT WILL DEFINE EVERYTHING WE'LL DO FROM THIS POINT FORWARD.
WHAT CAN *BATWOMAN* DO THAT BATMAN *CAN'T?*
I DON'T KNOW.
BUT I'M EXCITED TO FIGURE THAT OUT TOGETHER.

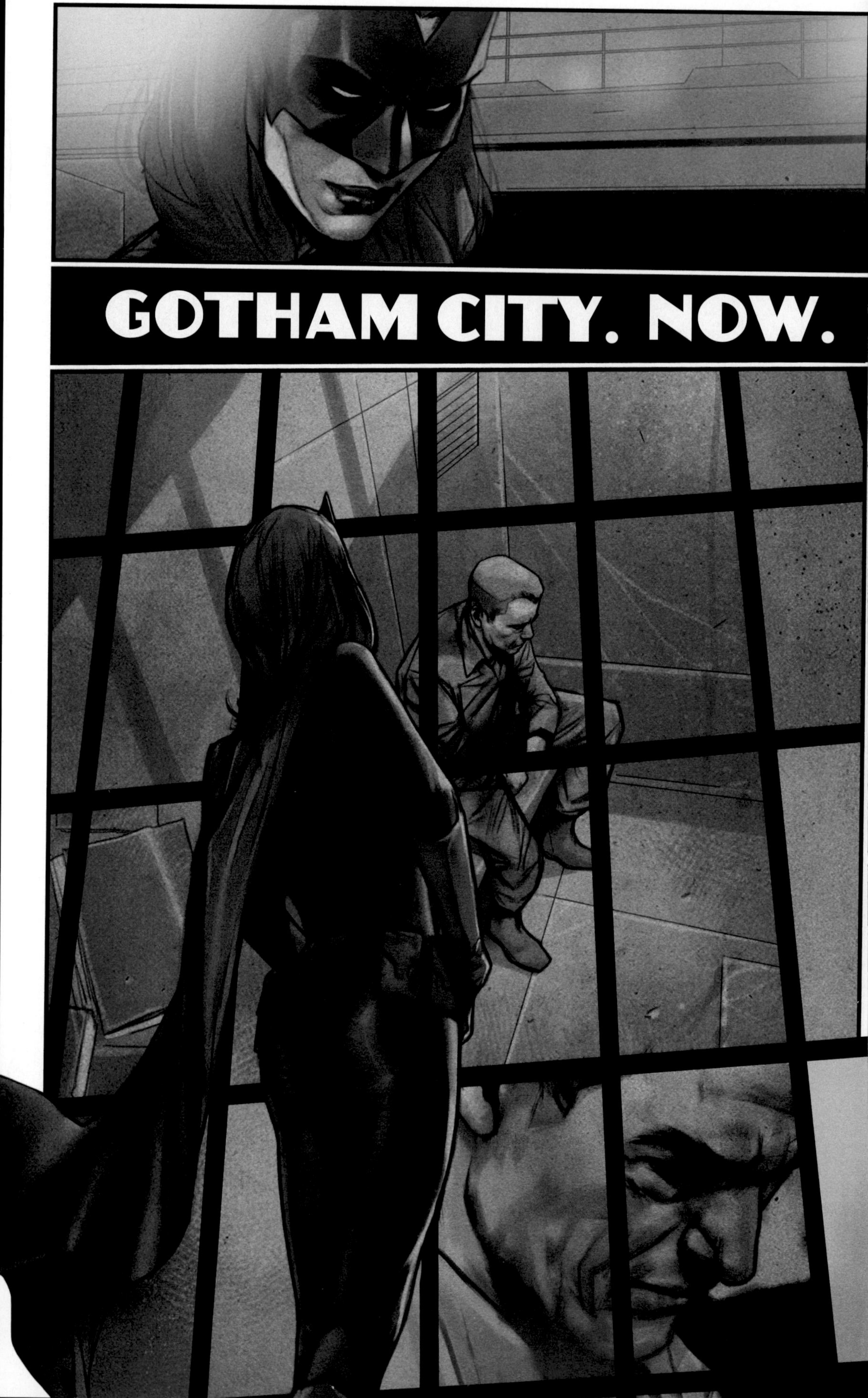
GOTHAM CITY. NOW.

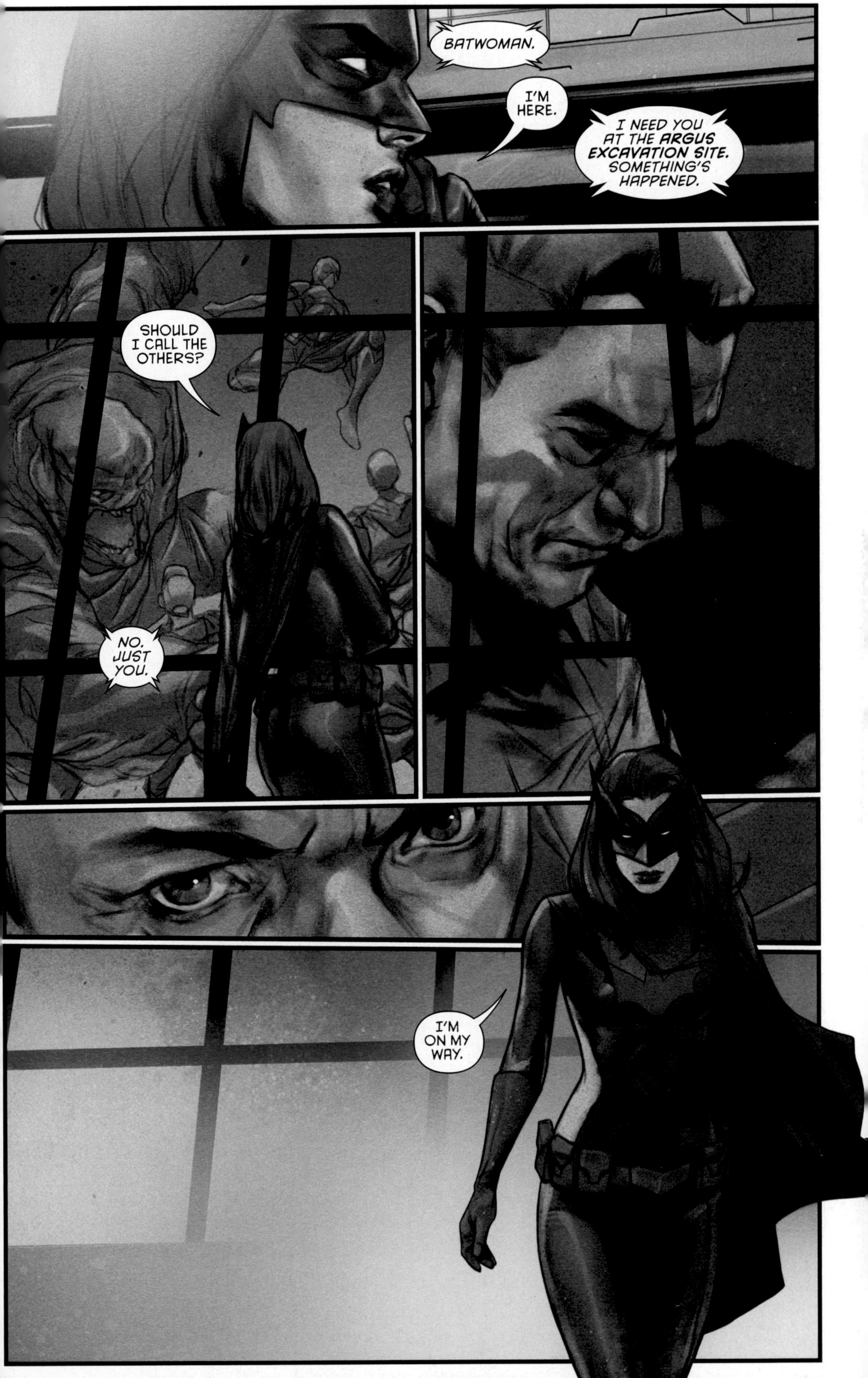
BATWOMAN.
I'M HERE.
I NEED YOU AT THE ARGUS EXCAVATION SITE. SOMETHING'S HAPPENED.
SHOULD I CALL THE OTHERS?
NO. JUST YOU.
I'M ON MY WAY.

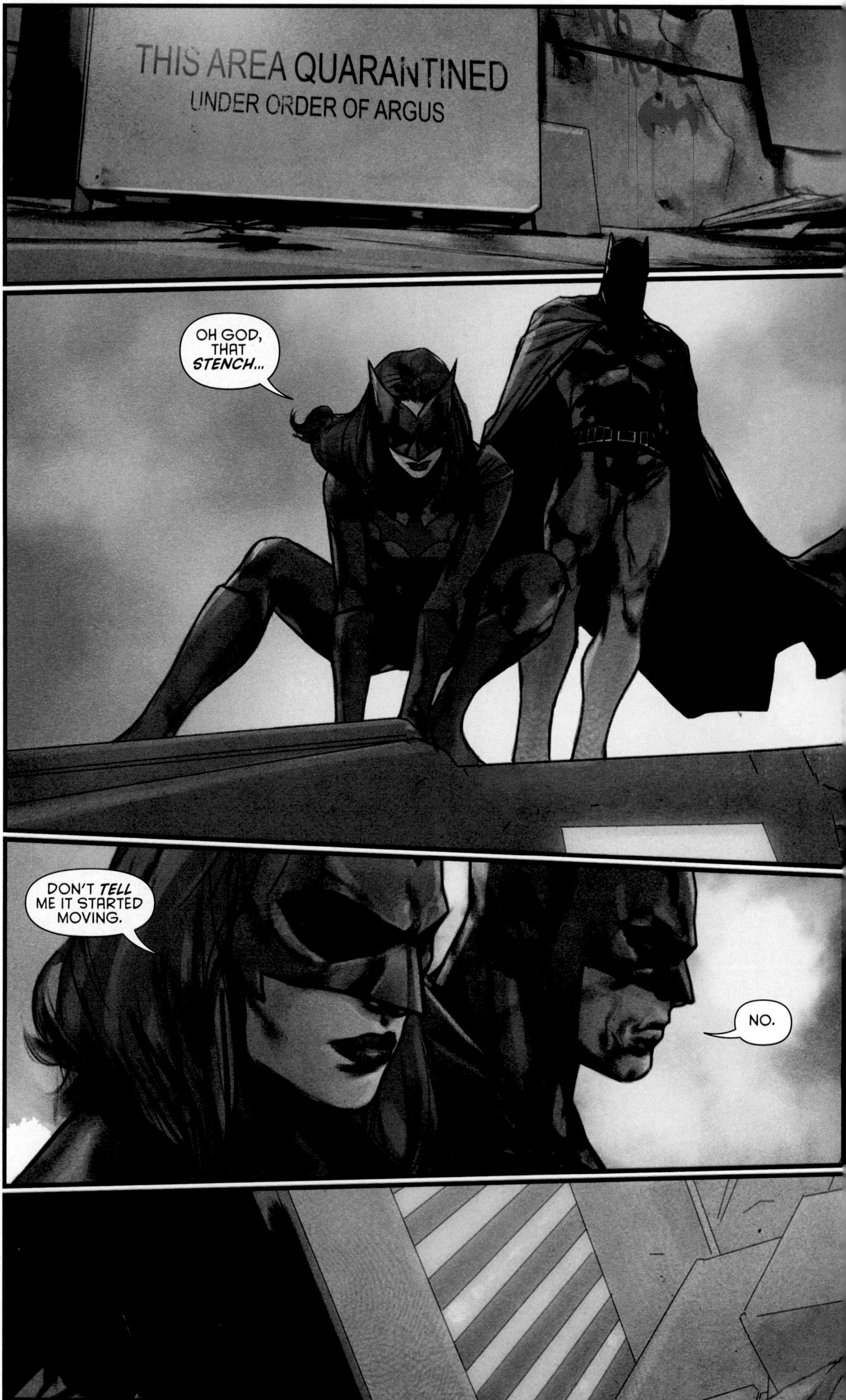
THIS AREA QUARANTINED
UNDER ORDER OF ARGUS
OH GOD, THAT STENCH...
DON'T TELL ME IT STARTED MOVING.
NO.

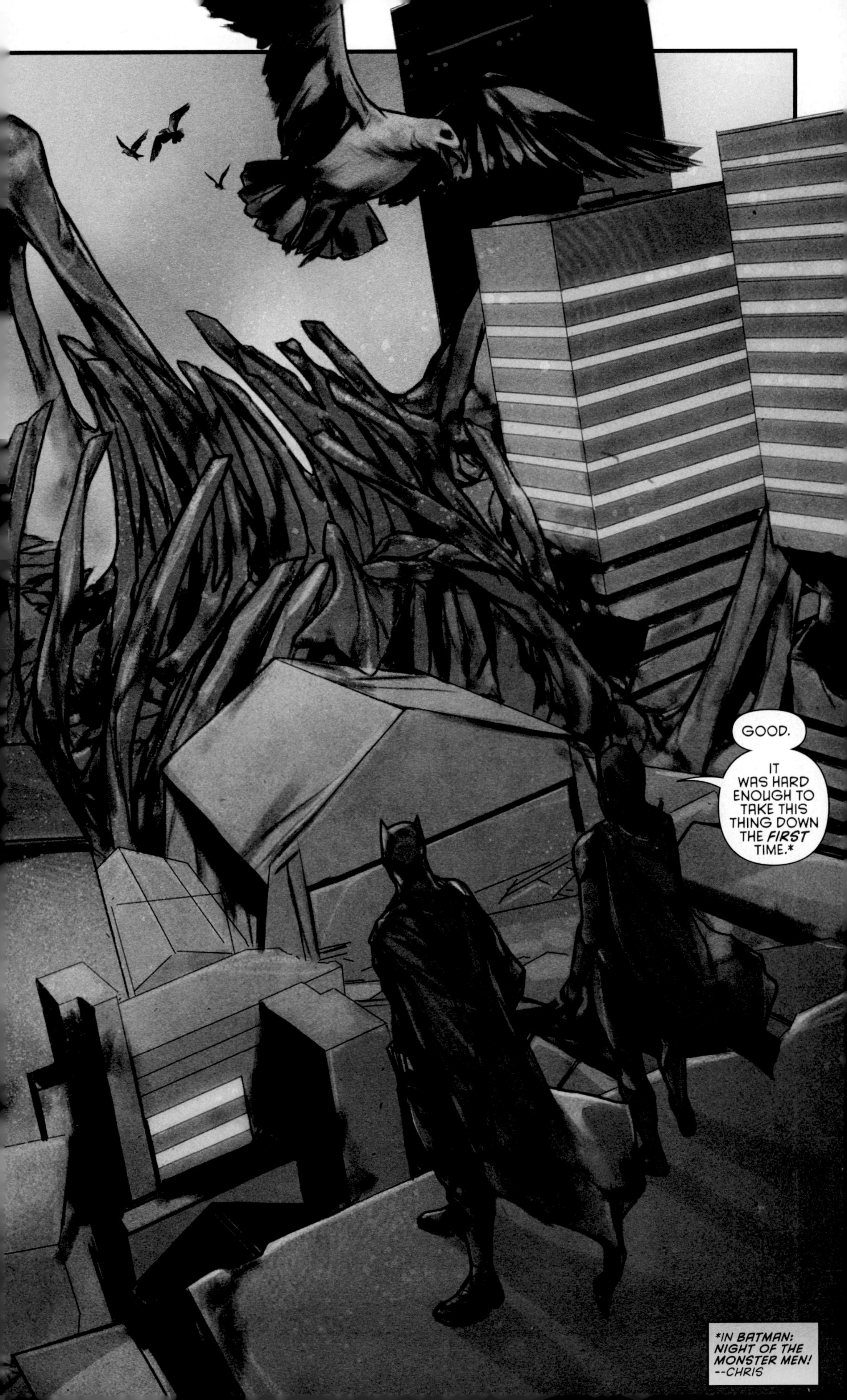
GOOD.
IT WAS HARD ENOUGH TO TAKE THIS THING DOWN THE *FIRST* TIME.*
*IN *BATMAN: NIGHT OF THE MONSTER MEN!* --CHRIS

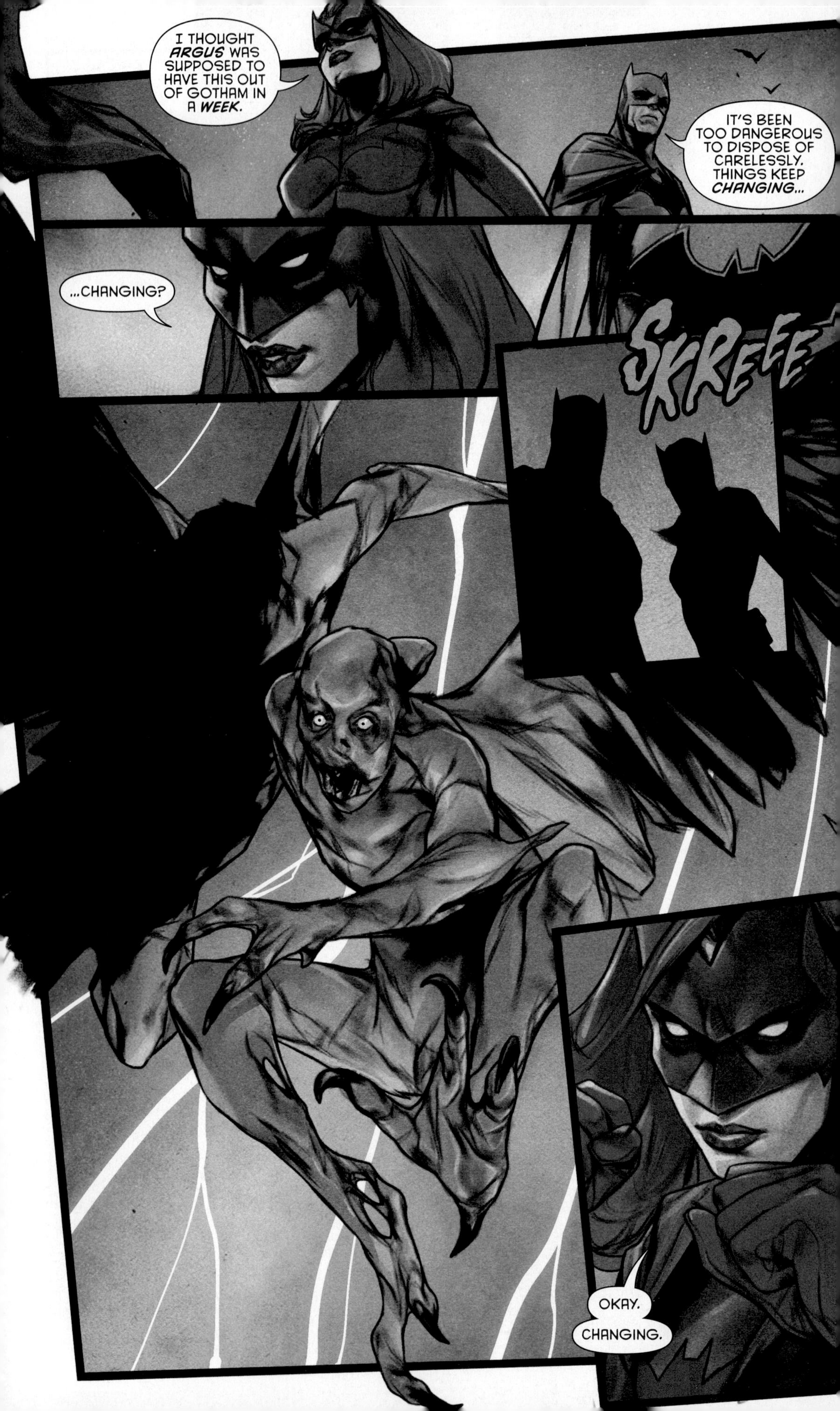
I THOUGHT ARGUS WAS SUPPOSED TO HAVE THIS OUT OF GOTHAM IN A WEEK.
IT'S BEEN TOO DANGEROUS TO DISPOSE OF CARELESSLY. THINGS KEEP CHANGING...
...CHANGING?
SKREEE
OKAY.
CHANGING.

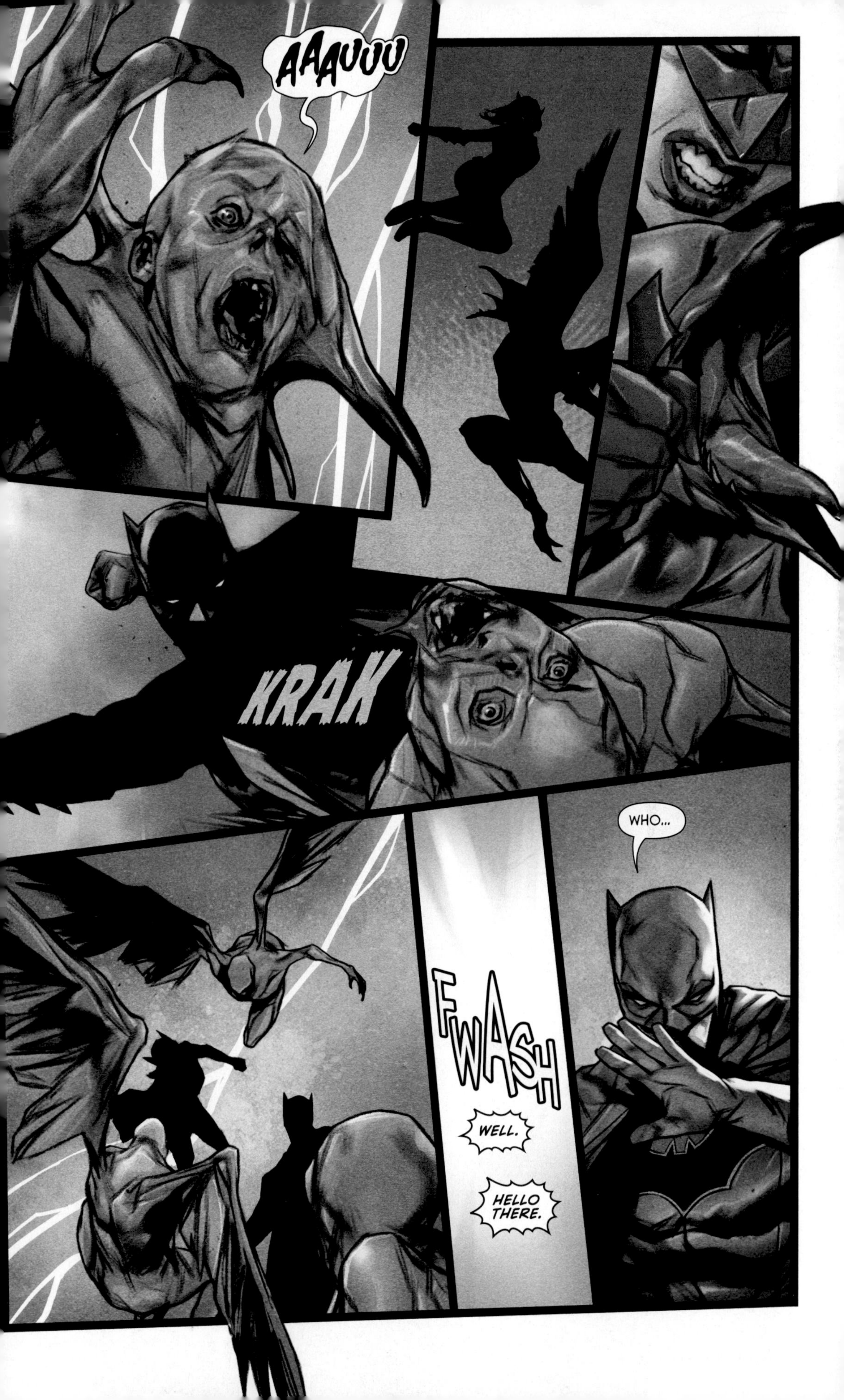
AAAUUU
KRAK
WHO...
FWASH
WELL.
HELLO THERE.

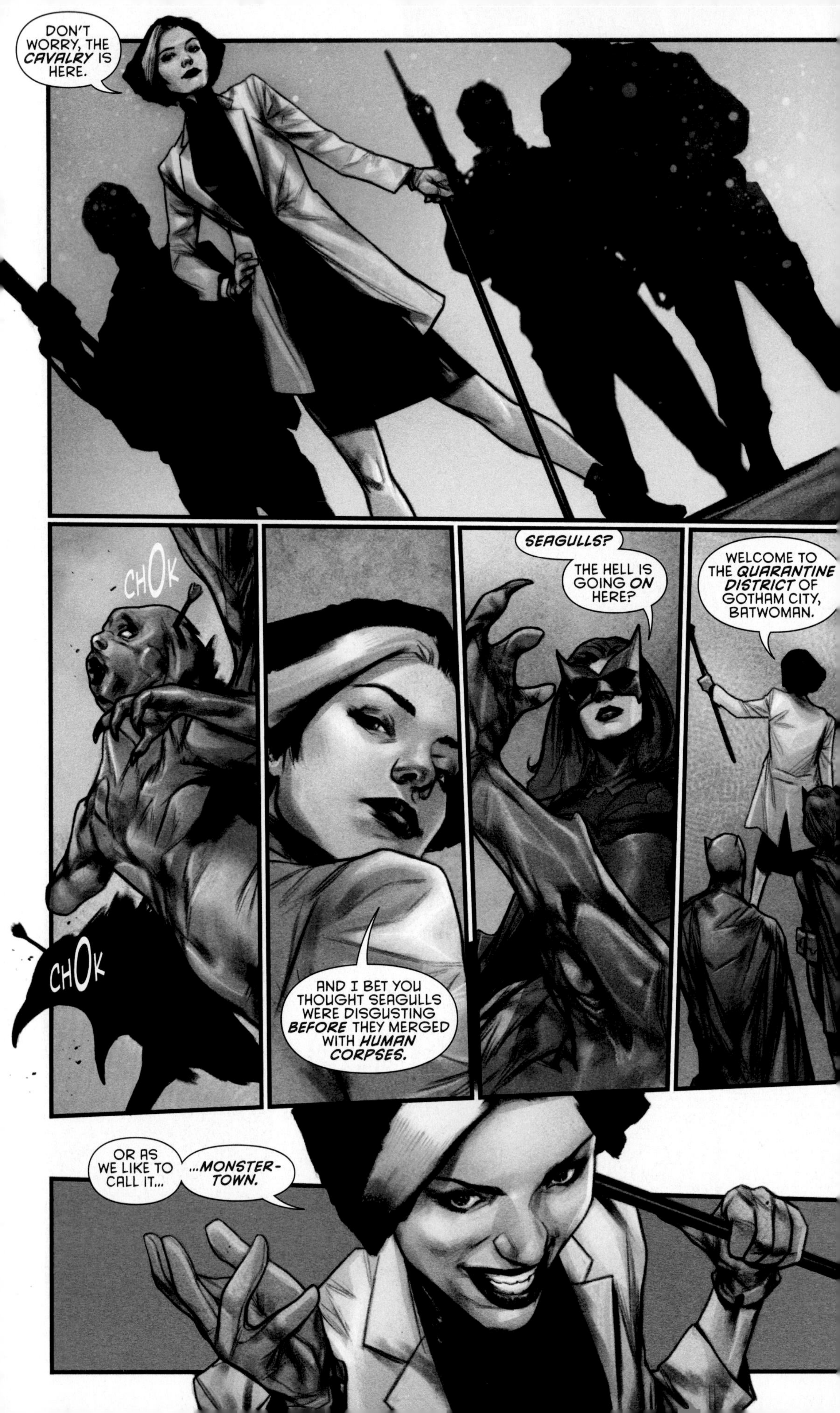
DON'T WORRY, THE CAVALRY IS HERE.
CHOK
CHOK
AND I BET YOU THOUGHT SEAGULLS WERE DISGUSTING BEFORE THEY MERGED WITH HUMAN CORPSES.
SEAGULLS?
THE HELL IS GOING ON HERE?
WELCOME TO THE QUARANTINE DISTRICT OF GOTHAM CITY, BATWOMAN.
OR AS WE LIKE TO CALL IT...
...MONSTER-TOWN.

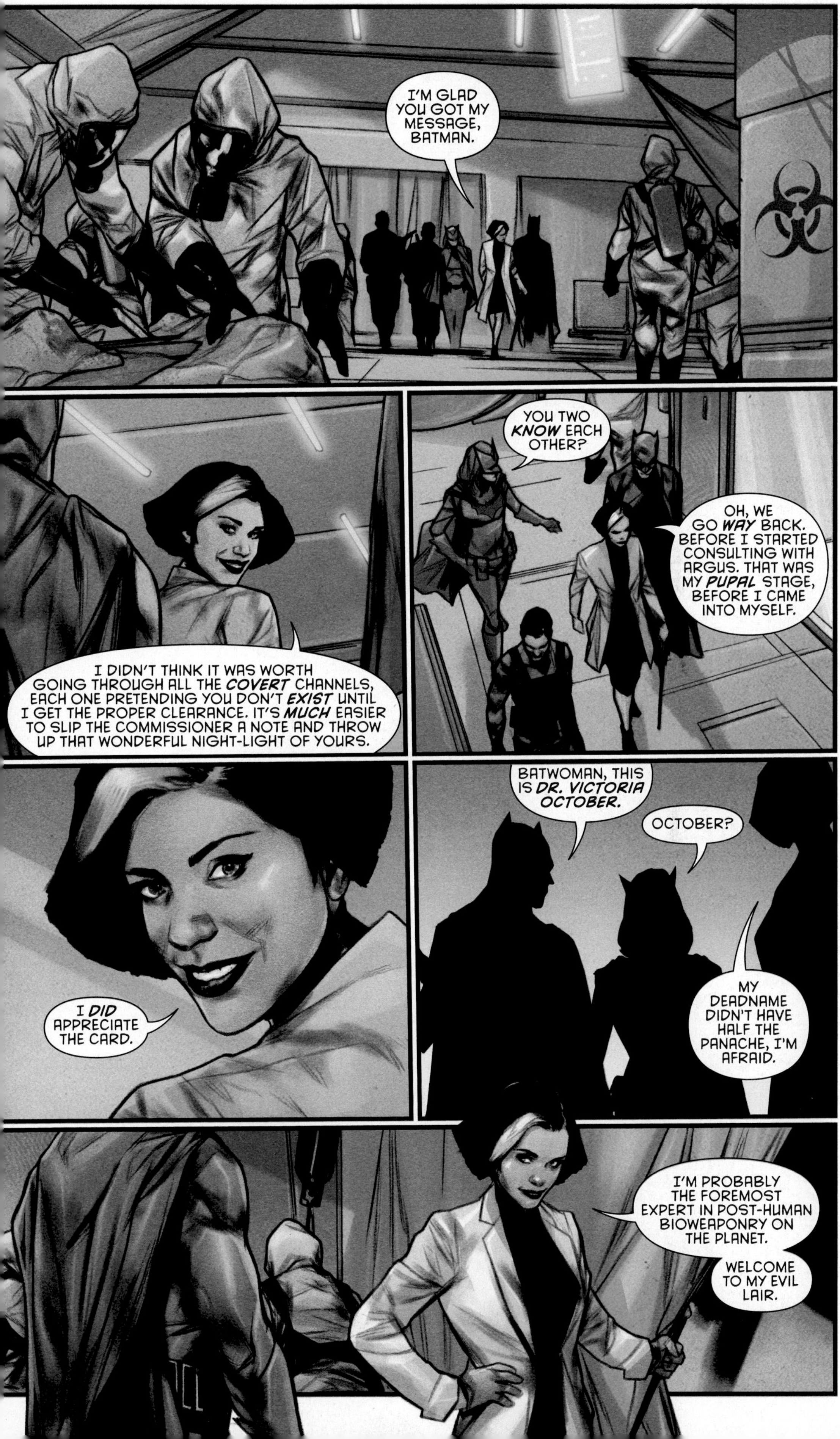
I'M GLAD YOU GOT MY MESSAGE, BATMAN.
I DIDN'T THINK IT WAS WORTH GOING THROUGH ALL THE COVERT CHANNELS, EACH ONE PRETENDING YOU DON'T EXIST UNTIL I GET THE PROPER CLEARANCE. IT'S MUCH EASIER TO SLIP THE COMMISSIONER A NOTE AND THROW UP THAT WONDERFUL NIGHT-LIGHT OF YOURS.
YOU TWO KNOW EACH OTHER?
OH, WE GO WAY BACK. BEFORE I STARTED CONSULTING WITH ARGUS. THAT WAS MY PUPAL STAGE, BEFORE I CAME INTO MYSELF.
I DID APPRECIATE THE CARD.
BATWOMAN, THIS IS DR. VICTORIA OCTOBER.
OCTOBER?
MY DEADNAME DIDN'T HAVE HALF THE PANACHE, I'M AFRAID.
I'M PROBABLY THE FOREMOST EXPERT IN POST-HUMAN BIOWEAPONRY ON THE PLANET.
WELCOME TO MY EVIL LAIR.

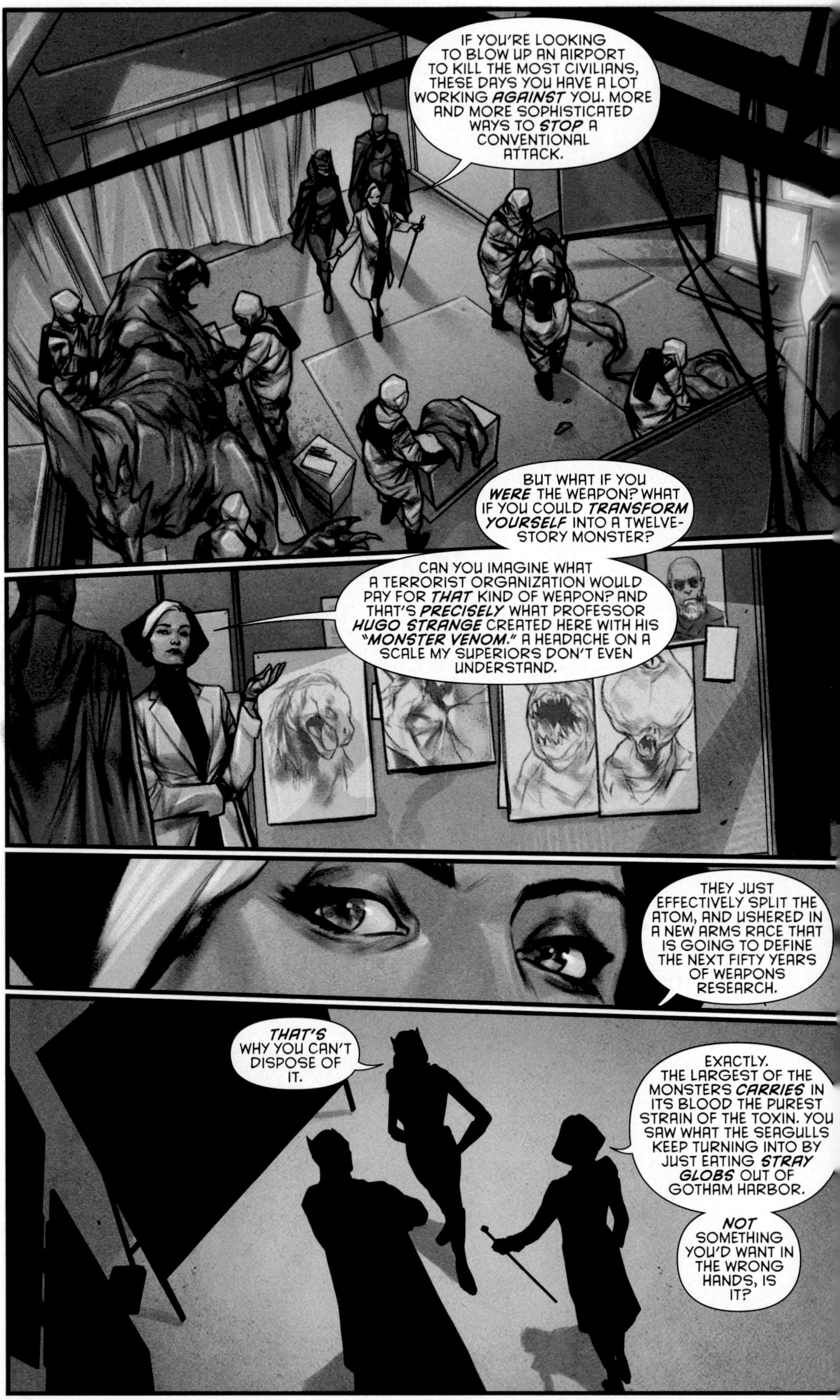
IF YOU'RE LOOKING TO BLOW UP AN AIRPORT TO KILL THE MOST CIVILIANS, THESE DAYS YOU HAVE A LOT WORKING *AGAINST* YOU. MORE AND MORE SOPHISTICATED WAYS TO *STOP* A CONVENTIONAL ATTACK.
BUT WHAT IF YOU *WERE* THE WEAPON? WHAT IF YOU COULD *TRANSFORM YOURSELF* INTO A TWELVE-STORY MONSTER?
CAN YOU IMAGINE WHAT A TERRORIST ORGANIZATION WOULD PAY FOR *THAT* KIND OF WEAPON? AND THAT'S *PRECISELY* WHAT PROFESSOR *HUGO STRANGE* CREATED HERE WITH HIS *"MONSTER VENOM."* A HEADACHE ON A SCALE MY SUPERIORS DON'T EVEN UNDERSTAND.
THEY JUST EFFECTIVELY SPLIT THE ATOM, AND USHERED IN A NEW ARMS RACE THAT IS GOING TO DEFINE THE NEXT FIFTY YEARS OF WEAPONS RESEARCH.
THAT'S WHY YOU CAN'T DISPOSE OF IT.
EXACTLY. THE LARGEST OF THE MONSTERS *CARRIES* IN ITS BLOOD THE PUREST STRAIN OF THE TOXIN. YOU SAW WHAT THE SEAGULLS KEEP TURNING INTO BY JUST EATING *STRAY GLOBS* OUT OF GOTHAM HARBOR.
NOT SOMETHING YOU'D WANT IN THE WRONG HANDS, IS IT?

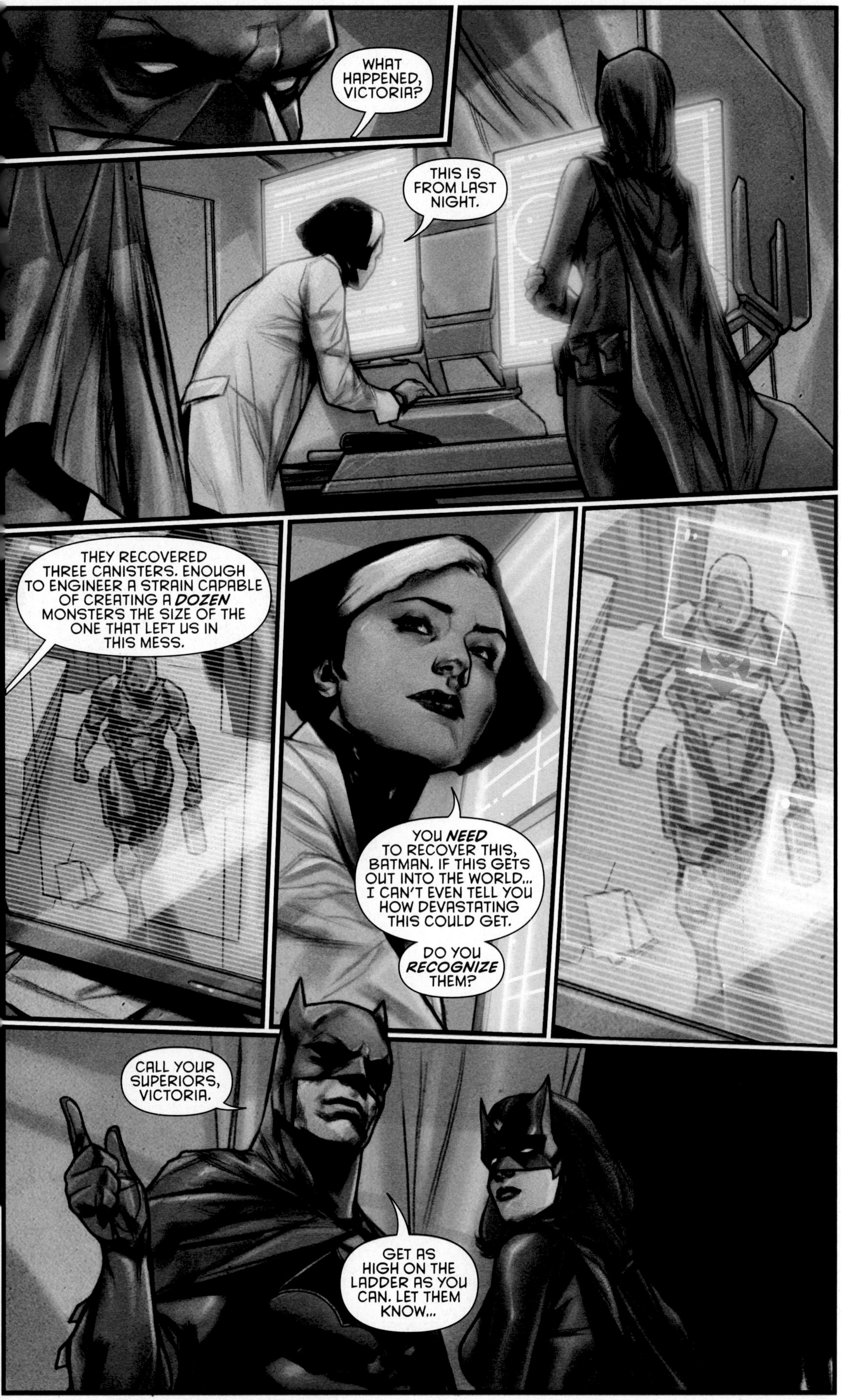

WHAT HAPPENED, VICTORIA?
THIS IS FROM LAST NIGHT.
THEY RECOVERED THREE CANISTERS. ENOUGH TO ENGINEER A STRAIN CAPABLE OF CREATING A *DOZEN* MONSTERS THE SIZE OF THE ONE THAT LEFT US IN THIS MESS.
YOU *NEED* TO RECOVER THIS, BATMAN. IF THIS GETS OUT INTO THE WORLD... I CAN'T EVEN TELL YOU HOW DEVASTATING THIS COULD GET.
DO YOU *RECOGNIZE* THEM?
CALL YOUR SUPERIORS, VICTORIA.
GET AS HIGH ON THE LADDER AS YOU CAN. LET THEM KNOW...

"...*THE COLONY* IS BACK IN GOTHAM CITY."

SIR.

THIS IS *COLONY PRIME*. READY TO GET YOU THE HELL OUT OF HERE.

HA. I GUESS *THANKS* WILL COME LATER, SIR.

I'VE GOT THE FREQUENCY YOUR INTERC WIRED INTO SUIT. I NEED TO TELL ME H TO GET YOU OF HERE WITH SOUNDING ALARMS.

THERE'S NO WAY IN *HELL* YOU WERE AUTHORIZED TO EXTRACT ME, SIMON.

THIS IS *FOOLISH* OF YOU.

SORRY. THAT'S *NOT* HAPPENING.

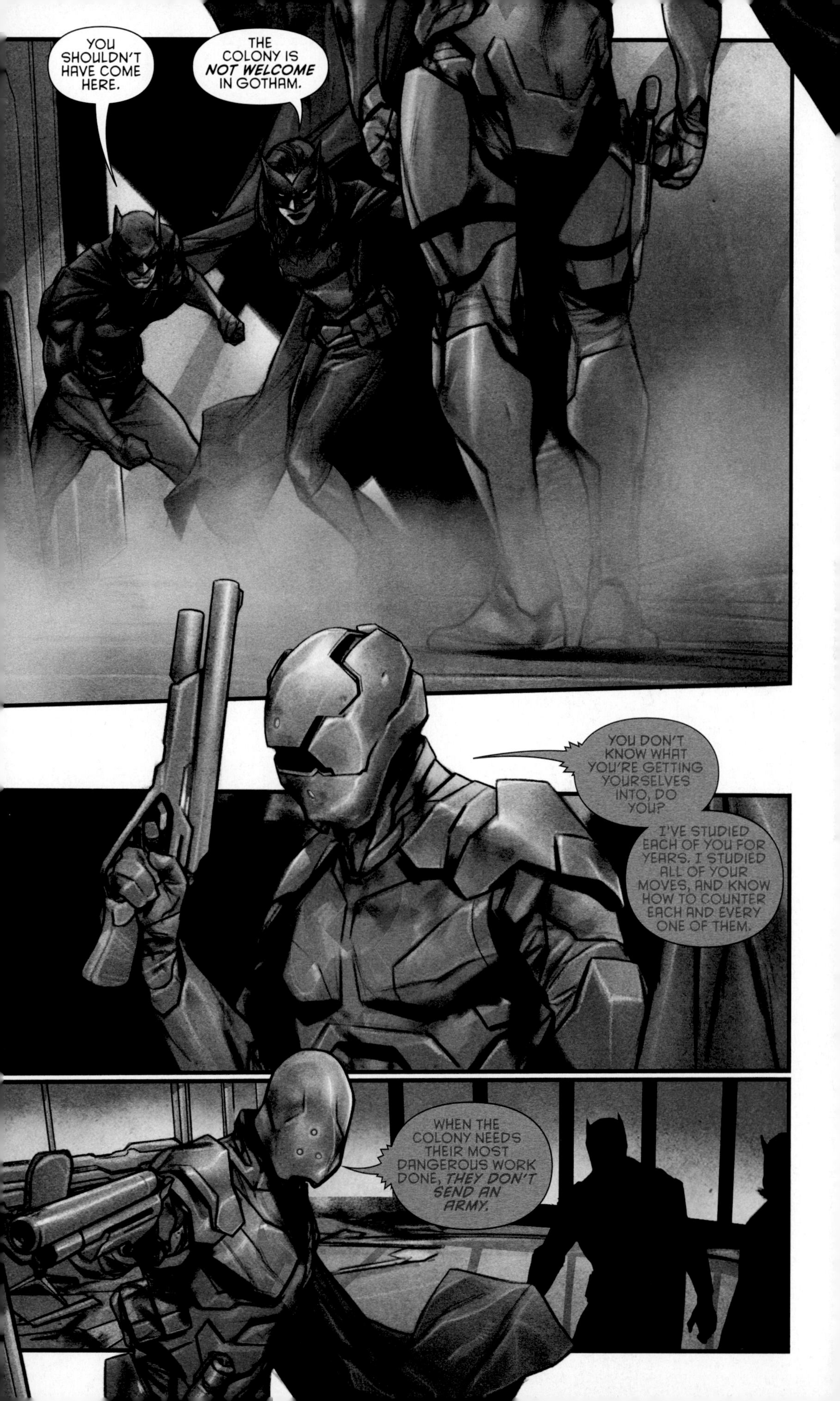
YOU SHOULDN'T HAVE COME HERE.
THE COLONY IS *NOT WELCOME* IN GOTHAM.
YOU DON'T KNOW WHAT YOU'RE GETTING YOURSELVES INTO, DO YOU?
I'VE STUDIED EACH OF YOU FOR YEARS. I STUDIED ALL OF YOUR MOVES, AND KNOW HOW TO COUNTER EACH AND EVERY ONE OF THEM.
WHEN THE COLONY NEEDS THEIR MOST DANGEROUS WORK DONE, *THEY DON'T SEND AN ARMY.*

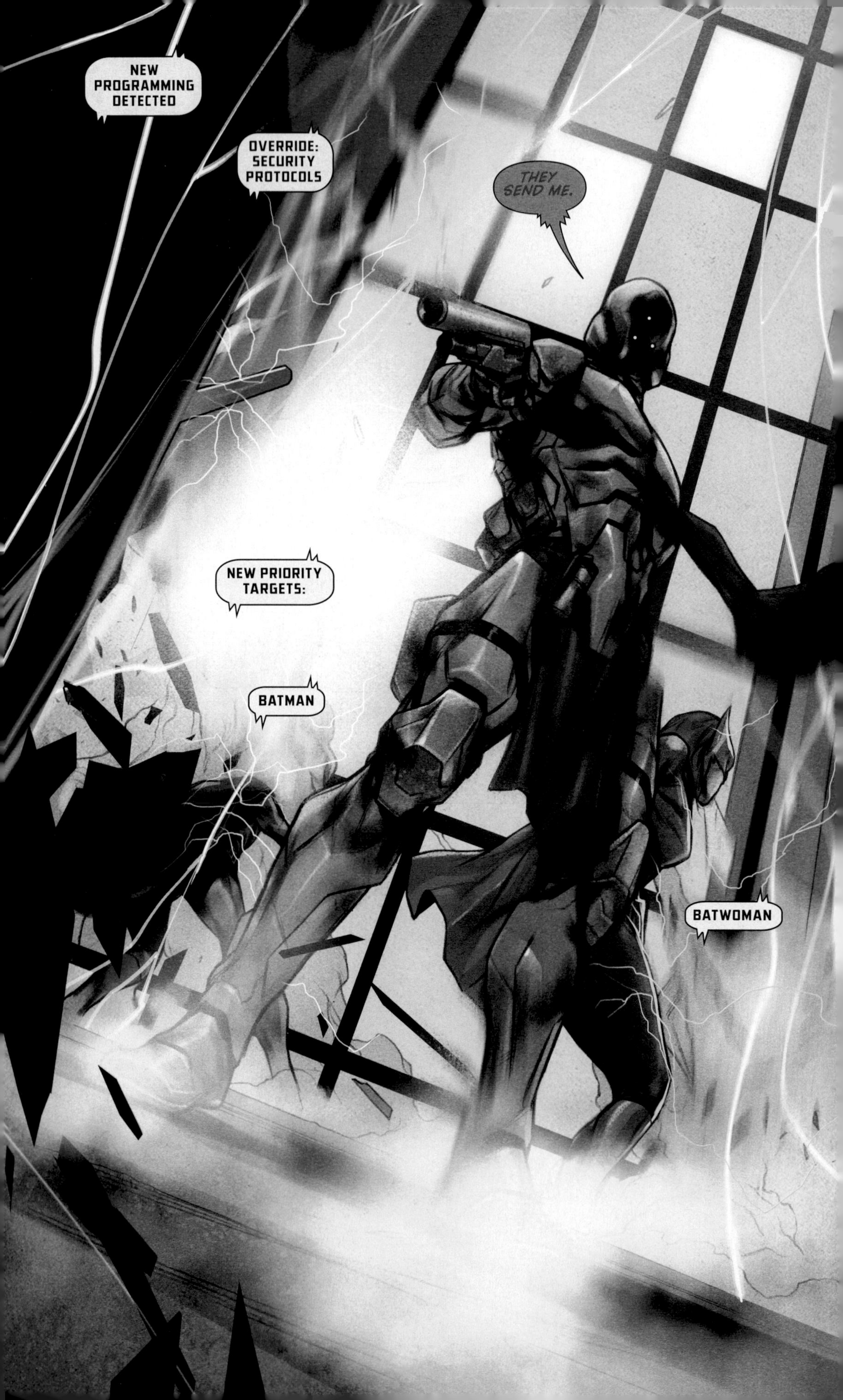
NEW PROGRAMMING DETECTED
OVERRIDE: SECURITY PROTOCOLS
THEY SEND ME.
NEW PRIORITY TARGETS:
BATMAN
BATWOMAN

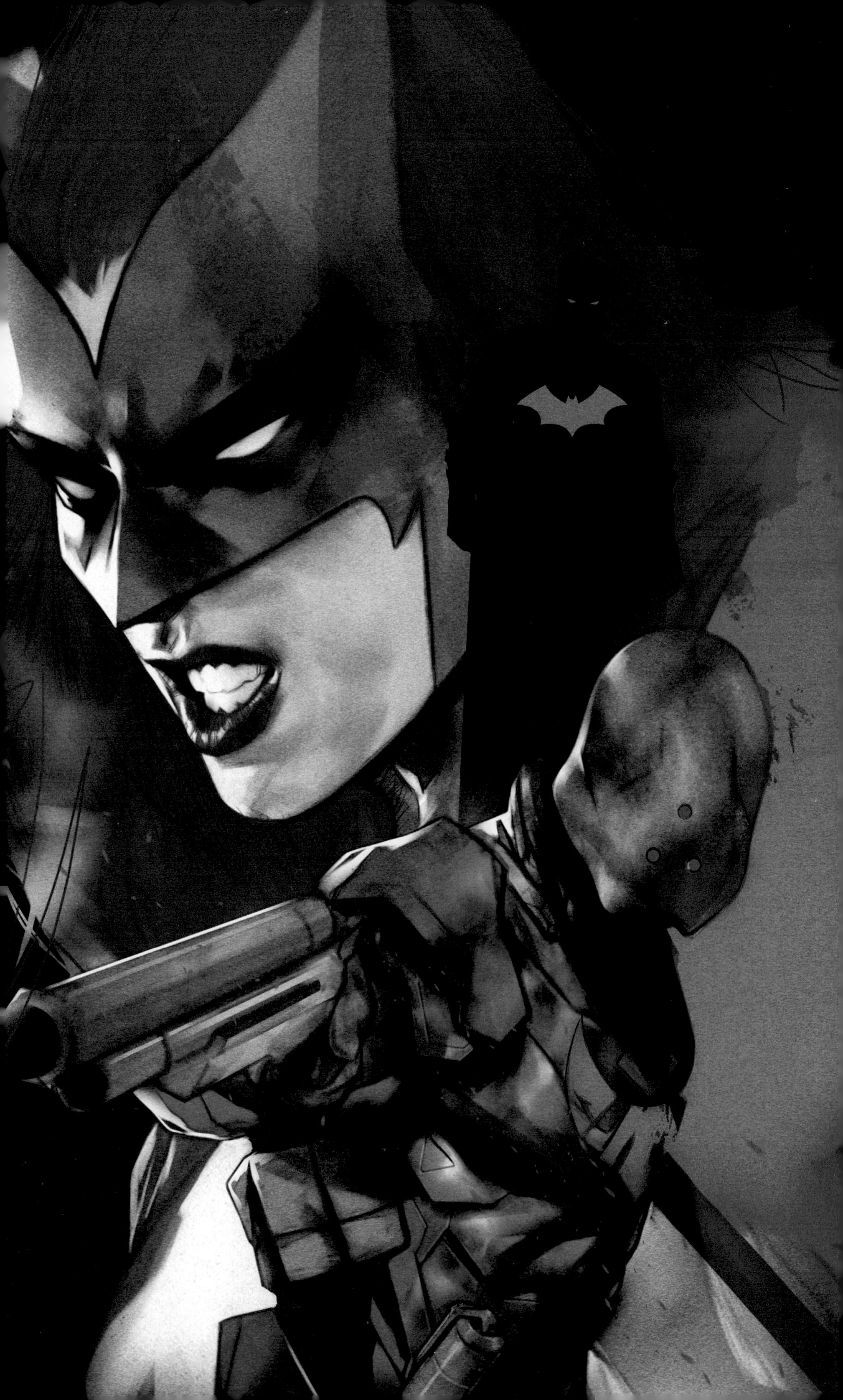

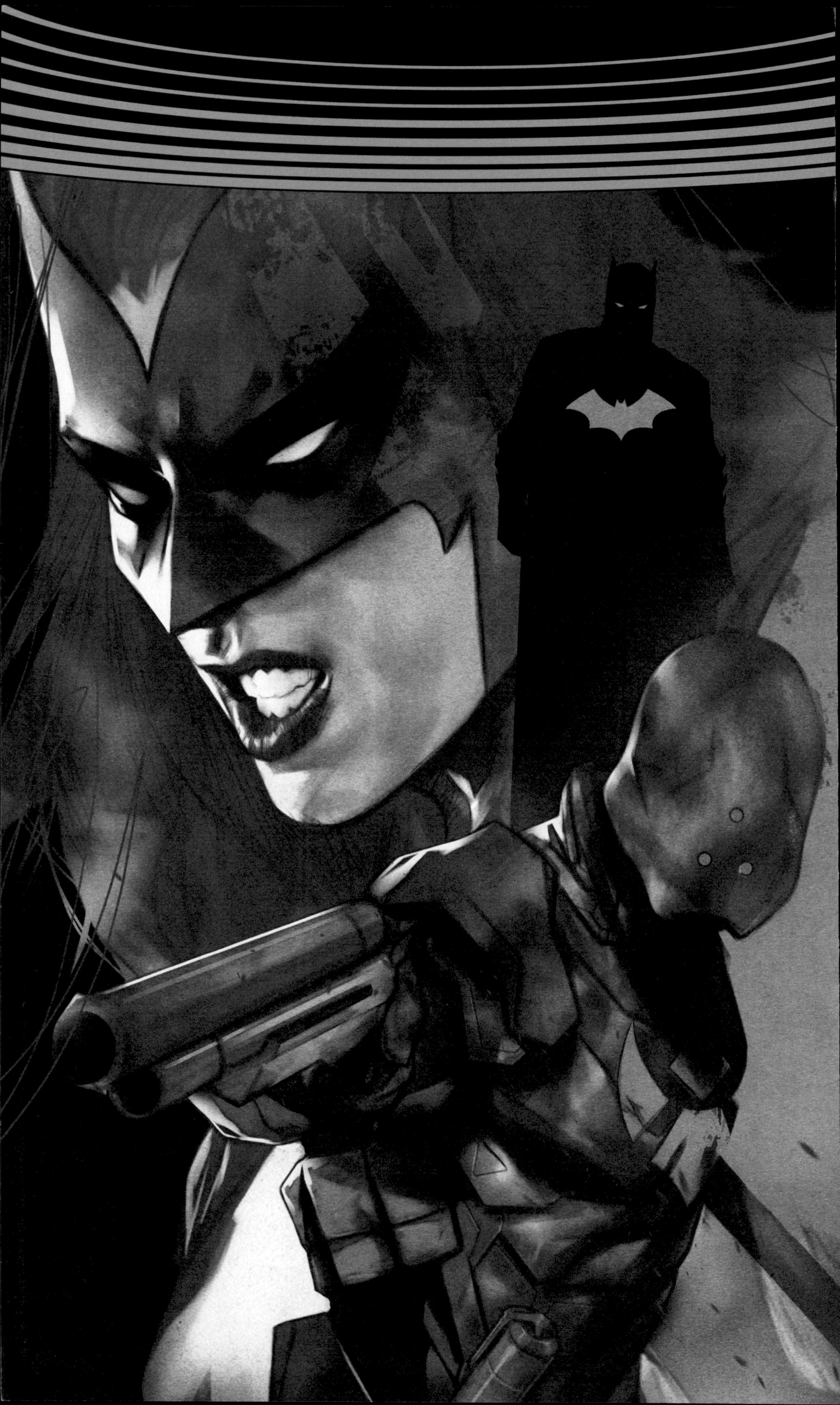

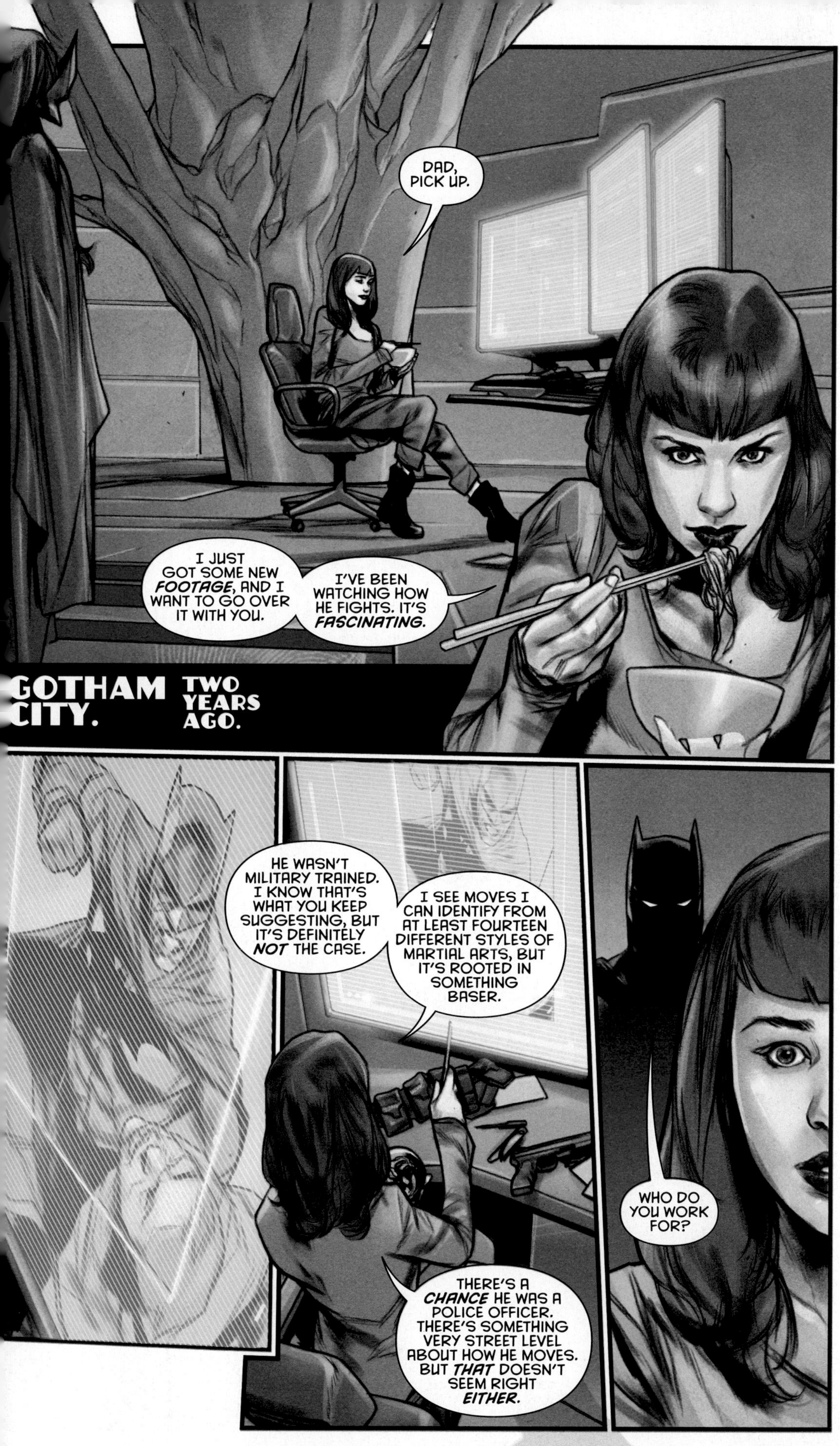
DAD, PICK UP.
I JUST GOT SOME NEW FOOTAGE, AND I WANT TO GO OVER IT WITH YOU.
I'VE BEEN WATCHING HOW HE FIGHTS. IT'S FASCINATING.
GOTHAM CITY.
TWO YEARS AGO.
HE WASN'T MILITARY TRAINED. I KNOW THAT'S WHAT YOU KEEP SUGGESTING, BUT IT'S DEFINITELY NOT THE CASE.
I SEE MOVES I CAN IDENTIFY FROM AT LEAST FOURTEEN DIFFERENT STYLES OF MARTIAL ARTS, BUT IT'S ROOTED IN SOMETHING BASER.
THERE'S A CHANCE HE WAS A POLICE OFFICER. THERE'S SOMETHING VERY STREET LEVEL ABOUT HOW HE MOVES. BUT THAT DOESN'T SEEM RIGHT EITHER.
WHO DO YOU WORK FOR?

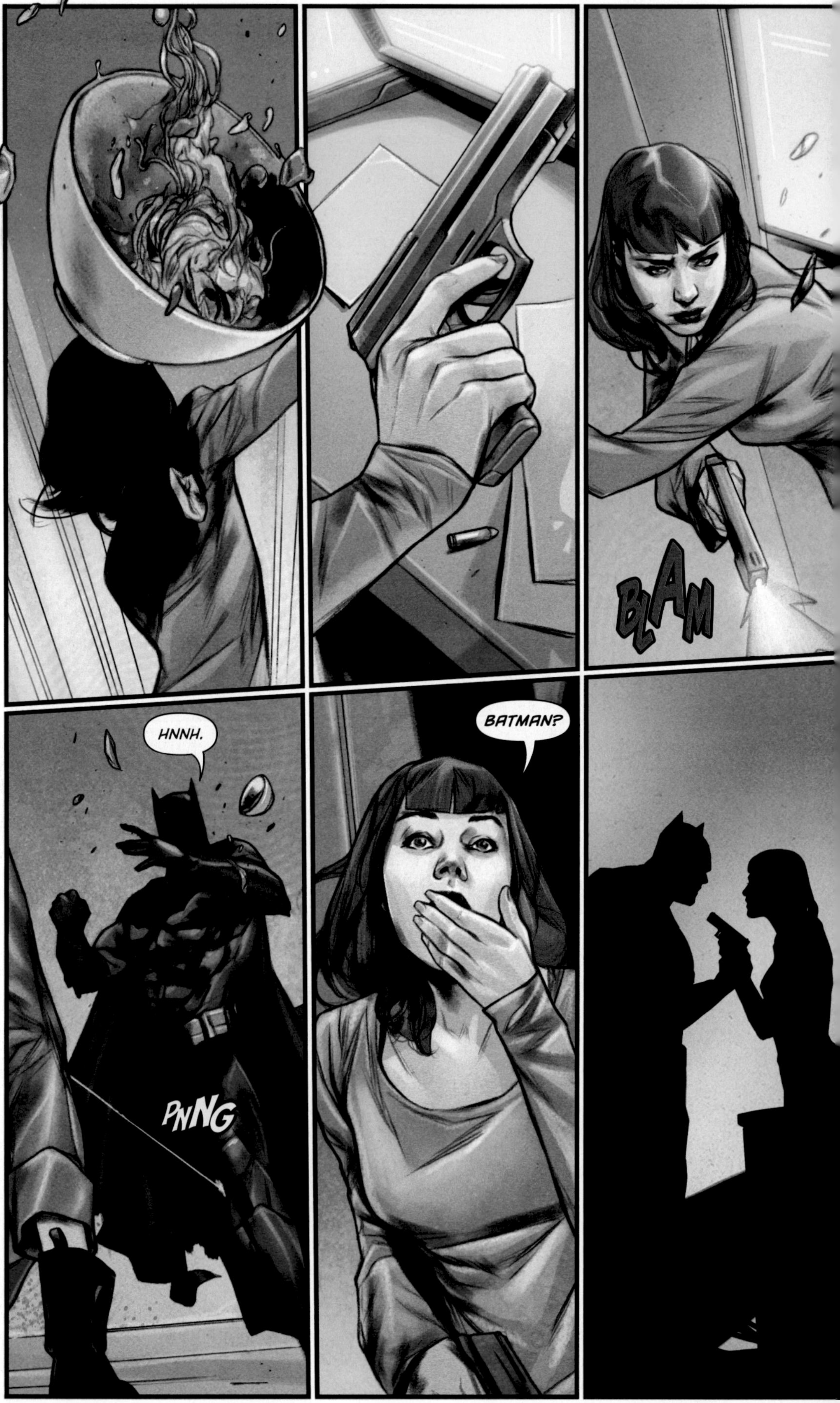
BLAM
HNNH.
PNNG
BATMAN?

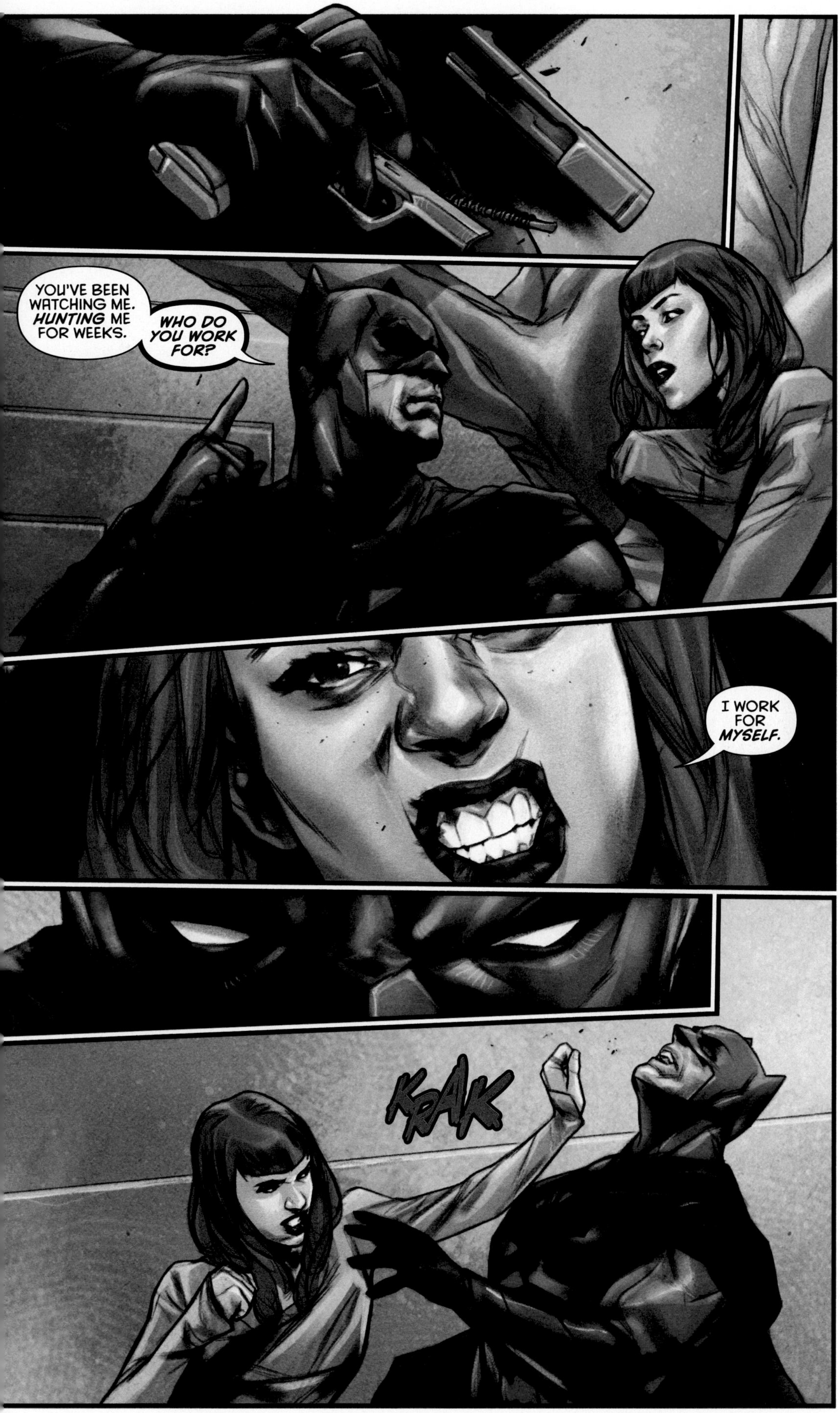

YOU'VE BEEN WATCHING ME. HUNTING ME FOR WEEKS.
WHO DO YOU WORK FOR?
I WORK FOR MYSELF.
KRAK

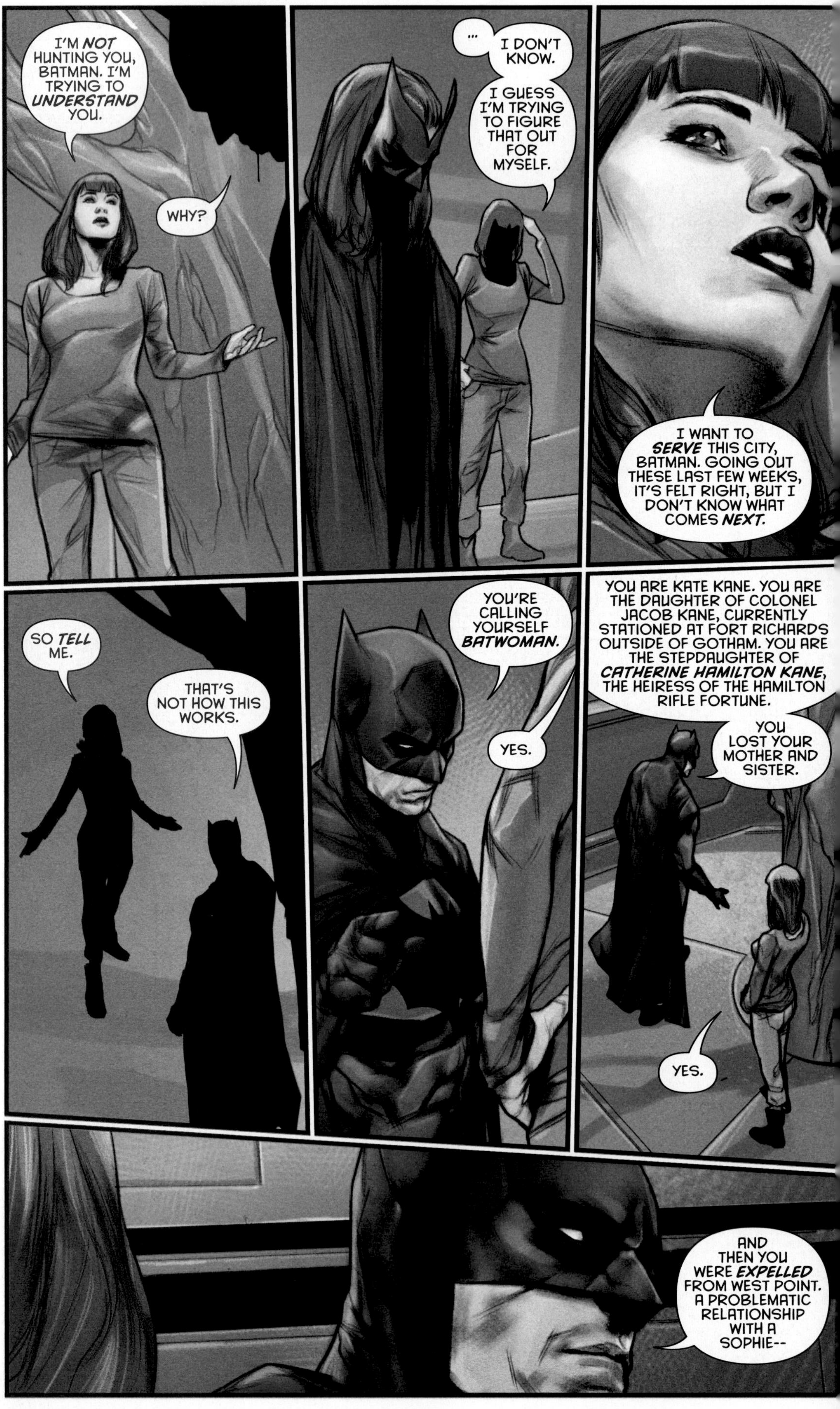
I'M NOT HUNTING YOU, BATMAN. I'M TRYING TO UNDERSTAND YOU.
WHY?
...
I DON'T KNOW.
I GUESS I'M TRYING TO FIGURE THAT OUT FOR MYSELF.
I WANT TO SERVE THIS CITY, BATMAN. GOING OUT THESE LAST FEW WEEKS, IT'S FELT RIGHT, BUT I DON'T KNOW WHAT COMES NEXT.
SO TELL ME.
THAT'S NOT HOW THIS WORKS.
YOU'RE CALLING YOURSELF BATWOMAN.
YES.
YOU ARE KATE KANE. YOU ARE THE DAUGHTER OF COLONEL JACOB KANE, CURRENTLY STATIONED AT FORT RICHARDS OUTSIDE OF GOTHAM. YOU ARE THE STEPDAUGHTER OF CATHERINE HAMILTON KANE, THE HEIRESS OF THE HAMILTON RIFLE FORTUNE.
YOU LOST YOUR MOTHER AND SISTER.
YES.
AND THEN YOU WERE EXPELLED FROM WEST POINT. A PROBLEMATIC RELATIONSHIP WITH A SOPHIE--

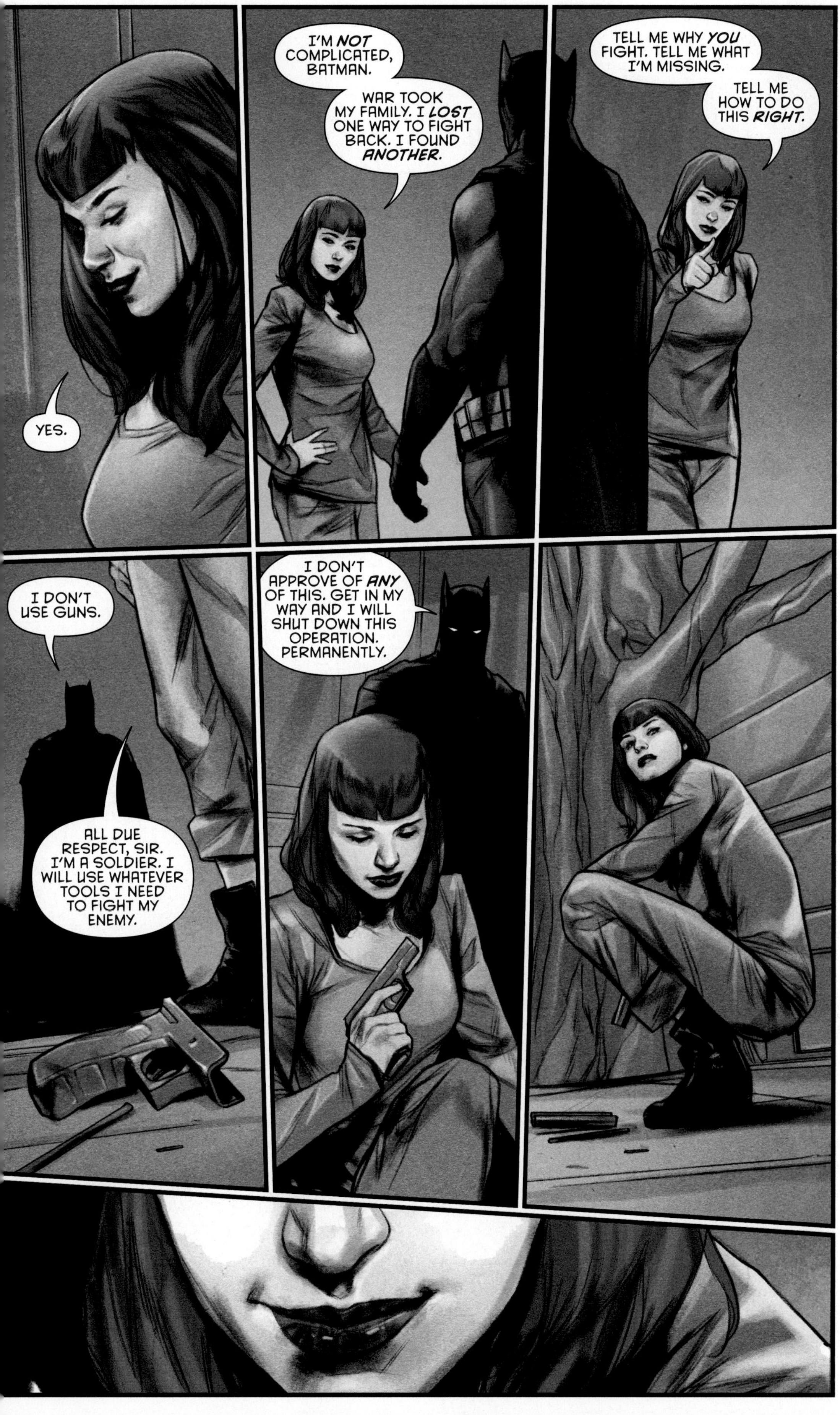
YES.
I'M NOT COMPLICATED, BATMAN.
WAR TOOK MY FAMILY. I LOST ONE WAY TO FIGHT BACK. I FOUND ANOTHER.
TELL ME WHY YOU FIGHT. TELL ME WHAT I'M MISSING.
TELL ME HOW TO DO THIS RIGHT.
I DON'T USE GUNS.
ALL DUE RESPECT, SIR. I'M A SOLDIER. I WILL USE WHATEVER TOOLS I NEED TO FIGHT MY ENEMY.
I DON'T APPROVE OF ANY OF THIS. GET IN MY WAY AND I WILL SHUT DOWN THIS OPERATION. PERMANENTLY.

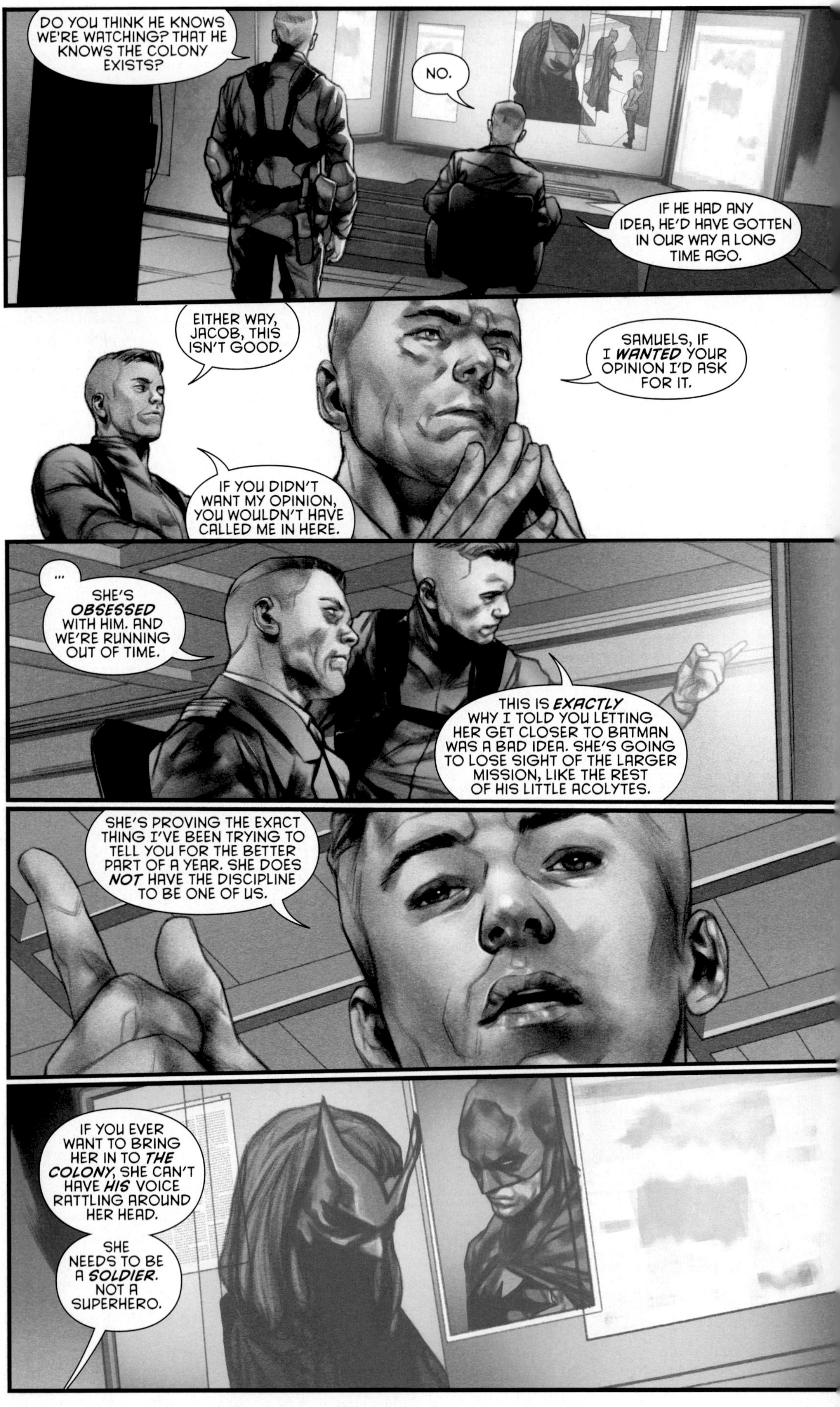
DO YOU THINK HE KNOWS WE'RE WATCHING? THAT HE KNOWS THE COLONY EXISTS?
NO.
IF HE HAD ANY IDEA, HE'D HAVE GOTTEN IN OUR WAY A LONG TIME AGO.
EITHER WAY, JACOB, THIS ISN'T GOOD.
SAMUELS, IF I *WANTED* YOUR OPINION I'D ASK FOR IT.
IF YOU DIDN'T WANT MY OPINION, YOU WOULDN'T HAVE CALLED ME IN HERE.
... SHE'S *OBSESSED* WITH HIM. AND WE'RE RUNNING OUT OF TIME.
THIS IS *EXACTLY* WHY I TOLD YOU LETTING HER GET CLOSER TO BATMAN WAS A BAD IDEA. SHE'S GOING TO LOSE SIGHT OF THE LARGER MISSION, LIKE THE REST OF HIS LITTLE ACOLYTES.
SHE'S PROVING THE EXACT THING I'VE BEEN TRYING TO TELL YOU FOR THE BETTER PART OF A YEAR. SHE DOES *NOT* HAVE THE DISCIPLINE TO BE ONE OF US.
IF YOU EVER WANT TO BRING HER IN TO *THE COLONY*, SHE CAN'T HAVE *HIS* VOICE RATTLING AROUND HER HEAD.
SHE NEEDS TO BE A *SOLDIER*. NOT A SUPERHERO.

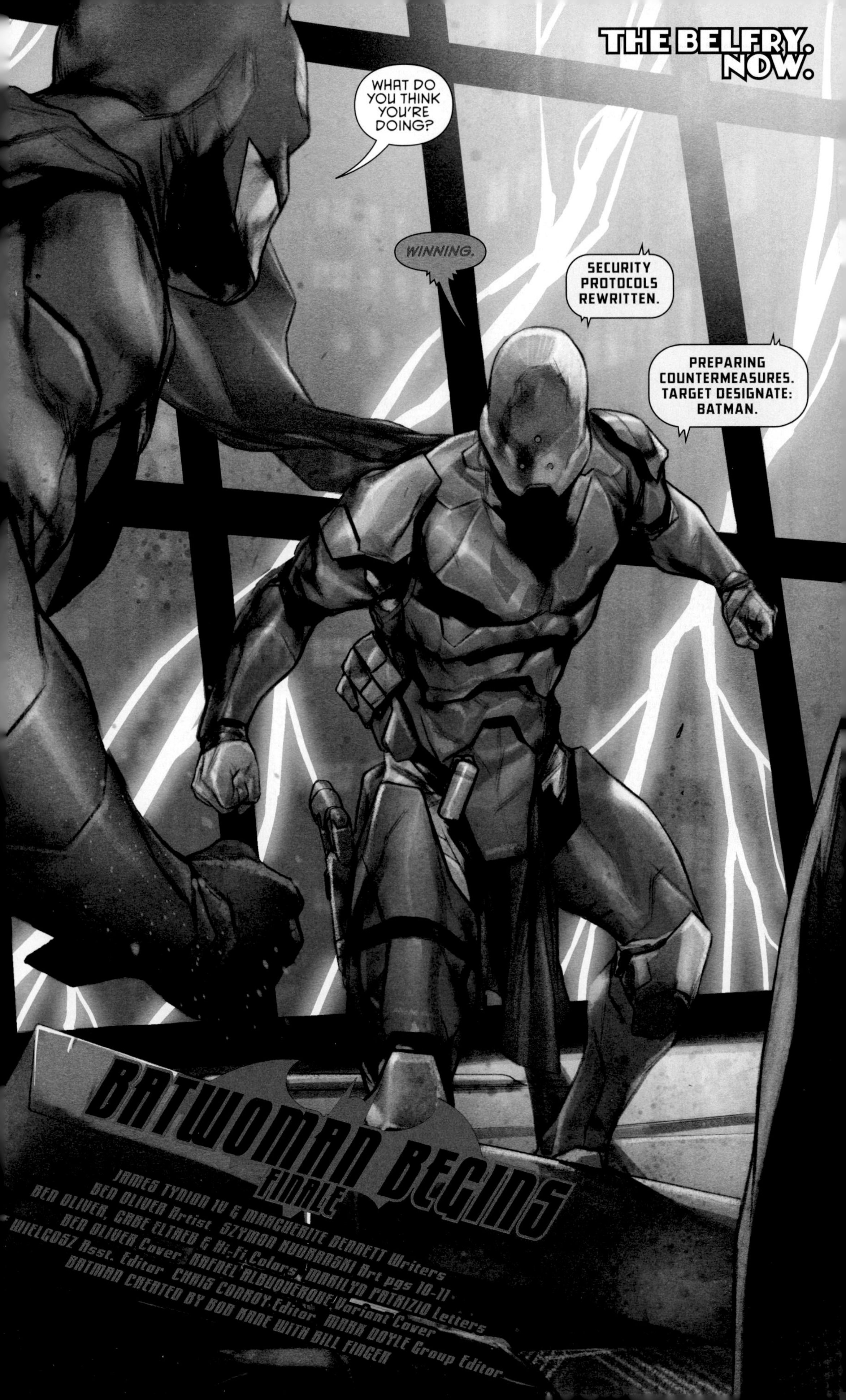
THE BELFRY. NOW.
WHAT DO YOU THINK YOU'RE DOING?
WINNING.
SECURITY PROTOCOLS REWRITTEN.
PREPARING COUNTERMEASURES. TARGET DESIGNATE: BATMAN.
BATWOMAN BEGINS FINALE
JAMES TYNION IV & MARGUERITE BENNETT Writers
BEN OLIVER Artist SZYMON KUDRANSKI Art pgs 10-11
BEN OLIVER, GABE ELTAEB & Hi-Fi Colors MARILYN PATRIZIO Letters
BEN OLIVER Cover RAFAEL ALBUQUERQUE Variant Cover
WIELGOSZ Asst. Editor CHRIS CONROY Editor MARK DOYLE Group Editor
BATMAN CREATED BY BOB KANE WITH BILL FINGER

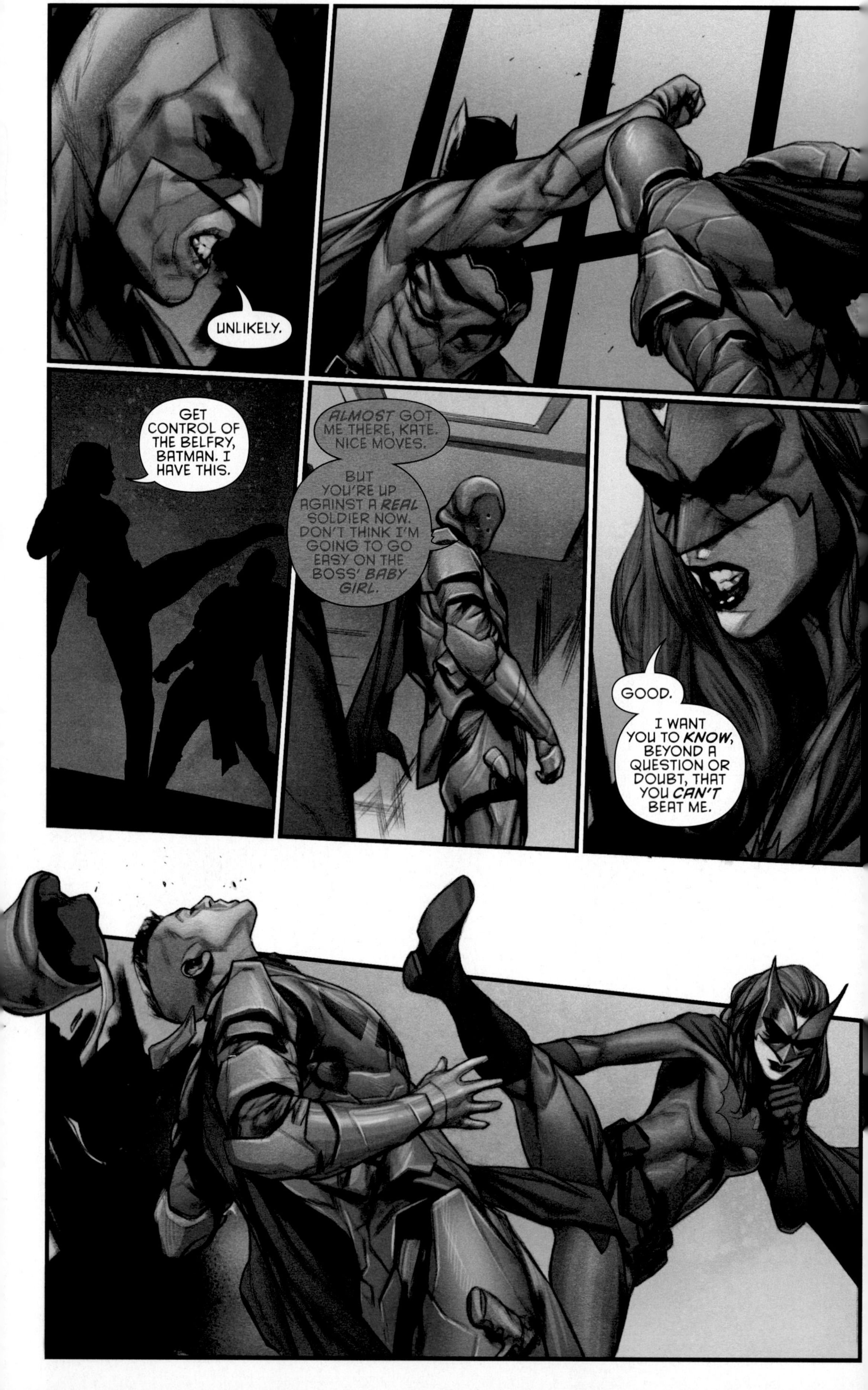
UNLIKELY.
GET CONTROL OF THE BELFRY, BATMAN. I HAVE THIS.
ALMOST GOT ME THERE, KATE. NICE MOVES.
BUT YOU'RE UP AGAINST A REAL SOLDIER NOW. DON'T THINK I'M GOING TO GO EASY ON THE BOSS' BABY GIRL.
GOOD.
I WANT YOU TO KNOW, BEYOND A QUESTION OR DOUBT, THAT YOU CAN'T BEAT ME.

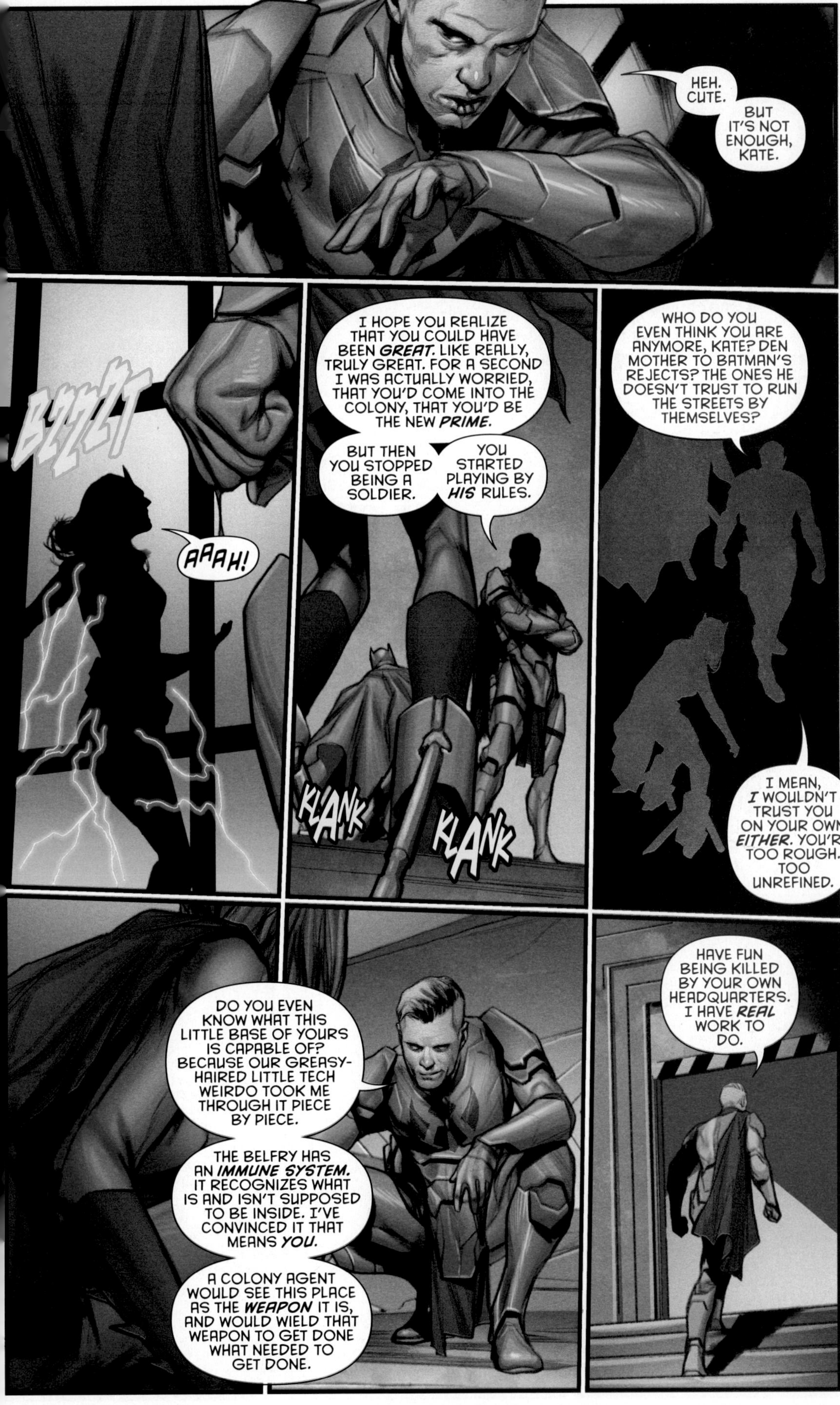
HEH. CUTE.
BUT IT'S NOT ENOUGH, KATE.
BZZZT
AAAH!
I HOPE YOU REALIZE THAT YOU COULD HAVE BEEN GREAT. LIKE REALLY, TRULY GREAT. FOR A SECOND I WAS ACTUALLY WORRIED, THAT YOU'D COME INTO THE COLONY, THAT YOU'D BE THE NEW PRIME.
BUT THEN YOU STOPPED BEING A SOLDIER.
YOU STARTED PLAYING BY HIS RULES.
KLANK
KLANK
WHO DO YOU EVEN THINK YOU ARE ANYMORE, KATE? DEN MOTHER TO BATMAN'S REJECTS? THE ONES HE DOESN'T TRUST TO RUN THE STREETS BY THEMSELVES?
I MEAN, I WOULDN'T TRUST YOU ON YOUR OWN EITHER. YOU'RE TOO ROUGH. TOO UNREFINED.
DO YOU EVEN KNOW WHAT THIS LITTLE BASE OF YOURS IS CAPABLE OF? BECAUSE OUR GREASY-HAIRED LITTLE TECH WEIRDO TOOK ME THROUGH IT PIECE BY PIECE.
THE BELFRY HAS AN IMMUNE SYSTEM. IT RECOGNIZES WHAT IS AND ISN'T SUPPOSED TO BE INSIDE. I'VE CONVINCED IT THAT MEANS YOU.
A COLONY AGENT WOULD SEE THIS PLACE AS THE WEAPON IT IS, AND WOULD WIELD THAT WEAPON TO GET DONE WHAT NEEDED TO GET DONE.
HAVE FUN BEING KILLED BY YOUR OWN HEADQUARTERS. I HAVE REAL WORK TO DO.

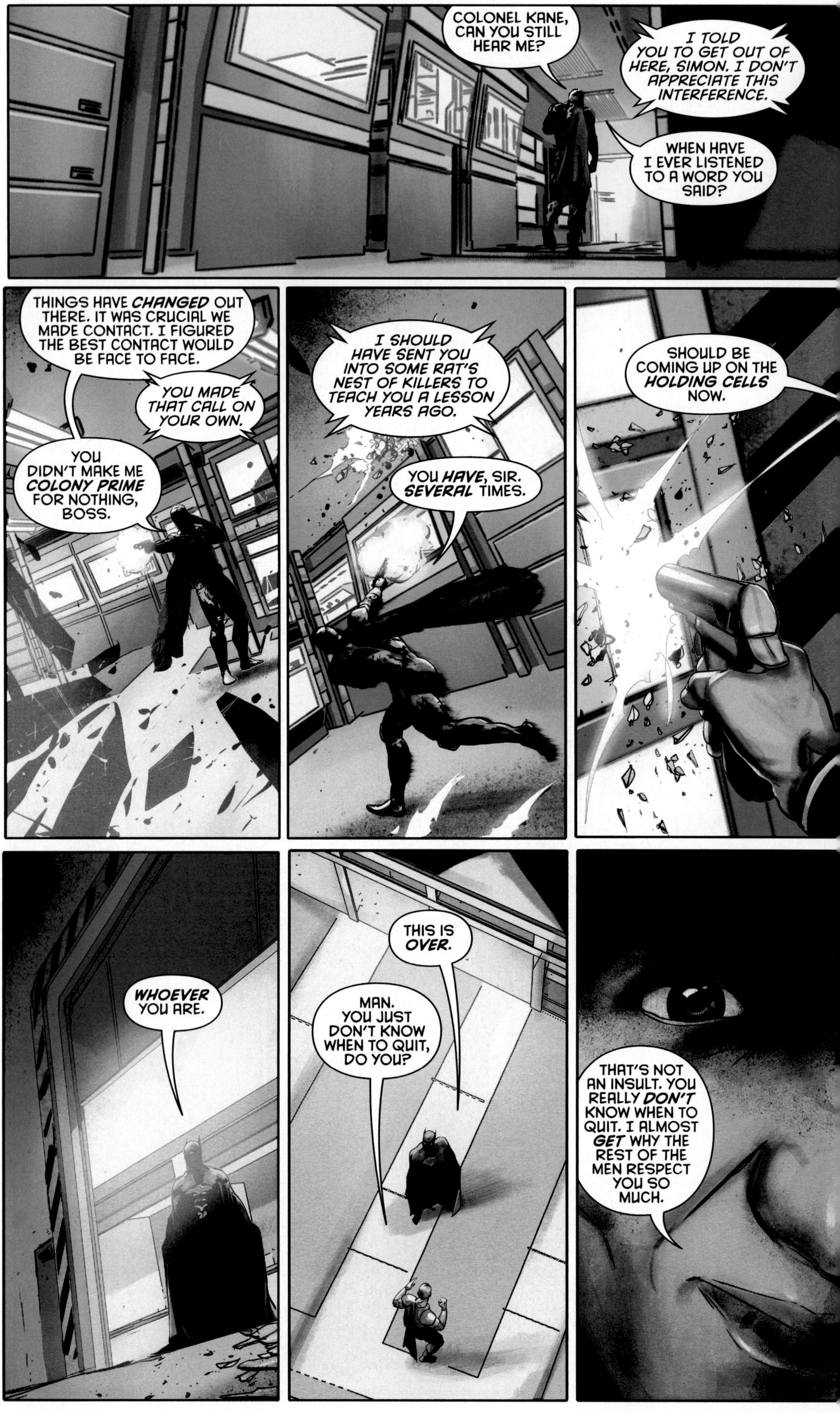
COLONEL KANE, CAN YOU STILL HEAR ME?
I TOLD YOU TO GET OUT OF HERE, SIMON. I DON'T APPRECIATE THIS INTERFERENCE.
WHEN HAVE I EVER LISTENED TO A WORD YOU SAID?
THINGS HAVE CHANGED OUT THERE. IT WAS CRUCIAL WE MADE CONTACT. I FIGURED THE BEST CONTACT WOULD BE FACE TO FACE.
YOU MADE THAT CALL ON YOUR OWN.
YOU DIDN'T MAKE ME COLONY PRIME FOR NOTHING, BOSS.
I SHOULD HAVE SENT YOU INTO SOME RAT'S NEST OF KILLERS TO TEACH YOU A LESSON YEARS AGO.
YOU HAVE, SIR. SEVERAL TIMES.
SHOULD BE COMING UP ON THE HOLDING CELLS NOW.
WHOEVER YOU ARE.
THIS IS OVER.
MAN. YOU JUST DON'T KNOW WHEN TO QUIT, DO YOU?
THAT'S NOT AN INSULT. YOU REALLY DON'T KNOW WHEN TO QUIT. I ALMOST GET WHY THE REST OF THE MEN RESPECT YOU SO MUCH.

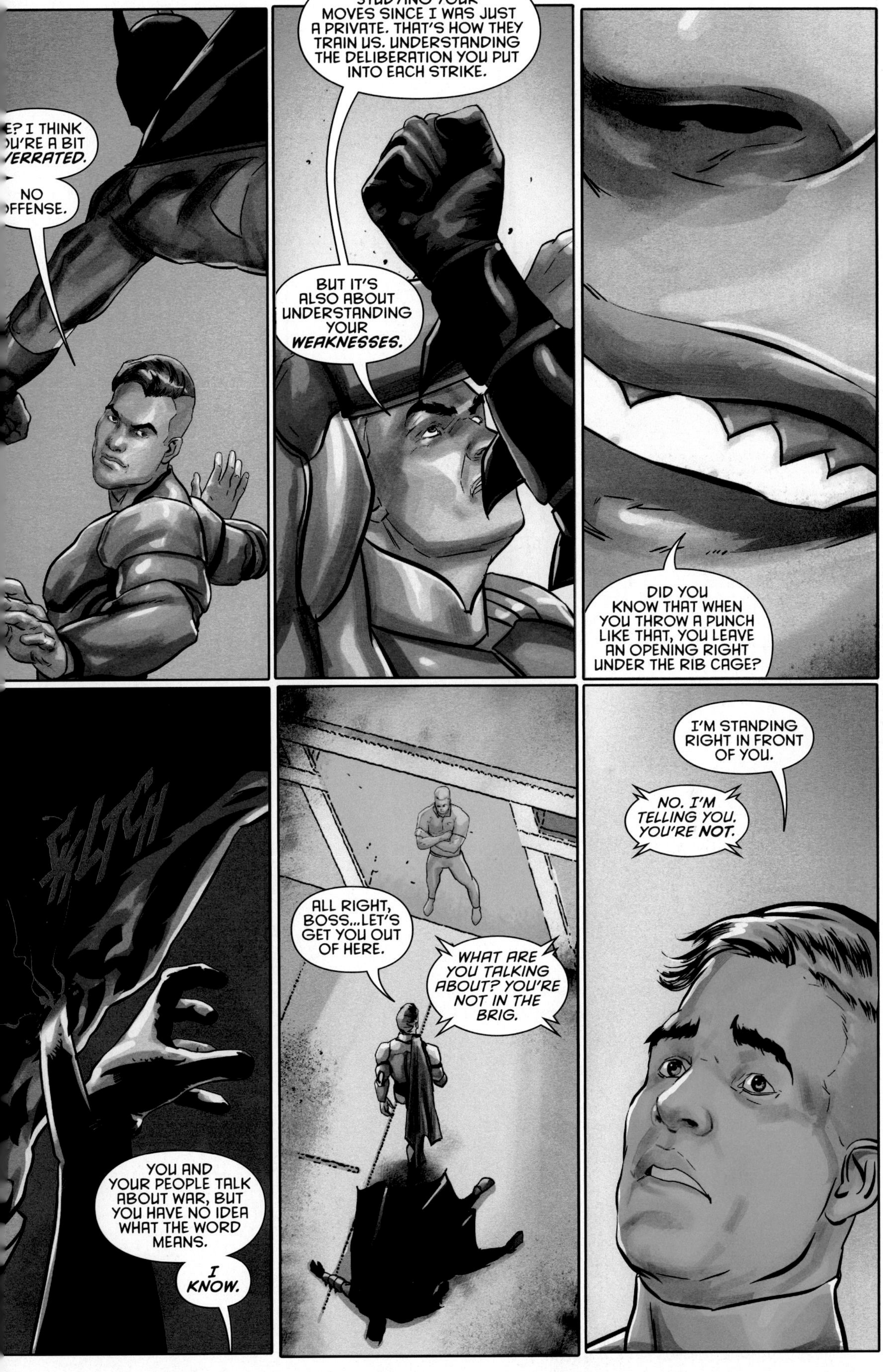
E? I THINK OU'RE A BIT VERRATED.
NO FFENSE.
I'VE BEEN STUDYING YOUR MOVES SINCE I WAS JUST A PRIVATE. THAT'S HOW THEY TRAIN US. UNDERSTANDING THE DELIBERATION YOU PUT INTO EACH STRIKE.
BUT IT'S ALSO ABOUT UNDERSTANDING YOUR *WEAKNESSES.*
DID YOU KNOW THAT WHEN YOU THROW A PUNCH LIKE THAT, YOU LEAVE AN OPENING RIGHT UNDER THE RIB CAGE?
YOU AND YOUR PEOPLE TALK ABOUT WAR, BUT YOU HAVE NO IDEA WHAT THE WORD MEANS.
I KNOW.
ALL RIGHT, BOSS...LET'S GET YOU OUT OF HERE.
WHAT ARE YOU TALKING ABOUT? YOU'RE NOT IN THE BRIG.
I'M STANDING RIGHT IN FRONT OF YOU.
*NO. I'M TELLING YOU. YOU'RE **NOT**.*

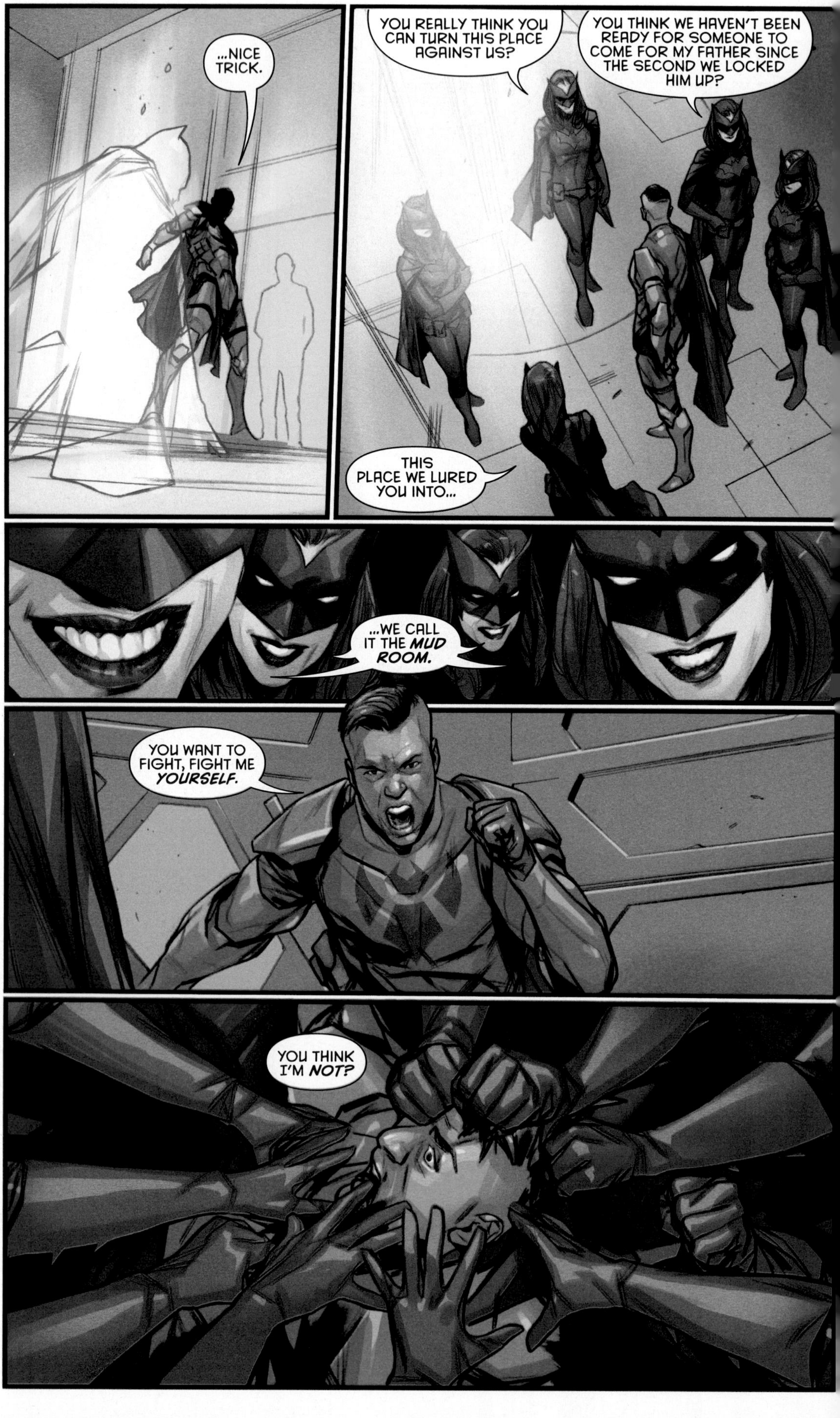
...NICE TRICK.
YOU REALLY THINK YOU CAN TURN THIS PLACE AGAINST US?
YOU THINK WE HAVEN'T BEEN READY FOR SOMEONE TO COME FOR MY FATHER SINCE THE SECOND WE LOCKED HIM UP?
THIS PLACE WE LURED YOU INTO...
...WE CALL IT THE *MUD ROOM.*
YOU WANT TO FIGHT, FIGHT ME *YOURSELF.*
YOU THINK I'M *NOT?*

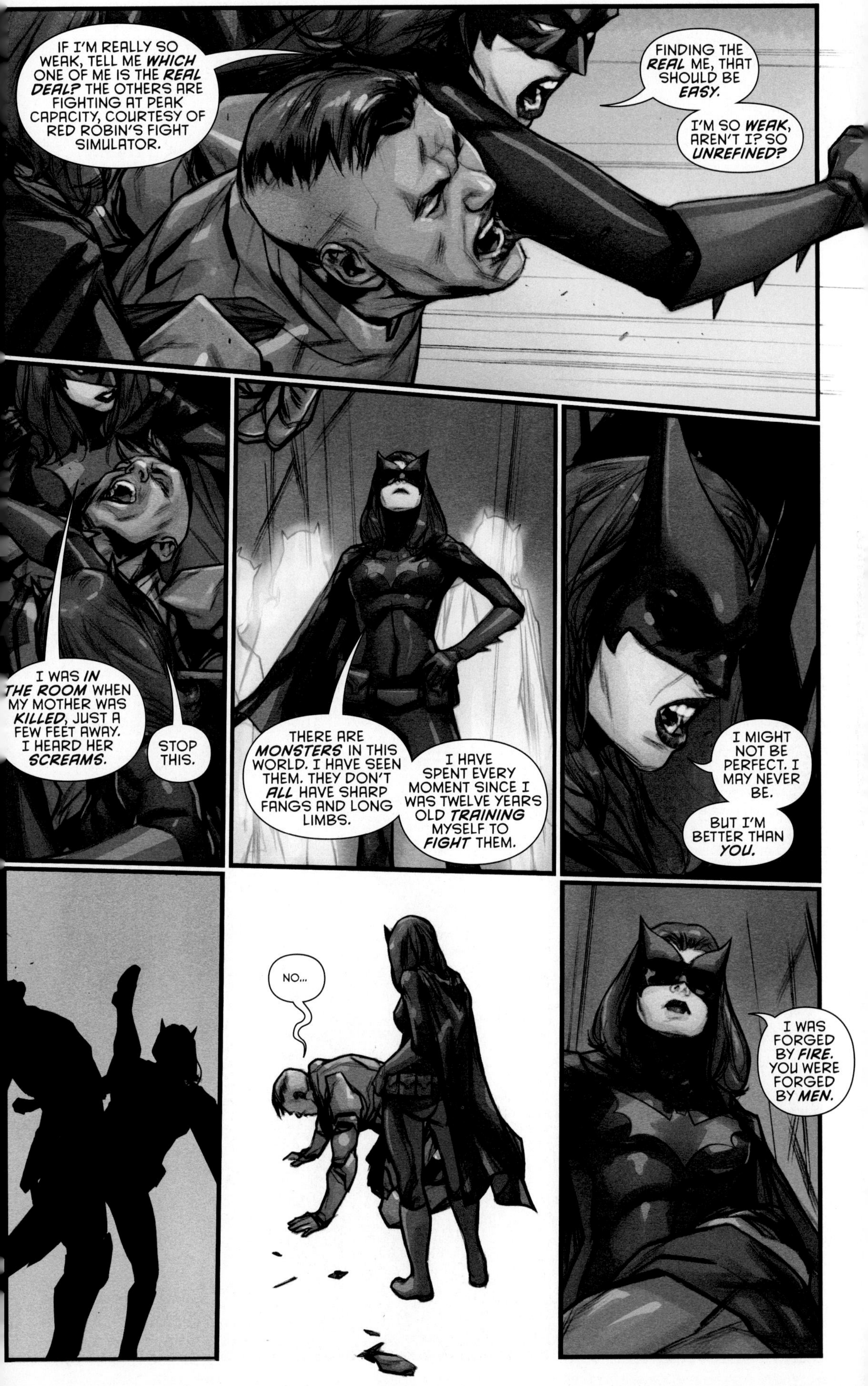

IF I'M REALLY SO WEAK, TELL ME WHICH ONE OF ME IS THE REAL DEAL? THE OTHERS ARE FIGHTING AT PEAK CAPACITY, COURTESY OF RED ROBIN'S FIGHT SIMULATOR.
FINDING THE REAL ME, THAT SHOULD BE EASY.
I'M SO WEAK, AREN'T I? SO UNREFINED?
I WAS IN THE ROOM WHEN MY MOTHER WAS KILLED, JUST A FEW FEET AWAY. I HEARD HER SCREAMS.
STOP THIS.
THERE ARE MONSTERS IN THIS WORLD. I HAVE SEEN THEM. THEY DON'T ALL HAVE SHARP FANGS AND LONG LIMBS.
I HAVE SPENT EVERY MOMENT SINCE I WAS TWELVE YEARS OLD TRAINING MYSELF TO FIGHT THEM.
I MIGHT NOT BE PERFECT. I MAY NEVER BE.
BUT I'M BETTER THAN YOU.
NO...
I WAS FORGED BY FIRE. YOU WERE FORGED BY MEN.

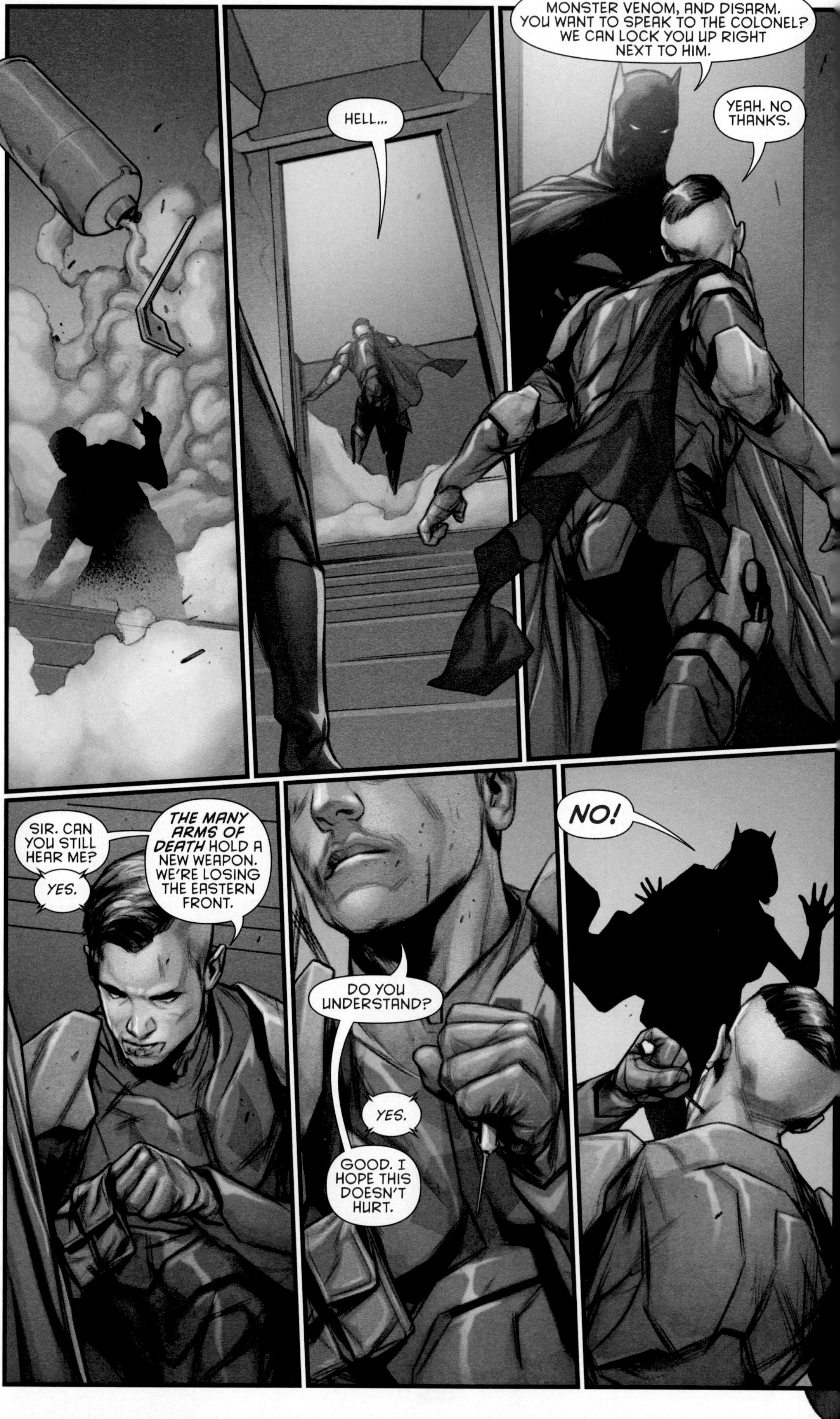
HELL...
HAND OVER THE MONSTER VENOM, AND DISARM. YOU WANT TO SPEAK TO THE COLONEL? WE CAN LOCK YOU UP RIGHT NEXT TO HIM.
YEAH. NO THANKS.
SIR. CAN YOU STILL HEAR ME?
YES.
THE MANY ARMS OF DEATH HOLD A NEW WEAPON. WE'RE LOSING THE EASTERN FRONT.
DO YOU UNDERSTAND?
YES.
GOOD. I HOPE THIS DOESN'T HURT.
NO!

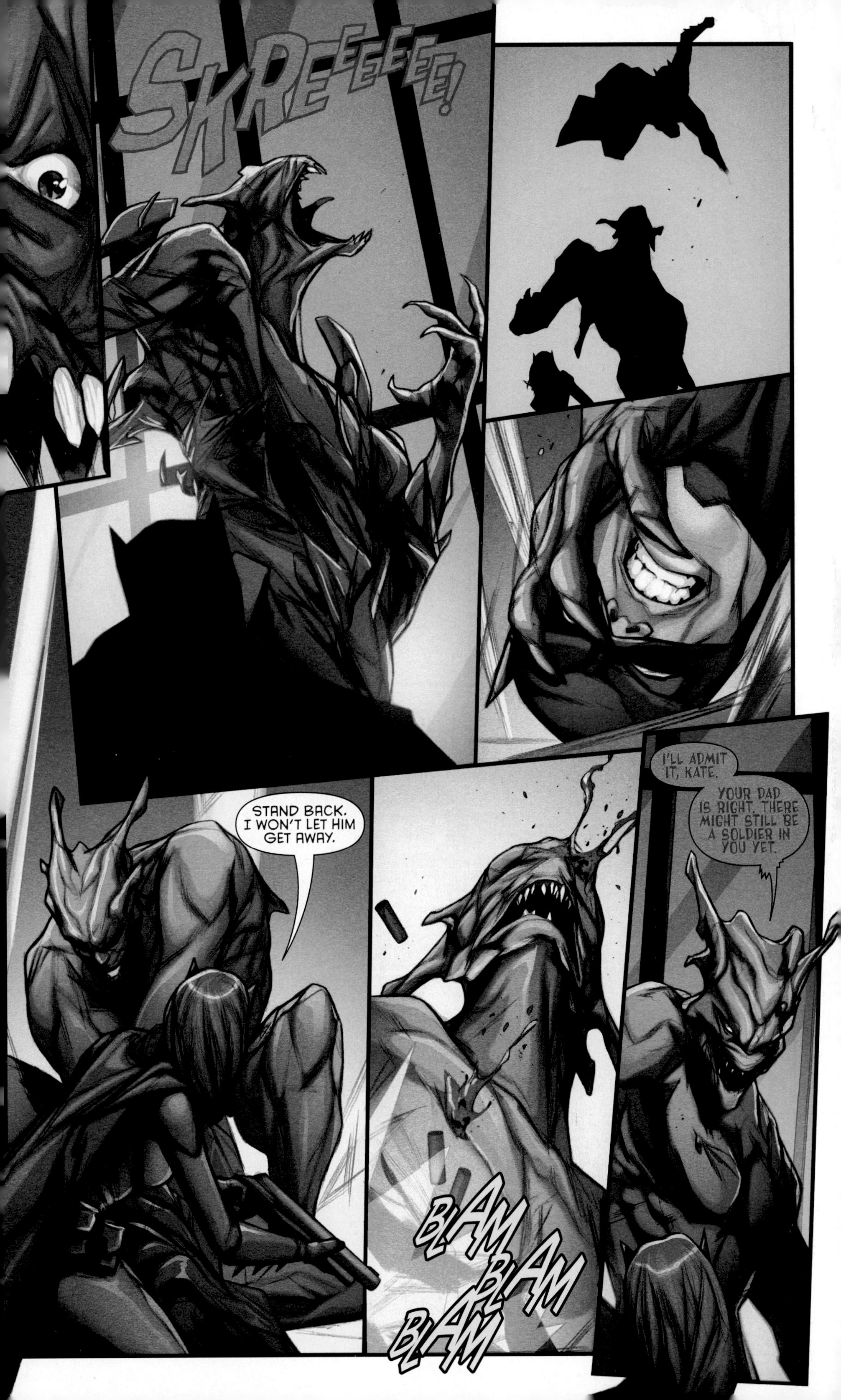

SKREEEEEE!
STAND BACK.
I WON'T LET HIM GET AWAY.
BLAM BLAM BLAM
I'LL ADMIT IT, KATE.
YOUR DAD IS RIGHT. THERE MIGHT STILL BE A SOLDIER IN YOU YET.

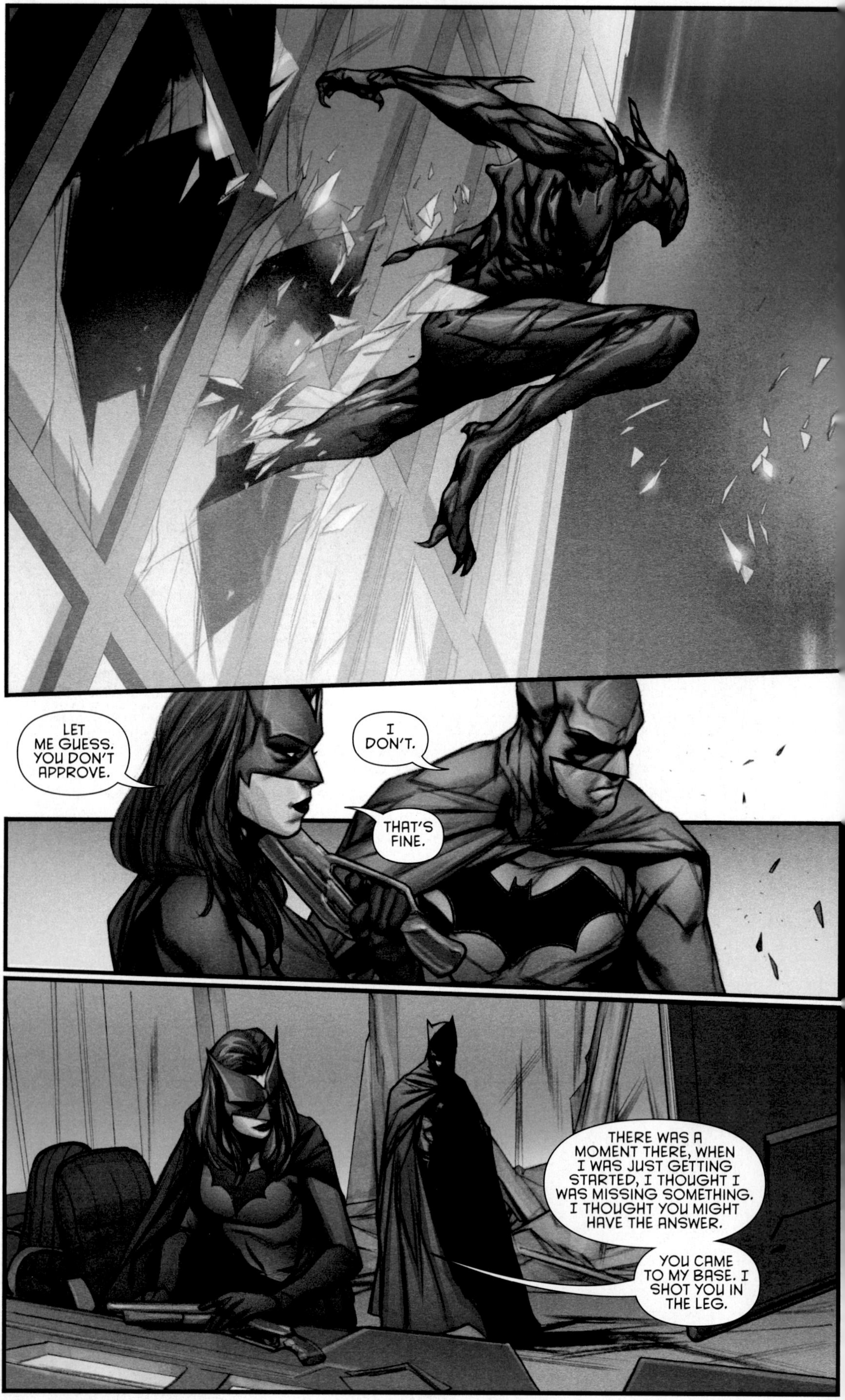
LET ME GUESS. YOU DON'T APPROVE.
I DON'T.
THAT'S FINE.
THERE WAS A MOMENT THERE, WHEN I WAS JUST GETTING STARTED, I THOUGHT I WAS MISSING SOMETHING. I THOUGHT YOU MIGHT HAVE THE ANSWER.
YOU CAME TO MY BASE. I SHOT YOU IN THE LEG.

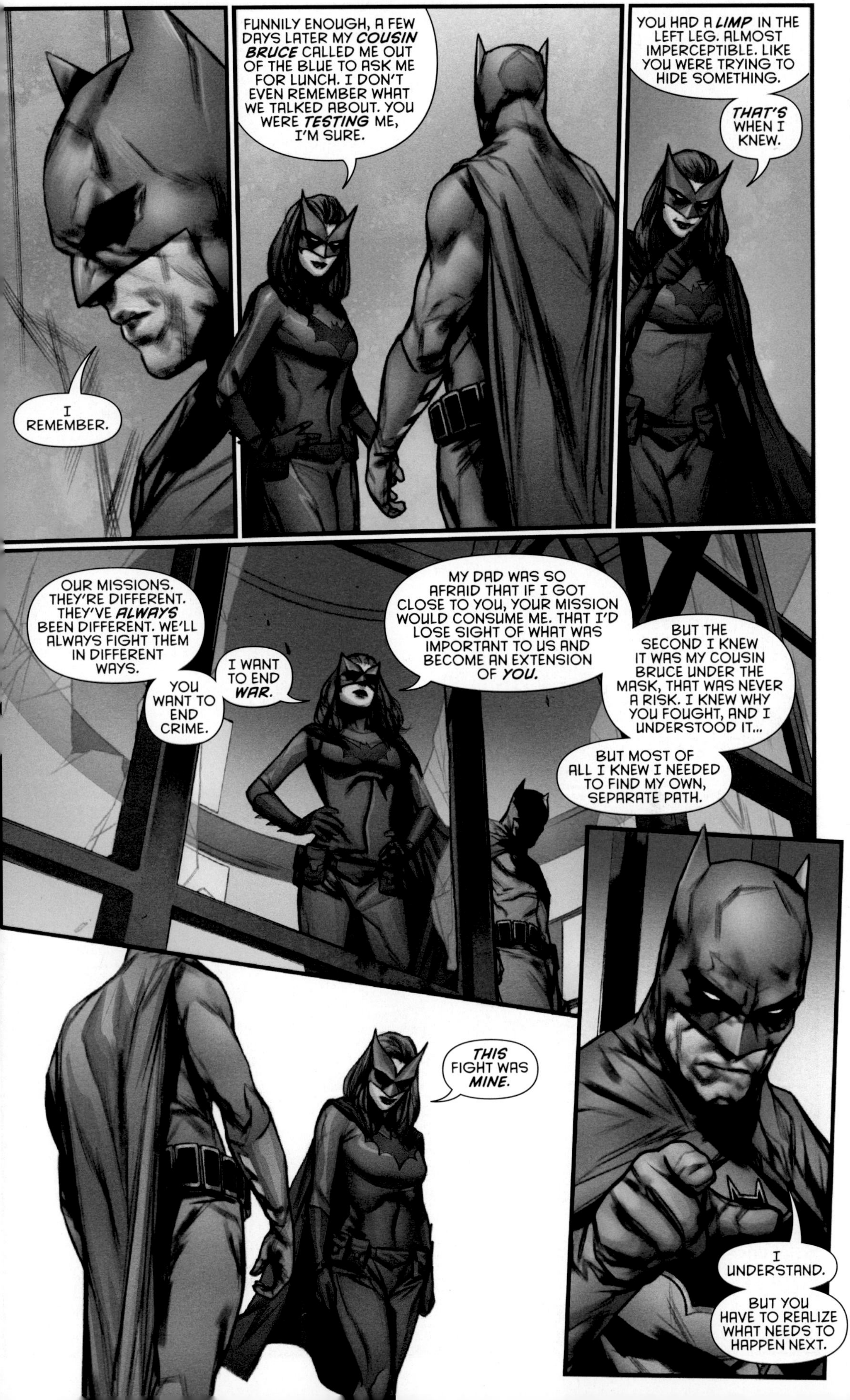
I REMEMBER.
FUNNILY ENOUGH, A FEW DAYS LATER MY *COUSIN BRUCE* CALLED ME OUT OF THE BLUE TO ASK ME FOR LUNCH. I DON'T EVEN REMEMBER WHAT WE TALKED ABOUT. YOU WERE *TESTING* ME, I'M SURE.
YOU HAD A *LIMP* IN THE LEFT LEG. ALMOST IMPERCEPTIBLE. LIKE YOU WERE TRYING TO HIDE SOMETHING.
THAT'S WHEN I KNEW.
OUR MISSIONS. THEY'RE DIFFERENT. THEY'VE *ALWAYS* BEEN DIFFERENT. WE'LL ALWAYS FIGHT THEM IN DIFFERENT WAYS.
YOU WANT TO END CRIME.
I WANT TO END *WAR*.
MY DAD WAS SO AFRAID THAT IF I GOT CLOSE TO YOU, YOUR MISSION WOULD CONSUME ME. THAT I'D LOSE SIGHT OF WHAT WAS IMPORTANT TO US AND BECOME AN EXTENSION OF *YOU*.
BUT THE SECOND I KNEW IT WAS MY COUSIN BRUCE UNDER THE MASK, THAT WAS NEVER A RISK. I KNEW WHY YOU FOUGHT, AND I UNDERSTOOD IT...
BUT MOST OF ALL I KNEW I NEEDED TO FIND MY OWN, SEPARATE PATH.
THIS FIGHT WAS *MINE*.
I UNDERSTAND.
BUT YOU HAVE TO REALIZE WHAT NEEDS TO HAPPEN NEXT.

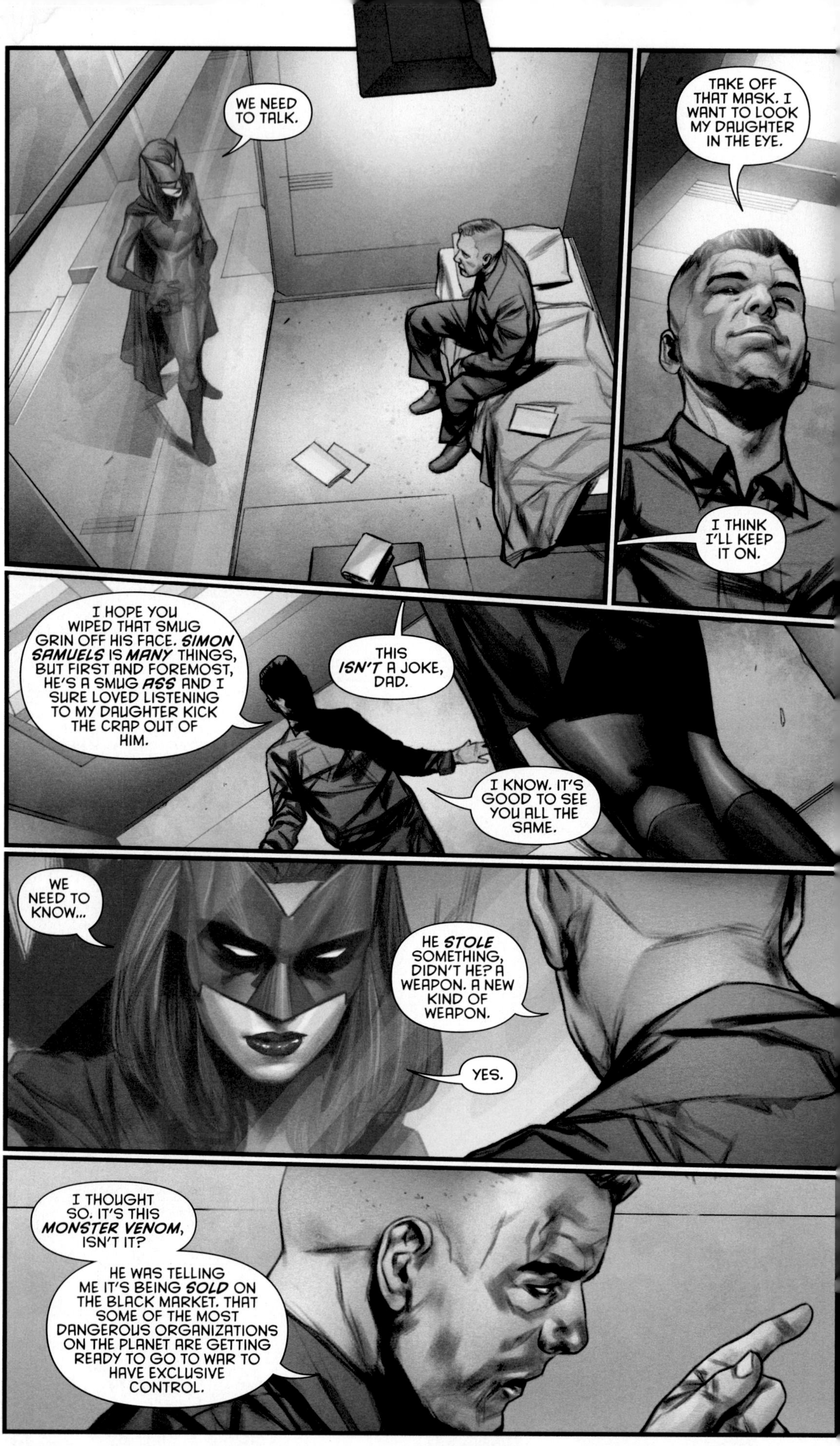
WE NEED TO TALK.
TAKE OFF THAT MASK. I WANT TO LOOK MY DAUGHTER IN THE EYE.
I THINK I'LL KEEP IT ON.
I HOPE YOU WIPED THAT SMUG GRIN OFF HIS FACE. SIMON SAMUELS IS MANY THINGS, BUT FIRST AND FOREMOST, HE'S A SMUG ASS AND I SURE LOVED LISTENING TO MY DAUGHTER KICK THE CRAP OUT OF HIM.
THIS ISN'T A JOKE, DAD.
I KNOW. IT'S GOOD TO SEE YOU ALL THE SAME.
WE NEED TO KNOW...
HE STOLE SOMETHING, DIDN'T HE? A WEAPON. A NEW KIND OF WEAPON.
YES.
I THOUGHT SO. IT'S THIS MONSTER VENOM, ISN'T IT?
HE WAS TELLING ME IT'S BEING SOLD ON THE BLACK MARKET. THAT SOME OF THE MOST DANGEROUS ORGANIZATIONS ON THE PLANET ARE GETTING READY TO GO TO WAR TO HAVE EXCLUSIVE CONTROL.

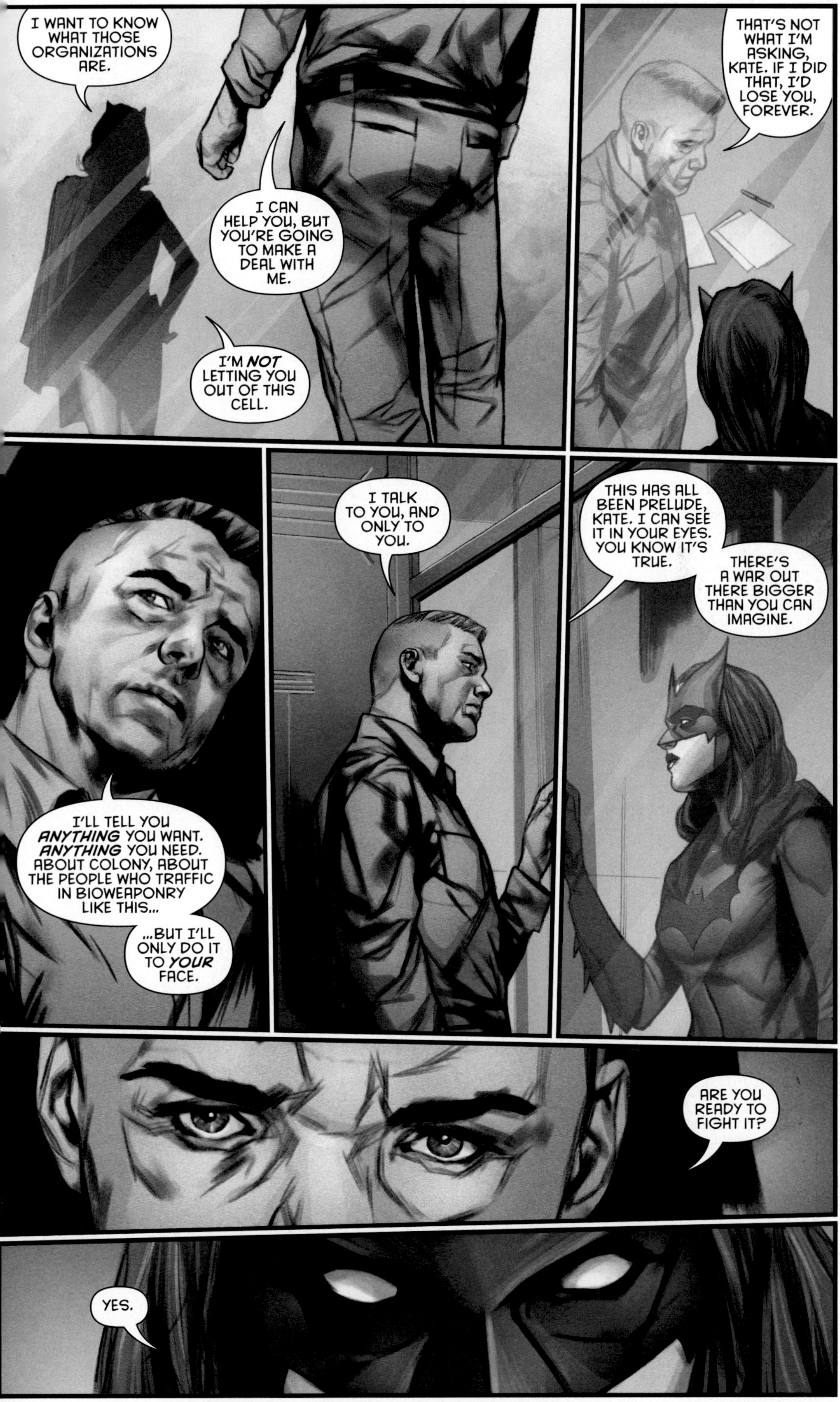
I WANT TO KNOW WHAT THOSE ORGANIZATIONS ARE.
I CAN HELP YOU, BUT YOU'RE GOING TO MAKE A DEAL WITH ME.
I'M *NOT* LETTING YOU OUT OF THIS CELL.
THAT'S NOT WHAT I'M ASKING, KATE. IF I DID THAT, I'D LOSE YOU, FOREVER.
I'LL TELL YOU *ANYTHING* YOU WANT. *ANYTHING* YOU NEED. ABOUT COLONY, ABOUT THE PEOPLE WHO TRAFFIC IN BIOWEAPONRY LIKE THIS...
...BUT I'LL ONLY DO IT TO *YOUR* FACE.
I TALK TO YOU, AND ONLY TO YOU.
THIS HAS ALL BEEN PRELUDE, KATE. I CAN SEE IT IN YOUR EYES. YOU KNOW IT'S TRUE.
THERE'S A WAR OUT THERE BIGGER THAN YOU CAN IMAGINE.
ARE YOU READY TO FIGHT IT?
YES.

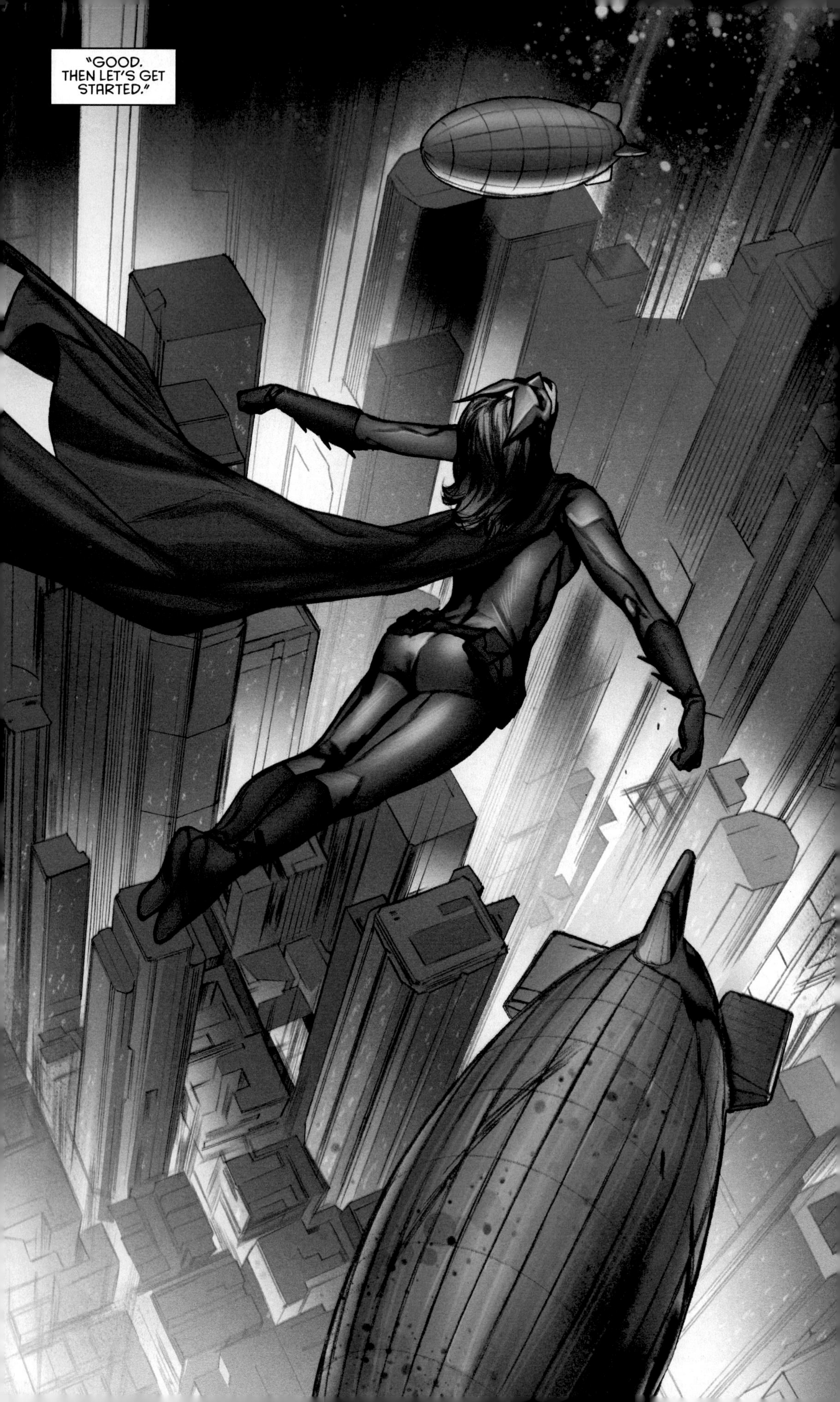
"GOOD. THEN LET'S GET STARTED."

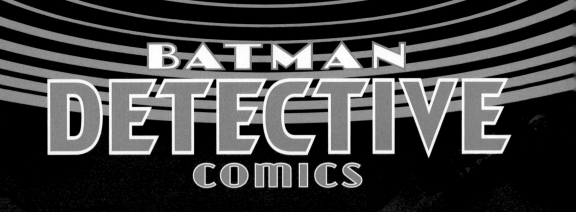

BATMAN

DETECTIVE COMICS

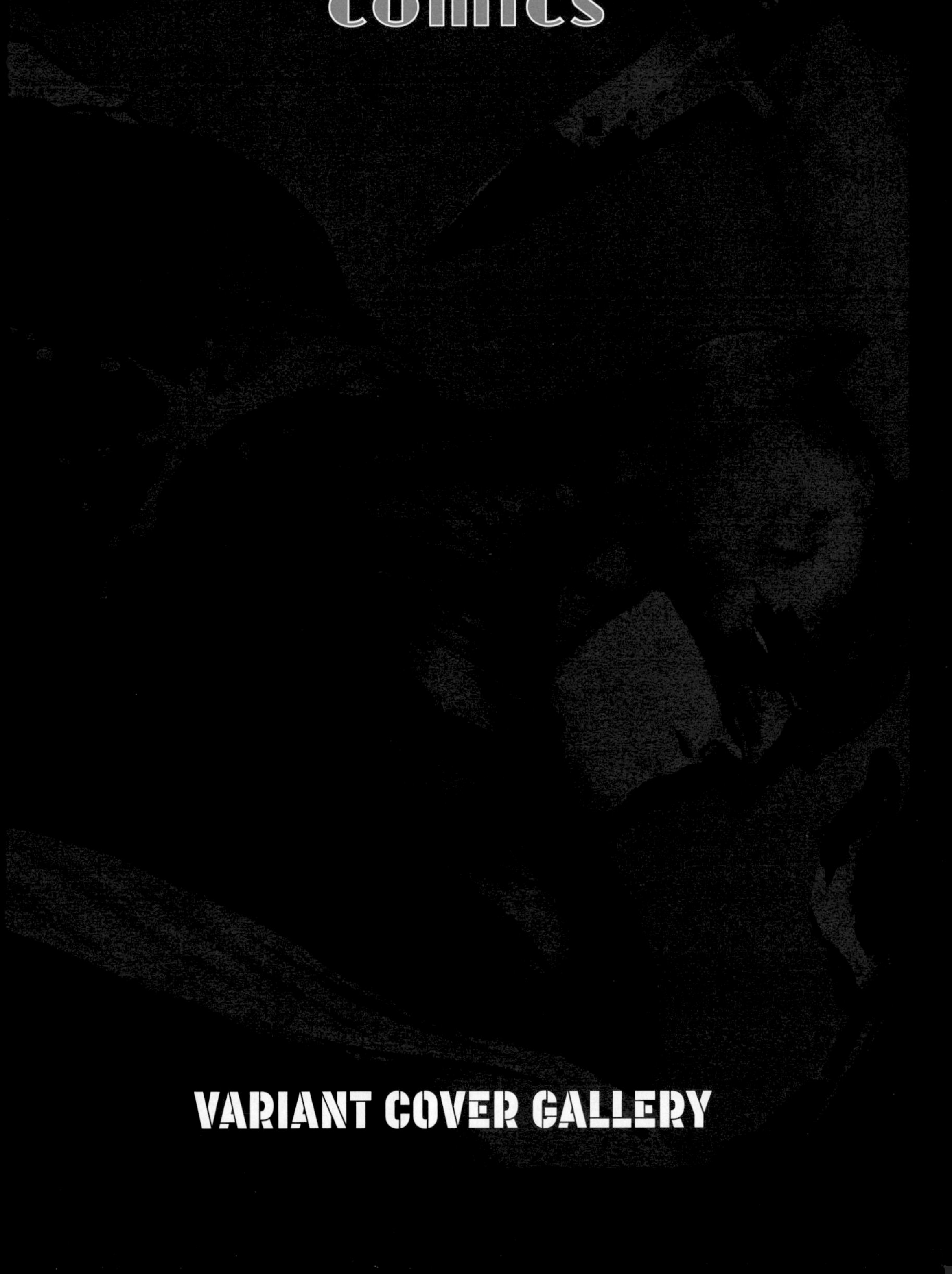

VARIANT COVER GALLERY

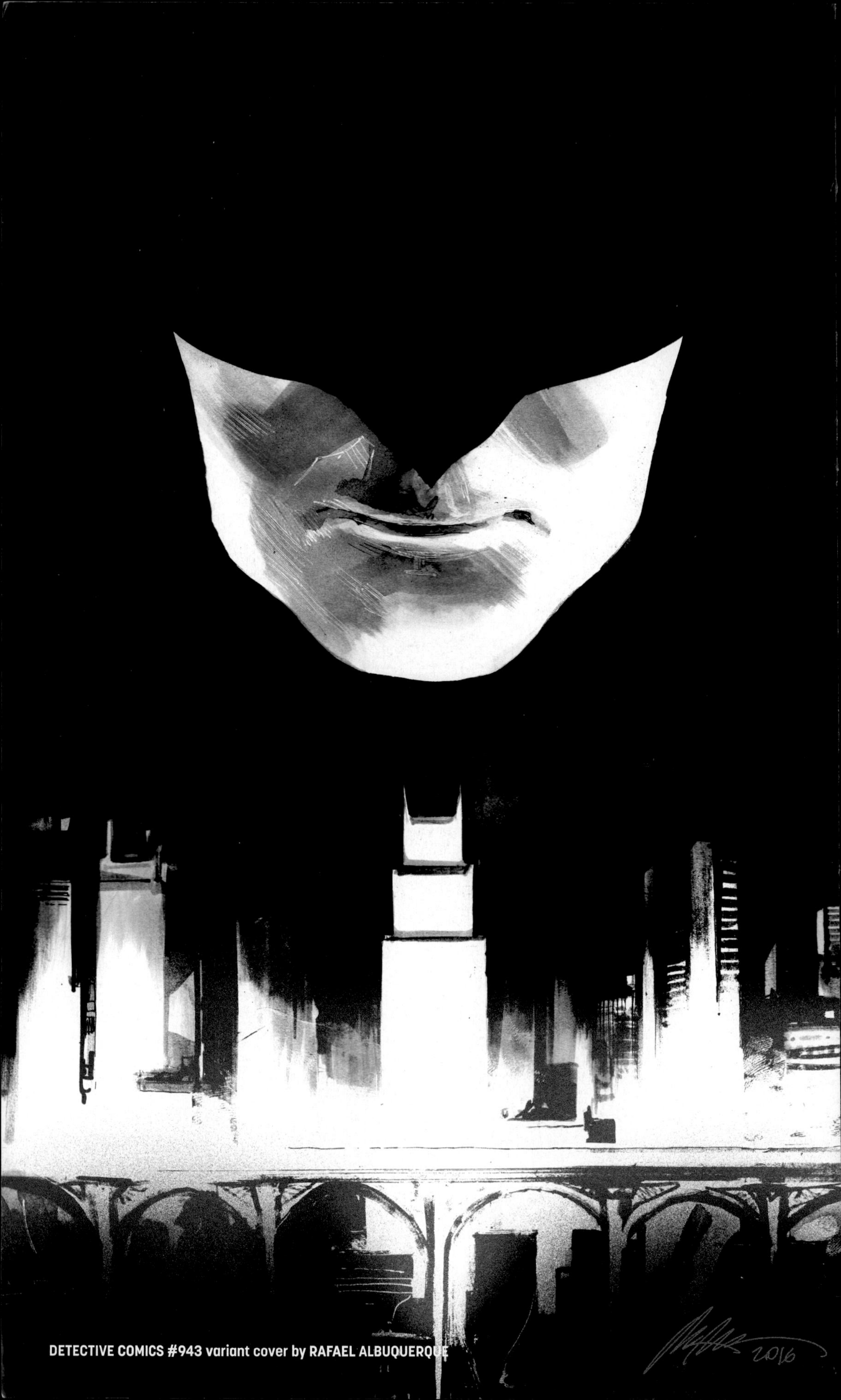

DETECTIVE COMICS #943 variant cover by RAFAEL ALBUQUERQUE

DETECTIVE COMICS #944 variant cover by RAFAEL ALBUQUERQUE

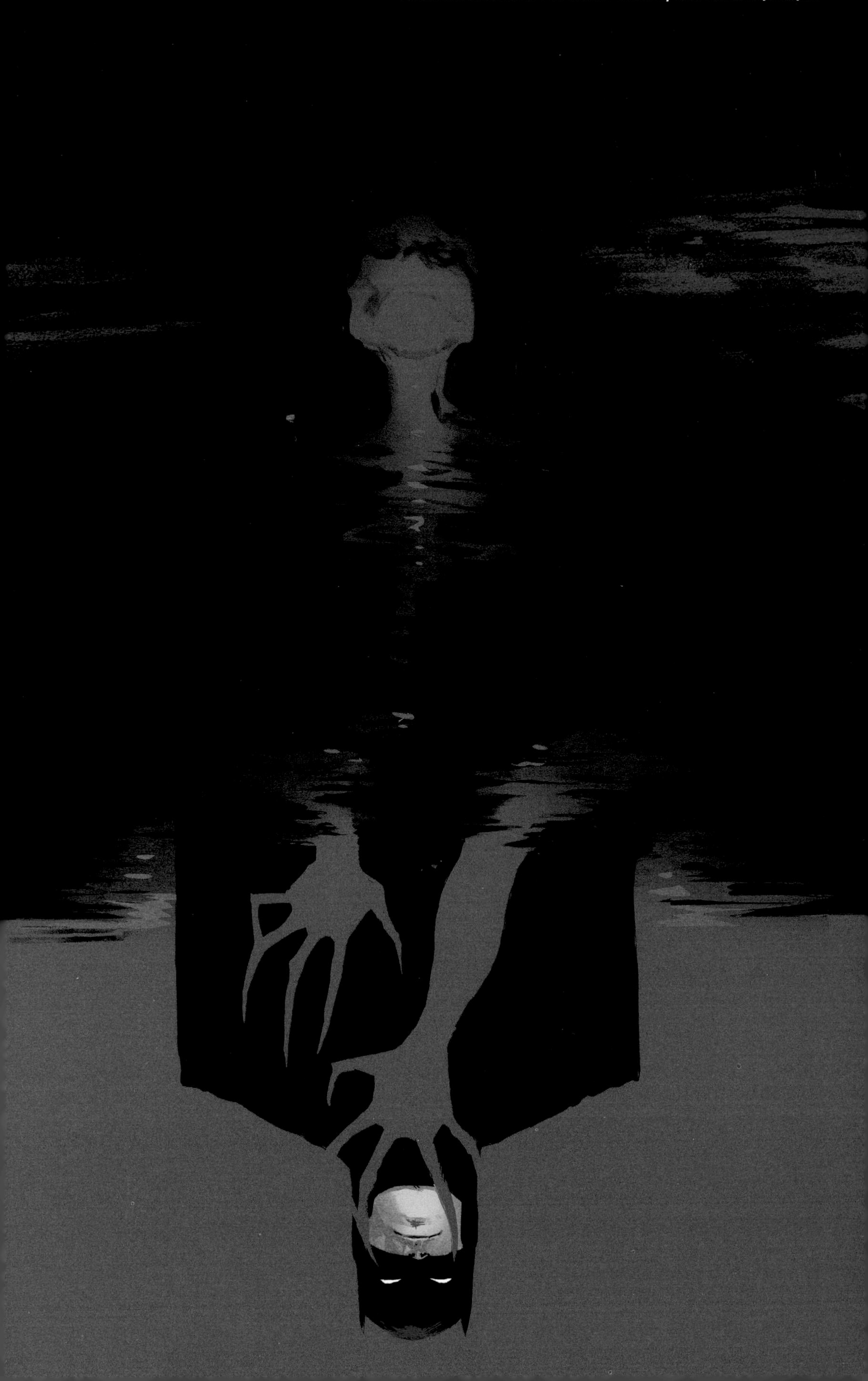

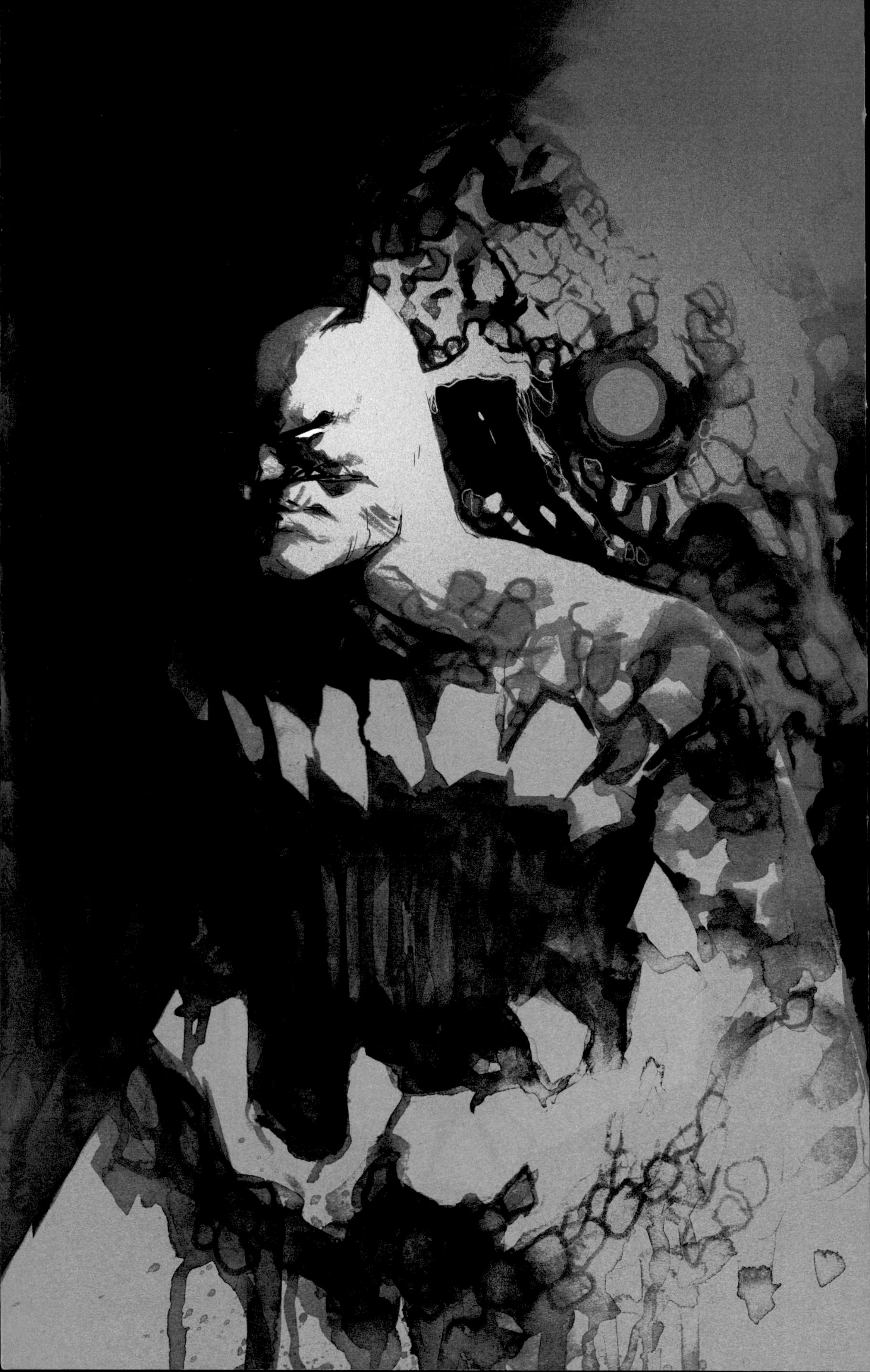
DETECTIVE COMICS #945 variant cover by RAFAEL ALBUQUERQUE

DETECTIVE COMICS #946 variant cover by RAFAEL ALBUQUERQUE

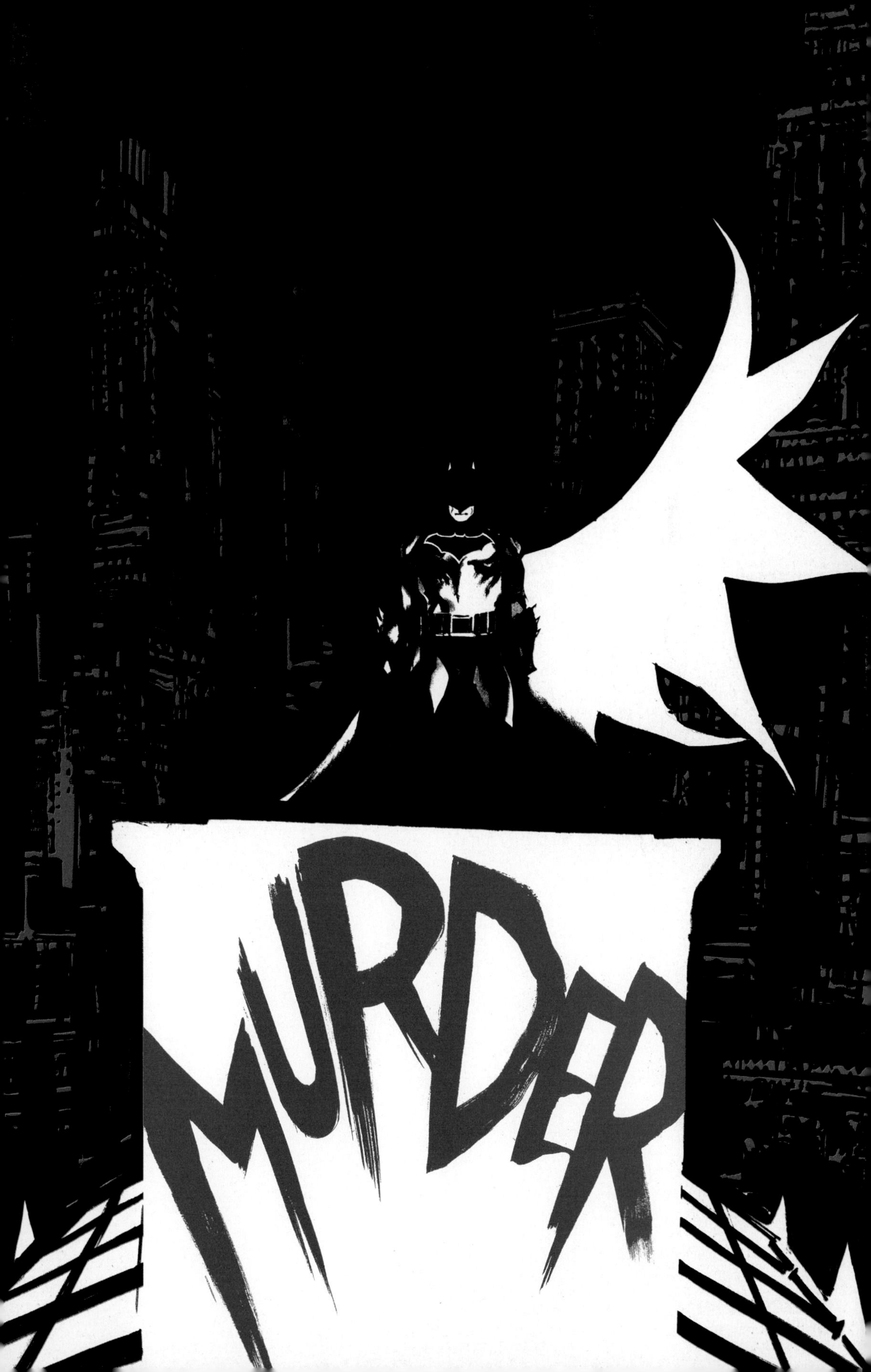
MURDER

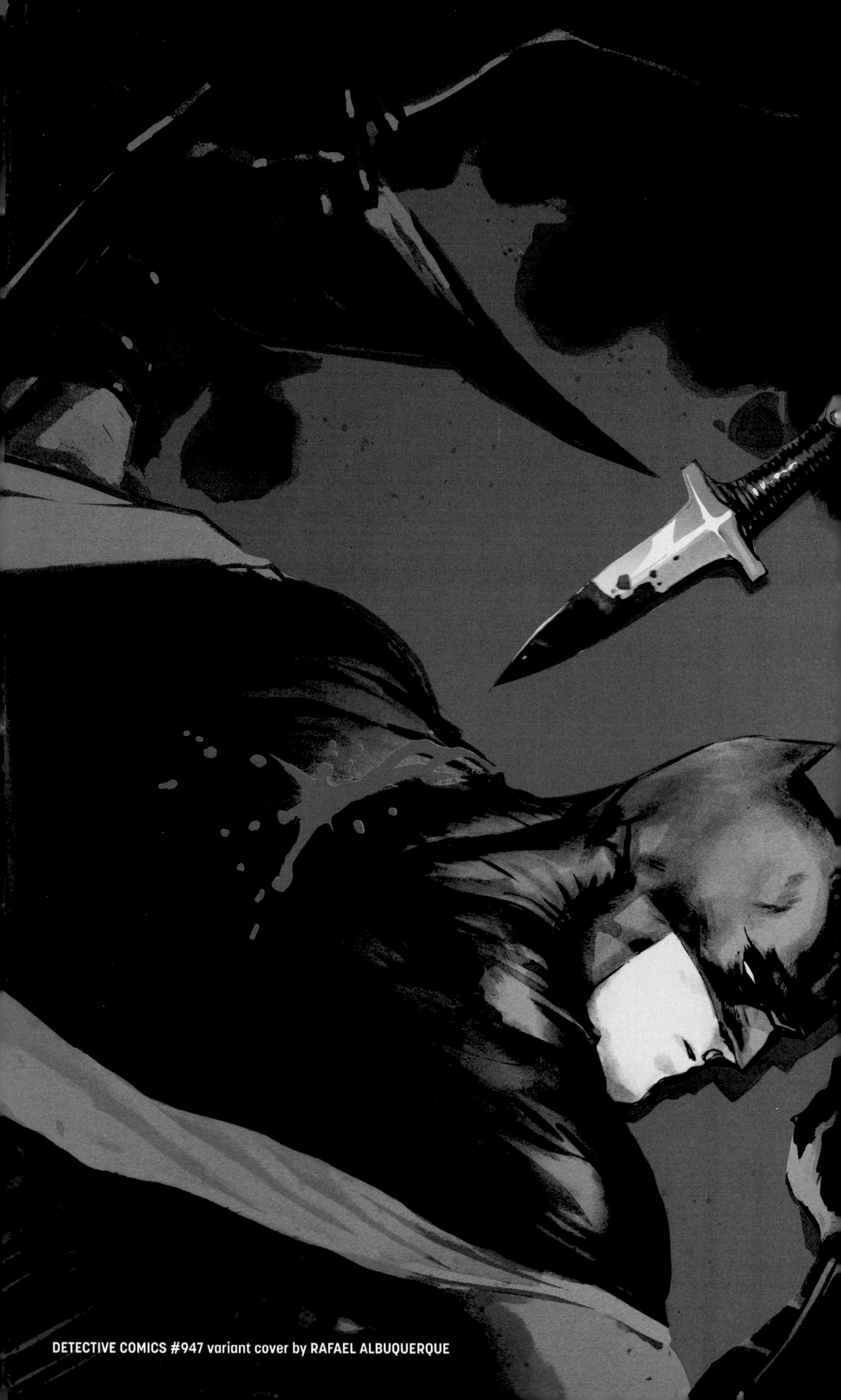

DETECTIVE COMICS #947 variant cover by RAFAEL ALBUQUERQUE

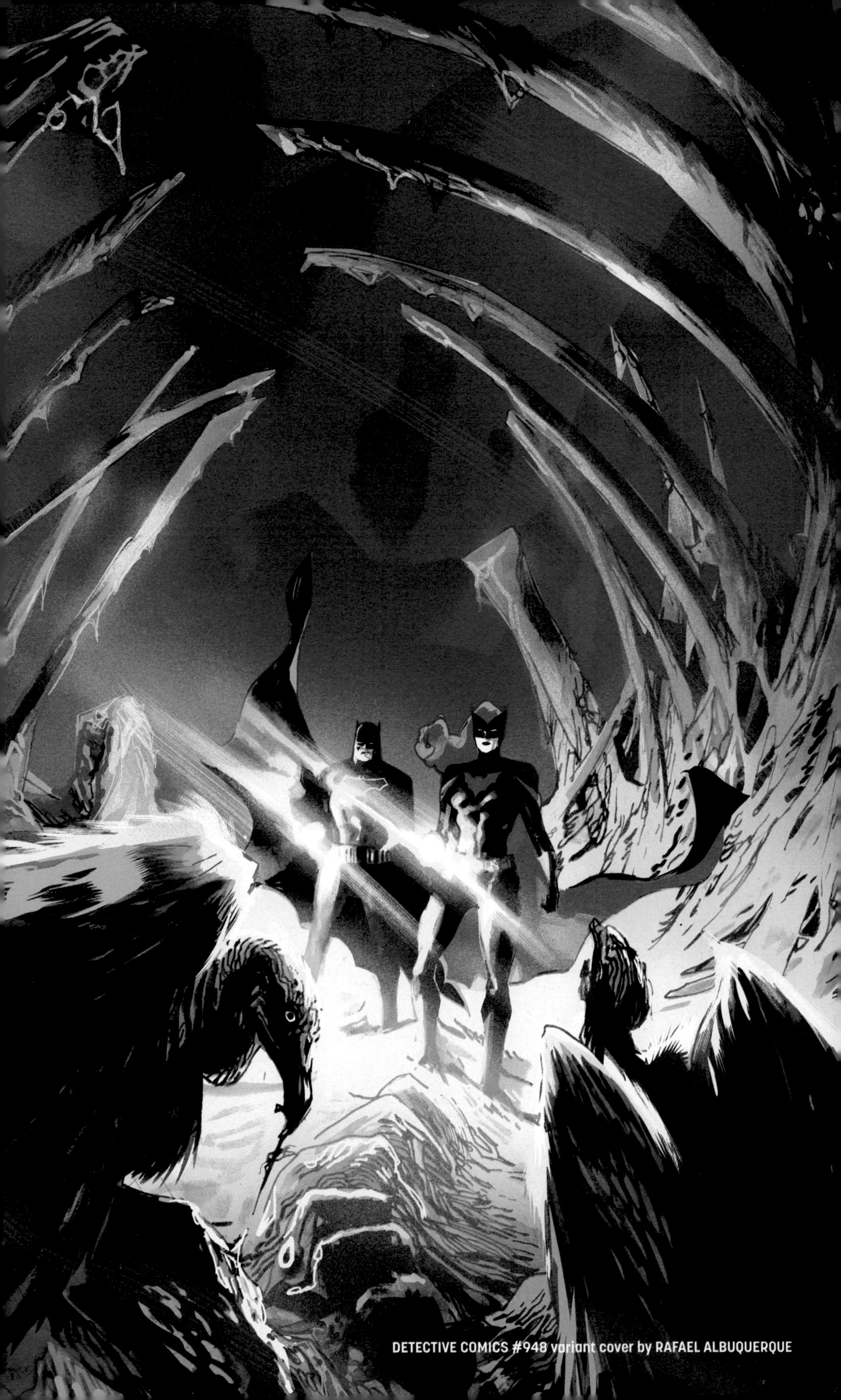

DETECTIVE COMICS #948 variant cover by RAFAEL ALBUQUERQUE

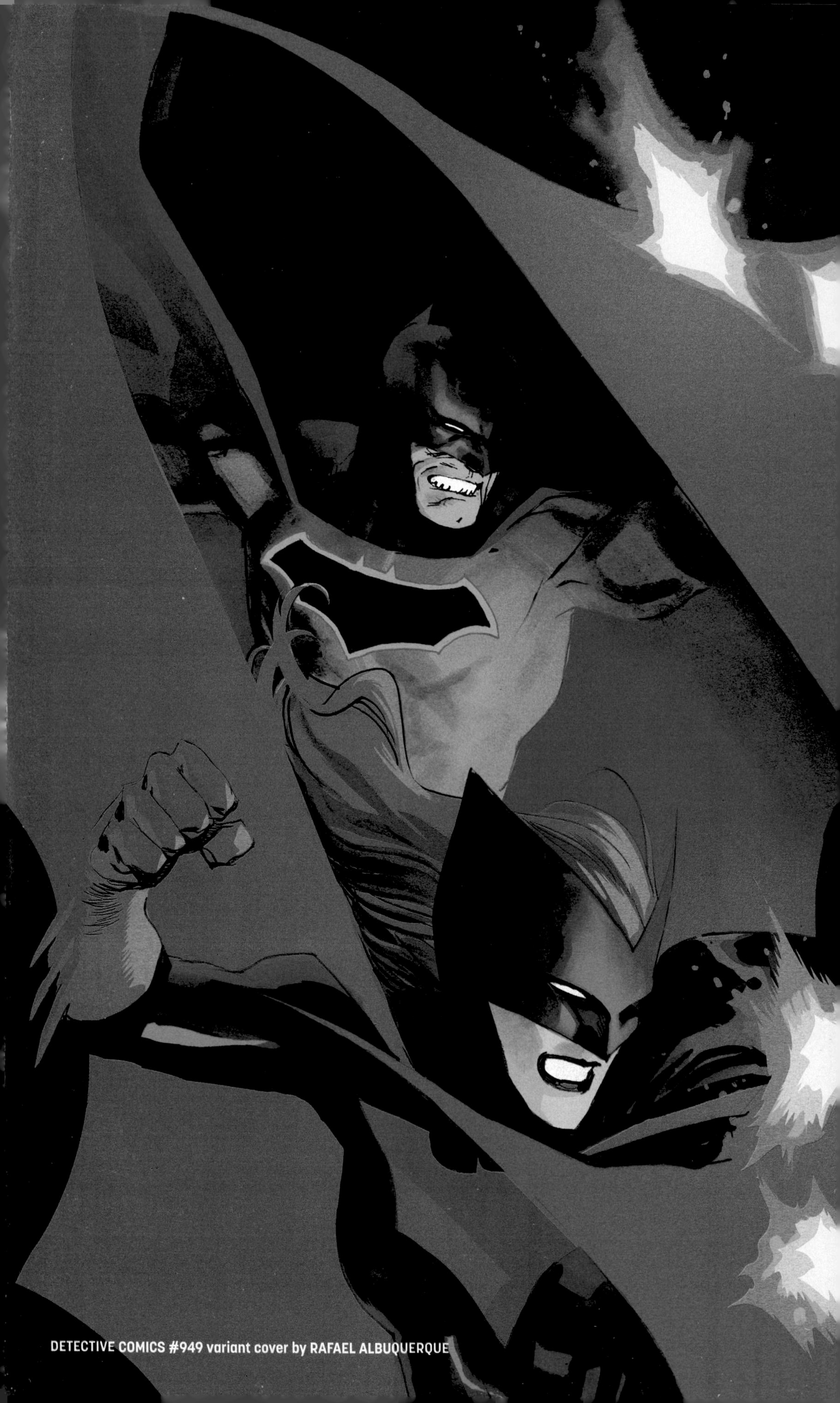

DETECTIVE COMICS #949 variant cover by RAFAEL ALBUQUERQUE

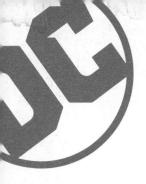

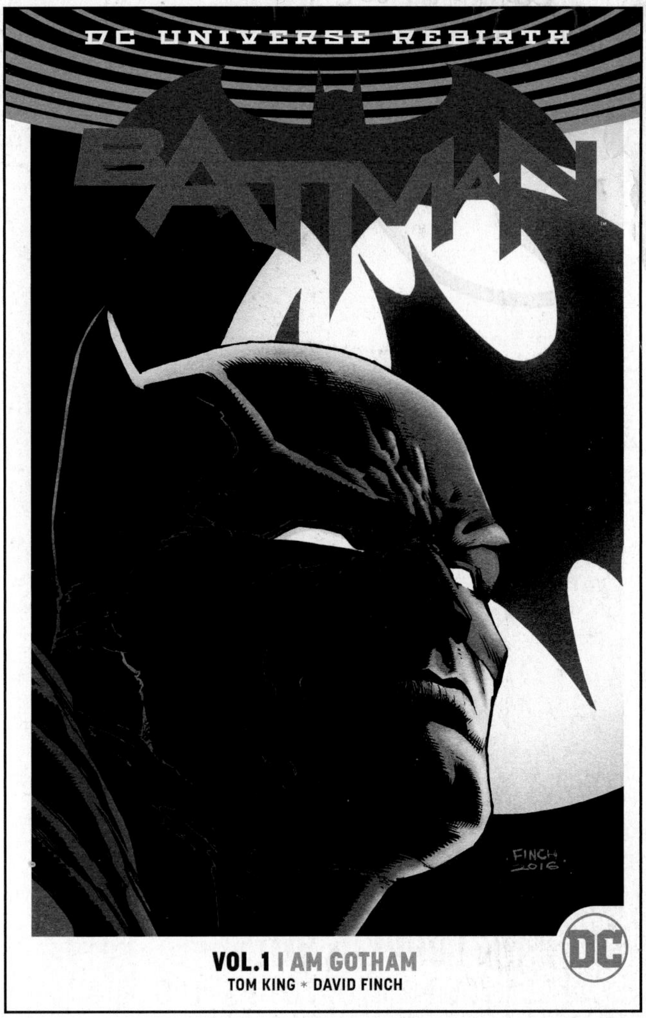
DC UNIVERSE REBIRTH
BATMAN
FINCH 2016
VOL.1 I AM GOTHAM
TOM KING * DAVID FINCH

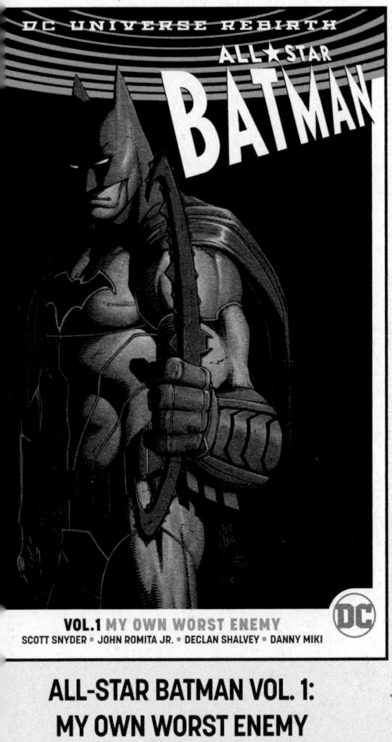
DC UNIVERSE REBIRTH
ALL★STAR
BATMAN
VOL.1 MY OWN WORST ENEMY
SCOTT SNYDER • JOHN ROMITA JR. • DECLAN SHALVEY • DANNY MIKI

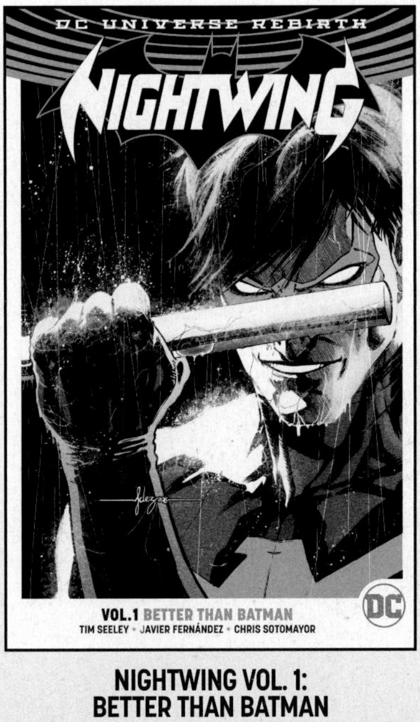
DC UNIVERSE REBIRTH
NIGHTWING
VOL.1 BETTER THAN BATMAN
TIM SEELEY • JAVIER FERNÁNDEZ • CHRIS SOTOMAYOR

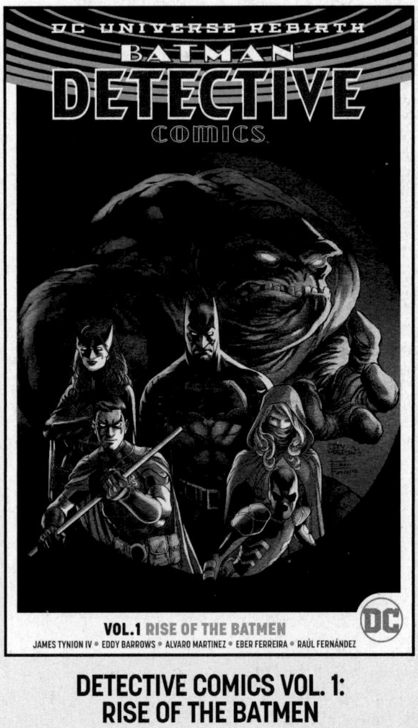
DC UNIVERSE REBIRTH
BATMAN
DETECTIVE
COMICS
VOL.1 RISE OF THE BATMEN
JAMES TYNION IV • EDDY BARROWS • ALVARO MARTINEZ • EBER FERREIRA • RAÚL FERNÁNDEZ

"[Writer Scott Snyder] pulls from the oldest aspects of the Batman myth, combines it with sinister-comic elements from the series' best period, and gives the whole thing terrific forward-spin."
– ENTERTAINMENT WEEKLY

THE #1 NEW YORK TIMES BESTSELLER
THE NEW 52!
BATMAN
VOLUME 1
THE COURT OF OWLS
"SNYDER MIGHT BE THE DEFINING BATMAN WRITER OF OUR GENERATION."
— COMPLEX MAGAZINE
SCOTT SNYDER GREG CAPULLO JONATHAN GLAPION

START AT THE BEGINNING!

BATMAN

VOL. 1: THE COURT OF OWLS

SCOTT SNYDER with GREG CAPULLO

THE #1 NEW YORK TIMES BEST-SELLING SERIES
THE NEW 52!
BATMAN
"ONE OF THE BEST TITLES ON THE MARKET."
—THE ONION / AV CLUB
VOLUME 2
THE CITY OF OWLS
SCOTT SNYDER GREG CAPULLO JONATHAN GLAPION JAMES TYNION IV
RAFAEL ALBUQUERQUE JASON FABOK

BATMAN VOL. 2: THE CITY OF OWLS

THE NEW YORK TIMES #1 BEST-SELLING SERIES
THE NEW 52!
BATMAN
"THIS IS A BOOK YOU NEED TO READ."
— HUFFINGTON POST
VOLUME 3
DEATH OF THE FAMILY
SCOTT SNYDER GREG CAPULLO JONATHAN GLAPION

BATMAN VOL. 3: DEATH OF THE FAMILY

READ THE ENTIRE EPI

BATMAN VOL
ZERO YEAR – SECRET C

BATMAN VOL
ZERO YEAR – DARK C

BATMAN VOL
GRAVEYARD SH

BATMAN VOL
ENDGA

BATMAN VOL
SUPERHEA

BATMAN VOL
BLO

BATMAN VOL.
EPILOG

Get more DC graphic novels wherever comics and books are sold!

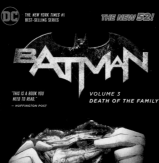

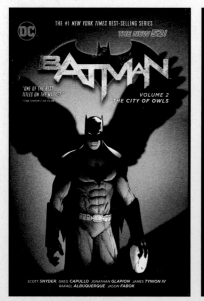

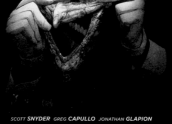

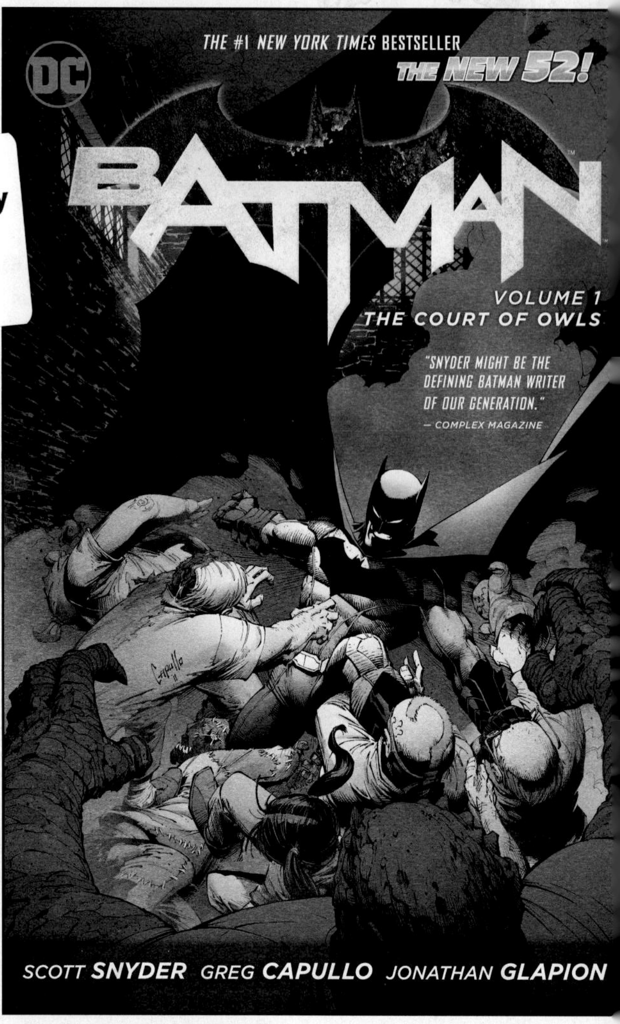